Aya Fujiwara and David R. Marples (eds.)

## **Hiroshima-75**
Nuclear Issues in Global Contexts

Aya Fujiwara and David R. Marples (eds.)

# HIROSHIMA-75

Nuclear Issues in Global Contexts

**Bibliografische Information der Deutschen Nationalbibliothek**
Die Deutsche Nationalbibliothek verzeichnet diese Publikation in der Deutschen Nationalbibliografie; detaillierte bibliografische Daten sind im Internet über http://dnb.d-nb.de abrufbar.

Bibliographic information published by the Deutsche Nationalbibliothek
Die Deutsche Nationalbibliothek lists this publication in the Deutsche Nationalbibliografie; detailed bibliographic data are available in the Internet at http://dnb.d-nb.de.

Cover picture: ID 116300747 © Guillohmz | Dreamstime.com

The papers herein were presented originally at a conference held at the University of Alberta in 2015. The authors comprise both senior and new scholars who work in disparate disciplines in universities in North America and Japan.

ISBN-13: 978-3-8382-1398-9
© *ibidem*-Verlag, Stuttgart 2020
Alle Rechte vorbehalten

Das Werk einschließlich aller seiner Teile ist urheberrechtlich geschützt. Jede Verwertung außerhalb der engen Grenzen des Urheberrechtsgesetzes ist ohne Zustimmung des Verlages unzulässig und strafbar. Dies gilt insbesondere für Vervielfältigungen, Übersetzungen, Mikroverfilmungen und elektronische Speicherformen sowie die Einspeicherung und Verarbeitung in elektronischen Systemen.

All rights reserved. No part of this publication may be reproduced, stored in or introduced into a retrieval system, or transmitted, in any form, or by any means (electronical, mechanical, photocopying, recording or otherwise) without the prior written permission of the publisher. Any person who does any unauthorized act in relation to this publication may be liable to criminal prosecution and civil claims for damages.

Printed in the EU

For our daughters, Akiko and Kaella

# ACKNOWLEDGEMENTS

The editors would like to acknowledge the financial support for this manuscript received from the Social Sciences and Humanities Council of Canada, the Faculty of Arts, the Kule Institute of Advanced Studies, the Prince Takamado Japan Centre, and the Department of History and Classics, University of Alberta, Canada. We are grateful for the editorial assistance of Eduard Baidaus and to Chris Schoen, Malisa Mahler, and Valerie Lange of ibidem-Verlag for their support at the final stages.

# CONTENTS

Acknowledgements .................................................................................... 5

Introduction ............................................................................................. 11
*Aya Fujiwara and David R. Marples*

**1. New Analyses of American Views on the Dropping of Atomic Bombs on Hiroshima and Nagasaki ............................................. 19**

Encountering the Atomic Bomb: The US Strategic Bombing Survey in Hiroshima and Nagasaki ......................................................................... 21
*Atsuko Shigesawa*

How to Celebrate the Deployment of the Atomic Bomb: Truman's Statement After Hiroshima ..................................................................... 49
*Yuko Shibata*

**2. Control or Not? Thinking on Atomic Power in the Cold War Context ... 63**

Early British Thinking on Atomic Energy Control .................................. 65
*James Keeley*

Soviet Atomic Internationalism, Egypt, and the Soft Power of Science ................. 89
*Frederick V. Mills*

What Made Japan Rely on Atomic Energy for Its Power Needs? A Historical Perspective on the Early Cold War ..................................... 125
*Mayako Shimamoto*

**3. Atomic Bombs and Cultural Representation in the World ................. 145**

Japan's Collective Memory of Hiroshima Seen Through the Eyes of a Child: The National and Global Impact of "Barefoot Gen" .................. 147
*Tomoko Masumoto*

Nuclear Noir: *Kiss Me Deadly* and Postwar Anxiety in America ......................... 163
*William Beard*

"Hiroshima" in France: Forgetting "Hiroshima" to Accept French
Ultra-Modernity and Its Nuclear Policies ...................................................... 177
*Chris Reyns-Chikuma*

## 4. Memoirs and Medicine: Japan, Ukraine, USA ......................... 197

My Path from Hiroshima to Houston ........................................................ 199
*Ritsuko Komaki*

"Atomic Soldiers and Downwinders": Health Legacies of the Nevada
Test Site ...................................................................................................... 215
*Susan L. Smith*

Chernobyl and Its Legacy: A Memoir ........................................................ 231
*David R. Marples*

## 5. Thinking on Nuclear Proficiency and Disarmament in the Current World ......................................................................... 251

Nuclear Proliferation and Double Standards .............................................. 253
*Jin Hamamura*

Ukraine's Nuclear Disarmament, 1990–2015:
Overview and Historiography .................................................................... 279
*Jordan Vincent*

Contributors ............................................................................................... 305

# INTRODUCTION

*Aya Fujiwara and David R. Marples*

An international conference took place at the University of Alberta in 2015 to commemorate the 70th anniversary of the dropping of the atomic bombs in Japan. Since then, selected contributors to the conference revised their essays for publication, reflecting our discussion. The anniversary was a very significant turning point that reminded the world of the catastrophe caused by the harmful use of the atom as a weapon. At the same time, this conference was held during the period in which the Japanese government, led by Prime Minister Sinzo Abe and his Liberal were working to pass the bill to recognize collective defence as a constitutional right. Such a move was controversial as Japan's Peace Clause 9 denounced Japan's involvement in any military action. Japan saw national protests rising in many parts of Japan in the spring and summer of 2015, mainly initiated by young people. These public demonstrations also embraced anti-nuclear movements that opposed the reoperation of Sendai nuclear plant following its closure after the Fukushima nuclear accident in 2011. This leftist-oriented movement was strongly supported by the opposition to Prime Minister Abe, and developed into an anti-Abe phenomenon. In Canada, Douglas Roche, O.C., a former Senator, MP, Canadian Ambassador for Disarmament, and honorary citizen of Hiroshima, who spoke at the conference, and said, "Japan is wasting a great opportunity to become a global leader in creating peace and stopping nuclear proliferation in this world."

In other parts of the world, nuclear proliferation is one of the most preeminent problems, as a nuclear weapon is often used as a tool of diplomacy and military threat. In March 2014, Russian president Vladimir Putin declared that he was prepared to use nuclear weapons had it been necessary during the annexation of Crimea from Ukraine. Similarly, North Korea under leader Kim Jong-un, has conducted many nuclear missile tests and its sixth such test in September 2017 demonstrated that nation's capacity to fight against other powers, including the United States.

The atom is also posing many concerns in the era of terrorism and extremism. In reality, nuclear plants, modified, could often contribute to the accumulation of plutonium, increasing a nation's capacity to produce nuclear weapons. Nuclear accidents and nuclear weapons, thus, are not separate issues in that both involve imagination and tactics in the use of the atom. Furthermore, nuclear plants could be targets of terrorist activities. In 2015, the US and five European nations concluded the Joint Comprehensive Plan of Action that ended Iran's longstanding attempt to put into operation a nuclear power station (Bushehr) based on Russian technology in return for the removal of economic sanctions that the US and EU imposed on this country. Such efforts well reflect concerns about the politically unstable situations in the Middle East, particularly due to the rise of extremist Muslim organizations.

But can we completely remove the atom from the world? Or even from continents? In 1985, Mikhail Gorbachev took over the leadership of the Soviet Union. Among his key stated policies was "removing nuclear weapons from the face of the Earth in the year 2000." In his quest to achieve this goal he spoke of "our common European home." A year later, after the accident at the Chernobyl nuclear power station in Ukraine, Gorbachev declared (3 May 1986) that the disaster illustrated the wisdom of such a policy. Subsequently, anti-nuclear movements developed around the world, including in the Soviet Union. By the 21$^{st}$ century, however, with the Soviet Union dissolved, Russia once again placed faith in the atom, as did Ukraine, while Belarus, one of the countries most affected by radiation fallout, embarked on the construction of a Russian-made nuclear power plant on its border with Lithuania. Memories are short, and ultimately economic needs often take precedence over moral stances and long-term safety interests.

Historically, human beings have lived with the atom since its discovery, incorporating, rejecting, and accepting it, and often changing course midstream. Despite its devastating nature or perhaps because of it, this source of energy has not disappeared and will not disappear from the world. As Joy Parr has shown in her study of "Canadian nuclear work culture" workers at the nuclear plants were often trained to "embody the insensible."[1] This argument could be applied to Japan specifically and to the rest of the world, whose history concerned the embodiment of the atom.

The first use of atomic bombs by US planes on the cities of Hiroshima and Nagasaki opened the nuclear era. During the Cold War (1946–89), the threat of the nuclear war was at its height, peaking with the Cuban Missile Crisis in 1962, shaping the international politics around the atom. North Americans were forced to prepare for the worst and embrace the atom in their everyday lives. Cold War psychology is evident in phrases such as "Mutually Assured Destruction" (MAD),

---

[1] Joy Parr, *Technologies, the Environments, and the Everyday, 1953–2003* ((Vancouver: UBC Press, 2010), 54.

which came to prominence after the Soviet Union detonated its first atomic bomb in August 1949, and initiated what became a frantic arms race. MAD was based on the premise that the two Super Powers had accumulated enough weaponry to destroy both the attacker and defender; thus, it embraced a form of deterrence based on nuclear strength. In the late 1950s when ballistic missiles were carried by submarines, the concept of MAD no longer applied, but throughout the Cold War, the concept of a "first strike" held sway in some military circles, i.e. the notion that the enemy could be destroyed before he had an opportunity to retaliate.

By the mid-1980s, the US' Strategic Defense Initiative (Star Wars) took the confrontation to potential new levels with the theoretical application of research on an anti-nuclear weapon shield that could protect US territory from a nuclear attack by the Soviet Union. While it was never put into practice, it sparked a dramatic transformation in international relations. Under the new Soviet leader Gorbachev (1985–91), the USSR initially tried to match Star Wars research, but ultimately chose a path of accommodation with the United States and dismantling medium range nuclear weapons. This process accompanied the opening of Soviet society and the eventual collapse of the Communist regimes of Europe (1989) and of the Soviet Union itself (1991). In turn, however, the Star Wars concept undermined the security of Western Europe, hitherto under the American protective umbrella. Though there were many factors behind the collapse of the Soviet Union,[2] the nuclear arms race was a key one. The end of the Cold War, however, paradoxically destabilized the international system and made it more unpredictable. It left nuclear stockpiles in four newly independent states (Russia, Ukraine, Belarus, and Kazakhstan), and placed the burden of initiating the decommissioning of nuclear weapons predominantly on the United States.

Atomic weapons have had an impact on international societies far beyond the well-researched Cold War confrontations. They have been incorporated into popular culture as the way to cope with the fear of global destruction and to motivate people's creativity. Anti-nuclear feelings were featured in numerous films and TV programs, some of which—like *The Day After* (1983), which was aired on the ABC Television network and watched by over 100 million viewers—tried to imagine life after a nuclear conflict. Other films ridiculed nuclear attack safety measures, with perhaps the most famous example being the 1964 movie directed by Stanley Kubrick, *Dr. Strangelove: How I Learned to Stop Worrying and Love the Bomb*

---

2   David R. Marples, *The Collapse of the Soviet Union, 1985–1991* (London: Longman, 2000); Serhii Plokhy, *The Last Empire: The Final Days of the Soviet Union* (New York: Basic Books, 2014).

(1964), portraying a deranged US air force general (played by Peter Sellers) who decides to order a first-strike nuclear attack on the Soviet Union.

Alongside nuclear weapons is the parallel development of the civilian nuclear power program, which began in the 1950s and has continued to the present. Nuclear energy is perhaps the most divisive issue in the debate on energy alternatives, whether on the Prairies of Alberta or the heartlands of Europe. Major accidents in nuclear plants have been relatively rare, but when they occur they inevitably make world headlines. This source of energy has been utilized in a number of ways since its initiation, particularly in the medical field. Medical imaging based on nuclear medicine applies miniscule quantities of radioactive material for both diagnosis and treatment of a wide variety of common diseases, including those that cause the most mortalities in the world today: heart disease, different types of cancers, etc. To the destructive force of the atom therefore can be added its benefits in curing or moderating diseases and prolonging the human lifespan.

With these broad and disparate applications of nuclear technology in mind, this volume brings together international scholars whose topics deal with a wide range of issues. It is divided into five thematic parts. The first section starts with the period just after the dropping of the atomic bombs on Japanese cities, adding new analyses of American views to the historiography. Two scholars, Atsuko Shigesawa and Yuko Shibata, revisit challenging questions as to how the United States dealt with the aftermath of the two atomic bombs. They both reveal that American attitudes towards the new discovery were complex, facing contradictory impulses to justify the use of the nuclear weapons and to discount their effects because of the possible nuclear wars in the future. Shigesawa examines the political circumstances in which seven survey groups, including the largest, the United States Strategic Bombing Survey (USSBS), produced their reports. She points to their deliberate effort to discount the impact caused by the atomic bombs in bringing about Japan's defeat. Shibata's article, which analyzes mainly American President Harry Truman's statement, also points out its ambivalent nature. It tends to conceal the real environmental and health consequences of the bombs. But undoubtedly, it expressed joy over the fact that the United States had gained the status of a military superpower as a result of the invention.

The second part examines the issue of atomic control during the early stages of the Cold War. Three articles by James Keeley, Frederick Mills, and Miyako Shimamoto analyze the different international approaches that Britain, the USSR, Egypt, and Japan applied to the newly invented power. Nuclear energy undoubtedly changed the power balance in international politics, consolidating the American lead though only for a short period. Keeley's analysis of British thinking shows how Britain approached the atom initially, leaning towards international atomic control. As one of the most significant American allies in the West, British thinking had obvious limitations—the war reduced Britain to a secondary power. Obviously, the USSR, which led the other ideological part of the world, concentrated its manpower and resources in nuclear research.

Mills' chapter, which examines the USSR's expansion of nuclear programs with specific focus on its relationship with Egypt, adds new perspectives to the Cold War stories that examine the ideological race between Communist nations and the West. Japan, as the only country in the world to have witnessed the horror of atomic bombs, regarded the military use of the atom as evil conduct. The atom itself, however, appeared a very attractive source of energy to fill the lack of natural resources. Shimamoto explains why the government of Japan, even after the Bikini Incident of 1954 in which Japanese fishermen were exposed to radiation due to an American nuclear test, moved to the use of nuclear energy. She reveals that there were vigorous American campaigns for the "peaceful" use of the atom and the construction of nuclear reactors in Japan.

The scars of Hiroshima and Nagasaki continued to dominate the world, but to a different extent and in diverse ways. Three authors—Tomoko Masumoto, Bill Beard, and Chris Reyns-Chikuma—investigate how the atom was represented in films and comics in Japan, the United States, and France respectively. It became an integral part of Japan's post-World War II collective memories. Masumoto's chapter analyzes the impact of a *hibakusha* manga, *Barefoot Gen*, and argues that manga indeed became one of the most effective expressions of the horror and catastrophe that the atomic bombs had caused. The military use of the atom and the possible nuclear war continued to define the Cold War. As people needed to find ways to deal with fear, and anxiety, their expressions were well integrated into Cold War popular culture.

Beard's article adds a new perspective to the studies of Hollywood films, arguing that "nuclear neurosis" was reflected in how they were created. Focusing on film noir, it argues that this genre presents the complex and metaphoric anxiety, applying gender analysis into atomic discourse. In France, however, such expressions were not apparent. Reyns-Chikuma questions why "Hiroshima," in general, was absent from French cultural industry. He argues that French official policies for the promotion of nuclear industry as well as the presence of the other human tragedy, "Auschwitz," have caused this silence.

We wanted to provide examples of memories and changing perceptions of the impact of the atom, both in 1945 and subsequently. Concerning Japan, which remains the only country to suffer the unique experience of an attack by atomic bombs, a medical doctor, Ritsuko Komaki, provides a poignant example of how she lived with the atom for more than seventy years. Her family home was in Hiroshima when the first atomic bomb was dropped on that city in 1945. Although she was in Osaka at that time, she moved back to Hiroshima two years later, and lived through the reconstruction era in this city. Her life thus was shaped by the notion of the atom, prompting her to pursue a career as a radiation oncologist. Thus, for us, she was the living embodiment of the negative and positive effects of the atom. Interestingly, she keeps a neutral stance on the nuclear discussion.

In the Cold War era, people in both communist and western spheres ascertained that nuclear threats would come from their respective enemies. Ironically, however, much real danger was caused in their backyard of their own states thanks to policies initiated in Washington, DC and Moscow. Two historians—Susan L. Smith and David R. Marples—assess the long-term health damage that was caused as a result of exposure to high levels of radiation. Smith sheds light on domestic victims in the United States, whose fates were less publicized, focusing on the nuclear tests at the Nevada Test Site from 1951 and 1963. Overshadowed by the state's propaganda, she suggests, local residents did not receive enough information about possible adverse health effects from the project. Marples' chapter, which looks back at his association with Chernobyl, also reveals the consequences of domestic failure to control the atom. Further, it argues that consequences of the accident, however devastating at the time, have now slipped from collective memory in the face of the collapse of the Soviet Union and the successor states' economic and technological projects that derive from earlier Soviet plans.

Should the use of the atomic energy be controlled internationally? Nuclear weapon states (NWS), in general, regard military and civilian uses of the atom as separate issues as long as their states are concerned. In global politics, however, such a dichotomy does not seem to exist. Jin Hamamura and Jordan Vincent question how the non-proliferation movement operates in the world. Hamamura analyzes the inequality of international politics and the ironic nature of non-proliferation, pointing out NWS's interference in domestic nuclear energy programs. Such an inherent contradiction was imbued in the current non-proliferation regime, and he nuances that universal abolition of nuclear weapons is the most effective method to resolve this dilemma. Vincent offers an illuminating example of how a state chose to sign the Treaty of Non-Proliferation of Nuclear Weapons, focusing on Ukraine. The path that Ukraine took to abandon its inherited nuclear arsenal from the Soviet Union in return for compensation and promised protection, he implies, could offer some lessons to other countries. He puts this conclusion in perspective following the Russian annexation of Crimea and events in Ukraine's eastern Donbas region, particularly in 2014–17. These actions indicate that political events can quickly undermine international guarantees and conceivably prompt states to keep their nuclear weapons if the partners in question demonstrate duplicity.

The world marked the 75th anniversary since the dropping of the atomic bombs in 2020, reminding us once again of the legacy of this energy source. This human invention has changed and shaped international politics, human imagination, and domestic politics. The authors of this volume aim to reopen the discussion by promoting awareness of the atom's direct and indirect power. During the early preparation of this volume, rhetoric about a possible nuclear war reverberated from Washington, DC to the capital of North Korea, Pyongyang, with Japan caught in the crossfire. In late November 2017, a missile fired by North Korea in a nuclear test landed in Japanese ocean territory, 1000 kilometres away. In response to the ensuing war of words between President Donald J. Trump and Kim Jong-Un, as well as North Korea's frequent weapons tests, *The Bulletin of the Atomic Scientists* in Chicago set its Doomsday clock to two minutes to midnight; the closest it had been to the fatal hour since 1953, when the Soviet Union detonated its hydrogen bomb for the first time (its original setting was seven minutes to midnight).

We believe that this volume is an important addition to the field of nuclear humanities. Like the earlier volume of Taylor and Jacobs,[3] it delves deeply into the impact of the atom beyond the former Cold War rhetoric that focused solely on how to prevent a global thermonuclear war and how humanity has learned to live with the atom in a variety of ways. One of our goals has been to highlight these different dimensions and different international perspectives from both Japan and the West. The study of atomic theory, as far as we know, originated with the Ancient Greek philosopher Democritus (c460–c370 BC) while the use of radiation in medicine dates from the late 19th century. The history of the atom does not begin in August 1945, but that date, justifiably, continues to demonstrate the horror it can inflict. Thus, we begin there while keeping in mind the other aspects of the

---

3   N.A.J. Taylor and Robert Jacobs, eds., *Reimagining Hiroshima and Nagasaki: Nuclear Humanities and in the Post-Cold War* (New York: Routledge, 2017).

atom that have helped frame modern society, its culture, medicine, and production of energy.

The reality is that the 75th anniversary is no time for complacency. The message of Douglas Roche, who offered a keynote speech at our conference, is as pertinent today as it was when he wrote his book *Bread not Bombs* in 1999.[4] Our book is not a political or anti-nuclear tract. Rather, it is intended as a reflection of the complex relationship between humankind and the atom. We would be well advised also to remember the comment of J. Robert Oppenheimer, one of the creators of the first such weapon that "The atomic bomb made the prospect of future war unendurable. It has led us up those last few steps to the mountain pass; and beyond there is a different country."

---

4    Douglas Roche, *Bread Not Bombs: A Political Agenda for Social Justice* (Edmonton, AB: University of Alberta Press), 1999.

# 1. New Analyses of American Views on the Dropping of Atomic Bombs on Hiroshima and Nagasaki

# ENCOUNTERING THE ATOMIC BOMB: THE US STRATEGIC BOMBING SURVEY IN HIROSHIMA AND NAGASAKI

*Atsuko Shigesawa*

## Introduction

When the first atomic bombs were used against Japan in August 1945, the effects of the new weapon inevitably became the focus of international attention and curiosity. The main questions raised were: how powerful is the new weapon? What are its effects on cities and their residents? As soon as occupation forces poured into Japan two weeks after her capitulation on 15 August, journalists competed to make their way to Hiroshima and Nagasaki, the two cities that suffered the first atomic blows, in the hope of providing the very first coverage. "No story was of more importance than a visit to Hiroshima … we were determined to get to Hiroshima ahead of other correspondents," William H. Lawrence of *The New York Times*, one of about a dozen American correspondents who visited Hiroshima on 3 September, recalled in his memoir.[1]

    Not only journalists, but also scientists, military officials and other experts of many fields, rushed to the cities. From September to December 1945, seven survey missions are known to have worked in Japan; the Special Manhattan Engineer District Investigating Group (Hereafter, "MED Group"),[2] Office of the Chief Surgeon of the General Headquarters, U. S. Armed Forces in the Pacific (GHQ Group),[3] Naval Technical Mission to Japan (NavTechJap),[4] and the British Mission to Japan, as well as the United States Strategic Bombing Survey (USSBS), Postwar Scientific Intelligence Mission to Japan led by physicist Karl T. Compton (Compton-

---

1    Bill Lawrence, *Six Presidents, Too Many Wars* (New York: Saturday Review Press, 1972), 137. Lawrence was in a press tour organized by the US Strategic Air Forces in the Pacific.

2    For its background and activities, see "Investigation of the After Effects of the Bombing in Japan," Chapter 6, Manhattan Project: Official History and Documents, Vol. 4, Book 1, Reel 1 (University Publications of America, 1977).

3    Ashley W. Oughterson et al., *The Report of the Joint Commission for the Investigation of the Effects of the Atomic Bomb in Japan*, Vol. 1 (U. S. Atomic Energy Commission, 1951), 17.

4    It was established to determine the position of the Japanese in the field of naval technology. Winthrop Slocum, "The Naval Technical Mission to Japan," *United States Naval Institute Proceedings* 75, no. 1 (1949): 1–11.

Moreland Group),[5] and Army Air Forces' Scientific Advisory Group, directed by world-famous aerospace engineer Theodore von Karman (von Karman Commission).[6]

Of these seven, the first two, together with the NavTechJap's Bureau of Medicine and Survey,[7] comprised the Joint Commission for the Investigation of the Effects of the Atomic Bomb in Japan, which would eventually publish the most authoritative report on the medical effects of the atomic bomb.[8] The commission and the British Mission were predominantly engaged in analysis of the military impact of the atomic bomb. They were motivated by a belief, which Col. Ashley W. Oughterson, surgical consultant to MacArthur and a member of GHQ's medical corps, expressed as follows: "A study of the effects of the two atomic bombs used in Japan is of vital importance to our country. This unique opportunity may not again be offered until another world war. Plans for recording all of the available data therefore should receive first priority."[9]

This sense of urgency and need to study the effects of the atomic bomb was also shared by the USSBS, the largest of all the post-war study groups that worked in Hiroshima and Nagasaki. Preserved USSBS documents attest to this intention. Of its four regional headquarters in Japan, for example, establishments of those in Hiroshima and Nagasaki were prioritized over those in Osaka and Nagoya, with larger numbers of personnel to be assigned in the areas.[10] Roughly one-third of the

---

5  Slocum, who joined NavTechJap first as Liaison Officer to G-2, SCAP, and later became the mission's Chief, wrote: "A special target of considerable interest at the time involved the medical effects of atomic bombing." Slocum, "The Naval Technical Mission to Japan," 3.

6  It conducted a study to determine what military weapons the US should develop in the future. Theodore Von Karman with Lee Edson, *The Wind and Beyond: Theodore von Karman, Pioneer in Aviation and Pathfinder in Space* (Boston: Little, Brown and Company, 1967), 290–293.

7  Slocum, who joined NavTechJap first as Liaison Officer to G-2, SCAP, and later became the mission's Chief, wrote, "A special target of considerable interest at the time involved the medical effects of atomic bombing." Slocum, "The Naval Technical Mission to Japan," 3.

8  Oughterson et al., *The Report of the Joint Commission for the Investigation of the Effects of the Atomic Bomb in Japan*, 6 vols. (U. S. Atomic Energy Commission, 1951).

9  Memorandum to Brig. Gen. Guy Denit, chief surgeon, GHQ, 28 August 1945, Appendix 1 (1), Oughterson et al., *The Report of the Joint Commission for the Investigation of the Effects of the Atomic Bomb in Japan*, Vol. 1, 23.

10  The operation orders established Hiroshima and Nagasaki headquarters to open on 8 and 12 October with 34 and 33 personnel, and Osaka and Nagoya on 18–19 October with 28 and "at least 10" personnel, respectively. "Operation Orders & Areas," Folder: 300.4 Orders-Operations (USSBS) Tokyo; "Operations orders," Folder: 300.4-E Operations (USSBS) Tokyo, both in Box 12, Entry 1, RG 243, National Archives and Records Administration, College Park, MD (hereafter, NARA).

Survey's some 200 operations in the Pacific took place either in Hiroshima, Nagasaki, or both.[11] Contrary to what historian Barton J. Bernstein notes,[12] the issue of the atomic bomb had become intrinsically the Survey's central task in the Pacific. Paul H. Nitze, a vice chairman for USSBS Pacific, stated that "Obviously the atomic bomb was a new element in Japan which warranted a great deal of attention."[13] USSBS was established in November 1944 by the US Secretary of War Henry L. Stimson, pursuant to a directive from President Franklin D. Roosevelt, to provide an impartial evaluation of the effects of the American strategic bombing against Germany. A group of civilian experts was recruited to lead the survey, including Franklin D'Olier, president of the Prudential Insurance Company, Henry Alexander, Vice-President of J. P. Morgan and Company, and John Kenneth Galbraith, an economist and war-time deputy administrator at the Office of Price Administration. It was expected that such a study would benefit the planning of air attacks on Japan and of postwar defence establishment.[14] The results of the European Survey, with 1,287 personnel, including 1,116 from the military at the peak time of 21 July 1945,[15] were filed in 216 reports published by May 1947.

The survey was reorganized and sent to Japan at the request of President Harry Truman when the Pacific War came to an end on 15 August 1945, to examine "the effects of all types of air attack."[16] The number of personnel counted 1,345—172 civilians, 513 officers and 675 enlisted—on 25 November, just before their departure from Japan.[17] The results of the survey in Japan by its fifteen divisions were published in the form of reports, with a total of 109 titles, by July 1947.

---

11  "Operation Orders & Areas," Folder: 300.4 Orders-Operations (USSBS) Tokyo; "Operations orders," Folder: 300.4-E Operations (USSBS) Tokyo, both in Box 12, Entry 1, RG 243, NARA.

12  "The issue of the atomic bomb, as construed by the survey, was not its central task, and only a few reports focused heavily upon issues of the bomb." Barton J. Bernstein, "Compelling Japan's Surrender Without the A-bomb, Soviet Entry, or Invasion: Reconsidering the US Bombing Survey's Early-Surrender Conclusions," *The Journal of Strategic Studies*, Vol. 18, no. 2 (June 1995): 106.

13  Statement by Paul H. Nitze, 15 February 1946, in the Hearings before the Senate Special Committee on Atomic Energy, S. Res. 179, 79th Cong., 2nd sess., pt. 5; 515.

14  Letter from Franklin Roosevelt to the Secretary of War, 9, September 1944, Folder: 300.6(A) Administrative Directives USSBS (G-2 Files), Box 14, Entry 1, RG243, NARA.

15  "Strength of United States Strategic Bombing Survey Pacific Theater;" "Strength of United States Strategic Bombing Survey in all theaters," both in Box 33A, Entry 1, RG 243, NARA.

16  Letter to Franklin D'Olier from Harry S. Truman, 15 August 1945, Folder: MISC Papers connected with USSBS, Box: United States Strategic Bombing Survey, Ari Force Historical Research Agency, Maxwell Air Force Base, AL (hereafter, AFHRA).

17  "Strength of United States Strategic Bombing Survey Pacific Theater;" "Strength of United States Strategic Bombing Survey in all theaters," both in Box 33A, Entry 1, RG 243, NARA.

A phrase in two of three reports published in July 1946 from the Chairman's Office—*Summary Report* and *Japan's Struggle to End the War*—has been a subject of controversy over the past seventy years. The phrase reads:

> Based on a detailed investigation of all the facts, and supported by the testimony of the surviving Japanese leaders involved, it is the Survey's opinion that certainly prior to 31 December 1945, and in all probability prior to 1 November 1945, Japan would have surrendered *even if the atomic bombs had not been dropped*, even if Russia had not entered the war, and even if no invasion had been planned or contemplated.[18]

The conclusion has been repeatedly referred to by journalists and scholars, including Nobel-laureate and Pulitzer-prize-winning writers as P. M. S. Blackett, Hanson W. Baldwin and Herbert Feis. Especially at the height of the Vietnam War, it was cited by so called revisionist historians as evidence to support their arguments against the decision made by President Truman. Whatever doubts it raised, the conclusion had "often been accepted, uncritically, by analysts"[19] because of the Survey's status as Presidential commission and eventual prestige of some of its civilian members in the government.

The tide turned in 1995 when studies by two scholars claimed that the Survey's opinion was unreliable and should not be trusted. Robert P. Newman and Barton J. Bernstein made a scrutiny of the USSBS transcripts of interrogations of Japanese military and political leaders[20] in which they claimed the conclusion was biased, and argued that there was not enough basis in the records to support the "early-surrender hypothesis."[21] Drawing on Nitze's recollection that he had suggested the Joint Chiefs of Staff (JCS) in June 1945 that Japan would likely surrender by November 1945 without the atomic bomb, even though JCS decided differently with the plan of invasion of the Japanese mainland,[22] the two assumed that Nitze, principal author of *the Summary Report*, had already formed his conclusion by the time he arrived in Japan.[23]

---

18  USSBS Chairman's Office, *Summary Report (Pacific)* (US Government Printing Office, 1946), 26; *Japan's Struggle to End the War* (US Government Printing Office, 1946), 13.
19  Bernstein, "Compelling Japan's Surrender," 101.
20  USSBS Transcripts of Interrogations and Interrogation Reports of Japanese Industrial, Military, and Political Leaders, 1945–1946, NARA, available in microfilm from Wilmington, DE: Scholarly Resources, 1992.
21  Robert P. Newman, "Ending the War with Japan: Paul Nitze's 'Early Surrender' Counterfactual," *Pacific Historical Review* 64, No. 2 (May 1995): 167–194; Bernstein, "Compelling Japan's Surrender," 101–148.
22  Paul H. Nitze, *From Hiroshima to Glasnost: At the Center of Decision* (New York: Grove Weidenfeld, 1989), 36–37.
23  Newman, "Ending the War with Japan," 169; Bernstein, "Compelling Japan's Surrender," 107.

The two historians made persuasive cases. Yet this author cannot fully agree with them since such a conclusion was not based on the opinion of a single individual, but rather on the results of an organizational effort. In the following paper, I will explain what led me to reach this conclusion.

On 30 June 1946, two weeks before the publication of the *Summary Report*, another report from the Chairman's Office, *The Effects of Atomic Bombs on Hiroshima and Nagasaki*, was published. Although it did not include the exact phrase of the early-surrender hypothesis, it still contained a conclusion of similar finality.[24] This report is important in two respects—first, because of the USSBS's prestige as a presidential and third-party commission, and second, because of its availability to the public,[25] it has been predominantly cited as a source for atomic bomb literature;[26] and second, it was the first published among the three reports from the Chairman's Office. Actually, this report and other atomic bomb reports published by five USSBS divisions that conducted studies in Hiroshima and Nagasaki laid the groundwork for the two other reports from the Chairman's Office.

In this article, I seek to explore how these divisions encountered the new weapon. How did they attempt to evaluate the effects of the atomic bomb? What elements did they consider in writing the report? To do so, I examine the materials these divisions used, and compared final and preliminary reports written by the divisions—mostly found in the Survey's collection at the National Archives in College Park, MD—to prove that these reports in effect prepared the way for the Survey's conclusion in question.

---

24  Part of the report reads, "It cannot be said...that the atomic bomb convinced the leaders who effected the peace of the necessity of surrender." USSBS Chairman's Office, *The Effects of Atomic Bombs on Hiroshima and Nagasaki* (US Government Printing Office, 1946), 22.

25  The three reports from the Chairman's Office were widely distributed. *The Effects of the Atomic Bombs on Hiroshima and Nagasaki*, for example, was reprinted in the *News and World Report*, 5 July 1946.

26  Most notably, John Hersey's *Hiroshima* draws on the Survey's findings for the descriptions of the effects of the atomic bomb on Hiroshima. For details, see, Atsuko Shigesawa, "John Hersey's Hiroshima Revisited: From the Vantage Point of 66 Years Later," *Hiroshima Journal of International Studies* 18 (November 2012), 19–37.

## Disaster Uncovered

Of the Survey's fifteen study divisions,[27] four—Physical Damage, Urban Areas, Civilian Defense and Medical—published reports especially on Hiroshima and Nagasaki, from the perspective of their own expertise.[28] Moral Division also published a report with special attention to the people in Hiroshima and Nagasaki.[29] These five divisions sent their teams, comprising from four to twenty-three people, to the two cities for the period of from four days to seven weeks during the period 8 October–16 December 1945, where they collected information mainly through questionnaires and interviews of Japanese officials and citizens.[30]

The results of the study produced eight reports. Physical Damage Division (PDD), in its 1081-page, three-volume *Effects of the Atomic Bomb on Hiroshima, Japan* and 1030-page, three-volume *Effects of the Atomic Bomb on Nagasaki, Japan*, discussed in detail the extent of the destruction the atomic bomb had caused on buildings. It examined the materials, with which they were built, and the design and quality of the construction, as well as the degree of damage to these buildings in accordance with their distances from Ground Zero (GZ).

Urban Area Division (UAD)'s fifty-seven-page *Effects of Air Attack on the City of Hiroshima* and 53-page *Effects of Air Attack on the City of Nagasaki* perhaps best describe what the individual communities were like during the war, their involvement in the government's war efforts and how they suffered from the conflict. Aimed at determining the effects of the atomic bombing on the two cities with a particular interest in their commercial and industrial facilities and activities, the Division examined the number and conditions of people mobilized to work there, and damage to the industrial capacities, and if and how fast they were recuperating.

---

27    The ten other divisions other than the five mentioned in this paragraph are: Aircraft, Basic Material, Capital Goods, Equipment, and Construction, Electric Power, Manpower, Food, and Civilian Supplies, Military Supplies, Oil and Chemical, Transportation, Military Analysis, Naval Analysis.

28    PDD, *Effects of the Atomic Bomb on Hiroshima, Japan I–III* (May 1947); *Effects of the Atomic Bomb on Nagasaki, Japan I–III* (June 1947); CDD, *Field Report Covering Air Raid Protection and Allied Subjects, Nagasaki* (February 1947); *Civilian Defense Report No. 1: Hiroshima, Japan, Field Report* (Nov. 15, 1945); Medical Division, *The Effects of Atomic Bomb on Health and Medical Services in Hiroshima and Nagasaki* (March 1947); UAD, *The Effects of Air Attack on the City of Nagasaki* (April 1947); *The Effects of Air Attack on the City of Hiroshima* (June 1947), all from US Government Printing Office.

29    Morale Division, *The Effects of Strategic Bombing on Japanese Morale* (US Government Printing Office, June 1947).

30    For the members and their overall activities, see, James Beveridge, *History of the Strategic Bombing Survey (Pacific) 1945–1946* (Wilmington, Delaware: Scholarly Resources, 1992). Beveridge was the official historian of the Survey and belonged to the G-2 Section of the Service Division.

Civilian Defense Division (CDD) studied wartime program of civilian defence and how it responded to the bombings. In its 127-page *Field Report Covering Air Raid Protection and Allied Subjects, Nagasaki*, and 60-page *Civilian Defense Report No. 1: Hiroshima, Japan, Field Report*, the division discussed the history, the organization and operations of civil defence agencies, air raid warning system, fire service, emergency medical services, and shelters of the two cities, as well as, in the case of Nagasaki, of mortuary and rescue services.

Medical Division's main task was to study the Japanese system of public health and medical services, people's health condition, and their nutritional state during wartime. It did not assume an active role in the study of the medical effects of the atomic bomb, as, by the time the division arrived, the Joint Commission had already been at work, and it would be "needless repetition and since so little time was available."[31] Fortunately, however, the Joint Commission cooperated with the division "to the greatest extent and made all of their records available for examination."[32] Its eighty-six-page *Effects of Atomic Bombs on Health and Medical Services in Hiroshima and Nagasaki* inevitably focused on the effects of the atomic bomb on human beings, including those of radiation.

Moral Division's 256-page *Effects of Strategic Bombing on Japanese Morale* is the compilation of its analysis of interviews of 3,135 individuals—2,887 in fifty-two cities and towns across the country, excluding Hokkaido, Shikoku, and southeastern Kyushu, as well as 129 in Hiroshima and its three vicinity towns and 119 in Nagasaki and its three vicinity towns. The division attempted to determine what affected people's morale during the war and what made them believe Japan had lost the war.[33]

The bulk of Japanese records, both of government and private industries, had been destroyed by the bombing, and by the following typhoon especially in case of Hiroshima,[34] or on the orders of the military at the time of the surrender. Many of the key Japanese personnel had been killed by the bombing.[35] The Survey could only depend on the interviews they had with whatever remaining Japanese

---

31  Medical Division, *Hiroshima and Nagasaki*, 1, 21.
32  Ibid, *Hiroshima and Nagasaki*, 21; Beveridge, *Pacific*, 206–207.
33  Report No. 14a(22). Actual interviews per sample point; Report No. 14a(26), both in Roll 93, USSBS RSD; Morale Division, *The Effects of Strategic Bombing on Japanese Morale*, 11; Beveridge, *Pacific*, 181–200.
34  The typhoon resulted in 2,012 people, including eleven members of a scientific survey team from the Kyoto University, either killed or missing.
35  UAD, *Hiroshima*, 51; PDD, *Hiroshima* I, 62–63.

officials or survivors they could find. It also based much of the data on reports prepared by Japanese officials or scholars.[36] The divisions naturally described the attack as experienced by the Japanese themselves:

> All of the persons outside of the shelter were burned to death ... flesh was charred and burned off in many places, tongues were hanging out, and eyeballs and teeth were knocked out as if from heavy pressure. ... the whole area was enveloped in a black or gray smoke through which they could see flames shooting high into the air. ... trees had been uprooted and burned, and all houses had collapsed.[37]
> ... many people were trapped in the debris of buildings demolished by the explosion and could not be extricated before being burned, casualties were of unprecedented proportions ... Those who were engaged in clearance and evacuation activities suffered very heavy casualties. It is estimated that over 20,000 of the killed and missing were school children.[38]

The extent and authenticity of the devastation was reinforced by the firsthand eyewitness accounts of the Survey members themselves:

> ... at the time the Medical Division visited Hiroshima, 3 months after the bombing, the first street car was beginning operation, people wandered aimlessly about the ruins, and only a few shacks had been built as evidence or reoccupation of the city. Leaking water pipes were seen all over the city with no evidence of any attention ... All in all, there appeared to be no organization and no initiative.[39]
> The stench of decomposed flesh was said to have hung heavily over the devastated area for weeks. In a casual inspection of one small section of the ruins the skeletal remains of one body which had not been located by the mortuary service was personally observed.[40]

While these accounts convey some terrifying pictures of the atomic bomb disaster, the majority of narratives in the reports written and published by the five study divisions seem to be directed at another end: denial of awe of the atomic bomb. The trend is more apparent when we trace the changes made to the manuscripts of different stages. Often these changes were made in a way to downplay the effects of the atomic bomb.

---

36   PDD, *Hiroshima* I, 10, 84. Certain information about the atomic bomb likely could not be shared even among USSBS divisions. For example, UAD used data for the height of the epicenter of explosion from a report of the Japanese scientific team, while PDD had obtained the information by their own measurement. UAD, *Nagasaki*, 12.
37   CDD, *Nagasaki*, 70, 72.
38   UAD, *Hiroshima*, 20.
39   Medical Division, *Hiroshima and Nagasaki*, 19.
40   CDD, *Nagasaki*, 37.

## Denial of the Awe

There are some informational gaps in these analyses. PDD, for example, never discussed how many people were inside the buildings and what happened to these people. Other than as witnesses of the phenomena that took place at the time of the bombing, the local population only appears as figures—numbers of population and casualties.[41] Their houses were not included in subjects of analysis, either. The effects on human beings were being taken care of by other divisions or groups. Yet, why was there such a disregard of Japanese dwellings?

While the reports made detailed investigations of every structure—173 in Hiroshima[42] and 567 in Nagasaki,[43] which were either industrial or public buildings—they only made passing and vague reference to dwellings. For example, there is only one reference on the number of houses destroyed or damaged—20,686—in one volume of the PDD Nagasaki report.[44] In Hiroshima reports, there is one reference to the alleged total number of buildings damaged in the city, which barely gives one a vague idea on the number of houses destroyed: "Approximately 60,000 of 90,000 buildings over an area of 9.5 square miles were totally or severely damaged."[45]

There is a section and references in the reports on Japanese dwellings,[46] but the division never discussed in detail as they did with other structures that remained standing. PDD analyzed typical style, construction, and materials of houses in Japan, and they discussed in detail how flimsy they were and how they were unable to withstand any attacks. A report reads; "The practice [of Japanese carpenters] ... placed their residential construction far below American standards of strength, rigidity, and weather tightness;"[47] "The light weight, slender columns,

---

41    PDD, *Hiroshima* I, 9, 68–69, 84–86.
42    "The 173 buildings in this study included virtually every reinforced-concrete, every steel-frame and every load-bearing, brick-wall building from GZ to a distance beyond which there was no further effective damage." PDD, *Hiroshima* I, 16; *Hiroshima* II, 97.
43    PDD, *Nagasaki* I, 99; Nagasaki II, 5.
44    PDD, *Nagasaki* I, 12.
45    PDD, *Hiroshima* I, 9. PDD obviously knew the number of houses destroyed since all reports submitted by Japanese authorities included the figures. See, Report No. 92f(1)(j) Report by Col. Oya, 8; Report No. 92f(1)(c) Report by the Governor of Hiroshima, 5, both in Roll 327; Report No. 93a(4)(b) Report from Governor of Nagasaki, 35–36, Roll 330; Report No. 93h(1) translations of official and industrial documents obtained in Nagasaki, 6, 61–62, 75, 148, Roll 332, USSBS Pacific Survey Reports and Supporting Records (hereafter, USSBS RSD).
46    PDD, *Hiroshima* I, 96–115; Hiroshima II, 21; PDD, *Nagasaki* I, 10; Nagasaki III, 121, 125. Photos of Japanese dwellings are included in 135–137 of the Nagasaki report.
47    PDD, *Hiroshima* I, 12, 107.

and weak mortise and tenon joints were points of weakness which rendered the Japanese residence highly vulnerable to damage by blast."[48]

It is likely PDD made a study of what survived the atomic bomb, rather than a study of damage caused by the atomic bomb. And that was actually one of the purposes of the Survey. An earlier preliminary draft made this stance clear: "It is the opinion of this Team that in planning for the future the facts bared and the lessons learned by the Hiroshima investigation into the characteristics and extent of physical damage from the atomic bomb can be of inestimable value in minimizing the vulnerability of our cities to air-burst atomic bomb."[49]

In fulfilling this purpose, PDD tried not to base their study on the Japanese dwellings. Its reports read: "Although much of the residential area of Nagasaki was composed of typical Japanese structures of primitive construction, almost all of the public and municipal buildings were of modern design. They were comparable with those found in cities of the same size in America or Europe, and, in many cases, were even more strongly constructed to withstand earthquakes;"[50] "These structures were studied in considerable detail, since they offered excellent evidence from which the effectiveness of the bomb against occidental construction might be deduced."[51]

While they tried to present the Japanese dwellings as flimsy and Japanese fire fighters as incompetent and ill-equipped, PDD intentionally avoided discussing the extent of the damage inflicted on Japanese houses. When the division found out that the atomic bomb report from the Chairman's Office contained a figure of 98.4% as the ratio of residential buildings in the city destroyed or severely damaged, the division's team in charge of Hiroshima argued as follows: "PDD Team 1 does not know where the figure of 98.4 per cent of all residential construction within the city was destroyed or severely damaged was obtained. We did not try to determine this figure and can only protest that the figure is believed to be seriously in error."[52]

---

48  PDD, *Hiroshima* I, 115.
49  Probable effects on other targets, Report No. 92f(1)(b), frame 31, Roll 327, USSBS RSD.
50  PDD, *Nagasaki* II, 5.
51  PDD, *Hiroshima* II, 98.
52  Composite Report on the Atomic Bomb: Its Power, Effects, and Limitations, Reviewed by PDD Team 1, Report No. 92f(1)(g), frame 175, Roll 327, USSBS RSD. This figure of 98.4% can be found in: The Secretariat, USSBS, "Preliminary Composite Report on the Atomic Bomb: Its Power, Effects and Limitations," March 26, 1946, 47, in Report No. 3, frame 356 (also 272 in 5 March ver.), Roll 51, USSBS RSD. It obviously came from UAD's preliminary report on Hiroshima. Report No. 1c(5) Hiroshima, frame 410, Roll 9; Report No. 60h(1), frames 766, Roll 304, both of USSBS RSD. The figure was not included in the final report.

The team also suggested that the USSBS Secretariat should not use the word "factory" to refer to home industries employing only one or two men, many of which were located around GZ, because that would give "a serious misimpression of the importance of the city to the industrial economy of Japan." The comment continued: "This is particularly true since only the small shops in Hiroshima were destroyed and the major factories producing by far the majority of goods were undamaged. Consequently, this paragraph gives a distinctly false impression."[53] Obviously, PDD wanted to avoid any impression that the atomic bomb was effective and powerful.

This trend is also found with other divisions. For example, UAD's reports conclude that the atomic bomb was indecisive from a strategic point of view. The reports read: "The Atomic Bomb attack on Hiroshima effectively destroyed the administrative, commercial, and residential heart of the city and caused an unprecedented number of casualties, but it failed to damage seriously the war production potential of the urban area."[54] "From the standpoint of neutralization of enemy industrial war potential, therefore, the atomic bombing of Nagasaki was strategically ineffective. It merely precipitated the same extinction of industrial Nagasaki which the internal economy of Japan would itself have brought about within a very few months."[55]

Knowingly or unknowingly, both reports proved the Truman administration's selection of the target wrong. What aimed to be "the vital war plant employing a large number of workers and closely surrounded by workers' houses"[56]

---

53   Composite Report on the Atomic Bomb: Its Power, Effects, and Limitations, Reviewed by PDD Team 1, Report No. 92f(1)(g), frame 175, Roll 327, USSBS RSD.

54   UAD, *Hiroshima*, 33. A slightly different version can be found in Report No. 60h(1), frame 736, Roll 304; Report No. 1c(5) Hiroshima, 3, Roll 10, both USSBS RSD. The earlier preliminary report contained another possibly discrediting phrase, which was omitted from later preliminary reports and final version: "All of these [important factories], with one exception where dispersal was in progress, were operating at nearly peak production, and any successful attack would have had a direct effect on output." Report No. 1c(5) Hiroshima, 15, Roll 10, both USSBS RSD.

55   UAD, *Nagasaki*, 15. The paragraph is followed by a sentence: "As has been shown above, the atomic bomb by no means neutralized the productive capacity of Nagasaki." There is a similar account in a preliminary report. "One conclusion only emerges from the aggregate. Nagasaki was within three to four months of her extinction as a factor in Japanese war economy. That eventuality was only precipitated by the atomic bombing of 9 August." Report No. 1c(5) Nagasaki, frame 658, Roll 10, USSBS RSD.

56   Notes of the Interim Committee Meeting, 31 May 1945, 14, folder no. 100, Harrison-Bundy Files, Microform publication (M1108), Roll 8, RG 77, MED Records, NARA. The actual aiming points were left to later determination at the base by military commanders when weather conditions would be known. It is apparent those who selected the targets knew they were city centers rather than war plants since they also concluded "to neglect location of industrial areas as pin point target, since on

turned out to be residential and commercial centers surrounded by war plants, some of which, on the contrary, escaped major damage. In Hiroshima, the entire heart of the city, approximately 4.7 square miles of densely built-up commercial and residential district, was devastated, while large, important plants were "well outside the area of devastation and in most cases sustained only minor damage."[57] In Nagasaki, a congested residential district, an oval area of 4.4 square miles, was completely destroyed or severely damaged, while the Mitsubishi Dockyard, the largest military plant employing over half of the city's labor force, was outside the periphery of destruction and suffered only superficial damage.[58]

The two reports, however, based their conclusions on totally different standpoints. In the Hiroshima report, the authors took great pains to place emphasize the city's potential for recuperation. The Nagasaki report, explained that the city's war potential had already been on the verge of collapse due to the lack of fuel and raw materials. The Hiroshima report repeatedly states that the large factories began partial operations immediately after the bombing and "could have been restored to practically normal production within 30 days,"[59] had the war continued. The evidence in USSBS documents, however, suggests otherwise.[60]

For example, the chief clerk of the Toyo Industries, the third largest plant with over 7,000 workers that produced 19% of the ordnance, told UAD that 900 workers, most of whom lived in dormitories, showed up to work on 7 August, but "their ability to produce was very poor."[61] More importantly, the company decided to close down the plant on 15 August "due to the general disruption."[62] Yet the description of this firm in the final report states "If the war had not ended, it would

---

these three targets (Kyoto, Hiroshima and Niigata) such areas are small, spread on fringes of cities and quite dispersed." Minutes of Third Target Committee Meeting, 28 May 1945, File No. 5d, Correspondence ("Top Secret') of the Manhattan Engineer District, 1943–1946, RG 77, NARA.
57   UAD, *Hiroshima*, 19.
58   UAD, *Nagasaki*, 5, 12–13, 23.
59   UAD, *Hiroshima*, 24, 25, 27. This trend is also found in all the preliminary drafts. Report No. 60h(1), frames 746–747, 805; Report No. 60h(2), frame 934, both in Roll 304; Report No. 1c(5) Hiroshima, 5, 52, 53, Roll 10, all in USSBS RSD.
60   Transcripts of the interviews are found in Report No. 60h(6), frames 1170–1213, Roll 304, USSBS RSD.
61   Interrogation of M. Nakamura, chief clerk, Toyo Industries, Nov. 12, 1945, Report No. 60h(6), frames 1172–1173, Roll 304, USSBS RSD. The final report of this part reads, "About 900 employees (12.5 percent of the total) reported for work 7 August, the day following the bombing. Most of these were from among those living in the dormitories."
62   Interrogations of Yosiro Kaizuka, head of the planning section, and Nakamura, chief clerk, Toyo Industries, 21 November 1945, Report No. 60h(6), frame 1196, Roll 304, USSBS RSD. Their dormitories were cleared and served as temporary hospitals. UAD, *Hiroshima*, 30.

have been possible to resume approximately normal operations on that date [15 August]."⁶³

Officials at the Mitsubishi Heavy Industries, Ujina Shipyard Division, the fourth largest war plant with 6,020 workers, which was responsible for 57% of the shipbuilding, told the interrogators, "The plant suffered only slight damage, and work was commenced again on 7 August. However, although 1,000 showed up for work on the morning of the 7$^{th}$ compared to 2,660 on the 6$^{th}$, only 600 showed up on the 8$^{th}$, and the number decreased on each following day. On 20 November there were 600 employees at work and of this number 15 percent were working on ship construction."⁶⁴ The report, however, stated that: "Nearly 50 percent of the normal work shift reported for work on 7 August, the day following the bombing, but only 30 percent reported on 8 August. The number continued to decrease for several days, but repairs went forward, and operations were resumed on 17 August with 70 percent of the normal number of workers."⁶⁵

UAD's Nagasaki report defied such attempts to place importance on the potential for industrial recovery. Unlike Hiroshima, which was almost intact until the atomic attack, Nagasaki had experienced five pre-atomic raids from August 1944, which resulted in 346 killed, 600 wounded and 43 missing in the entire city.⁶⁶ While the Dockyard sustained only 1.4% structural damage and 0.8% damage to property value from the atomic bombing, the 1 August raid, the fifth and worst of the pre-atomic attacks by 24 B-29s and 26 B-25s, killed 169, wounded 215 and left 40 missing among its employees.⁶⁷ It substantially damaged its facilities as well.⁶⁸ The raid

---

63 UAD, *Hiroshima*, 30. The report often cites "Industrial questionnaire" as a source of its date. However, the author could not find any such material in USSBS RSD. Most of the materials for UAD's Hiroshima report in the collection are processed data and not raw data with sources.
64 Interrogations of Sato, assistant general manager, and Yanaga, head of the planning section, Shipyard Division, Mitsubishi Heavy Industries, 27 November 1945, Report No. 60h(6), frame 1205, Roll 304, USSBS RSD.
65 UAD, *Hiroshima*, 30.
66 UAD, *Nagasaki*, 7–9; Air-raid Casualties, Report No. 59o, frames 103–106, Roll 303B; Interrogation No. D-22, Messrs. Mikawa, Toyoshima, Mizogoshi, Fujimoto, 29 November 1945, in Report No. 59f, frames 1221–1223, Roll 303A, USSBS RSD. The UAD Nagasaki report has "347" killed, but it must be a typological error.
67 UAD, *Nagasaki*, 7–9; Air-raid Casualties, Report No. 59o, frames 103–106, Roll 303B; Interrogation No. D-20, Mr. Muto present general manager of the Mitsubishi Dock Yard and Mitsubishi Engineering Co., 27 November 1945, Report No. 59f, frame 1210, Roll 303A, USSBS RSD. The UAD report states 199 killed, which is clearly an error.
68 Interrogation No. D-15, Mr. Ogawa, former head of Mitsubishi Dockyards, 24 November 1945; Interrogation No. D-20, Mr. Muto, present general manager of the Mitsubishi Dock Yard and Mitsubishi Engineering Co., 27 November 1945, both in Report No. 59f, frames 1198, 1210, Roll 303A, USSBS RSD.

also directly struck the Mitsubishi Steel Works, the smallest of the conglomerates located 0.75 miles (1.2 kms) north of GZ with 2,800 workers, severely damaging some of its machinery.[69]

> The UAD's Nagasaki Team argued, however, that neither pre-atomic raids nor the atomic bombing reduced Nagasaki's industrial potential for war. The report reads: "… from the standpoint of destroyed industrial capacity, the atomic bombing of Nagasaki was extremely effective. Such an attack visited upon any industrial center operating at capacity would seriously curtail the war potential of that nation. In the case of Nagasaki, however, the picture is radically different. At the time of the attack and for several months previously, Nagasaki industry had not been operating at more than a small fraction of capacity."[70]

By contrast, the Hiroshima report argued that the war plants in the city enjoyed sufficient resources during the war. It reads: "The trend of production, electric power consumption, and number of industrial workers in the Hiroshima urban area was generally upward during the period studied."[71] However, again, factory interviews and evidences attest otherwise.[72] For example, consumption of charcoal had decreased from 2,100 metric tons for home use as of May, 1944; 2,100 metric tons for industry use as of September 1944; and 482 metric tons for transportation

---

69   UAD, *Nagasaki*, 7–9.
70   Ibid, 14. Records of interviews of Nagasaki officials attest to this view. For example, to a question "To what extent could Nagasaki have recovered, had the atomic bomb not ended the war immediately?" Wakamatsu Nagano, Nagasaki Governor responded, "No recovery was possible." Officials of the Mitsubishi Steel Works also told the USSBS interrogator they were always short of certain materials that they were only able to produce no more than 60% of quota. Officials of the Mitsubishi Electric Manufacturing in their response to a questionnaire also wrote to the same effect. Interrogation No. D-1, Mr. Nagano, 11 November 1945; Interrogation No. D-17, Mr. Hirai, Mr. Tanaka, and Mr. Ogasawara of the Mitsubishi Steel Works, 26 November 1945, both in Report No. 59f, frames 1189, 1203, Roll 303A; Report to the questionnaire for Companies, in Report No. 59j, frame 35, Roll 303B, USSBS RSD.
71   UAD, *Hiroshima*, 8.
72   Five of thirteen firms interviewed mentioned lack of raw materials—Toyo Industry, Shipyard Division of Mitsubishi Heavy Industries, Asahi Arms, Mitsubishi Heavy Industry's Gion Machine Tool Works, Kirihara Barrel Factory—six firms reported shortage of labour—Nippon Steel, Chugoku Electric, Army Shipping, Mitsubishi Engineering, Kirihara Barrel Factory and Asahi Arms—and five firms shortage of either fuel, electric power or gas—Nippon Steel, Mitsubishi Heavy Industry's Gion Machine Tool Works, Toyo Industries, Mitsubishi Engineering and Asahi Arms—during the war. Only three firms, Japan Steel, Ujina Shipyard and Chugoku Electric, told they had sufficient raw materials. All in Report No. 60h(6), Roll 304, USSBS RSD.

as of October 1943, to 330 metric tons, 660 metric tons, and 210 metric tons, respectively in July, 1945.[73] Industrial consumption of gas decreased from 96,000 cubic meters in June 1944 to 36,000 cubic meters in July 1945.[74] Both the consumption and incoming shipping of almost all goods and raw materials had decreased over the last year of the war, and rapidly so in the final few months.[75] To reduce the consumption of electricity there were electric holidays initiated twice a month at many plants.[76]

Both the labour force and labour hours in Hiroshima started to decrease from August 1944 to early spring of 1945 in all categories, except for chemicals and metals.[77] The shortage of labour was aggravated by the lack of food. "Absenteeism was very great and was mainly due to the lack of sufficient food: (1) because of insufficient food, men including soldiers, could not hold up under the heavy work; and (2) the workers had to take time off to scrounge the countryside for additional food."[78] "Workers were not receiving sufficient food and at different times many left their jobs to go out in the country to try and scrounge food. Others were forced to remain at home because of sickness caused by lack of food. The women could not stand the strain as well as male employees, and the food shortage seemed to affect them more."[79]

The possible distortion of the facts seems more apparent in the final report than preliminary reports. For example, while a preliminary report mentioned that the incoming tonnage of truck freight had "dropped from 118% in June 1945 to 68% in July,"[80] that part was deleted from the final report to make the outgoing

---

73   Frame 631, Report 60e(2) Fuel consumption, Roll 304, USSBS RSD. The report reads, however, "Industrial and domestic consumption of charcoal was approximately equal over the period studied." "There were no reports of essential war production having been curtailed because of insufficient charcoal." UAD, *Hiroshima*, 12.
74   Report No. 60e(2) Fuel consumption, Frames 628, 640, Roll 304, USSBS RSD. The report reasons "Since there was no concomitant decline in the production of the larger plants, it can be assumed that gas was not a critical item in their manufacturing processes." UAD, *Hiroshima*, 13.
75   Report No. 60e(2) Fuel Consumption, Roll 304, USSBS RSD.
76   Interrogations of Yosiro Kaizuka, head of the planning section, and Nakamura, chief clerk, Toyo Industries, 21 November 1945, frame 1196; Interrogation of T. Yamazaki, Comptroller of Nippon Steel, 20 November 1945, frame 1189, both in Report No. 60h(6), Roll 304, USSBS RSD.
77   Urban Areas Section Hiroshima Team, 60b(2) Industrial labor, Roll 304, USSBS RSD.
78   Interrogations of Lt. Col. Hara, Commander, Jiro Kataoka, civilian consultant, of the shipyard repair division, Army Shipping Headquarters, Shipyard repair Division, 26 November 1945, frame 1197, Report No. 60h(6), Roll 304, USSBS RSD.
79   Interrogations of Kishimoto and Samura of Chugoku Electric, 21 November 1945, Report No. 60h(6), frames 1194, 1197, Roll 304, USSBS RSD.
80   Report No. 1c(5), frame 422, Roll 10, USSBS RSD.

tonnage, which remained above 100% at the end of the war, look like the total tonnage.[81]

Possibly acting out of the same motivation, the authors or reviewers of the report might have manipulated some figures. The ratio of the large industries on the perimeter, which could have resumed production within approximately thirty days after the bombing, was increased to 74% in the final report[82] from 50% in preliminary reports.[83] That of the industrial capacity of the urban area destroyed was decreased to 26% in the final report[84] from "less than 35%" or "less than 30%" in preliminary reports.[85] That of industrial workers in the ten largest plants who returned to work by 15 August was increased to 42% in the final report[86] from 18.6% or 24% in preliminary reports.[87] And that of workers housed in company barracks was raised to 31% in the final report[88] from 25% in preliminary reports—all without any grounds.[89]

While displaying more integrity, however, the Nagasaki report also contained a very critical alteration, namely that most of the population in the area surrounding the hypocenter "was killed outright and few of the wounded managed to escape to safety"[90] in preliminary reports was changed to "escaped to safety"[91] in the published version. It is obvious that, just like the case of PDD, UAD wanted the atomic bombings to sound indecisive. It may have something to do with the fear among American officials and military that "... the United States [would] get the reputation of outdoing Hitler in atrocities."[92] A careful reading of relevant materials, however, leads us to believe that it was more a matter of domestic concern than

---

81   UAD, *Hiroshima*, 12.
82   Ibid, 27.
83   Report No. 60h(1), frame 771, Roll 304; Report No. 1c(5) Hiroshima, 21, Roll 10, USSBS RSD.
84   UAD, *Effects of Air Attack on the City of Hiroshima*, 32.
85   Report No. 60h(1), frame 769; Report No. 60h(4), frame 1035, both in Roll 304; Report No. 1c(5) Hiroshima, 21, Roll 10, USSBS RSD.
86   UAD, *Hiroshima*, 24, 32.
87   Reports No. 60h(4), frames 1036, 1041; Report No. 60h(1), frames 772, 805, both in Roll 304; Report No. 1c(5) Hiroshima, 24, 46, Roll 10, USSBS RSD.
88   UAD, *Hiroshima*, 10.
89   Report No. 60h(1), frame 804, Roll 304; Report No. 1c(5) Hiroshima, 46, Roll 10, USSBS RSD.
90   Report No. 59m, Target Data, 11, Roll 303A; Report No. 1c(5) Nagasaki, frame 647, Roll 10, both of USSBS RSD.
91   UAD, *Nagasaki*, 11.
92   Entry of 6 June 1945, 4, Henry Lewis Stimson Diaries 51 (microfilm edition, reel 9), Manuscripts and Archives, Yale University Library, New Haven, CT, 1973, by courtesy of International Institute of American Studies, Doshisha University, Kyoto. An example of this classic interpretation is a case made by Swedish journalist/historian Monica Braw. She explains that MacArthur suppressed publications of news stories and other expressions of the horrors of the atomic bomb in fear of possible

of international reputation. USSBS was attempting to deny the awe of the atomic bomb and to display the atomic bomb as just another weapon for the sake of postwar civil defence. A preliminary PDD draft reads: "It is clear that despite the awesome power of the bomb and the unprecedented blotch of devastation left in its wake, it has limitations. Wise planning can decrease the bomb's destructiveness by taking advantage of the limitations as established by this report."[93] This attitude is also apparent in a UAD preliminary report, which explains the Survey's mission as follows:

> When the city of Nagasaki was made the target of the second atomic attack against Japan, it was publicly announced that this second, improved bomb had rendered the previous one obsolete. Lurid newspaper accounts by mission observers led the public at large to assume that the city must have been wiped from the face of the earth by the force of this new weapon ... On the other hand, wishing to utilize the enormity of the disaster, for propaganda purposes, as an instance of American brutality, Japanese news sources simultaneously exaggerated the extent of the destruction ... Surmise and rumor had created an almost superstitious attitude on the part of the world at large toward the atomic bomb and its destructive effect. In an effort to counteract this dangerous attitude, and at the same time provide a factual basis for future strategic thinking concerning the atomic bomb as an aerial weapon, the various divisions of the USSBS dispatched teams to the two atomic bombed cities to arrive at a true estimate ...[94]

However different in approach, both UAD's Hiroshima and Nagasaki reports had likely shared the same goal: to convince the public that it was possible to recover from the atomic disaster. Hiroshima proved this, while in Nagasaki it was not the atomic bomb that limited its recuperation but some other factors. It may have well been expressed most accurately in the following: "The atomic bomb is clearly the most effective area weapon yet devised. Its social and economic effects, however, are the result almost entirely of the area destruction and the casualties, and *do not differ essentially from the effects of a similar sweep of destruction from other means.* The ability of a city to recover from an attack with atomic bombs, then, will depend, as heretofore, upon the social and economic vitality of its people, and henceforth upon their foresight in applying the lessons of Nagasaki."[95] (Author's italics)

---

international criticism that the use of the weapon violated international law. Braw, *The Atomic Bomb Suppressed: American Censorship in Occupied Japan* (New York: M. E. Sharpe, 1991), 151–152.
93   "Probable effects on other targets," Report No. 92f(1)(b), frame 31, Roll 327, USSBS RSD.
94   UAD, preliminary report on Nagasaki, Report No. 55a(13), frames 373–374, Roll 283A, USSBS RSD. Most of these accounts are not included in the published report. It is beyond the scope of this article to discuss this in detail; however, this account obviously suggests Japanese propaganda inflated the effects of radiation, and especially the mysterious deaths of those who entered the cities after the explosion.
95   UAD, *Nagasaki,* 18.

## Atomic Bomb: Revolutionary, or Just Another Bomb?

In a similar vein, it was likely the responsibility of CDD to show that the atomic bomb was defendable.[96] And the division found shelters the most effective measure against the bomb. CDD's comprehensive report of its study in Japan reads, "At the present time, properly constructed and located shelters appear to be the only answer to that problem [protection for essential persons required to remain in cities], and shelters constructed of reinforced concrete of sufficient thickness to withstand the impact of the heaviest bomb anticipated, insulated against intense heat and atomic radiation, and provided with ventilation systems and self-contained oxygen unites to provide air in case of conflagration would meet nearly every test."[97]

This judgment on the feasibilities of shelters as protection against the atomic bomb was based on its Nagasaki report. In the report, CDD made detailed observations of five tunnel-type shelters in the city—some almost below the epicenter—their shapes, structures and distances from GZ, as well as physical conditions of people who were in these shelters, and their specific locations in the shelters at the time of the explosion.[98] The division concluded as follows:

> It was the opinion of all the subjects interviewed and of civilian defense officials questioned that if the people had been in the types of tunnel shelters ... and had taken the proper position therein (not in the entrance) that most of them would have suffered little or no injury and no apparent after-effects. This theory is further strengthened by statements from officials who estimated that about 400 persons were in tunnel shelters at the time of the explosion and that about 300 of them were unharmed or only slightly injured because they had taken the properly designated positions and had remained in those locations for a reasonable period of time after the explosion.[99]

The problem here is that CDD was not telling the whole truth. While photographically describing the horrible deaths of people outside the shelters, its Nagasaki report hardly mentioned that anyone died in the shelters except those standing at the "entrances" of the "Shelter 4," with all the others having only suffered mild injuries

---

96 Because CDD's Hiroshima report is so short and does not provide any tangible information, only Nagasaki report will be discussed in this essay.
97 CDD, *Final Report Covering Air-Raid Protection and Allied Subjects in Japan* (US Government Printing Office, February 1947), 6.
98 CDD, *Nagasaki*, 63–75. One of these seven individuals—Subject "F"—was not in the Shelter 4 at the time of the explosion but went there in the afternoon of that same day. It is difficult to understand how the Survey made him a witness of the scene and determined the location of individuals in the shelter at the time of the explosion.
99 CDD, *Nagasaki*, 73. Interestingly, this last sentence contradicts the official American view then that there would be no residual radiation in the two cities strong enough to harm people's health.

and radiation sickness, most of whom eventually recovered.[100] But the fact was that those who survived likely consisted of only a segment of people who were in the shelters. The rest of them died just like the people outside.

That comment will be more apparent if we compare CDD's study with another. According to a study conducted by a group of Japanese scientists from the School of Medicine at Tokyo Imperial University, who were members of the atomic bomb research committee assigned by the Japanese Education Ministry in September 1945, there were fifty-two people from a local block association working in the entrenched cave that CDD labeled as the "Shelter 1"[101] at the time the atomic bomb exploded.[102] The Japanese report states that only seven survived in this shelter.[103] The majority of the people, including those at the far end of the shelter, died, immediately or days later (see Figures 1 and 2).

It is true that a bare majority of people who were in "Shelter 2" were unharmed. But it was not because they had taken the "properly designated positions" and had "remained in those locations for a reasonable period of time after the explosion" as CDD argued. Shelters certainly provided a better survival rate for the people inside than those in the open-air;[104] however, whether one could survive in a shelter was rather a matter of unpredictable probability, on which no one would want to stake his or her life.

---

100  CDD, *Nagasaki*, 70–73. The report reads, "A woman (in Shelter 1)…was burned on the face, arms, and upper part of the chest but she recovered and was not suffering any after-effects" (70); "The persons (two in the Shelter 2)… were burned on the back and swelled up, but all of them have recovered with no apparent ill effects" (70); "A woman (in Shelter 3) was slightly burned and knocked over by the blast, but she has fully recovered with no apparent ill effects" (72).

101  CDD, *Nagasaki*, 69. According to Nagasaki's official atomic bomb history, these people, mostly women, were removing water from the cave flooded by the rain of a couple of days before.

102  Urabe, M., et al., "Reports of the Inspections of the Cave-Trenches Around the Hill of Prison in the City of Nagasaki," undated, Folder 4, Box 7407, Economic & Scientific Section, GHQ/SCAP Records, microfiche No. ESS(D) 06274, Ritsumeikan University Shugakukan Research Library. This author identified CDD's Shelter 1 as the same one cited as the "cave-trench I" in the Japanese report because of its shape, location at the hill, and the name of the person listed in the two reports.

103  Urabe, M., et al., "Reports of the Inspections of the Cave-Trenches Around the Hill of Prison in the City of Nagasaki," Folder 4, Box 7407, Economic & Scientific Section, GHQ/SCAP Records, ESS(D) 06274.

104  All the other study groups that studied which worked in Hiroshima and Nagasaki considered cave shelters effective with reservations. *Medical Report of the Joint Commission for the Investigation of the effects of the Atomic Bomb in Japan* 6, 238; British Mission to Japan, *The Effects of the Atomic bombs at Hiroshima and Nagasaki*, 9; NavTechJap, *Atomic Bombs, Hiroshima and Nagasaki, Article 1, Medical Aspect*, 6, 48; MED Group, *The Atomic Bombings of Hiroshima and Nagasaki*, 11.

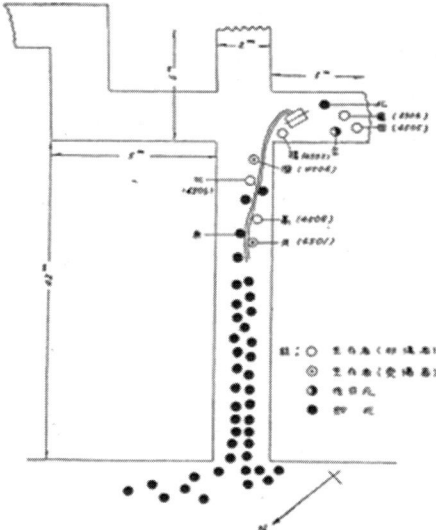

Figure 1. The shape of the Cave Trench I and positions of and extent of injuries suffered by people who were there, recorded by Japanese scientists. Black blank circles indicate survivors without injury, Black circles with center dots survivors with injuries, white/black circle those died afterwards, and black solid circles those died at once.

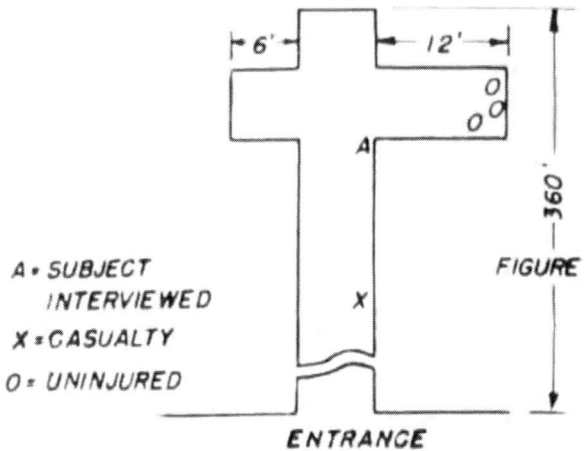

Figure 2. The shape of the Shelter 1 and positions of people who were there, recorded by the USSBS CDD. CDD, *Field Report Covering Air-Raid Protection and Allied Subjects, Nagasaki, Japan,* 68.

Actually, earlier drafts were showing likely more accurate pictures. These draft reports stated that "200 to 400 persons"[105] were in tunnel shelters at the time of the explosion and that "about 100 of them"[106] were unharmed or only slightly injured, instead of 400 and 300, respectively, in the final version. But these figures were changed in the later drafts without any grounds.

It is apparent that CDD attempted to make the report sound assuring that the atomic bomb was just another weapon, for which civilian defence was possible. A draft report explains the Survey's mission as follows:

> At first sight, the havoc caused by the atomic bombs in Hiroshima and Nagasaki seemed incredible, and such was the reaction of most observers who had the opportunity to make only cursory inspections of the two cities. The incidents provided field days for American newspapers, and their almost hysterical accounts proclaimed a new era in the science of warfare—all means and methods of combat up to that time had immediately become obsolete. To the journalistic chorus were added the voices of scientists, congressmen, "expert" commentators, the man-in-the street, and even some military authorities. The result was, of course, the formation of a distorted picture in the mind of the average person who was sincerely trying to evaluate the situation. A calm appraisal of the atomic bombing does not change any of the results but comparison of the devastation with that found in Kobe, Osaka, and Tokyo raises the question of, why there was so much emotion. The wasted areas in Hiroshima and Nagasaki do not differ materially, at least in outward appearances, from those in other Japanese cities which were ravaged by incendiary raids ... the ultimate result was identical—utter devastation. The suspicion, therefore, arises quite naturally that possibly this new method of destruction is not too unlike the old procedures, the results being the same, except that they are achieved with larger element of surprise and with greater concentration of force.[107]

Another draft comments that:

> From the civilian defense point of view, however, the problem is to develop protective measures which will minimize to some degree the effects of this new weapon. There is no reason for a "nothing-can-be-done" attitude in this field, for just as every revolutionary weapon of the past has caused the development of counter measures in active defense which tended to mitigate its effects, just so is it reasonable to expect that something can be done to lessen the effects of atomic bombs on civilian populations.[108]

---

105 Report No. 5b Manuscript, frame 758, Roll 66; Report No. 13a(8) Nagasaki field report, frame 430, Roll 92, both in USSBS RSD. In Report No. 1c(8), it is "some 400." (frames 86, 317, Roll 12)
106 Report No. 5b Manuscript, frame No. 758, Roll 66, USSBS RSD; Report No. 1c(8) Atomic Bomb Report, frames 86, 317, Roll 12; Report No. 13a(8) Nagasaki field report, frame 430, Roll 92, all in USSBS RSD.
107 Atomic Bomb Report, Report No. 1c(8), frames 68, 299, Roll 12, USSBS RSD. A similar account is found in Report 10ww(1) Special Atomic Bomb Report on Japanese Civilian Defense Forces for Inclusion in the Over-All Report of the United States Strategic Bombing Survey, 5 February 1946, 1–4, Roll 80, USSBS RSD.
108 Atomic Bomb Report, Report No. 1c(8), frames 69, 300, Roll 12, USSBS RSD. The writings are so straightforward and perhaps because of that they did not make it into the final reports.

A reviewer of this draft wrote the word "amplify" in handwriting in the blank margin next to the last sentence. It was the shared sense of purpose to explain to the American public that the atomic bomb could be terrifying but still manageable. It was important to show readers that there was a way to protect them against the bomb. The stories of people who survived in entrenched caves in Nagasaki had likely given the CDD members their *raison d'etre* at a time when civilian defence experts were struggling to bring the atomic bomb forward to be "recognized as a primary component of over-all defence and must be removed from its former inferior and haphazard role."[109]

The division also tried to blame the Japanese side for the lack of proper defence program. Throughout its final report on Japan, CDD criticized Japanese government, military, and emergency service providers, such as fire fighters, rescue workers, and medical personnel, for lack of adequate plans, equipment and training to combat with saturation incendiary bombing.[110] For example, it called equipment of Japanese fire departments "inferior," training "inadequate," and personnel "mediocre," which made it "impossible for them to meet even the lowest of fire-fighting standards in the United States."[111] For CDD, the loss of more than half the first-aid stations in Tokyo and its vicinities in Tokyo air raids was "responsible for the considerable but undetermined number of persons who died for lack of prompt and effective first aid."[112]

The same was true with the case of Nagasaki where "… possibly as many as 20,000 died over a period of weeks following the atomic bomb raid."[113] CDD's Nagasaki report argues: "… the physical condition of the streets and the inevitable confusion resulting from such a catastrophe placed insurmountable obstacles in the way of transporting the injured to places where they could receive medical attention. The conclusion is, therefore, inescapable that many persons did die from lack of medical care."[114] Obviously, their conclusion left no place for the delayed effects of the bomb's radiation. "Had more competent medical care been available, a still larger number would have been saved. It is the opinion of this Division that

---

109 Provost Marshal General, "Defense Against Enemy Action Directed at Civilians" (Study 3B-1), 30 April 1946 (hereafter, "Study 3B-1"), 3.
110 CDD, *Japan*, 7–9.
111 Ibid, 8.
112 Ibid, 9.
113 CDD, *Nagasaki*, 34.
114 Ibid.

optimum civilian defence measures can reduce injuries and fatalities to one-twentieth or less of the number that would be expected, were no such measures taken."[115]

Not all the divisions in the Survey agreed with the CDD's effort to downplay the effects of the atomic bomb, however. There seems to be a *certain* conflict between the Survey divisions over the evaluation of the effects of the atomic bomb—whether it was just another weapon, or a revolutionary and absolute weapon totally different from conventional weapons. Medical Division, which apparently stood on the latter position,[116] implicitly challenged some of the accounts CDD made to display it as just another weapon. For example, regarding the 20,000 people mentioned above who died weeks after the attack, Medical Division obliquely denied CDD's motion: "With large quantities of whole blood and adequate supportive treatment possibly 10 to 20 percent of those dying of radiation might have survived. However, it is doubtful that 10 percent of all the deaths resulting from the atomic bombs could have been saved with the best medical care; 5 to 8 percent is probably a more likely figure."[117]

While CDD attributed heavy casualties in Nagasaki to the military's failure to inform the people of the lesson of Hiroshima three days before,[118] Medical Division described the situation in Nagasaki as follows: "Even though it followed the bombing of Hiroshima by 3 days, wartime secrecy, general confusion and the short elapse of time did not allow the population of Nagasaki any particular advantage from the previous experience. The psychological reaction of the people was essentially the same and the chaos in the city seems to have been almost as great."[119]

---

115  CDD, *Japan*, 2.
116  It states, "…it is important for one to realize the magnitude of the destructive forces since they so completely surpass all previous concepts of destruction that one might have when thinking in terms of ordinary incendiary or high-explosive bombing." Medical Division, *Hiroshima and Nagasaki*, 2.
117  Medical Division, *Hiroshima and Nagasaki*, 55.
118  CDD states: "…the military authorities failed in their responsibility by (1) not advising the people of Nagasaki of the possibility of further raids similar to that made upon Hiroshima on 6 August 1945; (2) not directing all the public to take shelter when the appropriate signal was sounded; and (3) not ordering the "alarm" signal, inasmuch as it had been demonstrated that a single plane now could carry a destructive force equal to or greater than that carried by a large flight of planes." CDD, *Nagasaki*, 6, 75.
119  Medical Division, *Hiroshima and Nagasaki*, 20. The British Mission had a different opinion. It writes: "Since the population was aware that an atomic bomb had fallen on Hiroshima, the disaster was less unexpected. Nevertheless, it overwhelmed the medical and civilian services." Report of the British Mission to Japan on an Investigation of the Effects of the Atomic Bombs Dropped at Hiroshima and Nagasaki, December 1945, Report No. 3g(1), frames 230, 291, Roll 54, USSBS RSD. This part, however was not included in their published report.

Also, contrary to the CDD's argument that "a considerable number of students, nurses, and patients"[120] at Nagasaki Medical School survived because the school buildings were of concrete construction, Medical Division revealed a different picture: "Of the 850 medical students present 600 were killed and 12 of the 16 professors were also lost ... Almost all of the ... occupants of the buildings were killed outright."[121] Another report states that: "The destruction of the University Hospital and the Medical College was so great that the buildings left standing could not be reoccupied even for emergency medical care."[122] Even other than the 600 killed, "some others (students) may have died later. Of the survivors, practically every one was injured and at least half had radiation sickness later."[123]

Perhaps the difference between their stance and that of the CDD appears most conspicuous in their handling of the number of casualties of the atomic bomb. In its atomic bomb report, Medical Division questioned the casualty figures collected by Civilian Defense Division—25,761 dead, 30,460 injured, and 1,928 missing as of 6 November 1945.[124] It states: "The best figures available on the casualties in Nagasaki were prepared by the Japanese for the Civilian Defense Division of USSBS and they are admittedly inadequate. They include only the number of verified deaths and the figure for injured include only those hospitalized in Nagasaki." [125] The division then presented its estimates—about 80,000 deaths and 80,000–100,000 casualties in Hiroshima and about 45,000 deaths and 50,000–60,000 casualties in Nagasaki,[126] which are "the result of careful study by investigators who visited the cities."[127]

---

120 CDD's Nagasaki report also cites fewer number students killed—500. CDD, *Nagasaki*, 37.
121 Medical Division, *Hiroshima and Nagasaki*, 10. This account is supported by evidence, information provided by Prof. Kanehiko Kitamura and Prof. Raisuke Shirabe of Nagasaki Medical School. Statistics on Nagasaki Medical School, Report No. 13d(2)c, frame 746, Roll 92, USSBS RSD.
122 Medical Division, *Hiroshima and Nagasaki*, 20.
123 Ibid, 21.
124 Ibid, 56; CDD, *Nagasaki*, 2.
125 Medical Division, *Hiroshima and Nagasaki*, 56.
126 Ibid, 57. The report did not mention CDD's Hiroshima figures, but it was also much lower than Medical Division's estimates—46,185 dead, 64,670 injured and 17,429 missing. CDD, *Hiroshima*, 10. These figures remained the same from the earliest drafts. Report No. 1c(8), frames 71, 74, 302, 305, Roll 12; Report No. 10ww(1), frames 865, 867, Roll 80, both in USSBS RSD.
127 Medical Division, *The Effects of Bombing on Health and Medical Services in Japan* (Government Printing Office, 1947), 143. The division sounds almost dumbstruck that the Ministry of Education stated that only 399 students were killed at the Nagasaki Medical School whereas local authorities reported the number to be 600 (page 20).

Medical Division in fact considered the CDD's air-raid casualty figures of Japanese civilians for the entire country provided by the Japanese Home Ministry—269,187 deaths, 109,861 serious injuries and 195,517 slight injuries, or 574,565 casualties in total—too small.[128] Comparing the figures with those provided directly by prefectural health divisions, the report called the Home Ministry figures "conservative,"[129] and made its discussion using the prefectural figures—330,000 deaths and 473,000 injuries or 806,000 total casualties.[130]

Medical Division, in its inherent mission to study the effects of the bombings on the system of public health and medical care in Japan, inevitably had to deal with the problem of the morality of indiscriminate bombings. About 10% of hospitals across the country were totally destroyed, with more than 20% of their bed capacity lost.[131] In Tokyo, in particular, 233 of some 500 hospitals were completely destroyed and one-third of their 48,000 beds were lost.[132] While the division never openly criticized the American bombing campaign, it deplored what it found: "The destruction of the civilian population of any country, even if it occurs as an incident in the destruction of military objectives, is not pleasant to contemplate, especially when the majority of such casualties are women and children."[133] Having compared the damage with that of Germany, the division seems to have been awed by the extent of the overall destruction inflicted on Japan: "It is quite evident ... that whatever yardstick is used, whether fatalities per ton of bomb dropped, or fatalities per month, the number of fatalities caused by bombing in Japan was proportionately much greater than in Germany."[134]

"The blast effects of the atomic bombs as indicated by the effects on objects and persons in the target area are similar in most respects to those of other blast weapons,"[135] Medical Division's atomic bomb report reads. Yet, the bomb would also release a heat wave and radiation that could cause flash burns and, in case of radiation, a peculiar sickness that is characterized by such symptoms as leucopenia,

---

128  Medical Division, *Japan*, 142. These figures were calculated by adding the number of casualties of Kagoshima and two other cities, of which data was missing, to the figures shown in Appendix C-1 (242–244).
129  Medical Division, *Japan*, 142.
130  Ibid, 142–143.
131  Ibid, 10–11, 13.
132  Ibid, 11, 14, 21.
133  Ibid, 5. The photographs of charred bodies of mothers and their babies on page 152 of this report eloquently speak for themselves.
134  Ibid, *Japan*, 5.
135  Medical Division, *Hiroshima and Nagasaki*, 24.

epilation and petechiae, and which could cause eventual death.[136] Referring to the ongoing trend to make light of these aspects, Medical Division argued:

> The importance of radiation as a cause of death is definitely underrated by the foregoing presentation ... There is reason to believe that if the effects of blast and fire had been entirely absent from the bombing, the number of deaths among people within a half mile radius would have been almost as great and the deaths among those within a 1 mile radius would have been only slightly less. The principal difference would have been in the time of the deaths. Instead of being killed outright as were most of those people, they would have survived for a few days to 3 to 4 weeks, only to die of radiation disease.[137]

The preceding studies on USSBS predominantly discuss the aspect of the Pacific Survey in connection with the inter-service rivalry between the Army Air Force and Navy over who won the war with Japan and who should receive larger share in the postwar military establishment.[138] Careful reading of the USSBS atomic bomb reports, however, reveals that the Pacific Survey was as much an issue of the atomic bomb versus conventional bombing as that of the Army Air Forces vs. Navy, in that there were conflicts over the evaluation of the effects of the atomic bomb—if it was just another weapon, or revolutionary and absolute weapon, which is totally different from conventional weapons.

Such a conflict may be most apparent in the Morale Division's report. Whereas the draft report contained accounts that attributed the end of war to the atomic bomb,[139] they were replaced, in the published report, by those that emphasized the limited role the atomic bomb played in bringing Japan's surrender, including the following: "From the standpoint of the politics of surrender ... the atom bombing of Hiroshima and Nagasaki was not essential. From its studies of

---

136  Leucopenia is the reduction of white cells in the blood. Epilation is the removal of hair by the roots. Petechiae are red or purple spots caused by bleeding to the skin.

137  Medical Division, *The Effects of Atomic Bombs on Health and Medical Services in Hiroshima and Nagasaki*, 54. The NavTechJap, and the British Mission in their reports also made statements to this effect. NavTechJap, *Atomic Bombs, Hiroshima and Nagasaki, Article 1, Medical Aspect*, December 1945, 52; The British Mission to Japan, *The Effects of the Atomic bombs at Hiroshima and Nagasaki*, 16.

138  David MacIsaac, *Strategic Bombing in World War Two: The Story of the United States Strategic Bombing Survey* (NY: Garland Publishing, 1976), 119–135; Gian P. Gentile, *How Effective Is Strategic Bombing? Lessons Learned From World War II To Kosovo* (New York: New York University Press, 2001), 104–130.

139  "...the atomic bomb was the real Kamikaze, since it saved Japan from further useless slaughter and destruction...it was the atomic bomb which first offered certain government leaders the opportunity to sway the military;" "Breaking the confidence of the civilian population, however, was incidental to the more dicisive [sic] consequences of the bomb's use—elimination of the last ventiges [sic] of the government's determination to continue the war Report No. 14h(1) The effects of the atomic bombings on Japanese morale, Feb. 6, 1946, 13, 15, Roll 133, USSBS RSD.

Japanese resources, military position, and ruling class politics, the Survey estimates that the government would have surrendered prior to 1 November and certainly before the end of the year, whether or not the atomic bombs had been dropped and Russia had entered the war."[140]

## Conclusion

As we have seen there were narratives in some of the atomic bomb reports written by the five USSBS divisions that studied Hiroshima and Nagasaki that are similar to the early-surrender hypothesis found in the two reports published from the Chairman's Office. These were submitted to the USSBS Secretariat for the authors of the reports from the Chairman's Office to formulate their own statements. It is apparent that the narrative had been shared throughout the divisions in the Survey. It was certainly an organizational effort to downplay the effects of the atomic bomb.

In their reports, there were also many accounts designed to deny the awesome nature of the atomic bomb and to make it look like just another bomb, against which protection is possible. They likely targeted the American public, which the officials feared would go back to isolationism now that the United States had won the war. They were conceived both to assure and alarm the public to a certain degree, and to win their support to prepare for the next war.

When World War II broke out, only a little more than two decades after the end of World War I, the United States was caught ill-equipped and ill-prepared. Their leaders were determined not to repeat the mistake well before the end of the second war. The advent of the atomic bomb not only increased the need to be prepared for a possible atomic war, but also urged the importance of incorporating the new weapon in the American arsenal. The USSBS early-surrender hypothesis came just at the moment when the United States was making its transition from a conventional power to a nuclear one.

---

140   Morale Division, *The Effects of Strategic Bombing on Japanese Morale*, 4.

# HOW TO CELEBRATE THE DEPLOYMENT OF THE ATOMIC BOMB: TRUMAN'S STATEMENT AFTER HIROSHIMA

*Yuko Shibata*

## Gaining the Authority to Define the Atomic Bomb

When for the first time in history the American Forces used the atomic bomb in Hiroshima, how did they define the bomb and spread the news of this unprecedented event around the world? Although the idea of the atomic bomb was not new and was already shared among countries of both the Allies and the Axis powers, no military force in the world had ever succeeded in putting it to practical use before the US Forces did so on 6 August 1945. In this sense, the attacks on Hiroshima and Nagasaki have made the United States the only country whose articulation of the atomic bomb bears gravity and authority, no matter the content. To put it another way, in the wake of the atomic bombings, the US acquired not only the supreme military power to cause immeasurable damage to enemies, but also the predominant signifying power to pronounce how the advent of the new weapon should be understood by the rest of the world.

This world after Hiroshima started in tandem with this American possession of the atomic bomb both militarily and rhetorically. The position of the US as the sole nuclear power only lasted a few years and disappeared completely in the face of the nuclear proliferation of the 1950s. But some images of the atomic bomb and nuclear energy, as set in motion at the initial stage, not only resonated throughout the Cold War era, but have also exerted a far-reaching influence up to the present day. In order to explore how the US lead the production of discourses on the atomic bomb and nuclear power, this paper will look into American President Harry Truman's statement issued shortly after the bombing of Hiroshima—in fact it was the first statement that told the world of the employment of a nuclear weapon. I will discuss what kinds of images his statement conveys as to 1) the development and the use of the atomic bomb, 2) the definition of this bomb, and 3) the relationship between the bomb and American national identity.[1] These images

---

1   For my analyses of Truman's statement, also see Yuko Shibata, "The Valorization of the Atomic Bomb: Blast Power over the After-Effects of Radiation," in Yasuko Claremont ed., *Civil Society and Postwar Pacific Basin Reconciliation: Wounds, Scars, and Healing* (London: Routledge, 2018), 91–

attest to the strategies employed to dramatize the United States' position in the world after its development of the atomic bomb, as well as the framework of influential narratives about this bomb.

## Synchronization between American History and World History

The content of Truman's statement reflects how the US authorities wanted to portray the advent of the atomic bomb and their own conduct. It does not necessarily mean that everything that appears in the statement represents what really happened before and after the Hiroshima bombing. For instance, Truman's statement does not mention that the actual targets of the bombing of Hiroshima were the commercial and residential districts in the densely-populated city centre. From March 1945, the US Forces had engaged in indiscriminate air strikes against large Japanese cities such as Tokyo, Osaka, and Nagoya, as well as medium-sized cities and even small villages across the Japanese archipelago. Earlier, they had already destroyed most functions of Japanese military operations. US attacks had destroyed about 400 Japanese cities and towns in the wake of indiscriminate air raids by the end of the war;[2] the attacks on Hiroshima and Nagasaki were a prolongation of this extensive campaign against civilians.

But Truman's statement avoided mention of the entire development of these American military actions. This separation of the previous bombardment of other Japanese cities and towns from Hiroshima and Nagasaki at times generates a misleading view of the attack on the two southern cities as being isolated incidents, while forgetting and suppressing the memories of these other mass killings, which did not involve the atomic bomb, such as the Great Tokyo Air Raid of 9–10 March 1945. Although it is hardly conceivable that Truman's statement was the main and singlehanded cause of the prevalence of this misleading view, his statement became the first instance of disconnecting these air raids before and after Hiroshima. Another aspect absent in Truman's statement is any mention of the emittance of radiation, an invisible and deadly substance, from the atomic bomb at the moment of explosion. Instead, the statement puts a singular emphasis on its blast power. This lack of reference to radiation gives his description of the impact of the atomic bomb a lopsided nuance. I will return to this point later.

---

92, 95; and Yuko Shibata, *Hiroshima Nagasaki: hibaku shinawa o kaitaisuru* (*Hiroshima Nagasaki: Debunking a Myth of the Hibakusha's Narrative* (Tokyo: Sakuhinsha, 2015), Chapter 1.

2    Toshihiro Yoshida, *Han kubaku no shiso* (*Thought of Anti-Aerial Bombardment*) (Tokyo: Nihon hoso shuppan kyokai, 2006), 112.

Yet it is unsurprising that Truman's statement is structured in this way, and in its failure not only to situate the atomic bombing against the whole backdrop of American air raids against Japan, but also to reveal appropriate information about the bomb's precise features. Announced in the midst of the ongoing war, the American commander-in-chief's statement had to consolidate and justify both the reason and method of the American military air campaign. It should be added that the Japanese military also engaged in indiscriminate air raids against many cities in China; especially its attack on Chongqing in December 1938, which victimized many civilians. But during the war the Japanese Forces never mentioned this fact either.

Furthermore, from the outset the American authorities had no intention of disclosing much information about the atomic bomb. Truman's statement clearly states this:

> It has never been the habit of the scientists of this country or the policy of this Government to withhold from the world scientific knowledge. Normally, therefore, everything about the work with atomic energy would be made public. But under the present circumstances it is not intended to divulge the technical processes of production or all the military applications, pending further examination of possible methods of protecting us and the rest of the world from the danger of sudden destruction.[3]

Indeed, at that time detailed information on the atomic bomb was a military secret at the highest security level. Its disclosure ran the risk of jeopardizing the United States' overwhelming military power and the hegemonic status just attained by the sole possession of the atomic bomb. Thus, Truman's statement had already prepared well for the onset of a postwar world, and for what kind of role the US should play at this new stage of international politics.

It is also clear that Truman's statement embodies a completely new attitude of the American administration towards the world, as a sweeping power that enjoys a monopoly in atomic weaponry. As the statement claims, the ownership of the atomic bomb earns the US the position of protecting the world from "danger of sudden destruction."[4] But simultaneously this message implicitly indicates that the US had become powerful enough to define the world's fate. Furthermore, in

---

3   "Statement by the President of the United States," Press Release by the White House, 6 August 1945, Subject File, Ayers Papers, accessed 1 March 2016, http://www.trumanlibrary.org/whistlestop/study_collections/bomb/large/documents/index.php?documentdate=1945-08-06&documentid=59&pagenumber=1.
4   Ibid.

either case the outcomes were solely dependent on its own choice. Truman's statement operates as a declaration of such "freedom" that the US could savour from that time. Thus, it is inaccurate to take this statement as a mere announcement of the successful employment of the atomic bomb.

Rather, we should regard it as an historic intersection, not only in American history but also in world history. Without doubt American actions and behaviour weigh as decisively momentous in American history. But at that juncture these have also become significantly critical in world history. The atomic bomb made it possible to create such a sense of synchronization between American and world history. This synchronization was amplified inside the US throughout the Cold War, when the American nuclear arms race with the Soviet Union became one of the major political concerns of the international community. In this situation, not only military, but also political and economic crises taking place in the US have also been imagined as influencing the rest of the world. Postwar American national identity came into existence in conjunction with such psychological, but not always necessarily substantial, situations. In this way, the atomic bomb, which evolved later into more advanced nuclear weaponry, has burrowed deep within the American psyche as a conjunction of an imagined destiny of the US with that of the world. Historically speaking, we should deem Truman's statement to be one of the earliest manoeuvres that ushered in this phenomenon.

## Preclusion of Harmful Information about the Bomb

I have thus far discussed what Truman's statement indicates regarding the roles of the atomic bomb in establishing postwar American national identity—the demonstration of the new status of the US in international politics; the potentiality for the US to become either a protector or a destroyer of the world; the overlapping of US history with world history; and a sense of conflation between incidents that take place both in the US and in the world. But there is a very basic premise that sustains all these "features" in terms of the impact of the atomic bomb on American national identity; namely, the need to affirm and justify the use of the atomic bomb in Japan, along with the imperative to create a positive image of the atomic bomb and atomic energy.

On this basic premise, both the atomic bomb attack and the definition of the bomb *per se* should not be negatively understood. These imperatives also inevitably require a covering-up of the adverse consequences that the bomb has brought to human beings and the environment in its production process in the US, as well as after the attacks on the cities of Hiroshima and Nagasaki. The result of all of these factors is the focus on positive images of the atomic bomb, along with the preclusion of domestic and international criticism that may arise out of the political, economic, moral and ethical concerns about the Manhattan Project.

As mentioned, Truman's statement remains silent on the exact target of the atomic bombing in Hiroshima. Nor does it account for the effects of the bombing, but only addresses them generally and vaguely in the opening sentence: "Sixteen hours ago an American airplane dropped one bomb on Hiroshima and destroyed its usefulness to the enemy."[5] These words simply give an abstract idea of what was destroyed in Hiroshima. Instead of providing substantial information, this sentence prompts the audience to fill in the blanks on its own. Later in the statement, similar rhetorical strategies appear again. After explaining how the American Forces succeeded in producing the atomic bomb, the statement contends: "We are now prepared to obliterate more rapidly and completely every productive enterprise the Japanese have above ground in any city. We shall destroy their docks, their factories, and their communications. Let there be no mistake; we shall completely destroy Japan's power to make war."[6]

In displaying the American Forces' readiness to thoroughly destroy "Japan's power to make war," this time the statement affords more clues as to their military targets: "their docks, their factories, and their communications." They all suggest industrial facilities that can be put to use for Japanese military operations. Given this information, the audience naturally assumes that similar facilities were also destroyed in Hiroshima, despite the fact that ground zero was inside the inland residential and commercial areas, not the coastal industrial areas where docks and factories were centred. Truman's statement also assures the audience that there is no danger to the health of American workers engaged in the production of this harmful weapon in the Manhattan Project:

> The Secretary of War, who has kept in personal touch with all phases of the project, will immediately make public a statement giving further details. His statement will give facts concerning the sites at Oak Ridge near Knoxville, Tennessee, and at Richland, near Pasco, Washington, and an installation near Santa Fe, New Mexico. Although the workers at the sites have been making materials to be used in producing the greatest destructive force in history they have not themselves been in danger beyond that of many other occupations, for the utmost care has been taken of their safety.[7]

---

5    Ibid.
6    Ibid.
7    Ibid.

This passage also successfully gives the impression that no serious harm has been caused either to human beings or the environment. However, as an example, in Richland where plutonium used for the Nagasaki bombing was manufactured on the newly-built Hanford site, radioactive substances were released into the air, the ground and the adjacent Columbia River, and caused significant health damage to residents in the wide downwind and downriver areas.[8] The Hanford site itself has met great challenges. Although it has been a few decades since several nuclear reactors built during the Cold War were shut down, the American government has found no umbrella solutions in their decommissioning and decontaminating processes. In this regard, Truman's statement also became one of the first instances of being mute on damaging the well-being of Americans and contaminating American land due to the Manhattan Project. It is remarkable that Truman's statement never mentions any concern about residents near these sites in Oak Ridge, Richland and Santa Fe, but only about workers involved in the project, just as it ignores the residents in Hiroshima and Nagasaki.

## Creating a Masculine and Straightforward Image of the Atomic Bomb

But the exclusion of these matters is offset by the creation of the positive images of the atomic bomb. In Truman's statement, this is achieved in these three ways: 1) the glorification of the gigantic blast power of the bomb, 2) the metaphorical use of the sun as a source of the bomb's intrinsic power, and 3) the possibility of making use of atomic power for future industrial energy. All three dramatize the presence of the atomic bomb by creating awe-inspiring and future-oriented images far removed from its purpose for mass killing. The emphasis on the first feature, the atomic bomb's explosive power, comes at the beginning of Truman's statement. As mentioned, the very first sentence ("Sixteen hours ago an American airplane dropped one bomb on Hiroshima and destroyed its usefulness to the enemy") describes what the US Forces had just done, and when and where. At this point, the statement only says: "an American airplane dropped one bomb," without revealing its nature. Then, the second sentence offers more detailed information about its characteristics: "That bomb had more power than 20,000 tons of TNT. It had more

---

[8] See, for example, Karen Dorn Steele, "Hanford' Bitter Legacy," *Bulletin of the Atomic Scientists*, Vol. 44 (1988): 17–23.

than two thousand times the blast power of the British 'Grand Slam' which is the largest bomb ever yet used in the history of warfare."[9]

By comparing the atomic bomb only with the largest non-nuclear one to date, Truman's statement places it under the rubric of conventional weaponry. Here what distinguishes it from the others in existence is its massive blast power, as if the difference between them exists in terms of quantity, not quality. As mentioned earlier, Truman's statement again hides another characteristic of the atomic bomb, the greatest difference and the newest feature at its core: the emission of radiation that produces not only instantaneous, but also long-term effects on an unprecedented scale. Although it is true that some critics believe high-level policy-makers like Presidents Roosevelt and Truman had no knowledge of this perilous aspect of the atomic bomb, General Leslie Groves who led the Manhattan Project certainly did.[10] Groves also prepared Truman's statement together with his team. He even secretly recruited and hired the *New York Times* staff-writer William L. Laurence to effectively publicize the atomic bomb. Laurence was astounded at the enormous scale of the blast in the test undertaken at the Trinity site in July 1945. This experience had a big impact on his draft of the statement as well.

To simply define the atomic bomb according to its enormous explosive power helps to establish a clear-cut image of the bomb. The gigantic explosive power signifies a dynamism, an immense magnitude, and a gargantuan volume. Entrusted with a connotation of lionized masculinity, the explosive power comes to symbolize a sense of decisiveness, determination and decision-making. In so doing, this strong and straightforward "*macho* image" of the atomic bomb is transferred to an American national image. Reflecting this image of the atomic bomb, the idea of resoluteness, authority and pride is further projected onto the United States. In this way, the atomic bomb comes to exert an enduring influence on the creation of American national identity.

Obviously here, the inclusion of radiation in the feature of the atomic bomb would ominously disrupt the enactment of this positive image, insofar as radiation effects are invisible, cruel, and inhumane as poison gas. As a matter of fact, about a month after the atomic bombing of Hiroshima, the *Daily Express* correspondent Wilfred Burchett reported the disastrous outcomes of radiation in Hiroshima, with these shocking headlines: "The Atomic Plague; 'I Write This as a Warning to the World'; Doctors Fall as They Work; *Poison gas fear: All wear masks*" (emphasis in

---

9  Ibid.
10  Sean Malloy, "'A Very Pleasant Way to Die': Radiation Effects and the Decision to Use the Atomic Bomb against Japan," *Diplomatic History* 36-3 (June 2012): 520, 535, 537–38.

the original).¹¹ Immediately after this news appeared in early September 1945, the American Forces held a press conference in Tokyo to deny the occurrence of any ongoing loss of life and critical radiation symptoms in Hiroshima. At this conference, General Thomas Farrell, an assistant to Groves, made a false statement that no one in Hiroshima was dying or suffering from radiation aftereffects. Farrell's statement became an official narrative in Japan, and dictated the news media under censorship during the US occupation. As a result, a great number of the *hibakusha* (the atomic bomb victims) had to confront unknown diseases and severe injuries without any effective treatment.

## Misleading Association with the Image of Solar Power

The second positive image of the atomic bomb provided by Truman's statement is its close connection with solar power. After introducing the scale of the bomb's blast power in the first passage, the second one explains the reason for its use in Hiroshima as a retaliation against Japan's war efforts initiated at Pearl Harbor. Then in the third passage, a poetic description of the atomic bomb appears. The phrase "the atomic bomb" is revealed for the first time here. The passage continues: "It is an atomic bomb. It is a harnessing of the basic power of the universe. The force from which the sun draws its power has been loosed against those who brought war to the Far East."¹² While this part is short and terse, it also demonstrates a specific world view and its relationship with the US. Basically, it indicates that the US had comprehended the basic mechanism of the universe, as well as learning to apply the same driving force of the sun to the device of the atomic bomb. It is as if the US were also positioned not only as the centre of the world, but also of the universe, as being bestowed with knowledge of the power of the sun, together with a good command of the fundamental power of the universe. While omitting the actor involved (the US) from these sentences, the passage also obliquely implies that like an epic story, what had happened ("The force from which the sun draws its power has been loosed against those who brought war to the Far East") simply followed the principle of the universe and was beyond one nation-state's will.

---

11   Wilfred Burchett, "The Atomic Plague," in *Revel Journalism: The Writings of Wilfred Burchett*, ed., George Burchett and Nick Shimmin, excerpt (Cambridge: Cambridge University Press, 2007), 2, accessed 1 March 2016, http://www.chicagomanualofstyle.org/tools_citationguide.html.
12   "Statement by the President of the United States."

The positioning of the US at the centre of the world/universe also corresponds to the naming of the target of this force: "those who brought war to the Far East." By choosing to employ the term the "Far East" rather than the name Japan, the passage covertly creates a rhetorical juxtaposition between the centre and the periphery, the invisible "us" (whose presence is too evident to mention, like the sun in the solar system) versus those positioned in a remote, foreign area equivalent to an outlying frontier district. This juxtaposition is a palimpsest of the old-fashioned but long-established schematization between the hero and the villain in the American frontier tale, between white cowboys and belligerent Native Americans in the Wild West. As Tom Engelhardt points out, the conversion of this racialized scheme quickly took place in the representation of the war against Japan during the Second World War.[13] A Japan that attacked Pearl Harbor fits in with the image of this non-white savage, an image of the "sneaky enemy" that always ambushes the "white hero." In short, the rhetorical devices in Truman's statement, such as the valorization of the enormous blast power of the atomic bomb, the assumption of a command over solar power in the universe, and the equation of the US with the heroic figure, effectively promotes the positive image of the atomic bomb, and further justifies the bombing, as if it were executing a universal justice. Yet it is fundamentally problematic and misleading to portray the atomic bomb as something benefitting human beings by associating it with the sun, the origin of all life and the showering of blessings on nature, contrary to its fundamental motivation as a tool for massacre.

## The Successful Establishment of the Military-Industrial-Academic Complex

But Truman's statement also provides us with another positive image of the atomic bomb: a breakthrough in atomic power, a new energy source for the coming atomic age. It suggests the prospect of a realization of this new technology in the foreseeable future. According to Truman's statement:

> The fact that we can release atomic energy ushers in a new era in man's understanding of nature's forces. Atomic energy may in the future supplement the power that now comes from coal, oil, and falling water, but at present it cannot be produced on a basis to compete with them commercially. Before that comes there must be a long period of intensive research.[14]

---

13  Tom Engelhardt, *The End of Victory Culture: Cold War American and the Disillusioning of a Generation* (Amherst, MA: University of Massachusetts Press, 1995), 3–6.

14  "Statement by the President of the United States."

With the peaceful use of this power, it seems that atomic energy that initially derives from the manufacture of lethal weapons can outweigh the fear of nightmarish annihilation. Yet here the invention of atomic power is recognized as an epoch-making victory of science and technology. Indeed, it is also considered as a significant contribution to humanity and civilization. Concurrently this development of the atomic bomb recognizably signifies a victory of "American" science and technology. Truman's statement makes this clear by outlining the background and the production process of the bomb. This is the message that Truman's statement most passionately delineates in this short document. It begins with how this project was initially launched, informing that it was a joint project with Britain in the first place:

> Beginning in 1940, before Pearl Harbor, scientific knowledge useful in war was pooled between the United States and Great Britain, and many priceless helps to our victories have come from that arrangement. Under that general policy the research on the atomic bomb was begun. With American and British scientists working together we entered the race of discovery against the Germans.[15]

But then Truman's statement quickly turns to accentuating how in fact this accomplishment should be solely credited to Americans:

> The United States had available the large number of scientists of distinction in the many needed areas of knowledge. It had the tremendous industrial and financial resources necessary for the project and they could be devoted to it without undue impairment of other vital war work. In the United States the laboratory work and the production plants, on which a substantial start had already been made, would be out of reach of enemy bombing, while at that time Britain was exposed to constant air attack and was still threatened with the possibility of invasion. For these reasons Prime Minister Churchill and President Roosevelt agreed that it was wise to carry on the project here. We now have two great plants and many lesser works devoted to the production of atomic power. Employment during peak construction numbered 125,000 and over 65,000 individuals are even now engaged in operating the plants. Many have worked there for two and a half years. Few know what they have been producing. They see great quantities of material going in and they see nothing coming out of these plants, for the physical size of the explosive charge is exceedingly small. We have spent two billion dollars on the greatest scientific gamble in history—and won.[16]

This passage articulates the big stakes the American government had invested in terms of labour force and finance, in order to make the Manhattan Project fruitful. But the statement also asserts that its key to success was not just such heavy investments, but rather the nature of collaborative efforts in science and industry that were fostered under the military's leadership. It goes on to explain this phenomenon:

---

15   Ibid.
16   Ibid.

> But the greatest marvel is not the size of the enterprise, its secrecy, nor its cost, but the achievement of scientific brains in putting together infinitely complex pieces of knowledge held by many men in different fields of science into a workable plan. And hardly less marvelous has been the capacity of industry to design, and of labor to operate, the machines and methods to do things never done before so that the brain child of many minds came forth in physical shape and performed as it was supposed to do. Both science and industry worked under the direction of the United States Army, which achieved a unique success in managing so diverse a problem in the advancement of knowledge in an amazingly short time. It is doubtful if such another combination could be got together in the world. What has been done is the greatest achievement of organized science in history. It was done under high pressure and without failure.[17]

In other words, this "American victory of science and technology" came into being through a trinity of three different divisions: 1) scientific minds competent to synthesize divided and complicated pieces of knowledge as well as turn them into unified and practicable applications; 2) an industrial strength capable to invent completely new machinery, devices and production systems necessary for the manufacture of the atomic bomb; and 3) a high-quality labor force adept in operating and controlling these unfamiliar devices and systems never handled before. The successful integration of these three institutional divisions was indispensable for this victory of American science and technology. Hence, the well-organized formation of such a military-industrial-scientific complex was also necessary to be victorious in the era of modern total war. What Truman's statement has touted here is thus not only the successful development of a new weapon, but also the successful establishment of this military-scientific industry in the United States specifically. As we know, this powerful industry has remained at the core of postwar American politics.

## Who Is the Audience? Address to Rivals and Enemies

Ultimately, this triumphal integration of top-notch academic, military and industrial institutions is what Truman's statement aims to present to the world, especially to its rivals and enemies. This statement was created to suit a larger international framework, far beyond the scope of the American-Japanese War. Although its name never appears within the statement, it is hardly conscionable to exclude the Soviet Union from a list of its major audiences, judging from the political tension that had already existed between the two countries. Even at the Potsdam Conference, the disharmonious relationship between Truman and Stalin was evident; it already indicated a postwar leadership struggle between them in the near future.

Britain is also another major audience, though this has rarely been pointed out, especially during the Cold War era when the Western camp required a

---

17   Ibid.

demonstration of its solidarity. Truman's statement emphasizes the superiority of the US over Britain, as evident in its comparison between the magnitude of the atomic bomb and that of the British "Grand Slam." It also focuses on the British inability to co-develop the atomic bomb due to its subjection to constant threat from Germany during the war. The representation of these situations clearly suggests the transference of leading world power from Britain to the United States in the new international world order. Truman's statement also mentions Nazi Germany, but largely in terms of its failure in the race to develop the atomic bomb before the Americans. It gives the impression that Germany is mentioned merely to highlight the United States' success and triumph.

As for Japan, it is surely an anticipated audience, but not a major one. Rather, Japan's stake is lower than others, despite the fact that Japan was the victim of the atomic bomb. It should also be noted that Truman's statement makes no mention of saving the lives of American soldiers as well as those of the Japanese people, as the justification for the use of the atomic bomb; this is the mainstream narrative that later prevailed in American society. Rather, the statement issues a further warning of continuous attacks and invasion from the air, the ocean and even the ground: "If they do not now accept our terms they may expect a rain of ruin from the air, the like of which has never been seen on this earth. Behind this air attack will follow sea and land forces in such numbers and power as they have not yet seen and with the fighting skill of which they are already well aware."[18]

Furthermore, the statement does not touch upon the Japanese military's atrocities in Asia, nor the Showa Emperor and even the Japanese government. The only point of culpability of Japan is Pearl Harbor, the military event that directly concerns the US. Such a treatment of Japan and Asia indicates that not only Japan, but also the whole of Asia is excluded from Truman's statement. The timing of the statement also confirms this; its release took place sixteen hours after the atomic bombing of Hiroshima. It was before noon Eastern Standard Time, and early morning Western Standard Time in the US. Also, it was in the evening in Europe, but around midnight in Japan and other parts of Asia. In short, the statement was timed for optimal coverage in the US and Europe, but not in Japan and Asia. The designated audiences were obvious; this "victorious" news should promptly be delivered to the governments and peoples in the US and Europe, while the Asian counterparts might be asleep.

---

18   Ibid.

## Conclusion

As discussed so far, Truman's statement bestows positive images on the atomic bomb that indicate first, decisiveness and resolute leadership as symbolized by its enormous blast power; second, the absolute truth and necessity as associated with the principle of the universe and a source of solar power; and third, a contribution to humanity and civilization as the key to a new energy source through the peaceful use of atomic energy. Although Truman's statement is an example of discourse on the atomic bomb made at the initial stage, its ideas and information have had an impact as the very first articulation of the American government demonstrating the authority to define the atomic bomb. We can say that these discourses as represented in Truman's statement pre-empted what would follow.[19] The positive images of the atomic bomb became connected to American national identity, and enhanced America's self-image, as the only country that possessed the power to produce the atomic bomb at that time. These images as well as its dominant status in international politics and military situations dramatized the embodiment of postwar America. Most countries, including Japan, followed and accepted these new realities initiated by the atomic bomb and the particular status the US attached to it. As a result, an age emerged in which American domestic politics became intimately connected to international politics.

Overall, Truman's statement represents a desire of the American authorities to control the signification of the atomic bomb: to hide its negative aspects while valorizing the positive ones. Since the atomic bomb has a direct link with the nuclear weaponry that has dominated the postwar world, these valorized images of the atomic bomb in Truman's statement still linger today. Yet we should remember that Truman's statement was produced during wartime. It reflects a particular mindset and rationale typical during a war that took place a long time ago. There was no apt reason to continue them once peacetime resumed. We should reconsider the signification of the atomic bomb and the dependence of American national identity on it. Then we should find a way to come to terms with the disastrous outcomes that the atomic bomb and nuclear weaponry have caused in the world.

---

19   For instance, texts such as John Hersey's *Hiroshima* (1946), Takashi Nagai's *The Bells of Nagasaki* (1949), and Arata Osada's *Children of Hiroshima* (1951) were partially influenced by discourses of Truman's statement. See Yuko Shibata, *Hiroshima Nagasaki: hibaku shinawa o kaitaisuru* (*Hiroshima Nagasaki: Debunking a Myth of the Hibakusha's Narrative*) (Tokyo: Sakuhinsha, 2015).

# 2. Control or Not? Thinking on Atomic Power in the Cold War Context

# EARLY BRITISH THINKING ON ATOMIC ENERGY CONTROL

*James Keeley*

## Introduction

In the history of early post-war efforts to deal with the international implications of atomic energy, the Acheson-Lilienthal Report and the Baruch Plan to which it gave rise are justly given pride of place. These proposed a daring plan—a powerful Atomic Development Authority—to control the use and prevent the misuse of atomic energy. The subsequent struggle between the United States and its allies on the one hand and the USSR and its allies on the other in the United Nations Atomic Energy Commission (UNAEC) dominated the immediate post-Second World War control effort at the international level. The United Kingdom and Canada, junior and very junior partners in the Manhattan Project, and actively co-operating with the US in the post-war years through the Combined Development Trust, are generally treated as minor players, save perhaps, sometimes, by their own historians.[1] If, however, our interest is not in the course of post-Second World War policy and negotiations but in the ideas of the actors, we might look with greater interest on how those other than the main players approached the issues at stake.

---

1   The foundational sources for British nuclear history in the period are Margaret Gowing, *Britain and Atomic Energy 1939–1945* (London: Macmillan.,1964), and Margaret Gowing (assisted by L. Arnold), *Independence and Deterrence: Britain and Atomic Energy, 1945–1952, Vol. 1: Policy Making* (Houndsmills: Macmillan, 1974). See also Lorna Arnold, "A Letter from Oxford: The History of Nuclear History in Britain," *Minerva* 38 (2000): 201–219. For the United States, Richard G. Hewlett and Oscar E. Anderson, *The New World: A History of the United States Atomic Energy Commission Volume 1: 1939–1946* (Berkeley: University of California Press, 1990) is essential. There seem to be no real parallels to these for Canada. Brian Buckley, *Canada's Early Nuclear Policy: Fate, Chance, and Character* (Montreal and Kingston: McGill-Queens's University Press, 2000), 21–75, gives some coverage and some sources. For the period under review here, however, there are some sources, often focused especially on Lester Pearson and General Andrew McNaughton, and on the Washington meeting and the UNAEC: John Swettenham, *McNaughton, Vol. 3: 1944–1946* (Toronto: The Ryerson Press, 1969), 104–129; James Eayrs, *In Defence of Canada, Vol. 3: Peacemaking and Deterrence* (Toronto: University of Toronto Press, 1972), 258–318; John W. Holmes, *The Shaping of Peace: Canada and the Search for World Order, 1943–1957*, Vol. 1 (Toronto: University of Toronto Press, 1979), 196–225, and Vol. 2 (1982) 45–56; Albert Legault and Michel Fortmann, *A Diplomacy of Hope: Canada and Disarmament, 1945–1988* (Montreal and Kingston: McGill-Queens's University Press,1992), 55–65; Lester B. Pearson, *Mike*, Vol. I: *1897–1948* (Toronto; University of Toronto Press, 1972), 258–263; J.A. Munro and A.I. Inglis, "The Atomic Conference 1945 and the Pearson memoirs," *International Journal* 29 (1973–1974): 90–109.

This paper examines the approaches to and conclusions regarding the international control of atomic energy in the British government in the months surrounding the end of the war and the opening phases of the UNAEC. Schrafstetter and Twigge[2] argue, supposedly *contra* Gowing[3] and others, that the British government developed its own plan in early 1946, and took an active interest in the issue of control. However, Gowing, the premier early historian of Britain's atomic energy policy, does not, perhaps, so much suggest that the UK did not "attach great importance to the UN talks"[4] as "opt out of a leading part".[5] She writes: "The British Government put forward no proposals and exercised no initiative themselves. They had already, by the spring of 1946, become increasingly apprehensive about any control schemes which might in any way sacrifice their national security."[6]

The impression Gowing gives is not so much lack of interest as reluctance, tempered by the recognition that the United States must inevitably be the lead power on the Western side, with the UK (its own concerns notwithstanding) being the attentive ally. Prior to UNAEC deliberations, there was, by Gowing's account, active British consideration of issues of atomic control. But the approach *adopted* by the British was not, as Schrafstetter and Twigge[7] suggest, a "Baruch" plan; as we shall note below, this is a premature assessment. As events proceeded, British thinking had to adapt increasingly to the implications of both American dominance in the question of control, and the specifics of American thinking on the question.

Writing in 2002, Schrafstetter noted that:

> ... most British nuclear historiography of the 1940s has concentrated on three main areas: the origins of the British nuclear program; the foundations of British nuclear strategy; and Anglo-American defence relations ... Some of these works pay attention to the British role in the negotiations over international control, but no comprehensive and detailed study of the British position towards international control and London's contribution to the UNAEC has been presented as yet.[8]

---

2   Susanna Schrafstetter and Stephen Twigge, *Avoiding Armageddon: Europe, the United States, and the Struggle for Nuclear Nonproliferation, 1945–1970* (Westport, Conn.: Praeger, 2004), 18.
3   Gowing, *Independence and Deterrence*.
4   Schrafstetter and Twigge, *Avoiding Armageddon*, 18.
5   Gowing, *Independence and Deterrence*, 87.
6   Ibid. 90.
7   Schrafstetter and Twigge, *Avoiding Armageddon*, 18.
8   S. Schrafstetter, "'Loquaicious... and pointless as ever?' Britain, the United States and the United Nations Negotiations on International Control of Nuclear Energy 1945–48," *Contemporary British History* 16 (2002): 87–108. Quoted 88.

Her article and one by Bourantonis and Johnson in 2004[9] overlap with the analysis here, however Bourantonis and Johnson cover only November–December 1945. While this article differs with Schrafstetter and Twigge on certain points, its primary contribution is to fill in some of the scope and content of British thinking up to the opening of the UNAEC, including with respect to some documents cited by them and by Schrafstetter's 2002 article, but not presented in detail.

The examination here of the concerns and approaches of British policymakers is aided considerably by the narrow set of government actors involved. Gowing notes[10] that there was little or no discussion in Cabinet, as both Churchill and Attlee kept atomic issues very close to their chests. Some discussion occurred in limited Cabinet committees, especially the GEN 75 committee, but the only other major venue for policy consideration was the Advisory Committee on Atomic Energy (ACAE), chaired by Sir John Anderson. The focus of this paper will be particularly on GEN 75, on the work of the Advisory Committee, and on Attlee himself. It will also cover, however, a preliminary report on atomic energy prepared under Sir Ronald Campbell of the Foreign Office before the end of the war, and instructions given to the British representative on the UNAEC, Sir Alexander Cadogan.

## The Campbell Memorandum

Discussions of issues related to international atomic energy control prior to the spring of 1945 generally had little positive effect. Other considerations—expediting production of a weapon, problems of sharing technical information, Anglo-American collaboration both during and after the war, relations with the Soviets, and relations with the French, for example—complicated and discouraged serious attention to the matter until at least the fall of 1944 on the American side.[11] On the British side, Sir John Anderson, Chancellor of the Exchequer, then the cabinet minister responsible for Tube Alloys, raised the matter with Churchill in the spring

---

9   Dimitris Bourantonis and Edward Johnson, "Anglo-American Diplomacy and the Introduction of the Atomic Energy Issue in the United Nations: Discord and Cooperation in1945," *Contemporary British History* 18 (2004): 1–21.
10  Gowing, *Independence and Deterrence*, 19–32.
11  See, e.g., Hewlett, and Anderson, *The New World*, Chapters 8 and 10.

of 1944,[12] and helped arrange a disastrous meeting between Churchill and the Danish physicist Niels Bohr.[13] By the spring of 1945, as the prospect of the actual use of the atomic bomb approached, more attention turned to both how the accompanying announcement would be handled and to the international political implications, including arms control, which would follow. The British were anxious to develop their own views on these matters and to consult with the US regarding them while American thinking was still fluid. To that end, Sir Ronald Campbell of the Foreign Office developed a memorandum in the later days of May, 1945, which was considered by Anderson and others in early June and revised accordingly.[14]

The international control question was central, noted the memorandum:

> Until the Americans and ourselves have made up our minds how we are going to handle the T. A. [Tube Alloys] project in its bearing on international affairs we are clearly not in a position to make much headway on the drafting of a public statement nor obviously can we consider what kind of communication should be made to other Governments when the period of secrecy comes to an end (Para. 4).

Its driving argument was that the Anglo-American monopoly could not be maintained, and indeed other states, not having to replicate the vast, pioneering American effort, might have an easier and cheaper time of it. Various states could have the scale of industry and resources to develop a bomb: France and the USSR were

---

12  Gowing, *Britain and Atomic Energy*, 339–371. See also Sir John Anderson to Prime Minister, 27 April, 1944, Prime Minister's Office, PREM 3/139/2 UKNA; "Tube Alloys," 21 March 1944; PREM 3/139/2; Sir John Anderson to Prime Minister, 15 June 1944, Prime Minister's Office, PREM 3/139/11A, UKNA.
13  Gowing, *Britain and Atomic Energy*, 346–355. See also John Wheeler-Bennett, *John Anderson, Viscount Waverly* (London: Macmillan, 1962), 296–297, and Jacques C. Hymans, "Britain and Hiroshima," *Journal of Strategic Studies* 32 (2009): 780–781. By these accounts, Churchill was distracted, impolite, and probably highly unsympathetic to Bohr's approach to control, which was based on sharing scientific information. One outcome of the Bohr-Churchill meeting was the third clause of the Hyde Park Memorandum between Churchill and Roosevelt: "Enquiries should be made regarding the activities of Professor Bohr and steps taken to ensure that he is responsible for no leakage of information, particularly to the Russians." "Tube Alloys: Aide-memoire of conversation between the President and the Prime Minister at Hyde Park, 18 September 1944." Prime Minister's Office, PREM 3/138/8A, UKNA. Anderson, however, continued a strong relationship with Bohr, who submitted a summary of his views on international control to the ACAE. "Cabinet. Advisory Committee on Atomic Energy. International Control of the Use of Atomic Energy: Memoranda by Professor Niels Bohr," ACAE (45) 6, 28 August 1945, Cabinet Office, CAB 134/7 UKNA.
14  Ricketts to Campbell, 12 June 1945, Foreign Office, FO 800/530, UKNA. This had copies of the study attached: "Memorandum: International Treatment of the T.A. Project." "Tube Alloys," R. Campbell to Secretary of State, 8 June 1945, Foreign Office, FO 800/530, UKNA. A copy is also found in "Cabinet. Advisory Committee on Atomic Energy. International Policy on the Use of Atomic Energy: Note by the Secretary," ACAE (45) 3, 24 August 1945, Cabinet Office, CAB134/7, UKNA.

of the greatest practical concern with respect to this question (Para. 19), but Germany, Italy, Belgium, the Netherlands, Switzerland, Sweden, Czechoslovakia, and Japan were also noted. Norway was a later possibility, while China and India would require considerably more industrialization (Para. 11).

The memorandum briefly surveyed six broad approaches, from relying on the Anglo-US lead and not attempting to control other countries to a general agreement to forego production of explosive material. There were three variants on international control: an international authority to handle all explosive material, or to allocate the crucial raw materials, or a commission to which all governments would disclose their atomic activities. A final option was a ban on the use of atomic weapons, using the example of the prohibition on gas and bacteriological weapons. The first option could only give a temporary monopoly and could permit dangerous arms competitions, a possibility of surprise attack, and a charge of attempting to monopolize the industrial benefits of atomic energy. The variants on control would forego those benefits, and would require some form of inspection and enforcement. As for the disclosure option: "An agreement of this kind would not be to our advantage if we gave more information to the Commission than we received … But it might be regarded as a first step towards a fuller system of control and as a test of good faith of the parties to it (Para. 32)."

The ban option noted that even "unscrupulous nations" (Para. 33) had observed the Geneva Protocol, though only because it was to their advantage. Although it did not also refer explicitly to the problem of surprise attack, the memorandum did possibly note, at least indirectly, the deterrence element of the option and the implied arms race issue: "We should not … be absolved from taking the most strenuous steps to establish and maintain our supremacy over other countries in T.A. development and from taking all possible measures of defence (Para. 33.")) Such an agreement might, however, provide some hope and, "We should … be no worse off if we made such an agreement, unless it be assumed that we might wish in some future war to be ourselves the first to use this weapon (Para. 33)."

The memorandum's general conclusion was the following:

> None of the alternatives set out above, except possibly the last, is free from dangers and disadvantages. Any form of international agreement on T.A. would obviously carry with it great risks and would be open to evasion. If, however, we reject them for that reason it will be necessary to consider to carefully the grounds on which we shall defend to the world the alternative policy of seeking to exclude other nations from all participation in this new development; and we shall have to take steps to strengthen and maintain for as long as possible the lead which we at present hold (Para. 34).

It was a curious mix of hope and fear—and the last option reflected a reliance on a minimal legal solution rather than a more developed and institutionalized one. As Campbell himself noted of the 5 June 1945 meeting discussing the memorandum, "nothing very definite or positive emerged as far as our own attitude is concerned."[15]

A possible approach for a public statement was that, unable to arrive at an effective method of control, the US and UK should put the burden onto foreign governments and welcome any ideas they might put forward:

> In our view this attitude will have the advantage of putting upon other governments the onus of proposing a system of international inspection which would be the only hope of making control really effective. If the Russians chose themselves to put forward such an idea we think it would be worth considering but subject to American views it scarcely seems useful for us to make such a proposal to them ourselves.[16]

The Americans apparently confessed that they were also somewhat at a loss, and seemed to adopt a similar response:

> Bundy says that the American group have not achieved much result on the subject of international control. They are as yet unable to conceive of any system of control without a strict regime of inspection. They doubt whether the Soviet Government would accept such a regime, and even if they did, whether we could be sure of making inspection effective in the case of Soviet Russia. Nor, with this point in mind, can they see the Congress agreeing to strict inspection in the case of the A. Bundy was therefore considerably attracted by the suggestion ... that we should leave it to other countries to make proposals for control.[17]

On 26 June, 1945, Campbell noted to Sir Alexander Cadogan that: "We ... have not been able to think of any means of control, nor at present have the Americans, who unofficially approve our idea that in the circumstances we should leave it to other countries to make proposals for control."[18]

However, the statements of the two governments following Hiroshima made at best only very indirect, brief and passing references to any post-war control possibilities.

---

15 "Tube Alloys," R. Campbell to Secretary of State, 8 June 1945, Foreign Office, FO 800/530, UKNA.
16 Personal for Field Marshall Wilson from Chancellor of the Exchequer, CANAM 327, 9 June 1945, Foreign Office, FO 800/530, UKNA.
17 Following for the Chancellor of the Exchequer from Field Marshall Wilson, ANCAM 297, 23 June 1945, Foreign Office, FO 800/530, UKNA.
18 "T.A.," R. Campbell to Sir A. Cadogan, 27 June 1945, Foreign Office, FO 800/530, UKNA.

## Three Rounds to Washington

With the atomic bomb revealed, the new Labour government under Clement Attlee took up the control problem. Despite communications with the American and (more limited) the Canadian governments on the issue, British consideration of possible approaches prior to the meeting in Washington in November 1945 took place without much reference to what other states might be generally thinking other than the US. Indeed, it was not clear to the British with respect to the Americans that much detailed thinking was going on or progress on the issue was being made. Nonetheless, it was clear to British policy-makers that clarification of the American positions on both international control and on the future of Anglo-American collaboration in atomic energy was needed, as the US position would be the dominant one and the US would be the central actor. The Washington meeting of Attlee, Truman, and Mackenzie King was to secure more clarity and greater coordination on their positions on these issues. Before then, however, the British went through three rounds on the question of the international control of atomic energy: in the ACAE, leading to a memorandum in early October; the Bridges report of late October; and the approach that developed after these two had been rejected by the GEN 75 committee, and which then informed Attlee's approach in Washington in November 1945.

The ACAE, under the chairmanship of Sir John Anderson, was created in the last half of August 1945[19] to advise the government on the military and industrial use of atomic energy and to put forward proposals for its international treatment. To this latter end, a number of documents were eventually circulated to the members,[20] including:

---

19  "Cabinet. Advisory Committee on Atomic Energy. Composition and Terms of Reference, ACAE (45) 1, 20 August 1945, Cabinet Office, CAB 137/7, UKNA. The members initially were Anderson, Sir Alexander Cadogan (normally represented by Nevile Butler), Field Marshall Sir Alan Brooke, Sir Alan Barlow (Treasury), Sir Edward Appleton (Department of Scientific and Industrial Research), Sir Henry Dale (President of the Royal Society), Prof. P. M. S. Blackett, Sir James Chadwick and Sir George Thomson. The Secretary was Mr. D. H. F. Rickett.

20  "Cabinet. Advisory Committee on Atomic Energy. International Policy on the Use of Atomic Energy: Note by the Secretary," ACAE (45) 3, 24 August 1945, Cabinet Office, CAB134/7, UKNA. "Cabinet. Advisory Committee on Atomic Energy. International Control of the Use of Atomic Energy: International Policy on the Use of Atomic Energy. Note by the Secretary," ACAE (45) 4, 29 August 1945, Cabinet Office, CAB 137/7, UKNA; "Cabinet. Advisory Committee on Atomic Energy. International Control of the Use of Atomic Energy: Memoranda by Professor Niels Bohr," ACAE (45) 6, 28 August 1945, Cabinet Office, CAB 134/7, UKNA; "Cabinet. Advisory Committee on Atomic Energy. Atomic Energy: The International Background. Memorandum by the Foreign Office," ACAE (45) 11, 11 September 1945, Cabinet Office, CAB 137/7, UKNA; "Cabinet. Advisory

1. The Campbell memorandum (ACAE [45]) 3;
2. A set of memoranda from Prof. Bohr (ACAE [45]) 6;
3. A set of telegrams to and from British personnel in Washington in the period May 10–June 22, 1945 (ACAE [45]) 4;
4. A Foreign Office backgrounder (ACAE [45]) 11;[21]
5. A memorandum by Prof. Peierls (ACAE [45]) 12.

The Foreign Office piece briefly addressed three possible control alternatives. First, the "English-speaking states" could try to keep their secrets and control of raw materials, perhaps with an offer to keep the bomb in trust for the UN. This would move from state equality "towards a realistic concentration of authority in the hands of a minority of powerful states" but exclusive control of raw materials would be hard to justify without a UN mandate, and would be problematic if the UK planned on the use of atomic power for industrial purposes.

The second was to make a grand gesture to the USSR by offering to pool information, in the hope of reaching agreement on use and control, including inspection. Soviet gratitude, however, could not be relied on, and the offer could alarm smaller states to whom the UK had obligations[22] and some members of the British public. If, however, the "secrets" were a wasting asset anyway, these might not be overwhelming concerns as against developing the necessary will to peace.

Third, the Big Three or Big Five could pool their assets in trust for the UN as soon as an effective scheme could be worked out—while inviting all governments to contribute suggestions for effective control. Absent effective control, however, the Foreign Office paper asserted that this would be a "will-of-the-wisp and will make no great appeal to the Russians" (Para.24).

Another theme, only touched at the end of the memorandum, was that atomic energy could provide Britain an opportunity to recover its economic (and related diplomatic) strength. "Therefore in considering methods of control every effort should be made not to hamper our developments of commercial possibilities

---

Committee on Atomic Energy. Some Notes on the Future Implications of the Atomic Bomb: Memorandum by Professor Peierls," ACAE (45) 12, 17 September 1945, Cabinet Office, CAB 137/7, UKNA.

21 ACAE (45) 11, 11 September 1945, Cabinet Office, CAB 137/7, UKNA. This paper was drafted by Nevile Butler, Sir Alexander Cadogan's representative on the committee, and initialed by the Foreign Secretary, Ernest Bevin. Roger Bullen and M. E. Pelly, eds., *Documents on British Policy Overseas, Series I, Volume II 1985* (London: Her Majesty's Stationery Office, 1985): 532, footnote 1. The document is also available in Bullen and Pelley, 1985, No. 193, 532–540.

22 These were not specified.

more than these are for the time being restricted by the fourth Article of the Quebec Agreement."[23]

The Peierls memorandum, ACAE (45) 12, was developed after discussions with British scientists in the US and, he thought, was representative of their views. The Peierls and Bohr pieces discussed the exchange of information with the Soviets, though Bohr did not develop this theme much beyond constantly repeating it. Peierls noted the possibility of an exchange of information for some Russian concessions. He argued that the development of the weapon did not represent scientific discoveries that could long be kept from others, and that there was little prospect for a convention on non-use (the example of gas perhaps being due to its inefficiency as a weapon). Inspections would have to cover all industrial facilities, not just those devoted to the production of atomic materials, in order to prevent secret work. But there would also be a problem of seizures of materials by states if other weapon components had been designed and built in advance. Peierls thus argued the need for all plants producing, storing, or using atomic material "in appreciable amounts" to be under the physical control of an international authority.

The memorandum produced by the Advisory Committee on 2 October 1945[24] assumed that: a monopoly on "atomic secrets" or on raw materials would be impossible to maintain for long; there was little point in sharing information about processes except within an international system of control; and it would be difficult to have a control system without inspections, though inspection's effectiveness would be in doubt. It proposed the following steps, which might be undertaken in stages:

1. A world-wide propaganda campaign to shape public opinion.
2. An agreement not to use the weapon, with the signatories also agreeing not to use it against non-signatories without each other's consent and on Security Council authority.
3. An exchange of information with a central authority.
4. Preparation of a plan to control raw materials, though this in itself could not be sufficient.

---

23  The various articles of the Quebec Agreement provided that: neither party would use the atomic bomb against the other, or against third parties without the other's consent, that information concerning the bomb would not be communicated to others save with the other party's consent, that the US would specify a division of the post-war industrial and economic advantages of the project, and that a Combined Policy Committee would be established to ensure full and effective collaboration. The text is available in Gowing, *Britain and Atomic Energy,* 439–440.
24  "Cabinet. Advisory Committee on Atomic Energy. "International Control of Atomic Energy (Reference ACAE (45) 3rd Meeting, Conclusion 1). Note by the Secretary covering revised memorandum." ACAE (45) 20, 4 October 1945, Cabinet Office, CAB 134/7, UKNA.

5. Inspection, "most close and thorough," whether under the Security Council or some other UN organ.
6. The possibility of a combination of control of material and inspection of its use in factories designated to receive it.
7. As an alternative and more far-reaching system, putting ownership and control of all establishments for the manufacture of atomic materials under an international body set up by the UN or the Security Council.

It noted that all of these presented great difficulties which "might at first seem insurmountable," but the consequences of no agreement would be grave.

By the time this memorandum was distributed to the Cabinet's GEN 75 committee, which dealt with atomic energy, that group had already received copies of an early memorandum by Attlee[25] and of the Campbell memorandum.[26] The Chiefs of Staff had also been asked to comment on the Advisory Committee's product. They had responded that the UK must aim at international control—"it is probably the only alternative to mutual destruction"—but it "should include the most unequivocal and comprehensive rights of inspection. It seems to them that the whole conception of international control necessarily stands or falls on the efficacy of the arrangements for such inspection." In the event of a failure to secure an international agreement, the UK would need to have its own atomic weapons.[27]

GEN 75 considered ACAE (45) 20 on 11 October,[28] and again on 16 October. While agreeing on the need for a propaganda campaign, it placed little faith in a non-use agreement ("Such agreements would only be observed as long as it suited the convenience of those who were a party to them"), in raw materials controls ("could only be relied on as a safeguard for a limited time"), or inspection (as unlikely to be workable or effective in practice). It was initially somewhat positive on information sharing and on the international ownership option. This last would require some derogation of sovereignty, but that might be a small price to pay. But by the next meeting, attitudes had hardened: the Foreign Secretary's thoughts on the efficacy of information sharing had been the subject of a note on policy towards

---

25 "The Atomic Bomb: Memorandum by the Prime Minister." GEN 75/1, 28 August 1945, Prime Minister's Office, PREM 8/116, UKNA.
26 GEN. 75/2nd Meeting, 29 August 1945, Foreign Office, FO 800/547, UKNA.
27 Nevile Butler, "International Control of Atomic Energy: Copy of a Minute (COS 1449/5) dated 10 October, from the Secretary, Chiefs of Staff Committee to the Prime Minister." Foreign Office, FO 800/547, UKNA.
28 GEN 75/4th Meeting, 11 October 1945, Prime Minister's Office, PREM 8/116, UKNA.

the USSR from Nevile Butler, who pointed out, among other problems, the impediment posed by the Quebec Agreement and the US attitude. An offer to share could, as well, be seen as a sign of weakness by the Russians.[29]

At the 16 October meeting the difficulties of inspection were again stressed:

> This seems to be the very crux of the matter. If international control is to mean that there is no national ownership of atomic weapons, what safeguards can we provide against the risk that while some countries observe the agreement, others might not? If we are prepared to take this risk, a simple agreement not to make or use bombs would be enough. But this idea had already been rejected.[30]

The option of international ownership and control of bombs came under the same objection, and a variety of additional problems were noted: the location and protection of such plants, immediate control over them, and guaranteeing that those in immediate control "would act only in a constitutional authority and in accordance with the instructions of the world organisation."[31] Persuading the US to dismantle its plants would also be a difficulty. As an alternative, allowing national production under international control over use was suggested—an option which would be developed in the next round of thinking.

The result in GEN 75 was a decision to have a group of officials under Sir Edward Bridges, the Secretary to the Cabinet, present another report. Just before the Bridges report was presented to the GEN 75 committee, the Chiefs of Staff again discussed the problem of use, and argued that a prohibition against use should be absolute, without exceptions, and authorized by the Security Council. Against a small power, use would be inconsistent with the humanitarian purposes of an agreement; against a Great Power, the Security Council would be hampered by the veto.

> Finally they point out that this country, being as it would be highly vulnerable to this form of attack, would have nothing to gain by the use of atomic bombs in future warfare. We are unlikely, therefore, ever to seek the authority of the Security Council or any other body to be ourselves the first to use them, knowing that this would call forth retaliation on the part of the aggressor nation.[32]

---

29 "Cabinet. International Control of Atomic Energy. Policy Towards the Soviet Government. Copy of a Minute dated 12th October, 1945, to the Foreign Secretary by Mr. Nevile Butler." 18 October 1945, GEN 96/1, Foreign Office, FO 800/547, UKNA. See also GEN 75/6th Meeting, 18 October 1945, Prime Minister's Office, PREM 8/116, UKNA. On the Quebec Agreement, see footnote 24 above.
30 "Cabinet: International Control of Atomic Energy: Copy of Minutes by Sir Edward Bridges and Mr. Rickett submitted to the Prime Minister on 16 October 1945." GEN 96/2, 18 October 1945, Foreign Office, FO 800/547, UKNA.
31 Ibid.
32 Rickett to Butler, 26 October 1945, Foreign Office, FO 800/547, UKNA.

This was a problem that neither the Bridges report nor Attlee's response would resolve.

The Bridges report, GEN 75/10,[33] was produced on 29 October. It doubted that the Big Five could be prevented from acquiring atomic weapons and "This criticism must apply equally to a proposal that the production of atomic weapons should be confined to an international organisation, which would also raise other difficulties."[34] While the technical possibility of inspection might be granted, it would not be practical politically, for example in the Soviet case:

> All our experience suggests that, if applied to Russia, such a system would give rise to a series of crises in which other parties to the scheme would constantly have to ask themselves whether the point had been reached at which Russia must finally be accused of a breach of the agreement … A system of inspection of the big Powers is thus bound to develop into a highly dangerous sham, productive of endless suspicion and friction. The agreement for Non-intervention in Spain provides a precedent (Para 14).

Control through raw materials was doubtful, while the problems of international ownership were noted anew. Though it might be possible to control the lesser powers, the report recommended that all be left "free to make atomic bombs, if they can," but that use should be prohibited.[35]

The report turned to the possibility of control over their use. This could be through a convention banning use of atomic weapons, save as an enforcement measure against those parties violating this ban—a system of collective retaliation. Such an agreement would be of indefinite duration, and any attempt to denounce it would itself be treated as a breach liable to this sanction. Significantly, this agreement would be outside of the Security Council, thus avoiding the veto. A ban on use, the report argued, would be simple, "and avoids building up a cumbrous façade of inspection which for the Great Powers could never be made a reality. While there could be no absolute guarantee of security under such an agreement, it would certainly be preferable to any arrangement under which in return for an illusory promise of security we gave up the means of self-defence (Para. 26)."

However, while echoing the Chiefs of Staff and arguing that "it is unlikely to be in our interests to be the first to use the bomb even with the authority of the Security Council," the report failed to see the same problem inherent in the proposed convention. A similar problem in having some mechanism (the Security

---

33   GEN 75/10, 29 October 1945, "Cabinet. International Control of Atomic Energy. Report by Officials: Summary of Conclusions and Recommendations." Foreign Office, FO 800/547, UKNA.
34   Ibid. A.—Conclusions, Para. 8.
35   Ibid. A.—Conclusions, Para 5.

Council or in such a convention) to establish the identity of an aggressor was noted and ignored. This, of course, would have its own difficulties, including a possible veto in the Security Council.

The report also recommended that the UK "should undertake production of bombs on a large scale for our own defence as soon as possible" (Para 39). In a separate note, Butler wrote Cadogan that it was easy to criticize a policy that provided for a convention against use but wanted urgent steps to produce bombs, yet "This just has to be faced."[36] Butler also noted that the report, as written, could oblige the UK to bomb the US, and that "the proposed almost total renunciation of the weapon would merely leave nations free to carry on wars in the old style."

The Bridges report came up for consideration in GEN 75 on 1 November. It was attacked by Attlee, at the meeting and in a Memorandum he produced on the subject.[37] The intended sanction, he argued, was an illusion:

> It was useless to suppose that if a war once began, any agreement not to use the atomic bomb would be observed. The sanction proposed would never be effective in deterring a country which was in danger of being destroyed in a war begun without the use of atomic weapons. It would also be a most dangerous obligation for us to assume.[38]

There seemed to be general agreement that it was impossible to prevent the manufacture of atomic bombs, and that their use could not be controlled. On that basis, Attlee argued, the only hope lay in the prevention of war altogether. He therefore proposed to take to Washington the following points:

1. The necessity of a strong United Nations;
2. That no attempt be made to restrict development of atomic energy by any state, given the impossibility of effective control;
3. That the bomb be available to restrain aggression—not by a special convention (Attlee noted the veto problem and suggested that it was better to make no specific provision regarding who could authorize use), but rather by the determination of all those who develop atomic energy to live up to the principles and purposes of the Charter, and to back up its authority by using their atomic weapons against any aggressor if the occasion arises.[39]

---

36  N. Butler to Sir A. Cadogan, 1 November 1945, Foreign Office, FO 800/547, UKNA.
37  GEN 75/7th Meeting, 1 November 1945, FO 800/548; "Cabinet. International Control of Atomic Energy. Memorandum by the Prime Minister." GEN. 75/12, 5 November 1945, Foreign Office, FO 800/548, UKNA.
38  GEN 75/7th Meeting, 1 November 1945, Foreign Office, FO 800/548, UKNA.
39  "Cabinet. International Control of Atomic Energy. Memorandum by the Prime Minister." GEN. 75/12, 5 November 1945, Foreign Office, FO 800/548, UKNA.

4. Endorsement of Truman's proposal for the free exchange of basic scientific information, but the rejection of any idea of sharing the more technical knowledge.
5. All states should establish effective control over the use of atomic energy on their territory.

Attlee's formula in point 3, of course, did nothing to address the questions of how the use of the bomb to prevent aggression might be decided, or why Britain, given its vulnerability, would be willing to take such a risk.

Commenting on the outcome of the discussions and on the Prime Minister's proposed instructions for Washington, Butler wrote to Cadogan:

> It is likely ... that the public will get something of a cold douche if and when they are told the hard fact that the British and the American Governments have considered all possible forms of control and rejected them as impracticable and dangerous. But the douche should be salutary. I would only venture to hope that the Government will present their views to the public as early as possible so as to forestall misguided campaigns chasing along to dead ends.[40]

## The Washington Declaration

By the time of the Washington meeting, the British had gone through a number of rounds of consideration of the problem of international control. Several approaches had been surveyed, with results that were not encouraging. The general conclusions which emerged and informed Attlee's thinking were:

1. The major powers at least would likely get atomic bombs—this could not be prevented.
2. The basic scientific (and also the technical) information behind the bomb was a wasting asset in terms of its importance and its negotiation value, though it might be used to obtain a *quid pro quo*.
3. Approaches to control through allocation of raw materials, inspection or even international ownership were doubtful, whether technically or politically.
4. An agreement simply to ban the use of the bomb, backed by atomic sanctions, would not be adequate.
5. The only hope was to develop an effective United Nations, to preserve the peace.

---

40   Note from Nevile Butler to Sir Alexander Cadogan accompanying an aide-memoire by Gen. Jacob, 5 November 1945, Foreign Office, FO 800/548, UKNA.

6. States with the bomb might agree to enforce the Charter, though (because of the veto problem) not necessarily through the Security Council.[41]

In effect, the movement was from a relatively technical approach to a more general—also much vaguer—political approach, which also seems (if only in retrospect) of doubtful efficacy.

Gowing characterizes the British preparations for Washington as inadequate: Attlee brought no agenda and no documents to present to Truman.[42] The lack of a prepared British position paper could have been a source of difficulty: as early as 29 September, Roger Makins in Washington noted that: "… neither Mr. Byrnes [the American Secretary of State] nor his advisors have been able to give any thought to this question and …they are not in any position to embark on any informed discussion of it."[43] It was doubtful, Makins suggested in his note, that any progress could be made until the UK had a plan to put before the US "which they could bite on."[44] But who would bite? The state of organized and high-level American thinking on the subject was, if anything, not even at the British point. Hewlett and Anderson[45] and Zachary[46] suggest an Administration not well-organized to address the issue, focusing on the creation of domestic control legislation, and broadly unwilling to share information at least beyond the basic level with the Russians. When the British arrived in Washington, they discovered that no Americans

---

41 "Documents relating to the Meeting in Washington between the President of the United States of America, the Prime Minister of the United Kingdom, and the Prime Minister of Canada on the subject of Atomic Energy, November 1945." Annex A: International Control of Atomic Energy: Memorandum by the Prime Minister. Annex B: C.M. (45) 51st Conclusions—Minute 4, 8 November 1945. Annex C: U.K. Delegation/1st Meeting, 11 November 1945. Prime Minister's Office, PREM 8/117, UKNA.
42 Gowing, *Independence and Deterrence*, 73–74.
43 P. J. Dixon to Rowan; Enclosure by Makins, 29 September 1945, FO 800/535. In Roger Bullen and M. E. Pelly, eds., *Documents on British Policy Overseas, Series I, Volume II* (London: Her Majesty's Stationery Office, 1985), No. 197, 548–549. Serious consideration was being given to the issue by various Americans, including Vannevar Bush, James Conant and Henry Stimson, and also the scientific community. However, these efforts, up until November 1945 and the Washington Declaration, or even after (up to the formation of the Board of Consultants that gave rise to the Acheson-Lilienthal Report) did not seem to bear much fruit at the highest political levels, which seemed to be focussing mostly on issues of domestic legislation for the control of atomic energy and of sharing atomic information internationally. See, e.g. James G. Hershberg, *James B. Conant: Harvard to Hiroshima and the Making of the Nuclear Age* (New York: Alfred A. Knopf, 1993), 242–250.
44 Dixon to Rowan; Enclosure by Makins, 29 September 1945, FO 800/535. In Bullen and Pelly, *Documents*, 1985, No. 197.
45 Hewlett and Anderson, *The New World*, 426–427, 456.
46 G. Pascal Zachary, *Endless Frontier: Vannevar Bush, Engineer of the American Century* (New York: The Free Press, 1997), 292–295.

who had been involved in the subject of the bomb had been included in the President's party. At least Attlee had brought Sir John Anderson.

Hewlett and Anderson[47] state that no preparations had begun in the US government even ten days before the British arrived. Into the breach stepped Vannevar Bush, a central figure in the creation and management of the Manhattan Project, and someone who *had* been giving the matter some thought. Bush believed that any power that could build the bomb might well do so once it had the capability, and supported sharing at least basic scientific information with the Russians: there was nothing to lose, and it could be a test of the Russian attitude.[48] Approached by Byrnes mere days before the meeting opened, he produced a memorandum on tactics, on the Quebec Agreement, and on dealing with the Russians. He proposed a three-step control approach:

1. Establish, with the UK and the US, a clearinghouse for basic scientific information.
2. Extend this exchange to practical information on the use of atomic energy, but under conditions of control and inspection of laboratories and plants dealing with or producing atomic materials (the US would keep some plants closed to this until it was sure the inspections would work).
3. Ban the production and possession of bombs by any state, and use atomic materials only for commercial purposes—though the elimination of the weapon might be many years away.[49]

Despite this apparently unpromising start, there seems to have been enough overlap to permit a considerable and early convergence: Bush was informed on 12 November that in effect his memorandum had been accepted, and was asked to draft an official statement for a meeting he had not himself attended.[50]

Nonetheless, drafting the final statement was a chore.[51] Early British drafts reflected their broad position—including the inadequacy of any system of inspection "of itself" and the importance of the United Nations—but also included a reference to the allocation of raw materials "in due course" after a world survey of

---

47   Hewlett and Anderson, *The New World*, 459.
48   Zachary, *Endless Frontier*, 284, 292–3.
49   Hewlett and Anderson, *The New World*, 459–461; Zacharay, *Endless Frontier*, 1997, 302–3.
50   Hewlett and Anderson, *The New World*, 461; Zacharay, *Endless Frontier*, 305.
51   See "Documents relating to the Meeting in Washington between the President of the United States of America, the Prime Minister of the United Kingdom, and the Prime Minister of Canada on the subject of Atomic Energy, November 1945." Annexes D–L. Prime Minister's Office, PREM 8/117, UKNA.

resources. There was a reference to the sharing of technical information, under UN auspices. In these British drafts, the parties stated their undertaking "never to use atomic weapons against any nation except in support of the principles and purposes of the United Nations. We invite all other nations to become parties to this undertaking." The American drafts introduced the idea of a Commission—though the UK initially found its terms of reference to be too broad—to provide "recommendations and conventions" (the reference to conventions was later dropped) on the exchange of basic scientific information, the control or elimination of atomic weapons, and effective safeguards through inspection and other means. However, technical information would not immediately be shared. The fourth British draft included the Commission but dropped the resources survey. It continued to emphasize the UN, but dropped the reference to the use of the bomb in support of the Charter.

The final declaration referred to the sharing of basic information, but the sharing of technical information was only to occur "just as soon as effective enforceable safeguards against its use for destructive purposes can be devised." Curiously, an earlier paragraph again asserted the inadequacy of inspections in themselves. Questioned on this by his Cabinet, Attlee responded that the safeguards envisioned with respect to technical information would only be instituted after confidence and co-operation had developed.[52] The Commission formed under the UN was to make recommendations regarding the exchange of basic scientific information for peaceful ends, for the control of atomic energy, for the elimination of atomic weapons (and other mass destruction weapons) from national armaments, and effective safeguards through inspection by other means. Again, the issue of enforcement and of the use of atomic bombs in support of the Charter were not present.

The British view was significantly watered down in this declaration, though not lost entirely: the UN was given a significant role through the Commission, but support for the organization was only mentioned in general terms and questions of enforcement were avoided. The questions of inspections and other safeguards were essentially postponed. Information-sharing could establish an initial basis for

---

52   "Documents relating to the Meeting in Washington between the President of the United States of America, the Prime Minister of the United Kingdom, and the Prime Minister of Canada on the subject of Atomic Energy, November 1945." Annex N: Record of Teletype Conversation between the Prime Minister and the Lord President (Washington and London) on 15 November, 1945.Prime Minister's Office, PREM 8/117, UKNA.

co-operation, but would not advance far beyond that unless and until confidence was established on which inspections and other safeguards could be based.

Noted Butler:

> The principal points of interest centre, I think, round the functions of the new Atomic Commission. The Commission was first proposed by the Americans in their draft dated November 13$^{th}$ (…). Up till then we had merely suggested that the United Nations Organization should arrange on a reciprocal basis international exchanges of visits by qualified technical personnel. The terms of reference suggested by the Americans for the Commission seemed to us too wide … The Americans, however, insisted on, and expanded, the scope of the Commission—…—so as to include certain points which Ministers in London had regarded as impracticable and dangerous. The final Communiqué commits us to asking the new Commission to put up proposals for elimination of the use of the weapons "from national armaments", and for Inspection. Contrast with this paragraph … the memorandum by the Prime Minister … and with the opposition of Ministers to Inspection.[53]

A turning-point had been reached: the Americans were now focusing on the problem of international control.

## To the Baruch Plan

With the acceptance of the Washington Declaration, and with the terms of the United Nations Atomic Energy Commission which developed out of it, the British had essentially also accepted the broad American plan for action. In effect, the UK returned to a consideration of proposals, especially with respect to ACAE (45) 20, which it had previously considered in general terms and found doubtful, while those other options which it had considered both before and after ACAE (45) 20 were at least held in limbo. While British thinking would develop in greater detail within the parameters of the Washington Declaration and the UNAEC—and, as well, the Acheson-Lilienthal Report and the Baruch Plan—it would henceforth be constrained by these parameters. Reconciling these with its own concerns would be a significant problem.

The United Nations General Assembly, on 24 January 1946, passed Res 1(1), establishing the United Nations Atomic Energy Commission. Its terms of reference drew from the Washington Declaration, calling for the Commission to make recommendations and proposals particularly with respect to: an exchange of basic scientific information; control of atomic energy "to the extent necessary to ensure

---

53   U 9660/6550/70, Minute of 27 November 1945. Quoted in Bullen and Pelly, *Documents*, 1985, No. 233, footnote 1, 620–621. However, Butler noted, "The P.M. was, of course, successful in getting the President to take a fence he had hitherto shirked—that this matter must be handled by the U.N."

its use only for peaceful purposes;" eliminating atomic weapons and other weapons of mass destruction from national armaments; and effective safeguards through inspection and other means.[54] This formed the context for further consideration in the ACAE, culminating in ACAE (46) 31 of 14 March 1946. This suggested draft instructions for the British delegation to the UNAEC. At the same time, however, the United States was also putting in place the Board of Consultants that would eventually lead to the Acheson-Lilienthal Report of March 1946.[55] At this point, the British were acting in ignorance of the results of that report. Noted Butler on 16 March, "The Americans are completing the formulation of their views, but we can only guess at their nature."[56] It is not simply the case that the ACAE's efforts were quickly overtaken by the Acheson-Lilienthal Report (and the later adaption of the Baruch Plan). *Pace* Schrafstetter and Twigge, far from being a coherent British position, they did not actually get approved in GEN 75 and thus cannot be properly considered government policy.[57]

ACAE (46) 31 suggested proceeding by stages, to build the necessary confidence for later stages on the successful performance of the earlier ones. The earliest stage could be the exchange of basic scientific information, but technical information would be held in reserve until later. This initial exchange could then be followed by a global raw materials survey—a point concerning which the Soviet attitude could be assessed. *Some* technical sharing could then follow the successful completion of this step. The ACAE suggested a safeguards approach based on both the control and allocation of raw materials and an inspection system linked to it. It still feared that, while technically feasible, political possibilities of an inspection system were more doubtful. This was precisely why proceeding in stages, to build confidence, was essential. (This reflected Attlee's response to his Cabinet after the Washington Declaration—see above.) Also essential to British thinking was the

---

54 United Nations, General Assembly, Res 1 (1), "Establishment of a Commission to Deal with the Problems Raised by the Discovery of Atomic Energy," 24 January 1946.

55 A succession of drafts leading to ACAE (46) 31 can be found in "Atomic Commission (Draft Instructions to British Delegate)," 1946, Foreign Office, FO 800/574, UKNA. The final version can be found as: "Draft Instructions to United Kingdom Representatives on United Nations Commission on Atomic Energy," ACAE (46) 31, 14 March 1946, Cabinet Office, CAB130/3, UKNA.

56 Minute by Mr. Butler to Sir O. Sargent, Secretary of State: "Atomic Energy: Draft Instructions for Sir Alexander Cadogan," 16 March 1946, U 3123/20/70. In Roger Bullen and M. E. Pelly, eds., *Documents on British Policy Overseas* (London: Her Majesty's Stationery Office, 1987), No. 50.

57 Earl of Halifax to Mr. Bevin, 13 April 1946, U 4081/20/70. In Bullen and Pelly *Documents* 1987, No. 68. Makins and Cadogan, calling on Acheson in April, told him about the ACAE study, but noted "It had, it is true, been submitted to Ministers, who had not endorsed it (though they had not repudiated it)."

question of sanctions. An effective system of sanctions for violation of an international agreement was necessary. Until both the inspection and control system and the sanctions system were satisfactory, Britain wanted the US to retain at least its current stock of atomic weapons (whether or not under arrangement with the UN), as the only acceptable—if transitional—guarantee available. The issue of the veto in the Security Council would also have to be addressed: the sanctions could not be subject to veto.

Action—as opposed to discussion—by stages was a central British requirement. Whatever was raised in discussion (and the British might have preferences regarding this), *action* on later stages could only be based on the successful completion of earlier stages, to provide the necessary confidence for otherwise unsure later measures of control.

The ACAE's suggested draft instructions thus noted and repeated a number of points already significant in earlier considerations. Butler's 16 March memo discussing the draft covered much the same ground, though with a rather more critical flavour. He concluded:

> The present proposals may serve the very useful purposes of ventilating difficulties and of making suggestions the discussions of which will gain time; but they do present certain dangers. Ministers therefore, when they consider the Committee's paper next week, may wish to qualify them.[58]

In GEN 75 on March 20, 1946, reservations were also expressed. Cadogan was directed to seek out American views, and to regard the ACAE report (with which he was provided) as a survey of "ground to cover" rather than as negotiating instructions.

It should also be made clear that Ministers were doubtful:

(a) Whether an exchange of basic scientific information would be of much value as a test of willingness to cooperate; and

(b) Whether a system of inspection could ever be made effective, and whether, therefore, to prohibit the manufacture of atomic weapons would be in our interest.

---

58  Minute by Mr. Butler to Sir O. Sargent, Secretary of State: "Atomic Energy: Draft Instructions for Sir Alexander Cadogan," 16 March 1946, U 3123/20/70. Bullen and Pelly, *Documents*, 1987, No. 50.

They were, however, willing that the exchange of basic scientific information should be discussed as a first step.[59]

With the release of the Acheson-Lilienthal Report and the proposals presented by Bernard Baruch[60] the British had, finally, a much more concrete sense of US thinking around which to adapt their own approach. The new features noted included: the apparent de-emphasis of inspection in favour of some degree (softened somewhat in the Baruch Plan) of international ownership and control by an Atomic Development Authority; a distinction between "safe" and "dangerous" activities (the latter to be under ADA control); a related reliance on "denaturing" explosive materials; and the questions of sanctions and the veto (found in the Baruch Plan). The British response to the Baruch Plan was much more positive than to the Acheson-Lilienthal Report.[61] With respect to the latter, "denaturing" as a control measure was suspect to begin with. It also affected the "safe/dangerous" distinction, with implications for national industrial efforts: if denaturing did not work a wider range of activities would have to come directly under ADA control. The very concept of the ADA—and by implication its status as itself a control measure through the ownership and control of "dangerous" facilities—was also seen as questionable. Aside from the problem of the extent of ownership with respect to mines, itself a point of concern:

> The only form of international organisation which we know to-day is not one which stands above and apart from individual nations, which is free from national rivalries and dissension and which possesses the means of enforcing its will upon any nation that may challenge it. A supra-national authority of this kind does not exist, and there is, unfortunately, little prospect of its emergence in the measurable future.[62]

---

59  "Cabinet. Atomic Energy." GEN 75/12th Meeting, 20 March 1946, Cabinet Office, CAB 130/2, UKNA.
60  United States, Department of State, *A Report on the International Control of Atomic Energy* (Washington, D.C.: March 14, 1946). A text of the Baruch Plan, as presented on 14 June 1946, may be found in United States, Congressional Research Service, *Non-Proliferation: A Compilation of Basic Documents on the International, Statutory, and Executive Branch Components of Non-Proliferation Policy*, CRS 91–85 RCO. (Washington, Library of Congress: 18 December 1990).
61  Memorandum by Mr. N. Butler, "Mr. Baruch's Proposals," 15 June 1946, FO 800/572. In Bullen and Pelly, *Documents*, 1987, No. 112. Minute from Sir J. Anderson to Mr. Attlee, 21 June 1946, and Annex (ACAE (46) 64, "The Proposals of the Lilienthal Committee," 20 June 1946 CAB 130/3. In Bullen and Pelly, *Documents*, 1987, No. 114. "Cabinet: Atomic Energy: International Control of Atomic Energy: The United States and Soviet Proposals: Memorandum by Officials," GEN. 75/37, 4 July 1946, Cabinet Office, CAB 130/3, UKNA.
62  Minute from Sir J. Anderson to Mr. Attlee, 21 June 1946, and Annex (ACAE (46) 64, "The Proposals of the Lilienthal Committee," 20 June 1946 CAB 130/3. In Bullen and Pelly, *Documents*, 1987, No. 114, footnote 7, 363.

The retention of atomic weapons, even if only as a transitional matter, was seen favourably, as was the implication in Baruch of sanctions and the avoidance of the veto in the UNSC. One British thought—overlapping with US thinking—was to link enforcement of any international agreement on the control of atomic weapons to action under Article 51 of the UN Charter. Both the place of the ADA relative to the UN and the question of the veto and its avoidance could raise delicate points of international law.

On many of these points, Soviet disagreement was easily foreseen. In general, the UK was willing to proceed with discussions, though it might hope and press for the most contentious issues to be dealt with later rather than earlier. While the US proposals were obviously more amenable to British interests and concerns, on some points in effect the UK would offer support in principle but defer final approval until it saw how the overall process of control was developing (the stages strategy) and until it could see the relevant details. When GEN 75 came to consider the matter on 9 July 1946, then, it expressed broad support for the American proposals but was not willing to write a blank cheque, particularly on the issues of inspection and control, the nature of the Atomic Development Authority, sanctions for violation, and the veto.[63]

## Conclusion: Possibilities, Probabilities and Preferences

Over the course of a year, the British government visited and revisited the problems posed by the development of the atomic bomb, at the levels of advisers and officials and of Cabinet Ministers in the GEN 75 committee, and in consultations with their Canadian and American partners in the Tube Alloys and Manhattan Projects. Initially, they could see no particular clear line of response. Through the Fall of 1945, their thinking developed, though it broadly steered towards a non-use agreement backed by the threat of sanctions (the essence of the Bridges report)—a conclusion rejected by Attlee in particular, though the need for enforcement of a ban was accepted. Though British thinking continued to develop on its own lines in early 1946, as indicated by the "Draft Instructions" of ACAE (46) 31, it was from the meeting in Washington in November 1945—one dominated by the American response—that the country began to turn its efforts, in an organized fashion, to a consideration of the problem.

This subordination in practice to American thinking was a reflection of the post-war reality of American domination, especially in things atomic. The British

---

63 "Cabinet. Atomic Energy." GEN. 75/14th Meeting. 9 July 1946, Cabinet Office, CAB 130/2, UKNA.

did not and could not, lead in this area once the Americans determined their own course of action—they had learned long before that their real influence might only be exerted before that point was reached. Once the Americans had decided on the course of action set forth in the Acheson-Lilienthal Report, and in the Baruch Plan which modified it, the British position was one of offering support— though not unreserved—and at best hoping to modify the direction of results in ways amenable to their concerns.

Even considered separately from the American proposals, however, it is not the case that the British were particularly hopeful about any plans they might come up with themselves. It is important to recognize that the "Draft Instructions" of March 1946 were not endorsed by the British government. While British thinking turned to the possibilities offered by a combination of resource allocation and inspection, they never had full confidence in this as a politically feasible solution, however technically feasible it might seem. The insistence on progress in stages reflected this dilemma. In modern terms, the earlier stages were to be exercises in confidence-building. The insistence on a ban on production and use—and on finding some means of avoiding the veto—also followed from this. "Progress by stages" also was reflected in their preference for some of the harder issues—like inspection, sanctions and the international authority—to be reserved for detailed consideration at a later stage of discussion, rather than being addressed immediately. The American proposals simply added to these additional details regarding control measures (such as "safe" and "dangerous" activities, and potential implications for post-war industrial development), while the proposal for an Atomic Development Authority opened new areas of profound doubt.

Gowing notes Britain's failure to put forward any initiatives of its own, its preference for relying on US weapons for security, and its increasing concern about control measures until effective control was achieved. She adds: "They could not possibly accept the Russian scheme and they supported only reluctantly the American plan for an international authority. As time went on, the reluctance increased…"[64]

Well aware of its vulnerability to atomic attack, Britain sought a solution to this threat. Among the possibilities, the following order of preferences might perhaps be seen in British considerations:

---

64   Gowing, *Independence and Deterrence*, 90.

1. A workable and reliable scheme for the control of atomic energy, including an acceptable enforcement machinery, which would remove that threat;
2. No scheme at all—and initial reliance on the US and then on a British bomb to provide for their security;
3. Reliance on an ineffective control scheme, with a weak or non-existent enforcement apparatus, which could leave them significantly exposed should some other state breach its obligations.

One might speculate about what the British reaction would have been had the Americans and Soviets reached an agreement which the British found fundamentally wanting. In the course of events that followed the dropping of the atomic bomb, the possibility of the first outcome—however much it might devoutly be hoped for—was always seen as a chancy and difficult thing, politically if not always technically. As that possibility became even less likely to materialize, the fallback position was the second choice. The third was no choice at all.

Over the course of a year, the British government visited and revisited the problems posed by the development of the atomic bomb. In so doing, they identified and anticipated, at least in outline, many of the issues and concerns that would arise over the next twelve months and over the next years and decades. Reading the documents retrospectively is an education. In fact, the Great Powers could not be stopped from producing bombs, though there would be greater hope with respect to lesser states. In fact, development of an inspection system would take time and effort, and that system would be vulnerable to suspicions as to its effectiveness. In fact, progress would have to be made in stages, but the timing and the content of these could not necessarily be foreordained.

# SOVIET ATOMIC INTERNATIONALISM, EGYPT, AND THE SOFT POWER OF SCIENCE

*Frederick V. Mills*

> *Unleashing the power of the peaceful atom will favourably alter the correlation of forces in the developing world.*[1]
>
> —Igor Kurchatov, Soviet nuclear physicist, writing to Efim Pavlovich Slavsky, Deputy Minister of the Ministry of Medium Machine Building
>
> *Without science popular authorities may inflame the enthusasm of the people. With science alone, can they hope to realise the demands of the people.*[2]
>
> —Gamal Abdel Nasser

## Introduction

On the afternoon of 27 June 1954, the cream of Soviet atomic science and engineering gathered in the main control room of the Institute of Physics and Power Engineering in the small city of Obninsk, roughly 100 kilometres southwest of Moscow. On the day's agenda was a single experiment—transforming the thermal energy of the Institute's modest 5,000-kilowatt research reactor into commercially available electricity. By 4:00 p.m., the first electrons generated by reactor *Atom Mirnyi*-1 [Peaceful Atom-1] entered the power grid. This successful test was the culmination of thousands of man-hours of research and labour, taking place eight years after the Soviet Union's first experimental research reactor, F-1 (*pervyi fizicheskii reaktor* [first physical reactor]), reached criticality, and four years after Josef Stalin signed a government decree stipulating the construction of an experimental power plant.[3] Those gathered witnessed nothing less than the dawn of the Soviet nuclear power era.

In a very short time, the Soviet Union had built an impressive archipelago of nuclear research institutes, academic publications, and specialized manufactories

---

1   R.B. Kuznetsova, *Kurchatov v zhizni: pis'ma, dokumenty, vospominaniia (iz lichnogo arkhiva)* (Moscow: Izdatel'stvo Ob"edinineniia "Mosgorarkhiv," 2002), 552.

2   Nasser, Gamal Abdel, *The Charter* (Cairo: United Arab Republic Information Department, 1962), 75.

3   Vladimir G. Asmolov, Andrei Iu. Gagarinskii, Viktor A. Sidorenko, and Iurii F. Chernilin, *Atomnaia energetika: Otsenki proshlogo, reali nastoiashchego, ozhidaniia budushchego* (Moscow: 2004), 6.

for nuclear industries.[4] Soviet atomic research produced striking technological innovation and cutting-edge scientific advancements in fields such as fusion and the study of transuranic elements.[5] Within the USSR, the country's scientific and technological ability to yoke the atom for peaceful purposes was a formidable symbol of its advanced industrial modernity and post-World War II recovery. Yet, Soviet nuclear power spoke not only in a domestic register. In the context of the Cold War, Russian atomic research and accomplishments were direct challenges to Western hegemony. In fact, atomic science and technology fuelled socialism's messianic visions. In energy generation, the atom offered the promise of reliable and inexpensive electricity; in industry, efficiency and productivity gains due to automation and mechanization; in agriculture, better quality food and perishable goods.

On the international stage, the decolonizing world was already showing interest in socialism's ability to rapidly transform the USSR, so ravaged by war and revolutionary struggle, into a world leading military and economic power. The transformative potential of the tamed atom, Moscow's place at the forefront of this emerging field, and the country's willingness to collaborate with post-colonial partners in nuclear research programs had the potential to revolutionize international political economy and further increase socialism's appeal among newly independent states. In other words, nuclear research could be an economic and social equalizer for the USSR and post-colonial countries—an international inflection of Josef Stalin's domestic incantation of catching up with the West in ten years, but without the brutality and deprivation of his Five-Year Plans.

According to Michael Adas, modern societies deploy "sophisticated technology to remake their environment and change their social systems in ways intended to advance the development of their societies as a whole."[6] This is certainly true of the history of nuclear research. The Soviet Union's explicitly articulated social and political goals, both at home and abroad, offer a clear example of the ways in which such "sophisticated technologies" were engaged with and embedded in

---

4   For scholarly works on the history of the early Soviet nuclear program, see: Viktor Sidorenko, ed., *Istoriia atomnoi energetiki Sovetskogo Soiuza i Rossii*, Vol. 1 (Moscow, 2001), Paul R. Josephson, *Red Atom: Russia's Nuclear Power Program from Stalin to Today* (Pittsburgh: University of Pittsburgh Press, 2005), and David Holloway, *Stalin and the Bomb: The Soviet Union and Atomic Energy, 1939–1956* (New Haven: Yale University Press, 1995).

5   For an overview of Soviet technological and research developments see Josephson, *Red Atom*, passim.

6   Michael Adas, *Machines as the Measure of Men: Science, Technology, and the Idea of Western Dominance* (Ithaca: Cornell University Press, 1990), 413.

larger political and economic programs. Nuclear energetics could potentially fulfil Vladimir Lenin's dream that "communism equals Soviet power plus electrification of the country," a dream that linked technological progress with social transformation.[7] Nikita Khrushchev's policy of peaceful coexistence, moreover, allowed technologies such as research reactors and nuclear power generators to gain a socialist-tinged international inflection. The USSR deployed legions of scientists and technicians with expertise in nuclear research and atomic energy to the Third World, exercising both hard and soft power in the form of socialist atomic development programs.[8] By 1960, for example, the Soviet Union had already signed agreements to build and operate atomic research reactors, cyclotrons, or isotope laboratories, or to train nuclear scientists, in four non-Warsaw Pact countries.[9]

This paper explores the early years of the Soviet-Egyptian nuclear relationship and the soft power of science and technology. Atomic links between the two states were extensive. On 17 February 1955, the Egyptian Atomic Energy Commission (EAEC) was established and its initial efforts were devoted to studying "everything related to atomic energy and its peaceful applications."[10] In a late-1955 interview with Dimitri Shepilov, then editor-in-chief of *Pravda*, Egyptian President Gamal Abdel Nasser appealed to the Soviet Union to assist in the advanced training of Egyptian scientists in various atomic energy fields.[11]

On 12 July 1956, the Soviet Union and Egypt formalized their atomic relationship, signing a treaty that provided for the construction of a two-megawatt research reactor at Inshas in the Nile delta, as well as the promotion of educational exchanges and joint scientific research projects. When the EAEC was abolished and its duties were taken over by the newly established Atomic Energy Institute in Cairo in 1957, six of the Institute's nine directors had already received training in

---

7   Vladimir Lenin, *Lenin's Collected Works* (Fourth English Edition, Progress Publishers: Moscow, 1965), 419. This quotation is from a speech titled "Our Foreign and Domestic Position and Party Tasks" delivered to the Moscow Gubernia Conference of the Bolshevik wing of the Russian Communist Party in November 1920.

8   Here I use the definitions of American political scientist Joseph Nye who wrote that hard power rests on "inducements" or "threats" to get the outcomes you want or to compel a change in position. Soft power, on the other hand, rests on the ability to shape the preferences of others. It is "the ability to attract and attraction often leads to acquiescence." Joseph S. Nye, *Soft Power: the Means to Success in World Politics* (New York: Perseus Books, 2004), 5–6.

9   Hans Hilger Haunschild, "Die bilateralen Atomabkommen der Sowjetunion," *Die Atomwirtschaft*, Issue 3 (March 1960): 130. These countries were China (27 April 1955), Egypt (12 July 1956), Iraq (1 August 1959), and North Korea (7 September 1959).

10  Anatol Surak, *Nuclear Reactor Development in Egypt—Summary of Data* (Washington DC: Aerospace Technology Division Library of Congress, 1966), 1–2.

11  "Interv'yu s Gamalem Abdelem Naserom, prezident Egipta," *Pravda*, 2 November 1955.

or had visited the Soviet Union.[12] In July 1957, Dr. Izzedden Abdul-Salaam Hallaba opened the Egyptian nuclear mission to the Soviet Union at the Institute of Nuclear Physics at Moscow State University. Ultimately, Soviet universities and institutes trained scores of Egypt's elite "atomerati," in fields as diverse as mechanical engineering, geology, nuclear chemistry, and experimental physics. Yet Soviet scientists and experts imparted more than knowledge of reactors and radioisotopes. They also nurtured a very political sense of the atom's potential to transform and modernize landscapes and agriculture, states and societies, peoples and places.

This paper begins by reviewing the historiography of science and technology in the Cold War, and continues along two main axes. The first examines events in the Soviet Union and contends that Soviet atomic scientists, in conjunction with bureaucrats, took the lead in promoting and advocating for the modernizing power of atomic energy and nuclear research. They celebrated nuclear energy's potential to transform social, economic, and political foundations, both within the USSR and abroad—a logical goal for a country that envisioned itself at the forefront of a global socialist revolution. Leading physicists created an atomic imagination that appealed to domestic and international utopian visions for states engaged in economic and social modernization. Against the backdrop of the Cold War, atomic scientists positioned their work as vital to national security and as internationally relevant symbols of socialism's transformative potential. The split atom, peacefully applied, was at the forefront of Moscow's enthusiastic and increasingly sophisticated effort to promote socialism globally. This effort, I contend, rode a wave of atomic enthusiasm among political, scientific, and bureaucratic elites that relied on a techno-political imagination to advance processes of social and economic modernization.

This enthusiasm dovetailed with the heady passions of newly independent regimes, such as Egypt, which were seeking to undo colonial legacies of poverty, exploitation, and economic underdevelopment. The second part of this chapter will look at the discourses surrounding the transformative potential of nuclear research specifically, and science and technology more generally, in Egypt. As the leading Arab state and co-founder of the non-aligned movement, Egypt under Nasser pursued political, economic, and social agendas enamoured with rapid transformation and modernization. Nasser also recognized the key role that scientific advancements would have to play in enabling such sweeping change, and recognized the Soviet Union's willingness to provide them. In a speech on 13 May

---

12  Haunschild, "Die bilateralen Atomabkommen der Sowjetunion," 131.

1958 at the Drinov Atomic Research Institute in Melekess, Ulyanovsk Oblast (now Dimitrovgrad), titled "Science for Peace," Nasser extolled Soviet efforts as "a model of international co-operation," thanked "the scientific progress made in the interests of peace," and welcomed "science and technology for the good of mankind at large."[13]

Though much has been written about the links between science, technology, and post-colonialism, I contend that recent scholarship has perhaps too readily dismissed the fervour with which newly independent regimes invested, literally and figuratively, in scientifically-inflected modernizing missions. This is not to deny the clear technopolitical power imbalance between either the West or the East and the global South. Indeed, science and technologies were often used to discipline the colonized or to maintain power imbalances in a post-colonial setting.[14] Nor should we discount the environmental degradation and exploitative practices of many techno-scientific enterprises.[15] But the states of the global South were independent actors, too. Egypt, in particular, developed its own atomic enthusiasm, which reflected both its anti-colonialism and its aspirations for the future. Ultimately, the USSR used the soft power of scientific co-operation to train and nurture a generation of Egyptian scientists and engineers. The Soviet Union hoped that a shared atomic imagination would translate into a shared atomic-powered socialist modernity in which closer scientific cooperation would mirror closer geo-political alignment during the Cold War. Analysis of the Soviet-Egyptian case makes clear that "Red technopolitics" can be best understood as a constellation of opportunities, both real and imagined, offered by the Soviet Union and embraced by newly independent states in order to ameliorate broadly defined "backwardness," a label that many countries, evaluating their new, independent positions in the global order, were willing to admit might apply to themselves.

---

13   *President Gamal Abdel Nasser on Consolidation of the Cause of World Peace—Speeches pronounced in International Conference and abroad and Joint Communiques with Heads of State* (Cairo: Ministry of National Guidance State Information Service, 1971), 43. The Institute's full name is the *Gosudarstvennyi Nauchnyi Tsentr-Nauchno-issiedovatel'skii Institut Atomnykh Reaktorov* [State Scientific Centre-Scientific Research Institute of Atomic Reactors] and at the time of Nasser's visit it had only recently opened on 15 March 1956.
14   Paolo Paladino and Michael Worboys, "Science and Imperialism," *ISIS*, Vol. 84, No. 1 (1993): 93.
15   Andrei Sakharov led Moscow's thermonuclear weapons program. Later in his life, he became a staunch advocate for disarmament and was a Soviet whistle-blower revealing the negative health effects of atmospheric nuclear testing and the loose safety standards of the national nuclear industry. See Andrei Sakharov, *Vospominaniia. v 2 Tomakh, Tom. 1* (Moscow: Prava Cheloveka, 1996), 171–173, 200–204. He was, however, an advocate for the peaceful uses of atomic technology. In the 1950s, for example, he co-developed a design for a nuclear fusion reactor, the Tokamak.

## Atomic Technopolitics in the Global Cold War

Moscow's modernizing mission at home owed much to the idea of science and technology as the motor of progress and much has been written that explores scientific and technological development during the Cold War. As flagship symbols of modernity, the actors, institutions, and policies of nuclear-industrial complexes on both sides of the Iron Curtain have received considerable attention. In the Soviet context, however, most of this research has been focused on either the military atomic project or the Chernobyl disaster of 1986.[16] More recently, scholars have taken a closer look at the social and cultural elements of atomic power.

Paul Josephson offered an early post-Cold War technological outline of the Soviet civilian nuclear program, focusing on overarching visions and decision-making processes. Framed by the Chernobyl disaster, his exploration of the cultural dimension of what he termed "atomic powered Communism" is a "cautionary tale of engineering hubris."[17] Josephson argues that the Soviet view of technology as infallible and manipulable by the common worker set in motion a system where those technicians and engineers tasked with the daily operation and maintenance of nuclear infrastructure were often undertrained and under aware of the extreme risks involved with nuclear technology.[18] In other words, the nuclear industry, like other Soviet industries, both shaped and embraced the notion that technologies could and should be mass produced, standardized, and operated by workers with only a rudimentary understanding of underlying theoretical principles. This proved to be a recipe for disaster. These radiant technopolitical dreams contained within themselves the fuel of technopolitical nightmares.

However, by using Chernobyl to understand thirty years of Soviet nuclear history, Josephson inadvertently invites us to write history backwards, attempting to seek out the origins of this political and environmental catastrophe in the cultures and organizations, the practices and the people, of the USSR's atomic industry. In this regard, the bureaucratization of Soviet nuclear energetics during the Brezhnev-era Empire of large-scale technologies was dedicated to increasing the

---

16   For additional examples that focus on the Soviet atomic bomb project, see Holloway, *Stalin and the Bomb* and Thomas B Cochran, Robert S. Norris, and Oleg A. Bukharin, *Making the Russian Bomb from Stalin to Yeltsin* (Oxford: Oxford University Press, 1995). For scholarship on the legacies of the Chernobyl disaster see Zhores Medvedev, *Legacy of Chernobyl* (New York: WW Norton & Co Inc.), 1992 and David R. Marples, *The Social Impact of the Chernobyl Disaster* (London: The Macmillan Press, 1988).
17   Paul R. Josephson, *Red Atom: Russia's Nuclear Power Program from Stalin to Today* (Pittsburgh: University of Pittsburgh Press, 2005), 2.
18   Ibid, 12–18.

power of the state but provided little to the average citizen.[19] More recently, Kate Brown's transnational analysis of Richland, Washington, and Ozersk, Chelyabinsk Oblast, for example—two respective plutonium production centres—reveals how Soviet nuclear leaders, like those in the United States, created limited-access, aspirational, and often photo-ready communities that satisfied their respective postwar societies' visions of a kind of innocent atomic energy but often masked the environmental calamities unleashed by the same. Calling these towns "plutopias," Brown uses their similarities across capitalist and socialist systems to suggest that science and technology, regardless of ideology, were as much about the consolidation of power and the securing of public buy-in, as about the public good per se.[20]

But even Brown's focus on atomic image—and atomic casualties—cannot do justice to the optimism and enthusiasm of the first-generation of Soviet nuclear scientists working on the USSR's peaceful atom program in the Khrushchev era; instead, both Josephson and Brown sweep them into a tragic narrative of arrogance, neglect, occasional resistance, and ultimate catastrophe. Other scholars, to be sure, have given more attention to the years between the birth of the Soviet bomb and the Chernobyl disaster. Sonja Schmid, for example, has traced the historical origins of Soviet atomic culture and the professional identities of nuclear specialists (*atomshchiki*) and power engineers (*energetiki*),[21] arguing that Soviet atomic scientists were excellent lobbyists who deployed economic, scientific, and political arguments to deepen the Kremlin's commitment to all things nuclear.[22] These nuclear leaders were deeply committed to scientific rationality and personally convinced about the necessity of nuclear energy, particularly in its capacity to facilitate economic and social development.[23] Though these visions were generated by elites, they quickly assumed popular prominence at venues such as the Pavilion for Atomic Energy at the Exhibition of the Achievements of the National Economy in Moscow [*Vystavka Dostizheniy Narodnogo Khozyaystv*].[24]

---

19   Ibid, 18.
20   Kate Brown, *Plutopia: Nuclear Families in Atomic Cities and the Great Soviet and American Plutonium Disasters* (New York: Oxford University Press, 2013).
21   Sonja D. Schmid, "Organizational Culture and Professional Identities in the Soviet Nuclear Power Industry," *Osiris*, Vol. 23 (2008): 82–111
22   Sonia D. Schmid, *Producing Power: The Pre-Chernobyl History of the Soviet Nuclear Industry* (Cambridge: The MIT Press, 2015) and Schimd, "Celebrating Tomorrow Today. The Peaceful Atom on Display in the Soviet Union," in *Social Studies of Science*, Vol. 36, no. 3 (2006): 331–365.
23   Schmid, "Organizational Culture," 82–83.
24   According to Schmid, "the pavilion had the goal of familiarizing visitors with atomic scientific disciplines and of rendering sophisticated technologies accessible." In Schimd, "Celebrating Tomorrow Today," 333.

But despite its attention to the domestic politics of nuclear technology, this scholarship gives us little sense of how we might understand Soviet nuclear technology's global reach in this period. For scholars working on other examples of global atomic energetics, the analysis often relies on the concept of "technopolitics." Gabrielle Hecht defines "technopolitics" as "the strategic practice of designing or using technology to constitute, embody, and enact political goals."[25] As such, technology and science are neither deterministic nor are they neutral handmaidens to ideological precepts. Rather, Hecht posits that ideology and science are mutually imbricated. Science and technology are designed and used to serve the interests of the state, both domestically and internationally, while the interests of the state are mediated or imagined through technopolitical futures.[26] Shelia Jasanoff's related concept of "sociotechnical imaginaries," which she defines as "collectively held ... visions of desirable futures ... attainable through, or supportive of, advances in science and technology," is also important in understanding the role of ideology and culture in allegedly rational scientific modernity.[27] This public dimension of science and technology means that scientific and technical futures need to gain assent outside the narrow communities of specialists in order to create truly viable futures in which societies can invest.[28] This was as true in the Soviet Union as it was in the West.

Global atomic energetics in the 1950s and 60s, however, must also be understood in terms of a field that has come to be known as "the Global Cold War."[29] Much work on international Soviet nuclear technopolitics has focused on the East-West or intra-Warsaw Pact encounters involving the USSR's atomic scientists,

---

25  Gabrielle Hecht, The Radiance of France: Nuclear Power and National Identity after World War II (Cambridge: The MIT Press, 1998), 9.
26  Gabrielle Hecht, *Being Nuclear: Africans and the Global Uranium Trade* (Cambridge: The MIT Press, 2012), 17–21 and Gabrielle Hecht, "Introduction," in *Entangled Geographies: Empire and Technopolitics in the Global Cold War* ed. Gabrielle Hecht (Cambridge: The MIT Press, 2011), 1–12.
27  Shelia Jasanoff, "Future Imperfect: Science, Technology, and the Imaginations of Modernity," in *Dreamscapes of Modernity—Sociotechnical Imaginaries and the Fabrication of Power eds.* Shelia Jasanoff and Sung-Hyun Kim (Chicago: University of Chicago Press, 2015), 13.
28  "Shelia Jasanoff, "A World of Experts: Science and Global Environmental Constitutionalism," *Environmental Affairs Law Review*, Vol. 40, no. 2 (2013): 439–452. Though her argument examines climate change, the role of the expert, and mass political participation, her claim that experts must work in both a techno-scientific and "accessible" register is an important observation about the practice and dissemination of scientific research.
29  See section in introduction.

helping provide some sense of the strategic stakes for the USSR.[30] Fabian Lüscher, for example, examines the internationalization of Soviet nuclear science and the creation of the International Atomic Energy Association in 1957, stressing the importance of personal encounters and direct contacts between scientists from both sides of the Iron Curtain.[31] In turn, Schmid, has argued that the domestic success of nuclear scientists as atom advocates took the Soviet nuclear industry international, starting with the sale of Soviet-designed reactors to eastern European satellite states in the mid-1950s.[32] These exports, she argues, were ideologically construed as instruments of modernization, and served as flagships for a Soviet-style "civilizing mission."[33] Although the Soviet Union claimed that science and technology are politically neutral subjects, the transfer of nuclear expertise specifically to Eastern European countries engendered a distinctive Soviet plan of influence and imperialism in these states.[34] However, in geographical terms, Schmid's analysis stops at the Elbe; when speaking in an international register, she focuses on Soviet actors in Eastern Europe.

In fact, during the Cold War, this technopolitical expertise quickly formed and informed the infrastructure of geopolitical competition beyond European borders. Hecht argues that nuclear nationalisms specifically have often obscured the colonial relationships and post-colonial exploitation necessary to their existence.[35] In this regard, technopolitical relationships between the global North and South have been conceived of as a watchword for forms of violence and exploitation—the continued environmental and economic pillaging of the periphery for the benefit of the metropole. However, the technopolitics of East-South relations—atomic or otherwise—stand ripe for scholarly investigation, and in the case of Soviet-Egyptian relations these neo-colonial claims of exploitation warrant closer scrutiny. As this chapter will show, by examining the nuclear relationship between Moscow and Cairo we can better appreciate the sophistication and exceptionalism of Soviet foreign policy, which involved actors and attractions well beyond military advisors

---

30  One notable exception is Eliza Gheorghe who examined Romania's nuclear cooperation with the United States in, "Atomic Maverick: Romania's negotiations for nuclear technology, 1964–1970," in *Cold War History*, Vol. 13, No. 1 (2013): 373–392.
31  Fabian Lüscher, "The Nuclear Spirit of Geneva: Boundary-Crossing Relationships of Soviet Atomic Scientists after 1955" in *Jahrbucher fur Geschichte Osteuropas* vol. 66, No. 1 (2018): 20–44.
32  Sonja Schmid, "Nuclear Colonization? Soviet Technopolitics in the Second World," *Entangled Geographies: Empire and Technopolitics in the Global Cold War* ed. Gabrielle Hecht (Cambridge: The MIT Press, 2011), 125–154.
33  Ibid, 125–127.
34  Ibid. 125 and passim.
35  Hecht, *Being Nuclear*, passim.

and arms sales. Similarly, Egypt's own confidence and interests as a state complicate our understanding of the role of techno-scientific factors in East-South relationships, which extend well beyond exploitation.

The USSR's dreams of creating atomic-powered futures found willing collaborators and partners on the Nile. Egyptian elites clearly understood the power of scientific research and the potential of unleashing technological development for social, political, and economic ends.[36] This was neither a Soviet imposition nor an exclusively Soviet-inspired process. Timothy Mitchell has traced the long history of the "expert" in Egyptian life dating back to Ottoman colonialism, whether that expertise lay in engineering, administration, or economics. He concludes that Egyptian leaders had long deployed technopolitical expertise for the sake of development and modernization.[37] In other words, Egyptian political culture was already disposed to favour techno-political solutions to economic problems, and the alacrity with which Nasser embraced solutions embedded in Soviet scientific cooperation itself required no major revolution. Though the relationship was clearly not between scientific "equals," as this chapter will show, evidence suggests that the Soviet Union did little to hinder the independence or activities of Egyptian scientists. This makes sense—the Soviet Union was not the only atomic game in town.[38]

The Cold War competition between East and West, so often depicted on the macro scale of states and ideologies, was also waged on the micro scale of individuals and institutes. If socialism displaced power from capital and the market, "Red Technopolitics" displaced power onto technical things in the service of constructing socialism. During the early Cold War, states such as Egypt, which were neither politically nor militarily dominated by Moscow, had latitude to manoeuvre between the competing interests of the superpowers in order to construct *à la carte* their own ideal societies. During the Khrushchev years, Soviet actors imagined an atomic powered future, the alleged benefits of which could not simply be imposed on newly independent states. Rather, Moscow had to support and nurture these collective visions internationally, using the soft power of science and technology in an attempt to influence favourably the outlook of post-colonial countries. To focus

---

36 Timothy Mitchell, *Rule of Experts: Egypt, Techno-Politics, Modernity* (Berkeley: University of California Press, 2002). Mitchell focuses specifically on the types of "political practice that produce the powers of science and the powers of modern states," 321. The power of science and technology also shaped the practice of politics.
37 Ibid., 52–77.
38 From 1957 to 1965, the Atomic Energy Institute sent 20 scientists overseas to obtain doctorates. Though a plurality was trained in the Soviet Union, West Germany and Austria were also popular destinations. Surak, *Nuclear Reactor Development in Egypt*, 6–7.

on the asymmetries of the USSR's and Egypt's respective power in the context of technopolitics is to miss the point; both states used technology to advance their own interests—a vision of strategic alliances and eventual global socialism in the case of the USSR, and self-determination and regional and political leadership in the case of Egypt.

## The Internationalism of Soviet Atomic Scientists

In August 1945, spurred by Washington's atomic attacks on Hiroshima and Nagasaki, the Soviet State Defence Committee appointed a Special Committee on the Atom Bomb tasked with initiating a well-funded accelerated nuclear program.[39] The scale of the Soviet project was enormous, and the USSR's command economy was ideally suited to marshal the resources and manpower required for its atomic project. According to Igor Kurchatov, father of the Soviet bomb and director of the Institute of Atomic Energy, "Comrade Stalin said that it is not worth spending time and effort on small-scale work, rather, it is necessary to conduct the work broadly, on a Russian scale."[40] The USSR's fourth Five Year Plan (1946–1950) was characterized by this "Russian scale" and saw considerable increases in defence spending related to the development of atomic weaponry, including the actual program to build the bomb, rocketry programs to deliver the eventual bomb, and enhancements to radar technology to improve defences against the American bomb.[41] This economy of scale was just as evident in the nuclear energy program as it was in the nuclear weapons program.[42] In fact, as early as 1946, Kurchatov had turned his attention, in part, towards civilian applications of nuclear research when he ordered an investigation on the use of graphite reactors for power production.[43]

Peaceful nuclear research was initially carried out under the umbrella of the defense industry.[44] According to a Central Intelligence Agency estimate, by 1951

---

39  The State Defence Committee (*Gosudarstvennyi Komitet Oborony*) was formed on 30 June 1941 in response to Operation Barbarossa. It was an extremely centralized organ of state power that coordinated the Soviet war effort. On 20 August 1945, it created the Special Committee on the Atom Bomb, chaired by the head of the People's Commissariat of International Affairs, Lavrentii Beria, and was tasked with building an atom bomb within five years.
40  Kurchatov's notes quoted in Yuli Khariton and Yuri Smironv, "The Khariton Version," *The Bulletin of the Atomic Scientists* Vol. 49, no. 4 (May 1993): 27–28.
41  Holloway, *Stalin and the Bomb*, 148–149.
42  Sonja Schmid, "Organizational Culture and Professional Identities in the Soviet Nuclear Power Industry," *OSIRIS*, Vol. 23, no. 1 (2008): 85–86.
43  V.V. Goncharov, "Pervyi period razvitiia atomnoi energetiki v SSSR," in *Istoriia atomnoi energetiki Sovetskogo Soiuza i Rossii* ed. V.A. Sidorenko (Moscow: Kurchatov Institute, 2001), 16.
44  Schmid, "Organizational Culture," 87–88.

the USSR employed between 350,000 and 500,000 people in nuclear research industries, including up to 9,000 technical professionals, at an estimated cost of 5% of annual state expenditures.[45] As Paul Josephson has persuasively argued, this critical mass of nuclear scientists sought to ensure continued funding by creating an atomic culture; they deployed popular pro-nuclear images and slogans, such as "let the atom be a worker, not a soldier."[46] More importantly, this nascent culture established a broad consensus on the feasibility and desirability of a civilian nuclear industry by rhetorically blending the promises of nuclear power with utopian visions of a communist future.[47] Under Khrushchev, these atomic powered visions of a communist modernity took on an international dimension supported by scientists, politicians, and bureaucrats alike.

Yet, even before Khrushchev rose to the top of the Party ranks, Soviet officials took note of the atom's catalytic potential. A June 1953 decree of the Supreme Soviet of the USSR transferred responsibility for coordinating military and civilian atomic research from the First Chief Administration to the newly created secret Ministry of Medium Machine Building and the Ministry of Energy and Electrification.[48] Funding for nuclear research increased dramatically. From 1945–1952, the average annual expenditure on this sector was R3.4 billion, whereas in 1953 alone it was R6.5 billion.[49] An anonymous report submitted to the Soviet Council of Ministers in January 1954, before the activation of the Obninsk reactor, concluded that atomic power should be pursued as it could aid growth and economic development in remote parts of the country.[50] A note from G. Kadomtsev, a fusion

---

45 CIA Memorandum, Director of Central Intelligence Hillenkoetter to Senator A.W. Robertson et al., "Update on Russian Atomic Energy Project," 1 April 1951, *Foreign Relations of the United States, 1951*, vol. I: 542. The term "employed" is used here euphemistically. Most workers affiliated with the nuclear program came from Lavrentii Beria's GULAG system and worked in mining or construction.
46 Josephson, *Red Atom: Russia's Nuclear Power Program from Stalin to Today* (Pittsburgh: University of Pittsburgh Press, 2005), 3.
47 Paul R. Josephson, "Rockets, Reactors, and Soviet Culture," in *Science and the Soviet Social Order*, ed. Loren Graham (Cambridge: MIT Press, 1990), 186–191; Josephson, "Atomic-Powered Communism: Nuclear Culture in the Postwar USSR," *Slavic Review* vol. 55 (1996): 297–324; Josephson, *Red Atom*, 6–46.
48 *Atomnyi proekt SSSR: Dokumenty i materialy T.2, Kn. 1* (Saratov, 1999), 11–12 and Schmid, "Organizational Culture," 84–88. Both discuss changes to the bureaucratic organization of the military and civilian nuclear research establishments.
49 *Atomnyi proekt*, 14–15.
50 Gosudarstvennyi Arkhiv Rossiiskoi Federatsii (State Archives of the Russian Federation, hereafter GARF) f R4459, op 27, d 15563, l 153.

researcher at the Institute of Atomic Energy, in the *Proceedings of the USSR Academy of Sciences* urged the government to increase expenditures on nuclear research dramatically in order to ensure the future security of the state.[51] He suggested that, beyond the military dimensions, atomic power could fuel economic growth and development at home and abroad, which would be one of the greatest guarantors of national security.[52] He touted the application of nuclear steam engines, for example, to help the Soviet Union transport its Siberian resources to its western industrial heartland and population centers.[53] Though the United States was the first to demonstrate the power of the nucleus to unleash unimaginable destruction, it was the Soviet Union that was the first to demonstrate and fully envision how that same power could be used to better all humanity.

Khrushchev triumphantly announced that "the Soviet Union wants to work with scientists and technicians of all peace-loving states to help develop domestic nuclear technology systems. These systems have the power to alter the international balance of capitalist exploitation."[54] Moscow's announcement of its functioning atomic power plant came on the heels of President Dwight Eisenhower's "Atoms for Peace" speech, which encouraged a "world-wide investigation into the most effective peacetime uses of fissionable material."[55] Ike may have imagined it, but the Soviets were doing it. This was a significant propaganda coup. At the first International Conference on the Peaceful Uses of Atomic Energy held in Geneva on 9 August 1955, head of the Indian Atomic Energy Commission, Secretary to the Government of India, and Conference Chair Homi J. Bhabha declared in his plenary remarks to more than 1,400 delegates and 900 journalists from seventy-three countries that "the activities of Soviet nuclear scientists have shown that atomic research has the potential to lift people out of poverty and backwardness."[56] V.S. Emelianov, chairman of the State Committee for the Utilization of Atomic Energy and a Soviet delegate at Geneva, declared that the achievements of Soviet

---

51  GARF f R4459, op 29, d 963, 13.
52  GARF f R4459, op 29, d 963, 14.
53  Ibid.
54  Nikita Khrushchev, "Nekotorye voprosy razvitiia atomnoi energetiki," *Pravda*, 18 May 1955, 6.
55  Digital National Security Archive (hereafter DNSA), United States: Executive Office of the President, *Atoms for Peace Speech with Handwritten Notes by President Eisenhower*, 7 December 1953, 16. Eisenhower's speech was delivered to the 470$^{th}$ Plenary Meeting of the United Nations General Assembly on 8 December 1953.
56  Homi J. Bhabha, "The Peaceful Uses of Atomic Energy," *Bulletin of the Atomic Scientists*, Vol. 11, no. 8 (October, 1955): 283.

nuclear science and technology symbolized the regime's legitimacy domestically and internationally.[57]

For the Soviet scientists at Geneva, their country's internationalism and world-leading research garnered them the respect of their Western counterparts and officials, who, according to Josephson, were previously hesitant to treat researchers from the USSR as equals.[58] In fact, one American General relayed that it was entirely appropriate to think of the Russians as "retarded folk who depended mainly on a few captured German scientists for their achievements."[59] In response to impressive Soviet research and tangible accomplishments, Melvyn Price, the subcommittee chair of the Congressional Joint Committee on Atomic Energy, declared "at stake is not only our national defense but our ability to compete with the Soviets in the struggle for men's minds throughout the free world."[60] For Soviet policy makers, Moscow' success in Geneva highlighted that an agrarian and illiterate nation could rapidly transform into a global leader of science and industry.[61] For American policy makers, that same success represented an existential threat to Washington's liberal democratic vision of economic and political modernization.

In the context of the Cold War, the consequences of scientific achievement were never apolitical. American policy makers were keenly aware of the Soviet atomic propaganda victory. A National Security Council Report listed as a "key objective" the need for "the United States and other appropriate Free World countries to regain the lead in peaceful atomic energy development and international cooperation."[62] More pointedly, it urged American leadership "to forestall successful Soviet exploitation of the peaceful uses of atomic energy to attract the allegiance of the uncommitted peoples of the world."[63] Moscow's early successes in developing atomic energy demonstrated socialism's apparent superiority over the West and the Soviet commitment to the peaceful atom. Nuclear research and atomic energy had the potential to electrify and transform the post-colonial world: for countries throwing off their oppressors, such programs were essential tools for affirming

---

57 For a transcript of his speech, see "Ispol'zovanie atomnoi energii v mirnykh tseliakh," *Vestnik Akademii Nauk SSSR*, no. 8 (1955): 19–21.
58 Josephson, *Red Atom*, 186.
59 Cited in Clarence Lasby, *Project Paperclip: German Scientists and the Cold War* (New York: Scribner, 1975), 6.
60 Cited in John Krige, "Atoms for Peace, Scientific Internationalism, and Scientific Intelligence," *Osiris* vol. 21, No. 1 (2006): 170.
61 "Atomnuyu energiyu-na sluzhbu miru," *Atomnaia Energiia* Vol. 1, no. 1 (1956): 3.
62 DNSA, National Security Council, *NSC 5625—Peaceful Uses of Atomic Energy*, 22 November 1956, 20.
63 Ibid., 21.

national autonomy and defining national identity. The balance of global power depended, in part, on who first brought atomic age technologies and science to the world's masses.

For the USSR's political elite, the potential benefits of nuclear energy were soon entangled with notions of economic modernization and socialist progress.[64] Khrushchev even invited Kurchatov to speak on the benefits of atomic research and nuclear power at the Twentieth Party Congress of the Communist Party of the Soviet Union held in February 1956.[65] Yet Party Congresses by their very nature had an international inflection, and more than 1,700 communist and socialist leaders from fifty-six countries converged on Moscow for the first Congress of the post-Stalin era. When Kurchatov confidently laid out a long-range plan for civilian nuclear energetics and projected that by 1960 nuclear power would add two million kilowatts of energy to the Soviet national grid, he was not only speaking to a domestic audience. In fact, his speech was simultaneously translated from Russian into Arabic, Chinese, English, German, and Spanish for Congress attendees.[66] Such translation, however, was not necessary for Khalid Bakdash, the Secretary of the Syrian Communist Party and the Arab world's first elected communist representative, who had attended the Baku Branch of the Communist University of the Toilers of the East in the 1930s. In response to Kurchatov's speech, Bakdash optimistically proclaimed that "the technology of atomic science will plant the seeds of communism throughout the Arab world."[67]

Though Kurchatov's assertion about the growth rate of nuclear power generation was wildly optimistic—as only the 5,000 kilowatt Obninsk reactor was online at the time of the Congress—it represented the Soviet scientist *cum* political actor.[68] His visions of gigantic energy complexes that took advantage of economies of scale "to power cities and plough fields" clearly impressed Congress attendees.[69] According to Benjamin Sovokool, "nuclear power was a way to instruct nature," to

---

64  Josephson, "Atomic Power Communism," 306 & Nekrasov and Khromov, "N.S. Khrushchev i novaia energeticheskaia politika," 128.
65  For a transcript of Kurchatov's speech, see: *XX s"ezd KPSS. Stenograficheskii otchet vol. 1* (Moscow: Gosizdatpolit, 1956), 595–609.
66  Rossiiskii Gosudarstvennyi Arkhiv Noveishei Istorii (hereafter RGANI) f. 1, op. 2, d. 162, l. 75.
67  RGANI f. 1, op. 2, d. 163, l. 12–13.
68  XX s"ezd KPSS. Stenograficheskii otchet, Vol. 1, 596.
69  Ibid., 597.

tame the USSR's hostile geographies and harness newly accessible resources to political ends.[70] Atomic energy would catalyze a national renaissance, and Kurchatov was not alone in plumping for nuclear research. Two sessions held on the afternoon of Thursday, 16 February 1956 spoke to the Soviet atomic imagination.[71] One panel dealt with the effects of the peaceful atom on Soviet mining and extractive industries, while the other featured discussions on atomic medical research.[72] Kurchatov's speech and related sessions simply offered a daring glimpse into one possible socialist future.

Imam Mustafayev, the First Secretary of the Azerbaijan Communist Party, was particularly taken by Kurchatov's vision of nuclear energy's potential to alleviate the Soviet Union's perennial problems of low agricultural productivity and output. Mustafayev, who received a PhD in biological sciences from the Azerbaijan Agricultural Institute in 1938 and who served as Minister of Agriculture of the Azerbaijani Soviet Socialist Republic from 1947–1950, was well acquainted with these problems. In response to Kurchatov's speech he optimistically proclaimed that "nuclear power will build our industry and agriculture ... and Azerbaijan will lead the way in peaceful atomic research. We are all inspired by the work of Comrade Kurchatov and others."[73] As the former Academician-President of the Azerbaijani Academy of Sciences, he also opined on an Azeri role in building cooperative international nuclear research programs. He stated, "we [Azeris] can guide the underdeveloped peoples of the East in establishing their own [atomic] programs. This will be an important weapon in combatting economic and political underdevelopment."[74] Though it is unclear to whom exactly he was referring to when he spoke of the "underdeveloped peoples of the East," his reference to an Azeri-guided scientific diplomacy could possibly refer either to an envisioned Azeri scientific leadership role among fellow Turkic peoples of the Soviet Union and non-Soviet Central Asia, or to the broad swathes of the Muslim world gaining their political sovereignty. At any rate, Mustafayev's nationalistic sentiments upset political masters in Moscow. In 1959, he was expelled from the Communist Party for reportedly

---

70 Benjamin K. Sovacool and Scott Victor Valentine, *The National Politics of Nuclear Power: Economics, Security, and Governance* (Routledge: New York, 2012), 139.
71 RGANI f. 1, op. 2, d. 6, l. 8.
72 Ibid.
73 RGANI f. 1, op. 2, d. 372, l. 16.
74 RGANI f. 1, op. 2, d. 372, l. 17.

trying to introduce the Azeri language into Baku's political organizations and institutions.[75] Developing autonomy through nuclear power met its limits at the Soviet border.

But optimistic scientists and policy makers both within and beyond the USSR quickly became enamoured with the potential of nuclear power. Aware of the importance of its atomic research program, in May 1956, the State Committee for Atomic Energy of the USSR and the USSR Academy of Sciences launched the theoretical and technical periodical *Atomnaia Energiia*. Though the periodical was published in Russian, it encouraged international submissions, occasionally printed foreign language articles, and after 1958, published abstracts in English and Mandarin. The journal served as a venue for cutting edge scientific and technical research, offering articles on topics such as nuclear fusion and the most efficient way to pre-cast concrete for sodium-cooled fast neutron reactors.[76] But even more importantly, articles and editorials often reflected enthusiasm about the ability of scientific research, particularly nuclear physics, to affect the development of states and societies, to contribute to political and economic modernization. The atomic imagination circulated both domestically and internationally. Indeed, the journal's alternation between scientific and socio-political registers reflects both the state's desire that scientists function as servants and propagandists of socialist ideology, and scientists' desire that the state support the growth of a scientific-expert-advisor culture, free from the type of political interference that decimated Soviet genetics and agronomics under Stalin.[77] For example, the opening article of the journal's first volume, titled "Atomic Energy in Service of Peace" boldly declared that "the peaceful atom can transform the word" and reflected the state's desire to wed science to the pursuit of international political objectives.[78]

During his short-lived tenure as Minister of Foreign Affairs, Dimitri Shepilov authored an article appearing in the same periodical that proclaimed that

---

75   Sevda Ismailli, "How did our language become a state language," *Radio Free Europe*, 25 June 2009. Accessed online 4 March 2018. https://www.azadliq.org/a/1762314.html.
76   A.N. Komarovskii, "Sbornye betonnye i zhelezobetonnye konstruktsii v stroitel'stve iadernykh ustanovok," Atomnaia Energiia Vol. 4, No. 1 (January 1959): 43–57. L.A. Artsimovich, "Vklad sovetskikh uchenykh v issledovaniia po fizike plazmy," *Atomnaia Energiia*, Vol. 3, no. 4 (August 1958): 324–336.
77   For a good discussion of the relationship between agriculture and the Soviet state, see: Nils Roll-Hansen, *The Lysenko Effect: The Politics of Science* (New York: Humanity Books, 2005) and David Jorovsky, *The Lysenko Affair* (Chicago: University of Chicago Press, 2010).
78   "Atomnuyu energiyu," 3.

atomic research must serve the interests of the international class struggle.[79] During his trip to the United Kingdom in May 1955, Khrushchev insisted on seeing the British Atomic Energy Research Establishment near Harwell, and he brought with him a retinue of physicists and atomic specialists.[80] Though Khrushchev knew little of the scientific or technical underpinnings of atomic energy, he had no problem boasting about the strength of Soviet nuclear science. A TASS (Telegraph Agency of the Soviet Union) news report from June 1955 quoted Khrushchev stating "British nuclear researchers can learn a lot from their Soviet counterparts."[81]

Scientists, in turn, worked to create a culture in which their expertise and authority were respected by their political masters. Soviet physicists under both Stalin and Khrushchev wielded a strong claim to political authority: atomic weapons afforded the nuclear research and engineering community considerably more autonomy from Party ideologues than other scientific communities.[82] Yet, they were still members of the Soviet technocratic intelligentsia. Physicists simultaneously held positions of some power yet were beholden to the domestic and international objectives of the political establishment. The USSR's quinquennial system of central planning required physicists to be both scientist and salesmen, combining showmanship with a scientific rigour that produced results. The inspirational rhetoric of a technocratic atomic future, free from want and deprivation, won sustained funding and political support in Khrushchev's 1956–1960 five-year plan; continued funding, however, was predicated on producing scientific results and technological breakthroughs that kept the Soviet Union ahead of its Western adversaries.

But though the Soviet atomic imagination had from the start an internationalist flavour, it was first given voice domestically. Indeed, in a 1957 speech to his Institute's Party organization, Kurchatov made the case that nuclear physics should spare no effort to improve the quality of life of Soviet citizens.[83] A. Markin,

---

79 Dimitri Shepilov, "Atomshchiki i klassovaia bor'ba na mezhdunarodnoi arene," *Atomnaia Energiia*, Vol. 1, no. 2 (1956): 1.

80 Malenkov visited the same research centre during his March 1955 visit, though without the academic entourage. Khrushchev's repeat visit, accompanied by the best Soviet nuclear minds, can perhaps best be read as domestic political posturing.

81 GARF f R4459, op 53, d 423, l 19.

82 On science in Stalin's USSR, see: Ethan Pollock, *Stalin and the Soviet Science Wars* (Princeton: Princeton University Press, 2006), 72–103 and Nikolai Krementsov, *Stalinist Science* (Princeton: Princeton University Press, 1998), 93–190. The second part of Krementsov's monograph details Stalin's personal intervention in the fields of biology and genetics and the implications that this had on the conduct of Soviet science as a whole.

83 Cited in Josephson, "Atomic Power Communism," 303.

a nuclear scientist at Kurchatov's Institute, was one of the first to suggest how the judicious application of peaceful nuclear explosions could transform the country, proposing to divert Siberian waterways for irrigation to arid Central Asian republics.[84] In a similar vein, V.A. Mezentsev suggested that atomic energy could revolutionize Soviet man's relationship to the natural world. Arguing that the rugged landscape and remoteness of the Soviet economic hinterland would be brought to heel under peaceful nuclear explosions, he proposed using atomic energy to strip mine entire mountains and build canals.[85] Another Soviet scientist envisioned the frequent use of nuclear devices to address issues relating to economic development in geology, metallurgy, and chemistry.[86] The Soviet atom would be used to electrify cities in the European USSR, where 70% of the population lived, and it would revolutionize the efficiency of extractive industries in the Siberian and Central Asian hinterlands. The image of a peaceful and productive atom was created by scientists, engineers, and technicians, who, with increasing confidence, proclaimed the myriad ways it would transform Soviet life.

In part, these pronouncements reflected a political calculus: the scientific literati needed to justify ever increasing state outlays. Yet the state's support of "big science" also reflects its own confidence in scientific authority and desire to see its transformative potential enacted. In a positive feedback loop, what Soviet science proposed, the Soviet state disposed. One scholar counted hundreds of peaceful nuclear explosions in the Soviet Union from 1955–1975, twenty of which were detonated in the densely populated Volga Basin, while another took place in Donetsk's Enakievo coal mine.[87] They were successfully used to create temporary earth works, construct canals, create subterranean storage for industrial toxic waste, and even to liquidate hydrocarbon deposits for easier extraction. In one instance, Ivan Vasilyevich Arkhipov, the Soviet Minister of Nonferrous Metallurgy, even suggested using nuclear devices to access a molybdenum ore deposit in the Urals,

---

84   A. Markin, "Atom na sluzhbe cheloveka," *Smena*, no. 1 (1955): 18.
85   V.A. Mezentsev, "Na poroge atomnogo veka," *Nauka i Zhizn'*, no.1 (1956): 7–8.
86   A.P. Vinogradov, "Atomnaia energiia i problem geologii, khimii, metallurgi, teknologii," *Vestnik Akademii Nauk SSSR*, no. 11 (1955): 31–39.
87   Milo Nordyke, "A Review of Soviet Data on Peaceful Uses of Nuclear Explosions," *Annals of Nuclear Energy*, no. 2 (1975): 658–659.

whose low quality made traditional mining techniques inefficient.[88] The environmental and health consequences of repeated nuclear explosions, however, were at most a secondary concern.

Soviet atomic enthusiasm is also reflected in the promised pantheon of nuclear devices, with proposals for floating, flying, and stationary reactors.[89] At the extraordinary Twenty-First Party Congress in 1959, Khrushchev spoke about "the advancements of nuclear science for the benefit of all mankind."[90] A TASS bulletin after the Congress offered more specifics, speaking to the potential of nuclear-powered machinery to revolutionize Soviet agriculture and to assist the Virgin Lands Program, for example.[91] Though weakened by a recent stroke, Kurchatov gave his full-throated support to accelerated nuclear research and its continued decentralization from Moscow and Leningrad to the constituent republics. Kurchatov argued that this would allow union republics to tailor nuclear research to suit their specific economic and industrial needs.[92] As usual, he strongly encouraged his fellow scientists "to tame the power of the atom to reach and surpass capitalist countries in production."[93] The Soviet atomic imagination envisioned the exploitation of its Siberian and Arctic regions as a testament to applied science's ability to help colonize hostile environments and to make the hinterland economically productive, both of which became linked to increasingly ambitious political goals and the further unification of the USSR. The Twentieth and Twenty-First Party Congresses, for example, mandated better living standards and the increased production of consumer goods, in addition to a continued focus on military and economic concerns.[94] The design of portable atomic engines, like the "Arbus," a 1,500 kilo-

---

88  V.S. Emelianov, *S chego nachinalos'* (Moscow: Sovetskaia Rossiia, 1979), 256. On 28 December 1950, the Presidium of the Supreme Soviet decided to split the Ministry of Metallurgical Industry in two, the Ministry of Ferrous Metallurgy and the Ministry of Nonferrous Metallurgy.
89  For a detailed discussion, see: Josephson, *Red Atom*, 187–215.
90  For a transcript of Khrushchev's speech, see: *XXI s"ezd KPSS. Stenograficheskii otchet*, Vol. 1 (Moscow: Gosizdatpolit, 1959), 5–12.
91  GARF f. 4459, op 27, d 20691, l 198.
92  For a transcript of Kurchatov's speech, see: *XXI s"ezd KPSS. Stenograficheskii otchet*, Vol. 1 (Moscow: Gosizdatpolit, 1959), 174–179.
93  Cited in: Josephson, "Atomic Powered Communism," 304.
94  Though it is true that all Party Congresses advocated for better living standards and increased production of consumer goods, the Twenty-First Party Congress was extraordinary as Khrushchev announced that the Soviet Union would *dognat' i peregnat' Ameriku* [catch-up to and overtake America] within twenty years. See Jutta Schrerer, "To Catch up and Overtake the West: Soviet Discourse on Socialist Competition," in *Competition in Socialist Society* eds. Katalin Miklóssy and Melanie Ilic (New York: Routledge, 2014), 10–22.

watt reactor and a larger 6,000 kilowatt reactor to power oil and gas extraction, designed for use in the far north and far east, generated much discussion among Congress attendees.⁹⁵ The 1959 launch of the world's first nuclear powered icebreaker *Lenin* was heralded as the first of many instances in which fission, applied to transportation, would change Soviet life for the better and allow the state to assert its territorial sovereignty.⁹⁶ As political calls to reach and surpass the material levels of the West grew in strength, so too did the pressure on Soviet science to provide faster and more efficient ways of contributing to growth.

This science-growth nexus was most evident at the Twenty-Second Party Congress of October 1961. Here, Khrushchev promised that communism "will be built in the main" by 1980: the final phrase of the CPSU's newly adopted program expected that "the current generation of Soviet people will live under communism."⁹⁷ Thus, the decisions of the Congress set new economic targets and priorities ideologically determined to form the material and technical basis for this communism. One of the largest obstacles to overcome was low productivity. In September 1958, in reports to the Presidium, Khrushchev lamented that a Soviet *kolkhoznik* (collective farmer) expended 7.3 times more labour on producing one unit of grain than their American counterpart.⁹⁸ Per pound of beef and pork produced, the Soviet worker was 15 times less efficient.⁹⁹ Khrushchev laid bare similar inadequacies in forestry and extractive industries. Though official statistics reported upticks in production and productivity across the board from 1955 to 1960, economic performance still lagged behind the West. The material technical basis of communism would not only require dramatic changes to sluggish productivity, it also demanded exponential growth. In order to fuel this "Red *Wirtschaftswunder*," at the Twenty Second Congress in 1961 Khrushchev proposed a comprehensive program of energy development. He called for oil extraction to increase from 147 million tons annually in 1960 to between 690–710 million tons annually in 1980, and for natural gas production to increase from 45.3 billion m³ to between 680–720 billion m³ over the same period.¹⁰⁰ He also called for

---

95  GARF f. 4459, op 27, d 20691, l 87–88.
96  GARF, f. 10201, op. 1, d. 133, l. 2.
97  William Tompson, *Khrushchev: A Political Life* (New York: St. Martin's Press, 1997), 238.
98  *Prezidium TsK KPSS. 1954–1964 T. 1*, 261.
99  Ibid., 262–263.
100 For a transcript of Khrushchev's speech, see: *XXII s"ezd KPSS. Stenograficheskii otchet*, Vol. 1 (Moscow: Gosizdatpolit, 1961), 32. For some perspective, in 2012 the International Energy Agency reported that Russia produced a world-leading 544 million tons of oil while the United States produced a world-leading 689 billion m³ of natural gas.

nuclear power generation to make up no less than 25% of total national electricity production by 1980.[101]

Atomic energetics, both in the form of contained reactions to generate power and peaceful nuclear explosions to facilitate previously inefficient or remote resource extraction, were key components of building the material basis for communism. Khrushchev himself hailed the results of five peaceful nuclear explosions in the Krasnovisherskii District of Perm in the early 1960s—oil production was five million tons a year above plan.[102] In 1961, roughly two weeks after the Party Congress, Efim Slavsky, the head of the Ministry of Medium Machine Building, wrote in the press organ of the All-Union Central Council of Trade Unions, *Trud*, that "the national nuclear research industry is on the leading edge of scientific and technological developments to meet and fulfil all economic targets."[103] By 1975, according to one estimate, the Soviet nuclear research establishment had grown to 1.5 million employees, 47 top secret locations, closed and open research, development, and production cities, and scores of engineering and physics institutes.[104] Judging by its size alone, the nuclear establishment was able to maintain official enthusiasm, advancing scientific, political, and economic interests.

Scientific and technical literature, cloaked in nationalistic and economic rhetoric, positioned nuclear research and technology as a possible panacea for comparative underdevelopment and backwardness, both in the USSR and abroad. Of course, the transformation of limited experimental reactors—whether into commercially viable power mega-complexes or miniaturized for portable community use—was always going to be an uphill battle. But the rhetoric and enthusiasm surrounding these programs positioned scientists as political actors and imbued this nascent nuclear culture with considerable authority. In the context of the early Cold War, Soviet accomplishments in nuclear energetics, coupled with the country's space program, presented challenges to Western scientific and technical leadership. Nuclear reactors and atomic research, as symbols of modernity, signified the strengths of the socialist paradigm. Moscow's eagerness to collaborate with newly independent states in atomic research spoke to the strength of the Soviet model of modernization and the technopolitical future made possible by socialism. It had only to be exported and socialist influence and socialist revolution the world over could be secured.

---

101  Ibid., 34.
102  *Prezidium TsK KPSS. 1954–1964 T. 2*, 71.
103  E. Slavsky, "Budushchie atomnaia issledovaniia," *Trud*, 2 November 1961, 5.
104  Josephson, *Red Atom*, 34.

## Nuclear Technopolitics on the Nile

In June 1955, Egypt's newly created Ministry of Education and Scientific Research released seven pamphlets about the potential benefits of nuclear energetics for the country. Taken as a whole, these booklets reflect a spirit of optimism and envision a better future made possible by harnessing atomic technology. The first, titled *Alṭaqat alnawawiat fi khidmat miṣr* [Nuclear Power in the Service of Egypt] declared that "just as the Revolution of 23 July guaranteed our political freedom, nuclear technology can help ensure our economic and social freedom."[105] The pamphlet's sanguine register boasted that the peaceful atom could do much to reverse the ill effects of colonialism and feudalism.[106] Another booklet, titled *Alṭaqat aldhariyat fi khidmat alriyf almiṣrī* [Atomic Power in Service of the Egyptian Countryside] foresaw sweeping changes in rural settings, from improved health to increased agricultural yields, stemming from Egypt's embrace of atomic futures.[107] Yet another, titled *Alṭaqat aldhariyat fi khidmat aliqtiṣad almiṣrī* [Atomic Energy in Service of the Egyptian Economy], laid out the economic benefits of a nuclear embrace, which included full employment [*tawẓiyf kamil*], electrification, and more leisure time for workers.[108] The pamphlets, written in simple language and illustrated with atomic nuclei and electrons, laboratory equipment, factories, and fields ripe for harvest, positioned science and technology as leading elements in a crusade for modernization and against "corrupt capitalist domination."[109] Moreover, they represent an elite faith in science and technology as agents of progressive social change. In a country where estimated illiteracy was almost 80%, these pamphlets presented atomic science as an easily understood benefit for the nation, a curative tonic for colonial underdevelopment, and a prophylactic against future exploitation.[110] Even before the first Egyptian physicist received any training in the Soviet Union, or the first Soviet scientist collaborated on the Nile, nuclear technopolitics had captured the imagination of Cairo's new pharaohs.

---

105   NAII, RG 0306, Entry P46, Container 94, *Alṭaqat alnawawiat fi khidmat miṣr*, 2. In Arabic the Revolution of 23 July [*thawrat 23 yuliu*] refers to the 23 July 1952 Free Officers Movement revolution, led by Mohammed Naguib and Gamal Abdel Nasser, which overthrew King Farouk.
106   Ibid, 7.
107   NAII, RG 0306, Entry P46, Container 94, *Alṭaqat aldhariyat fi khidmat alriyf almiṣrī*, 2
108   NAII, RG 0306, Entry P46, Container 94, *Alṭaqat aldhariyat fi khidmat aliqtiṣad almiṣrī*, 1.
109   Ibid, 2.
110   According to UNESCO, in 1947 Egypt's estimated illiteracy rate stood at just over 80%. In 1955, this figure had dropped slightly to 77%. *World Illiteracy at Mid-Century—A Statistical Study* (UNESCO: Paris, 1957), 52, 77.

The Egyptian Act 509 of 1955, which permitted the establishment of the Egyptian Atomic Energy Commission, was indeed an aspirational document based on this atomic imagination. An explanatory note to the Act proclaimed that:

> Atomic Energy has grown to be an important factor in military and political fields. Scientists unanimously believe that the utilisation of Atomic Energy for peaceful purposes in the scientific, technical and other fields, will in future play a major role. The very future of civilization itself will depend on harnessing this energy for constructive purposes.[111]

The Act continued, stating that

> the vast improvement achieved in scientific discoveries related to Atomic Energy compels us in Egypt to consider the drawing up of an appropriate plan ... Thus we can manage to keep pace with the progress of civilization instead of lingering behind.[112]

This Egyptian enthusiasm for the atom did not go unnoticed by the men stationed in the Garden City district of Cairo at 5 Tawfik Diab Street, otherwise known as the American Embassy. Three cables from Cairo to Washington in the summer of 1955 detailed how the United States could benefit from Egypt's desire for nuclear research and technology. The first, dated 9 July 1955 and written by John Foley Jr., the embassy's commercial attaché, contended that Washington could use the promise of future nuclear scientific cooperation to extract favourable conditions for American companies chafing under seemingly arbitrary regulations and high taxation.[113] The second cable, simply titled "The Situation in North Africa" and dated 15 July 1955, proposed that the United States should offer "financial, economic, and scientific inducements to the Egyptian government in order to temper its support of FLN [*Front de libération nationale*] forces in Algeria."[114] Though the cable was light on specifics, it did note Cairo's desire for cooperation and assistance

---

111   NAII, RG 59, Entry 3008-A, Container 486, *The Atomic Energy Commission: Its Law, Formation, and Program* (Cairo: The Republic of Egypt: The Presidency of the Council of Ministers, December 1955), 10.
112   Ibid, 10–11.
113   NAII, RG 84, Entry 320, Container 7, "American Business Interests at Risk," 2. In particular, he cited the travails of an American steel and pipeline company whose offices had been recently raided by Egyptian police.
114   NAII, RG 84, Entry 320, Container 7, "The Situation in North Africa," 1. In 1956, the French socialist Prime Minister Guy Mollet explained to his British counterpart Anthony Eden that Nasser's ultimate ambition was "to re-create the empire of Islam around Egypt." Cited in Matthew Connelly, "Rethinking the Cold War and Decolonization: The Grand Strategy of the Algerian War for Independence," *International Journal of Middle Eastern Studies*, Vol. 33, no. 2 (2001): 227. Though this was probably an overestimation of Nasser's ambitions, the quotation speaks to French perceptions and interpretations of Nasser's motivations stemming from Egypt's material and military support of FLN forces.

in the fields of civil aviation, agriculture, and nuclear research.[115] The cable also noted that the United States could use Public Law 480 (PL 480), otherwise known as the Food for Peace program of the United States Agency for International Development, to encourage bilateral cooperation and deepen trade ties.[116] Though it was unlikely that any amount of American aid could have matched the prestige accrued to Nasser in the decolonizing world for his rhetorical and material support of the FLN, that the American embassy thought the promise of nuclear cooperation would moderate Egypt's positions represents the value placed in this type of research by leaders in Cairo.[117]

The third cable was a summary and analysis of a conversation between Henry A. Byroade, the US Ambassador to Egypt, and Nasser, which took place on 30 July 1955. The ambassador recounted that Nasser was adamant "Egypt must get into the nuclear age in quick time. It was late getting into [the] Industrial Revolution and into [the] electrical age."[118] The ambassador also relayed to Washington that he had conveyed America's willingness to help Egypt construct a 150MW nuclear power reactor at Borg al Arab, forty-five kilometers south-west of Alexandria.[119] Indeed, this was not the first offer of atomic cooperation made by the United States to Egypt. In October 1954, the Egyptian ambassador in Washington formally requested American assistance in Egypt's atomic energy activities.[120] On 29 October 1954, Secretary of State Dulles even informed the ambassador that the US government had agreed to train Egyptian scientists in America and establish a radioisotope laboratory in Cairo.[121] It is unclear why the Egyptian government, however, did not proceed with this offer of American assistance. In summer 1955, Nasser clearly demurred, claiming that "now was not the right political climate" for America's involvement in such a show piece project.[122]

---

115  Ibid, 2.
116  On 10 July 1954, Eisenhower signed the Agricultural Trade and Assistance Act, which simultaneously created the Office of Food for Peace. The law's purpose was, in part, "to make maximum use of surplus agricultural commodities in the furtherance of foreign policy."
117  For a discussion of the international aspects of the Algerian War and Nasserite Egypt's involvement see Matthew Connelly, *A Diplomatic Revolution: Algeria's Fight for Independence and the Origins of the Post-Cold War Era* (Oxford: Oxford University Press, 2002), 67–116 and passim.
118  NAII, Record Group 59, Entry 5265, Box 3, "Record of Conversation with President Nasser," 3–4.
119  Ibid., 4.
120  NAII, RG 59, Entry 3008-A, Container 486, "Egyptian Atomic Energy Activities," 2. The Ambassador's personal interest in atomic science had been piqued by famed Egyptian singer Umm Kulthum's treatment for hyperthyroidism with radioiodine at the Naval Medical Centre in Bethesda.
121  Ibid. 3.
122  NAII, Record Group 59, Entry 5265, Box 3, "Record of Conversation with President Nasser," 4.

Why would Nasser, whose visions for a modern independent Egypt relied heavily on technocratic modernization, decline Washington's offers of assistance in 1954 and summer 1955, only to turn to Moscow in the fall? The answer most likely lies in Nasser's domestic and international manoeuvring. The summer of 1955 found the Egyptian president strengthened by his successful participation in the April conference of nonaligned nations in Bandung, Indonesia. Mohammed Fawzi, Egypt's foreign minister throughout the 1950s, claimed that "Bandung opened new vistas for Abdul Nasser, and helped him to discover better both the world and himself."[123] During his international travels that summer, Nasser visited Afghanistan, Burma, India, and Pakistan, and formed close friendships with Zhou Enlai, the first premier of Red China; Jawaharlal Nehru, the first prime minister of independent India; and Josip Broz Tito, the first president and nineteenth prime minister of Yugoslavia. James Jankowski has argued that Nasser's prominent role in Indonesia and the enthusiastic reception he received as "the champion of Asia and Africa" upon his return to Egypt crystallized his political ascendency and permitted him a tighter grasp on domestic and foreign affairs.[124] In short, openly turning to the United States for aid and assistance would have jeopardized Egypt's and Nasser's own recently won anti-imperialist and neutralist bona-fides, as well as the president's position at the fore of the global non-aligned movement. Such a volte-face would also have poisoned the wellspring of his domestic legitimacy and perhaps neutered his own political ascendency. Scientific diplomacy with the Soviet Union, however, posed no such risks to his domestic position and international standing. Moscow was a relative diplomatic newcomer to this part of the world and suffered from neither the original sin of global empire, as was the case of the United Kingdom and France, nor guilt by association, as was the case with the United States.

Nasser's desire for atomic cooperation coincided with bureaucratic changes within the Soviet nuclear establishment that facilitated and encouraged international scientific exchange. Moreover, they corresponded with Moscow's realization that during the Cold War, the peaceful uses of atomic energy had become an arena of competition between capitalism and socialism, which could potentially

---

123 Mahmoud Fawzi, *Suez 1956: An Egyptian Perspective* (London: Shorouk International, 1987), 13–14.
124 James P. Jankowsi, *Nasser's Egypt, Arab Nationalism, and the United Arab Republic* (Boulder: Lynne Rienner Publishers, 2001), 66. In June 1956, Nasser was confirmed as President through a popular referendum and his consolidation of power and control over foreign and domestic policies was complete.

align the USSR with the developing world and provide an opportunity—although not a guaranteed one—to display the superiority of the Soviet path to modernization.[125] In March 1956, the Soviets created the Chief Administration for the Use of Atomic Energy [*Glavatom*] within the Ministry of Medium Machine Building to handle all activities related to the peaceful use of nuclear technology and international cooperation.[126] Glavatom would be the atomic ministry's window on the world and ostensibly the USSR's official authority in matters of foreign relations in the field of nuclear research.[127] In this regard, the Ministry keenly positioned the Soviet nuclear program as pacific in its ambitions and dedicated to international cooperation and socialist-oriented development. Cold War tensions certainly primed the pump but Nasser's anti-colonialism—in which capitalism was synonymous with colonialism—made the Soviet-Egyptian atomic rapprochement almost a *fait accompli*. In a July 1956 speech in New Delhi, Nasser opined on the ongoing threat of imperialism:

> Our peoples still have to exert enormous efforts to make up for the underdevelopment imposed on them, so that they can catch up with the great future awaiting mankind, thanks to the new discoveries and the wide horizons provided by the fields of knowledge ... One would not be exaggerating if one said that the monopoly of science will be imperialism's new method.[128]

This cautionary language mirrors a speech given by Kurchatov at the Twentieth Party Congress just four months prior:

> We would like to work on the resolution of this most important scientific problem [atomic energy] for mankind together with scientists from all countries in the world whose scientific and technical achievements we highly value ... We all must be aware of the drive in certain countries to achieve nothing less than atomic colonialism.[129]

"Monopolized science" and "atomic colonialism" were effectively synonymous—even if cast in each country's preferred rhetoric—reflecting the position of atomic technopolitics and technopower as presumably capitalist and colonialist forces. As seen from Cairo, science was a chimera. It could either be an agent of post-colonial imperialism—if capitalist—or a tool to guarantee national self-determination—if socialist. As seen from Moscow, socialist science was not just a strategic tool; it was

---

125 Holloway, Stalin and the Bomb, 14.
126 Schmid, "Nuclear Colonization?" 126 and Maria Vasilieva, *Soleils rouges: L'ambition nucleaire soviétique* (Paris: Hist Industriel, 2010), 178–179.
127 Vasilieva, *Soleils rouges*, 179.
128 *President Gamal Abdel Nasser on Consolidation of the Cause of World Peace* (Cairo: Ministry of National Guidance State Information Service, 1971), 58.
129 *XX s"ezd KPSS. Stenograficheskii otchet*, Vol. 1 (Moscow: Gosizdatpolit, 1956), 600–601.

a sincerely modernizing force that could economically and politically transform developing nations. Capitalist science, however, was colonialist and retrograde. Though the atom could serve multiple masters, both countries agreed that it could advance only one agenda, that of socialist liberation.

In late-June 1956, Khrushchev sat for twenty minutes with Zakaria Nil, a correspondent for the Cairene daily *Al Ahram*, in Moscow. Appearing on the newspaper's front page on 1 July, the text of the interview covered a wide range of issues, from the Palestinians and Israel to American imperialism, communism, and nuclear weapons.[130] When asked pointedly about nuclear weapons and atomic research, Khrushchev replied, "we agree to direct our atomic research to the services of humanity and the happiness of the human race. [The west] strive[s] to produce greater quantities of weapons, and they devote the major part of atomic energy to military purposes."[131] Khrushchev's positioning of the USSR as an advocate for the irenic atom set up a contrast between Soviet and American policy. Khrushchev continued, claiming that the Soviet Union wanted to be a friend to the Egyptian people, "working together as equals in peace and advancing the interests of all mankind."[132] In a dispatch dated 12 July 1956, Alexander Schee, the American Embassy Counselor for Political Affairs in Cairo, claimed that Khrushchev's interview, in part, indicated that the Soviet Union was taking a new approach to relations with Egypt.[133] He argued that Soviet-Egyptian relations were entering a new phase in which "political and military aid will be soft pedalled and primary emphasis given to increasing scientific and cultural ties."[134]

In a sense, Schee's analysis accurately deduced Soviet intentions. Bilateral military aid often engenders aggression and unanticipated behaviours in the recipient state that can run contrary to the interests of the vendor. There was serious concern in Soviet ruling circles that unbridled arms transfers to the Middle East could destabilize the Israel-Palestine situation and embolden Arab states to act more aggressively.[135] Mohammed Heikal, the long-time editor of *Al Ahram* and a close friend of Nasser, argued during the Suez Crisis of 1956 that "Russia's support of Egypt's position played a vital role in the mobilization of world opinion against

---

130  "Muqābla ma' Nikita S. Khrushchev," *Al Ahram*, 1 July 1956, 1.
131  Ibid.
132  Ibid.
133  NAII, RG 84, Entry 320, Container 17, "Khrushchev's Interview in al-Ahram," 3.
134  Ibid.
135  Karen Dawisha, *Soviet Foreign Policy Towards Egypt* (New York: St. Martin's, 1979), 15–33.

the aggressors," but that the USSR was unable to either prevent the invasion or mediate an end to it.[136] Though Egypt, and by extension the Arab world, was impressed with the style, if not the substance, of Moscow's diplomatic activity surrounding these events, the Soviet Union quickly realized that it had little control over how war materiel was used by recipient states and could do little to mitigate the unintended geopolitical consequences wrought by martial aid. Khrushchev's focus on "the peaceful pursuit of shared interests" with Egypt thus speaks to an evolving Soviet foreign policy that acknowledged the USSR's regional weaknesses (limited naval presence in the Mediterranean and an inability to impose effective economic pressure to curtail adventurism) and sought to overcome them by deepening its bilateral relationship with Egypt.

This is not to deny the influence or prestige of hard power elements of Moscow's foreign policy with the decolonizing world. Indeed, Khrushchev was willing to sell arms to Middle Eastern states, as typified by the Soviet-sponsored Czechoslovak-Egyptian arms deal of September 1955.[137] However, this agreement should best be seen in the context of a broad, multi-faceted Soviet engagement with the Arab world. Arms sales and military transfers were but one element of Moscow's attempt to build influence in Egypt. In a 5 July 1956 letter to P.M. Zernov, the Deputy Minister of the *Glavatom*, Daniil Solod, former-Soviet ambassador to Egypt and Deputy Head of the Department of Near and Middle East Ministry of Foreign Affairs of the USSR, argued that the Soviet Union should give scientific and technical cooperation with Egypt the highest priority.[138] Specifically, he argued that "there is little risk to our position in the region and much to gain from this type of international cooperation."[139]

Ostensibly, Solod, a trained-Arabist and veteran of the Soviet Foreign Ministry, was cautioning against deeper regional martial involvement that might undermine the USSR's policy options by further militarizing the Middle East and reducing Moscow's role to that of an arms merchant. Techno-scientific collaboration would serve Russian interests by increasing elite interaction and ideally cultivating pro-Soviet sentiment within those communities. It would present the political and economic interests of the USSR as synonymous with those of developing states,

---

136 Mohammed Heikal, The Cairo Documents: The Inside Story of Nasser and His Relationship with World Leaders, Rebels, and Statesmen (London: Doubleday, 1973), 45.
137 John Lewis Gaddis, *We Now Know: Rethinking Cold War History* (New York: Clarendon Press, 1998), 170–172.
138 RGANI f 8, op 14, d 3, l 1.
139 Ibid.

and offer a low-risk, high-reward form of bilateral cooperation. In turn, the Egyptian regime and its interests would be served by gaining access to modern technology and establishing elite research and scientific centres to train a new class of future-oriented technocrats. Scientific cooperation thus posed few of the high risks associated with weapons transfers.

Following the 12 July 1956 Soviet-Egyptian atomic treaty, high ranking delegations from both states met in Moscow on 29 August 1956 to discuss and agree on specifics of this new dimension of their relationship. On 25 August 1956, just a few days before the Egyptian delegation's arrival, the Near Eastern Service of Moscow Radio hailed Egypt as "the first Islamic country taking the road of cooperation with the Soviet Union in the peaceful utilization of atomic energy."[140] Catering to the political and economic aspirations of the region, the broadcast said that the Soviet people perceive in the "Egyptian initiative" a desire to make the country "economically independent to the greatest possible extent."[141] It added that "economic prosperity could not be fulfilled in our times without the utilisation of atomic energy which has titanic latent productive power" and hinted that more extensive Soviet aid would be forthcoming in this field.[142]

In a preparatory memo, *Glavatom* chair Slavsky, in a letter to Kliment Voroshilov, the Chairman of the Presidium of the Supreme Soviet of the USSR, proposed the exchange of scientists, an increase in the number of spots available for Egyptian students at Soviet institutions, a plan to send engineers and atomic experts to teach and train Egyptians in Egypt, and the creation of a science and technology office at the embassy in Cairo.[143] In response, Voroshilov agreed that these would be positive initial steps but stressed that the Soviet position should underline the unity of Soviet science and the Soviet state.[144] In other words, Soviet scientific support could not be separated from the underlying political and economic system that created it. At a banquet held on the evening of Saturday 1 September 1956, Dr. Ibrahim Hilmi Abdul-Raham, the Egyptian undersecretary of the Ministry of Atomic Energy Affairs, praised the advances of the Soviet people, the strength of the socialist economy, and Moscow's leadership in the development of peaceful uses of atomic energy.[145] Additionally, he specifically acknowledged Khrushchev

---

140 For a transcript of the radio broadcast, see GARF f R4459, op 53, d 105, l 3.
141 Ibid, 3.
142 Ibid. 3–4.
143 RGANI f 3, op 39, d 24, l 14.
144 RGANI F 3, op 39, d 25, l 1.
145 A translated (Arabic–Russian) copy of his speech can be found at GARF f R4459, op 53, d 102, l 1.

for helping "to bring the wonders [*chudesa*] of the modern era to a country that no more than a few years ago was a relative stranger to you."[146] "Our strength," he continued "followed your example of democratizing national wealth so that we would be safe from the raids of forces hostile to political freedom."[147] In other words, Abdul-Rahman's speech indicates the clear entanglement of notions of socialist economics, social restructuring, and—for Egypt—political independence, all strengthened by techno-scientific modernization.

The rhetorical enthusiasm with which Egyptian elites imagined a bright technopolitical future, however, obscured the magnitude of the efforts required. On 10 May 1958, during a nearly month-long tour of the Soviet Union, Nasser spoke at an electrical plant in Leningrad. He told a group of factory workers and gathered dignitaries that "on my visit to the Soviet Union, I have seen how Russia was transformed from an agricultural state into a first-class industrial power, where the people were determined to work and to work with determination. We are inspired by your accomplishments"[148] The president, however, appeared focused on the result and not on the process; Soviet modernization's many casualties went unremarked. In an interview with the *Christian Science Monitor* published on 2 February 1959, Nasser argued:

> We were surprised by the age of the atom and I feel that we have to redouble our efforts now to make up for what we missed and to join the future with others. We have developed a plan, which needs several things: human capacity, capital to invest, and then expertise.[149]

But even if the Egyptians proceeded optimistically, the Soviets quickly realized that their colleagues' atomic eagerness surpassed their abilities. The founding document of the Egyptian Atomic Energy Commission laid out a clear vision for personnel training, capital outlays, and expertise development. The Commission posited that it needed fifty specialists in atomic energy sciences and 100 specialists in applied science related to atomic energy to form the nucleus of an independent research sector.[150]

---

146  Ibid.
147  Ibid.
148  "Kalimāt alrayis Gamal Abdel Nasser fi Leningrad athnā zyāratihi Soviet Union," http://nasser.bibalex.org/home/main.aspx?lang=ar. Last Accessed 3 July 2018.
149  "Ḥadith alrayis Gamal Abdel Nasser ilā William Stringer muḥarar garidat Christian Science Monitor," accessed 3 July 2018, http://nasser.bibalex.org/home/main.aspx?lang=ar.
150  NAII, RG 59, Entry 3008-A, Container 486, *The Atomic Energy Commission: Its Law, Formation, and Program* (Cairo: The Republic of Egypt: The Presidency of the Council of Ministers, December 1955), 18.

## TABLE 1.

| Trainees Requested in Atomic Energy Sciences[151] | | Trainees Requested in Applied Nuclear Science[152] | |
|---|---|---|---|
| Field | Number | Field | Number |
| Higher Mathematics | 10 | Atomic Plant Construction | 5 |
| Experimental Physics | 15 | Automatic and Electronic Machines | 10 |
| Theoretical Physics | 10 | Metallurgy of Radioactive Elements | 10 |
| Chemistry of Radioactive Elements | 5 | Radioactive Applications | 15 |
| Chemistry of Radioactive Ores | 5 | Statistical Machines and their Uses | 5 |
| Geology of Radioactive Ores | 5 | Medical Studies using Isotopes | 15 |
| | | Experimental Tracer Studies | 15 |
| | | Electronic Calculating Machines | 5 |
| | | Reactors and Atomic Motors | 20 |

The Commission's founding document declared that "all are to be trained experimentally up to the level of mastering their respective branches and assisting research workers."[153] Unfortunately, the Commission grossly underestimated the costs involved in not only training these specialists but in providing research expenses, laboratory equipment, and scientific apparatus. Egypt's total financial outlay for personnel training and research start-up costs was a paltry LE300,000.[154] Its total operating budget for its first year of operations was only LE1 million,[155] though this figure increased to LE4.5 million by 1960.[156] In comparison, in 1956 *Glavatom* estimated that during the previous two years the United States had spent $200 million on its nuclear industry while Great Britain had just unveiled a ten year plan in nuclear energetics costed at £300 million.[157] Atomic powered futures were

---

151  Ibid, 19–20.
152  Ibid, 20–21.
153  Ibid., 21.
154  Ibid, 22–23. LE was the currency symbol for the Egyptian pound (livre égyptienne). To add a bit of perspective, in 1955 the Egyptian Pound was pegged to the Pound Sterling at an exchange rate of 2.3:1. The Pound Sterling itself was pegged to the US dollar at a rate of 1:2.8. Thus, 300,000 Egyptian pounds would be roughly equivalent to $365,000. Adjusting for inflation, this would be roughly the equivalent of $3.4 million in 2018. A sizeable sum but a minor fraction of what was required to launch an atomic powered future.
155  Ibid, 4.
156  NAII, RG 59, Entry 3008-A, Container 490, "Review of Egyptian Atomic Energy Program," 3.
157  RGANI f 3, op 39, d 30, 12

expensive, and by signing an agreement on the peaceful uses of atomic energy with Egypt, the USSR in effect agreed to subsidize Egypt's chosen path to modernity.

Article Five of the bilateral atomic agreement committed the Soviets to "aid the Government of the Egyptian Republic in training Egyptian specialists in nuclear physics and other sciences connected with the atomic energy and its utilization for peaceful purposes."[158] In this, the USSR certainly fulfilled its obligations. In November 1956, the first group of nine Egyptian undergraduates and fourteen graduate students, all studying in fields related to atomic science, left for Moscow.[159] In 1956 and 1957, nine official missions relating to the peaceful use of the atom departed from the Cairo International Airport at Heliopolis for various destinations within the Soviet Union.[160] On 4 June 1957, Kamal al-Din Hussein, Egypt's Minister of Education, fresh off a tour of the Soviet Union where he headed a scientific delegation, announced that the USSR would create 300 fellowships for Egyptian students, teachers, and researchers in the sciences.[161] Accompanying the fellowships would be the reciprocal creation of Russian and Arabic language training programs in the two states. Hussein also agreed that the program for applying science in Egypt would be "in accordance with the system applied in the Soviet Union."[162] In practice, this meant that Egypt would emulate the Soviet model of scientific organization and research institutes.

During Hussein's scientific pilgrimage, the USSR also agreed to establish a chemical radiation laboratory in Alexandria and an atomic science museum in Cairo.[163] In 1958 and 1959, Moscow agreed to offer 220 additional fellowships to qualified Egyptian students and researchers.[164] By Egypt's own estimate, by 1961 over 1250 Egyptians had or were currently studying in the USSR.[165] In 1961, a report by the American State Department's Bureau of Educational and Cultural Affairs on Egypt's Atomic Energy Commission estimated that the Soviet Union had

---

158 NAII, RG 59, Entry 3008-A, Container 23, "Agreement on Cooperation Between the Union of Soviet Socialist Republics and the Egyptian Republic in the Utilization of Atomic Energy for Peaceful Purposes," 4,
159 Surak, *Nuclear Reactor Development in Egypt*, 7–8.
160 Ibid, 10.
161 *Pravda*, 5 June 1957, 3.
162 Ibid.
163 Ibid, 3.
164 NAII, RG 59, Entry 3008-A, Container 448, "USIA Telegram," 1.
165 *Statistical Handbook United Arab Republic 1952–1961* (Cairo: Central Agency for Public Mobilisation and Statistics, 1962), 141.

spent or lent $250 million to Egypt to help create that country's nuclear establishment.[166] Unfortunately, a *Glavatom* report from the 1962, though not attaching a monetary figure to Soviet assistance, detailed the deficiencies in Egypt's Atomic Energy Commission despite Moscow's enthusiasm and financial generosity.

The unauthored Soviet report laid out a litany of problems in Egypt, including issues with equipment, a shortage of qualified personnel, and the nature of Egyptian research projects themselves. "We now see in Egypt," the report noted "both extremes of the equipment situation. In general, there is a great dearth of equipment in universities, both for instruction and research in physics. The Atomic Energy Establishment has much more equipment than there is trained personnel."[167] In a package deal in early-1960, the USSR provided the AEE a chain reactor, a Van de Graaff accelerator, a mass spectrometer, a $\beta$-ray spectrometer, and other auxiliary equipment. Though Soviet personnel worked closely with Egyptians in installing and testing the equipment, the problems of maintenance, repair, and calibration of physics apparatus, according to the Soviet report, were extreme.[168] The American report, however, blamed substandard Russian equipment for delays and setbacks while the Soviet report blamed Egypt's lack of qualified personnel to repair electronic equipment.[169] Equipment concerns, regardless of their origin, were just one of myriad noted problems. Though the USSR subsidized the education of scores of Egyptian students and researchers, the *Glavatom* report noted how difficult it was for Soviet atomic specialists to work and train in Egypt. Language concerns aside, the report claimed that "there is no place where a highly trained physicist can expect to learn anymore about his speciality than he already knows."[170] As such, for Soviet personnel, the practice of scientific diplomacy on the Nile was seen as a hardship post, with few prospects for meaningful research. By Moscow's own estimations, Egypt's peaceful atomic program, despite more than half a decade of operation, was "unsatisfactory [*neudovletvoritel'no*]."

Indeed, Moscow's continued atomic scientific collaboration on the Nile was, in many tangible ways, a net loss for the USSR, but both states accrued enough benefits from scientific collaboration that neither were willing to abandon it entirely. During the Cold War, the Soviets benefited from leading the charge in en-

---

166  NAII, RG 59, Entry 3008-A, Container 450, "Egypt's Atomic Energy Commission," 3.
167  RGANI f 3, op 39, d 31, 16.
168  Ibid., 19–20.
169  NAII, RG 59, Entry 3008-A, Container 450, "Egypt's Atomic Energy Commission," 9.
170  RGANI f 3, op 39, d 31, l 24.

suring that the benefits of the peaceful atom be available for all mankind. For Nasser, the construction of an independent, anti-colonial state was deeply imbricated with political and economic modernization made possible by techno-scientific advancements. His continued support of the Egyptian Atomic Energy Commission, for all its practical shortcomings, represented in part his continued faith in the transformative potential of scientific and nuclear research. Additionally, Nasser could point to his state's advancements in "decolonized science" as an example of Egypt's strength in the Arab world specifically, and the global South generally. In a speech in Damascus in April 1960, he opined on the links between scientific advancement and political independence:

> We stand ready to assist any of our Arab brothers in resisting bastions of colonialism and we resent foreign efforts to divide us. The people of Egypt have chosen a path of unity. We know we have much work ahead of us ... Our scientists and engineers will lead the way for a better future for all Arabs, everywhere.[171]

Both the Soviet Union and Egypt shared this "vision for a better future" made possible by scientific research. In the Soviet Union, atomic power captured the imagination of the scientific, political, and economic intelligentsia; it had the potential to accelerate economic growth and usher in a new era of communist politics. For Egypt, already largely impressed by and amenable to Soviet-style central planning and state ownership of the "commanding heights" of the economy, atomic energy was a dazzling symbol and a potential harbinger of a modernity free of the exploitation and deprivation characterized by the colonial era. Ultimately, the USSR used the soft power of scientific co-operation to train and nurture a generation of Egyptian scientists and engineers. The Soviet Union hoped that a shared atomic imagination would translate into a shared atomic powered modernity in which closer scientific cooperation would mirror closer geo-political alignment during the Cold War, and, one day, a global socialist revolution.

Unfortunately, the Soviet atomic imagination—whether at the domestic or the international scale—was always a few steps ahead of its atomic capabilities. In his address to the Twentieth Party Congress in 1956, Kurchatov told his audience that atomic power plants would be built "as part of a large state experiment with the goal of finding more technologically feasible and economical paths for the creation of atomic power stations."[172] Yet the economic and technological barriers to

---

171 *President Gamal Abdel Nasser on Consolidation of the Cause of World Peace—Speeches pronounced in International Conferences and abroad and Joint Communiques with Heads of State* (Cairo: Ministry of National Guidance State Information Service, 1971), 86.
172 *XX s"ezd KPSS. Stenograficheskii otchet*, Vol. 1, 602.

nuclear-powered futures, to say nothing of the growing realization of radiation's health and safety risks, were simply too great to overcome. And if the Soviet Union could ill-afford its most indulgent nuclear fantasies for the peaceful atom, then the nuclear aspirations that the USSR nurtured in Egypt and throughout the decolonizing world would go unfulfilled.

Despite years of Soviet support, Egypt never developed anything remotely approaching a state-of-the-art autochthonous nuclear research industry and as of the late-2010s still has not constructed a nuclear power plant. Though the waves of nuclear enthusiasm broke against the shore, scientists and internationalists did not abandon the atom. That neither state was able to translate the rhetoric of atomic enthusiasm into a nuclear reality somewhat misses the point of Moscow's scientific diplomacy. *Glavatom*'s report on the shortcomings of Egypt's nuclear energetics industry ultimately concluded that the Soviet Union "should continue to encourage and support the development of Egypt's domestic scientific community. If we do not, it is almost certain that capitalist countries will move in and undo our years of work."[173] Ultimately, it was Cold War competition that initiated the internationalism of "Red Technopolitics," and this same Cold War competition would press the Soviet Union into other forms of diplomacy, as well.

---

173  RGANI f 3, op 39, d 31, l 31.

# WHAT MADE JAPAN RELY ON ATOMIC ENERGY FOR ITS POWER NEEDS? A HISTORICAL PERSPECTIVE ON THE EARLY COLD WAR

*Mayako Shimamoto*

## Introduction

Japan is faced with an extremely important question: Should the country abolish nuclear power plants? Nuclear energy is beneficial in terms of both the environment and economy. Moreover, it offers a stable supply of energy. Those benefits notwithstanding, Japan's public opinion is coming to favour the abolition of nuclear power plants after the Fukushima nuclear crisis of March 2011.[1] Abolitionists prefer decommission partly because, while all Japan's nuclear reactors stay offline (48 reactors as of 2014), a huge amount (approximately 17,000 tons) of nuclear stockpile of spent fuel-cycle material (nuclear-reactor waste) remains unprocessed.[2] The figures above illustrate that Japan has greatly relied on nuclear power for almost one-third of its entire electric power supply.

What made Japan so heavily reliant on nuclear power for its energy needs? To answer this question, this paper presents a historical analysis of nuclear policy in the early Cold War.

After the collapse of the atomic monopoly as a result of the Soviet atom bomb test in 1949, nuclear proliferation accelerated, as atomic scientists and Secretary of Commerce Henry A. Wallace[3] had previously cautioned. As the arms race

---

1. In mid-summer 2014 the following questionnaire was circulated among Japanese respondents: Do you agree to resume operations of the power plants which have been recently approved by the Nuclear Regulation Authority, indicating that the reactors have met the current, far more stringent, safety standards? Agree 36.1%, Disagree 56.2%, Others 7.7%. What do you think should be done with Japan's nuclear power plants in the future? Should increase 2.9%, Should maintain 23.2%, Should decrease 45.2%, Should decommission, 26.1%, Others 2.6%. *Sankei Shimbun*, 1 July 2014.
2. Of 17,000t, 2,900t are stored for reprocessing in the Rokkasho Reprocessor in Aomori Prefecture; 7,100t have been reprocessed abroad (in the UK and France). The remaining spent fuels were on the waiting list, announced in August 2014 by the Ministry of Economy, Trade and Industry (METI).
3. Henry A. Wallace (1888–1965) served as Secretary of Agriculture for two terms (1933–1941), Vice President (1940–1945), and Secretary of Commerce (1945) in the Franklin D. Roosevelt (FDR) administration, but was dismissed in 1946 by President Truman. Wallace is well-known not only as a New Dealer, but also as FDR's technical advisor, in which role he exhibited his deep scientific

intensified, the stockpile of fissile materials mounted in order to reduce giant military expenditure; commercialization of surplus uranium for the free world, notably for friendly nations, became the only available solution for the United States.

The United States started to promote the use of nuclear materials for peaceful purposes, a policy laid out in President Dwight Eisenhower's "Atoms for Peace" address to the United Nations Assembly in 1953. This policy had been altered drastically from Truman's "atomic monopoly" to "atomic usage for peace," to market fissile material and technology to friendly nations, aimed at catching up and reducing the supposed gap with the Soviet Union, which had already initiated a policy for the peaceful use of atomic energy.

Strangely, Japan, the world's first atom-victimized nation, became a beneficiary of an atomic sales promotion for commercial use. Why did Japan readily accept its role? A hypothesis explored in this paper is that the idea of atomic energy's non-military use matched the Japanese people's desire for sustainable, peaceful future energy technology. Only two years after Eisenhower's address, Japanese bureaucrats, as well as politicians, initiated agreements with the United States to allow Japan to buy enriched uranium for use in an experimental nuclear reactor. That was done, despite a group of dissenting scientists in the Science Council of Japan (SCJ), including Nihon Gakujutu Kaigi, who had insisted on multilateral agreements through the United Nations. From that point onward, most of the enriched uranium and related technologies were delivered to Japan's nuclear reactors under the Japan bilateral agreement of 1955.

## Monopoly of Nuclear Energy after Hiroshima

The theory of atomic energy was first put forward in the United Kingdom in 1941 by the Maud Committee.[4] Two years later, the United Kingdom and the United States together pursued the Manhattan Project, which moved the Anglo-American joint program on its road to producing an atomic bomb. Before this later date, British Prime Minister Winston S. Churchill persuaded US President Franklin D. Roosevelt (FDR) to commit to sharing the benefits of atomic energy in the Quebec Agreement of 1941. This commitment was later renewed in 1943, when the project

---

knowledge. Wallace and Dr. Vannevar Bush, scientific administrator in the Manhattan Project, shared atomic views during the FDR administration.

4    M.A.U.D. Committee, June 1941, 165–166, (CAB) 90/8, Public Record Office, The National Archives, Kew, London.

was still underway.⁵ However, contrary to this agreement, FDR's successor President Harry S. Truman did not want to share any atomic knowledge with the United Kingdom or other countries, e.g. Canada and France, and even less with the Soviets, a wartime ally. In fact, President Truman and his close advisor, Secretary of State James F. Byrnes, regarded atomic knowhow as a "sacred national asset."⁶

A member of the cabinet harboring a dissenting vision was Secretary of Commerce Henry A. Wallace, whose scientific knowledge was trusted in his role as Vice-President in the Roosevelt administration, not only by the president, but also by the fellowship of atomic scientists. Wallace's vision of postwar atomic energy shared many points with that of the atomic scientists, a group which believed that basic scientific knowledge could not be contained, because science neither knows nor recognizes any national boundaries.

Wallace strongly supported Stimson's proposal submitted to the Truman cabinet in September 1945, suggesting that atomic energy be internationally controlled with Soviet partnership. For his part, he also submitted his own plan for a postwar world order, in which people would benefit from the peaceful usage of atomic energy.⁷ President Truman, however, disregarded Wallace's plan. By enforcing the McMahon Law in February 1946, Truman decided to monopolize atomic technology legally both inside and outside of the nation. Truman's mistaken belief in retaining an atomic monopoly lasted until the Soviets tested their own atomic bomb in 1949. Consequently, the monopoly had collapsed within four years, leading to global proliferation of nuclear weapons and energy.⁸

As Wallace had predicted, an arms race began immediately after the monopoly ended. Following the United States' test of the hydrogen bomb in November 1952 and the Soviet hydrogen bomb test in August 1953, the military budget mushroomed. The country struggled with military expenses that were spiraling

---

5   Anglo-American differences produced an argument between Winston Churchill and FDR. In addition to the first Quebec Agreement, FDR agreed to resume discussions at Quebec, Hyde Park. The Second Quebec Agreement was concluded in 1943.
6   See "President Truman's Message to Congress on the Atomic Bomb. 3 October 1945," *Public Papers of the Presidents of the United States,* 362–366.
7   "Significance of the Atomic Age," Henry Wallace's Statement on 15 October 1945, *Henry Wallace's Oral History,* Reel No. 2, Ritsumeikan University, Kyoto.
8   See for details, Mayako Shimamoto, "Henry A. Wallace: Critic of America's Atomic Monopoly, 1945–1948," Ph.D. dissertation, Osaka University, 2011.

out of control ($44.2 billion as of 1953).⁹ Eisenhower tried to remove the distinction between conventional and nuclear weapons to reduce the budget,¹⁰ as nuclear preparation appeared to be cheaper than maintaining a large standing army.¹¹ To prepare for any surprise Soviet attack, Eisenhower transferred control of the atomic stockpile from the Atomic Energy Commission (AEC) to the military, ordering the AEC to relinquish control of nuclear weapons to the Department of Defense for deployment overseas to protect the periphery of the United States.¹² In this way, the United States was able to maintain its atomic supremacy, another version of the monopoly that Truman had desperately sought. The difference was that nuclear weapons were, for Eisenhower, readily usable as the foundation of the defence strategy, whereas for Truman, nuclear weapons would be used only as a last resort.¹³

Eisenhower sought a new strategy for using nuclear sources for non-military purposes, a plan already put forward by the Soviet Foreign Minister Andrei Vyshinsky at the United Nations in November 1949. Now Eisenhower needed to show the world another version of supremacy through the peaceful use of nuclear power.

## From Weapons to Peaceful Use

The concept of nuclear energy for peaceful usage was declared on 8 December 1953 in Eisenhower's "Atoms for Peace" address to the United Nations. He pledged that the United States would "devote its entire heart and mind to find the way by which the miraculous inventiveness of man shall not be dedicated to his death, but consecrated to his life."¹⁴ In this statement, he promised to distribute the benefits of peaceful atomic power both at home and abroad, and to create a new organ, the International Atomic Energy Agency (IAEA), at the United Nations to

---

9   In the Truman administration, the actual TOA for fiscal year of 1953 came to about $44.2 billion which Secretary of Defense Robert A. Lovett had reduced $13 billion from the prior year. See Historical Office of the Secretary of Defense: Robert A. Lovett, at.
10  Richard G. Hewlett & Jack M. Holl, *Atoms for Peace and War 1953–1961: Eisenhower and the Atomic Energy Commission*, (Berkeley: University of California Press), 15.
11  Oliver Stone & Peter Kuznick, *The Untold History of the United States*, (Ebury Press, A Random House Group Company. First published in the United States by Simon and Schuster in 2012, 254–255.
12  Arthur M. Schlesinger, Jr., *The Cycles of American History*, (New York: Mariner Books, Houghton Mifflin Company, 1986, 1999), 402–405.
13  Oliver Stone & Peter Kuznick, 256.
14  Dwight D. Eisenhower, text of the address delivered in 1953 at the UN Assembly. http://www.eisenhower.archives.gov/atom1, accessed on 16 January 2015.

safeguard against nuclear proliferation and stockpiling of nuclear weapons. The Western nations applauded Eisenhower's proposal,[15] but Soviet Foreign Minister Vyshinsky rejected Eisenhower's proposal the following day at the UN General Assembly, arguing that, without a total and unconditional mass reduction of nuclear weapons, peaceful use of nuclear energy would not and could not be safeguarded. He regarded this as an altered version of the Baruch Plan of 1947, which admitted neither the abolition of nuclear weapons nor any form of consistent control of nuclear military forces.[16]

As Vyshinsky aptly pointed out, while promising the merits of beneficial atomic energy on one hand, Eisenhower hoped on the other to "reduce the growing danger of a world holocaust by the development of fission and thermonuclear weapons"—a policy of balancing the nuclear threat with nuclear power.[17]

## The Fukuryu Maru Incident

On 1 March 1954, an unexpected incident caused by the US hydrogen "Bravo" test off the Bikini Atoll created a public relations headache for American officials. Fallout from the hydrogen-bomb test had contaminated 236 Marshall Islanders and 23 Japanese fishing boat crewmen, who were 120 km distance from the detonation and outside the designated danger zone. The US evasion of any legal responsibility for the incident stirred up much anger among the Japanese public.[18] The Operations Coordinating Board (OCB) insisted that the fishing boat had been outside the officially announced danger zone, thus emphasizing the high degree of safety in American nuclear tests in general, and concluded that the vessel's radio operator, Aikichi Kuboyama, had died of hepatitis and not radiation sickness. A contrary result came from the chemical investigation conducted a week later by physicist Mitsuo Taketani, who reported that the fallout at Bikini might have been the by-

---

15　"Genshiryoku Kanrini Kōkan [In favor of Nuclear Controls]," 8 December 1953, the *Mainichi Shimbun.*
16　"Soren Daihyo Aiku Teianwo Kyohi [The Soviet Representative Rejected Eike's Proposal]," the *Mainichi Shimbun.* 9 December 1953,
17　Hewlett & Holl, *Atoms for Peace and War 1953–1961,* 72.
18　John Dower, "The San Francisco System: Past, Present, Future in Japan-China Relations," *The Asia-Pacific Journal,* Vol. 12, Issue 8, no. 2, 14 February 2014, 19, accessed on 8 March 2014; Hiroko Takahashi, *Fuinsareta Hiroshima, Nagasaki: Bei Kaku Jikkento Minkan Boei Keikaku,* [*Classified Hiroshima and Nagasaki; US Nuclear Test and Civil Defense Program*], (Tokyo: Gaifusha, 2008), 151–181.

product of the hydrogen test explosion in Bikini Atoll.[19] Yet, the OCB altered its original plan only slightly. The *Fukuryu Maru* incident forced the OCB to assign greater priority to preventing communists' exploitation of the incident, while hydrogen testing continued.

Angry voices were spread rapidly throughout Japan,[20] a long-suppressed rage over the wartime atomic bombings: 32 million people, one-third of Japan's population, had signed petitions by the following year,[21] which called for a halt to the production of hydrogen bombs. In protest against future hydrogen explosion tests, the Council of Japan against Atomic and Hydrogen Bombs (CAHB) was formed in Hiroshima, spreading the anti-hydrogen message across the country.[22] The Japanese government reacted quickly. After many heated discussions, the four political parties, Jiyuto (Liberal Party), Kaishinto (Progressive Party), Shakaito Uha (Right wing of the Socialist Party), and Shakaito Saha (Left wing of the Socialist Party) agreed unanimously to issue a statement from the House of Representatives on 1 April 1954, urging the United Nations to support international control over atomic energy and the abolition of atomic weapons. It also demanded rapid UN intervention to take effective measures to prevent further deaths and injuries caused by experimenting with nuclear weapons.[23] Similarly, the House of Councillors issued a statement that called for the above requirements to the United Nations on 5 April 1954.[24]

---

19 "Bikini no Hai, [Ash from the Bikini]," An interview with Mituso Taketani, *Asahi Shimbun*, 17 March 1954,
20 "Beikoku yo Yogoreta Sakanade Hansei wo [The United States Must Reflect on the matter of Contaminated Fish]," *Mainichi Shimbun*, 19 March 1954.
21 Hiroko Takahashi, *Classified Hiroshima and Nagasaki*, 180; BS Asahi, "Genpatsu to Genbaku: Nihon no Genshiryoku to Beikoku no Kage [Nuclear Power Plant and Atomic Bomb: Japanese Nuclear Power and US Shadow]," broadcast on 12 August 2013.
22 See for details, "The Japan Council against Atomic and Hydrogen Bombs," [Gensuikyō]. "Gen/Suibaku Kinshi wa Zenjinrui no Mondai [An Annihilation of A- & H-bombs is the Problem for All Humans]," 30 May 1954. "Suibaku Huan wo Rikaiseyo [Call for a More Knowledge about the H-bomb],", *Mainichi Shimbun*, 3 April 1954.
23 Conference Minutes of 19th House of Representative, 1 April 1954.
24 Conference Minutes of 19th House of Councilor, 5 April 1954.

## Why was Japan targeted?

In the Department of State, "a timely and effective mode of countering the expected Russian effort" was put into action when the *Fukuryu Maru* Incident occurred off Bikini Atoll.[25] The Department of State quickly extended the temporary danger area, working out interim arrangements between the US Embassy and the Japanese government. Along the way, G. B. Erskine, Assistant to the Secretary of Defense, who had been concerned about the Communist reaction, recommended three weeks later, on 22 March 1954, to the OCB of the National Security Council (NSC) that a "vigorous offensive on the non-war uses of atomic energy" be taken to "counter timely and effectively the expected Russian effort and minimize *the harm* already done in (Berlin) and Japan" ("the harm" referred to the *Fukuryu Maru* Incident—author). Therefore, he concluded, "this action might take the form of a decision to build a reactor in Berlin and Japan."[26] With that in place, he added, it would have strong publicity value. Erskine's suggestion to build a reactor in Japan was a first for the United States, but it was motivated primarily by fear of Communist propagandists' potential exploitation of "peaceful" [as original] intentions.[27]

As for Berlin, the Department of Defense maintained that the city was regarded as the "free world's show-window," where "Russian and satellite officials could take a glimpse at the Western world."[28] Accordingly, the building of a nuclear power station in Berlin could "influence the thinking of such people," and, moreover, the operation would "highlight American willingness to side with the Germans and other peoples suppressed by the Soviets."[29] However, negative arguments were made, i.e. such a power station in Berlin would give the Germans the impression the United States regarded the division of Germany as permanent. In addition to this Cold War theory, their concern was about premature engagement in a program, which was not economically sound, viable, as well as not being fully competitive. In fact, they argued that to make available peaceful nuclear energy

---

25  Department of State, "Background Statement Relative to United States Action in Connection with the *Fukuryu Maru* Incident Prepared by the Department of State," 30 March 1954, Eisenhower Presidential Library, Abilene, Kansas, (hereafter referred to as EPL).
26  G.B. Erskin, "Japan and Atomic Tests," Memorandum for the Operations Coordinating Board (OCB), 22 March 1954, NSC Staff Papers. OCB Central File, Box 46, OCB 091, Japan. File #1, EPL.
27  Ibid.
28  "Nuclear Power Station in Berlin and Japan—Reasons Pro and Con," Memorandum from Stefen T. Possony to Mr. Robert Button, 29 March 1954, 1, Department of the Air Force, OCB 00091, [Natural and Physical Sciences] (File #1)(1) Box 11, EPL.
29  Ibid.

only to former enemies, Germany and Japan, might not be "accepted gracefully by the allies" (excluding the Russians).[30] Interestingly, they put a higher priority on Berlin and Japan based on the reason that the United States never overlooked the interests of other friendly nations once they decided to make their position on this matter fully clear and transparent.

After considering all the negative factors, OCB's plan for building a nuclear power station in Berlin evaporated, but Japan remained a major beneficiary of this decision because (1) "Japan was the first victim of atomic warfare," so it was *just and fair* that it be an early recipient of nuclear energy, and (2) "Japan stood to profit more from this new energy resource than many other nations," due to the historical fact that Japan, whose interests had been through trading with Manchuria and China, should know "that an alternate energy resource could be available," and therefore "their preoccupation with the China trade might be lessened."[31]

On 30 March, when Japanese media claimed dangerous radiation fall-out from the Bikini hydrogen test, the OCB Executive Officer Elmer B. Staats drafted possible actions: First, the US should emphasize that the harm incurred by the Japanese crew be attributed to *chemical "effects of coral dusting"* rather than radioactivity. Second, there should be no mention of legal aspects of injury and damage resulting from the Pacific nuclear test. Third, they should emphasize the necessity to implement the peaceful uses of atomic energy to "secure Japanese cooperation and to assist in realizing the climate of opinion desired by the United States."[32] Interestingly, this memorandum did not attribute the Japanese fisherman's death to radiation fallout, or concede that any harm was caused by the hydrogen experiment.[33] Though the OCB revealed data showing industrial tolerance levels of safety, it recommended holding a joint "US-Japanese permanent large-scale peaceful atom exhibit" in Japan. Specifically, the recommended US action was for the AEC to undertake an intensive publicity campaign "by booklet and motion picture" to eradicate Japanese people's misconceptions related to the effects of atomic weapons.[34]

---

30  "Nuclear Power Station in Berlin and Japan—Reasons Pro and Con," Memorandum from Stefen T. Possony to Mr. Robert Button, 29 March 1954, 3, EPL.
31  Ibid, 2, EPL.
32  Memorandum from Elmer B. Saats to the Operations Coordinating Board (OCB). Subject: Position with Respect to Industry and Damages Resulting from Pacific Nuclear Test, 30 March 1954, 2, NSC Staff Papers. OCB Central File, Box #46, OCB 091, Japan. (File #1) (2), EPL.
33  Mitsuo Taketani, *Genshiryoku Hatsuden* [*Atomic Power Plants*], (Tokyo: Iwanami Shoten, 1976, 1989), 69.
34  "Outline Check List of Government Actions to Offset Unfavorable Japanese Attitudes to the H-Bomb and Related Developments," 22 April 1954, OCB091 Japan (file #3) (3) September1956 to June 1957, EPL.

## Proposals for Building Nuclear Reactors in Japan

### a. Thomas E. Murry's Proposal

Apart from the OCB's recommendations, other proposals were voiced. Five months later, on 22 September 1954, a commissioner of the AEC, Thomas E. Murray, made a speech to the international convention of the United Steel Workers of America, recommending that the United States build a nuclear power reactor in Japan to generate electricity.[35] He confessed in his speech that the US position was not strong (compared to the Soviet position), and emphasized that his proposal was made out of the fear that the Soviet Union could take part in—possibly even win—an atomic electric power race in "have-not" countries. For that reason, he urged, the United States needed to take early action while the memory of Hiroshima and Nagasaki remained so vivid; construction of a nuclear power plant in Japan would be a "dramatic and Christian gesture which could lift all of us far above the recollection of the carnage of those cities."[36]

Another move that might have prompted the US commissioner to initiate a plan came from the UK nuclear development that had been underway in Scotland. Four months earlier on 5 March, the United Kingdom had stipulated the Atomic Energy Law, by which a special company was established with a plan to build a huge (the largest ever, except for the Calder Holder reactor now under construction) breeder type of nuclear reactor in Scotland. The original aim of the British was to supplement its energy shortage, coupled with a purpose to secure the British position in the world's marketplace for nuclear reactors.[37] Intentionally or not, Murray did not even suggest that the United Kingdom had already joined the nuclear power generation race.

### b. John J. Hopkins' Proposal

On 1 December 1954, John Jay Hopkins, the President and CEO of General Dynamics, proposed a "Plan for the Development of International Atomic Energy under the Leadership of American Industry."[38] His idea, what he called an "Atomic

---

35 "Nuclear Reactor Urged for Japan. T. E. Murray of A.E.C. Tells Steel Union Step Is Vital in Atom Race With Russia." By Stanley Levey, *New York Times*, 22 September 1954, ProQuest Historical Newspapers: New York Times (1851–2009), 14.
36 Ibid.
37 "Susumu Eikoku no Genshiryoku Heiwariyo [British Peaceful Usage of Atomic Energy is in Progress]: Shin Sangyo Kakumei Mezasu [British Aimed at a New Industrial Revolution]," *Asahi Shimbun*, 5 March 1954.
38 "A Plan for the Development of International Atomic Energy under the Leadership of American Industry," by John Jay Hopkins, Congressional Record, Vol.101, no.14, 692–695, 1955/1/27.

Marshall Plan," was that American industry and the federal government work together for the financing, construction, and implementation of atomic reactors in "have-not" nations, most notably in Asian-African nations, under a 100-year program. Hopkins emphasized that American activity in underdeveloped nations would help to increase the standard of living in those nations. In short, he believed that this program was the only effective means of stopping the spread of Communism. Hopkins was invited to Japan the following year by Matsutaro Shoriki, an owner of the *Yomiuri Shimbun*, to hold exhibitions for peaceful atomic use,[39] starting from Tokyo, and continuing throughout the main cities in Japan, e.g. Kobe, Nagoya, Fukushima, Sapporo, Yokohama, and Hiroshima. Originally, the mission's intension was to discuss the "question of how to industrialize atomic energy as Japan's private enterprises."[40] There were difficulties present, as professor of Rikkyo University Eizo Tashima pointed out, that "scholars and technicians were not ready to act in concert," and that unluckily "there were no technicians who did the work of atomic energy."[41] Gerald C. Smith, a special aide to the State Department, concluded that "it would seem better if the approach to Japan had been made on *engineering* grounds rather than by a *newspaperman*."[42] The State Department did not officially acknowledge Hopkins' plan, because its officials thought the technical issues came first, before sales activities had been promoted.

### c. Sydney R. Yates' Proposal

Agreeing with Murray and Hopkins, a member of the House of Representatives, Sydney R. Yates, submitted a proposal to Congress in January 1955, urging the building of nuclear reactors in Hiroshima. His reason was that, "A nuclear reactor in the land of rising sun, built by Americans and out of America's resources, would be a lasting monument to our technology and good will."[43]

---

39　Department of State, Memorandum of Conversation, "Matsutaro Shoriki Invitation to Mr. Hopkins, General Dynamics Corporation," Country File: Japan b Atomic Develop Program, Box 505, RG 59, General Records of the Department of State, General Records Relating Atomic Energy Matters, 1948–1962, 12 January 1955, 1, National Archives II; Masakatsu Yamazaki, *Nihon no Kaku Kaihatsu: 1939–1955 Genbaku kara Genshiryoku ye* [ *Japan's Nuclear Development: 1939–1955 From Atomic Bomb to Atomic Energy*] (Tokyo: Sekibundō, 2011, 2012), 214.

40　"Various Circles' Opinions on Atomic Energy," *Yomiuri* (Summary of Article-2/3 of full article), 8 January 1955, Country File Japan, b Atomic Development Program, Box 504, RG 59, 1, National Archives II, Maryland, (hereafter referred to as NAII).

41　Ibid.

42　Department of State, Memorandum of Conversation, "Matsutaro Shoriki Invitation to Mr. Hopkins, General Dynamics Corporation," 12 January 1955, 1–2, NAII.

43　Sidney R. Yates, "Proposed Atomic Reactor for Hiroshima Japan," Congressional Record, Vol.101, No.14, 687–695, 1955/1/27; "On the National Front," *Reno Evening Gazette*, 10 February 1955, 4;

### d. W. Sterling Cole's Proposal

House of Representative member W. Sterling Cole, who had previously advised the President to offer a gift of a nuclear power reactor to be created in Hiroshima on 10 May 1955, and was suspended by the President until the Japanese Prime Minister agreed to his proposal,[44] resumed his desire five months later on 28 October to "put into Hiroshima a *sizable* reactor" to Ambassador Masayuki Tani. This time Cole wanted to show the Japanese people that "atomic energy needed not be used exclusively for destruction," but it should be done "in exchange for erecting a plaque in Hawaii to express Japan's regret at the 14th anniversary of the attack on Pearl Harbor."[45] Otto Laporte, scientific attaché at the Embassy in Tokyo, felt like this was an example of a "gift with strings attached [as original], which was clearly resented by the Japanese."[46]

However, those proposals were gradually phased out, partly because the President had rejected them in 1953, when Lewis L. Strauss, Chairman of the AEC, proposed to build an atomic reactor in Hiroshima. The President thought it indicated "a sense of guilt which he felt was misplaced." Strauss shared the President's view.[47] Other reasons why the CAHB in Hiroshima opposed it on 30 January 1955 were based on the following arguments:

1. A nuclear reactor could be converted to be used for weapons at any time. This weapon could target Hiroshima.
2. Atomic ash, a by-product of atomic power, would do great harm to Hiroshima citizens.
3. A US-Japan joint program for building nuclear reactors would adversely influence Japanese electric industries, both economically and militarily, because of its restrictive systems.

---

"Hiroshima ni Genshiro: Kensetuhi 2,250 mandoru," (Nuclear Reactor in Hiroshima: Construction Costs $22.5 million) 28 January 1955, the *Yomiuri Shimbun* (evening).

44  Gerard C. Smith, "Memorandum for the Acting Secretary," Congressman Cole's Proposal for a Power Reactor Gift to Japan, Country File: Japan a Agreements, 1955, Part 1 of 2, 10 May 1955, 1–2, Box 503, RG59, NAII.

45  Memorandum of Conversation between Representative Cole, Ambassador Tani and Otto Raporte, to Department of State, 28 October 1955, for S/AE, from Embassy, Tokyo. 1, N AII.

46  Ibid.

47  Gerald Smith, "Memorandum for the File," Reactor for Japan—Discussion with Mr. Strauss. Country File: Japan a Agreements, 1955, Part 1 of 2, 20 May 1955, Box 503, RG59, NAII.

4. If the United States wished to offer its sincere atonement, it should be done in the form of medical treatment for the atom-bomb victims.[48]

Clearly, Hiroshima citizens had known well enough what the after-effects of the Bikini ash would do to humans. They had been well aware of atomic energy's incompatible dual nature through directly experiencing the catastrophic effects of a nuclear atom-bomb explosion.

An opinion leader, Akira Yoshioka, a physicist and critic of nuclear policy, wrote in a 2012 publication that utilization of atomic energy, either for military or non-military use, has the same origin. The theory of dichotomy—civil use and military use from an atomic nucleus—does not apply to the Hiroshima citizens, who are supposed to have a special right to benefit from atomic energy, simply because they are A-bomb victims.[49] It is particularly interesting that Yoshioka sharply criticized Murray's and Yates' twisted logic, which called for building a nuclear reactor in Hiroshima.

## What Motivated the SCJ to Draft Resolutions?

It was astonishing for the SCJ members that the Japanese Diet passed the budget bill of Y235 million for funding an atomic energy program only four days after the Bikini Incident of 1954.[50] The budget proposal was submitted unexpectedly by Yasuhiro Nakasone, a Kaishinto member of the Diet and a firm believer in the urgent utilization of atomic energy. The Japanese public was slow to respond to this proposal, because their lack of atomic knowledge hardly allowed them to understand sophisticated modern science and its applications. Quick and active reaction, however, came from the fourth estate and the academic community. Among them were the SCJ members who protested that any important issue related to atomic

---

48  "Genshiro Secchi ni Hantai no Noroshi [An Opposition to Nuclear Reactors to be Built in Hiroshima]," *Mainichi Shimbun*, 30 January 1955.
49  Akira Yoshioka, *Genshiryoku no Shakaishi: Sono Nihonteki Tenkai [A Social History of Atomic Energy: Its Japanese Development]*, New Version, (Tokyo: Asahi Shimbun Shuppan, 2011, 2012), 76–77.
50  *Nihon Genshiryoku Hatsuden 30nenshi* [A 30-Year History of the Japan's Nuclear Power Plants], 30 Years Anniversary Project Committee, eds. 31 March 1989, 2; Yasuhiro Nakasone, *Jiseiroku: Rekishi Hōteino Hikokutoshite* [Memoir: As a Defendant at Court of History], (Tokyo: Shinchosha, 2004), 41–46. Nakasone, a member of the Lower House of the Diet and an earnest supporter of Japan's future nuclear development, initiated the budget proposal. Nakasone writes that he got a hint from uranium 235 when deciding the amount of budget $235 million.

matters should be consulted in advance.[51] This led the SCJ members to create three principles, which were announced on 23 April 1954, in the following formal statement.[52]

> In view of the two statements issued from the House of Representatives, and the House of Councillors, we will never develop a nuclear weapons program of our own, much less related atomic weapons in foreign countries. To assure this principle,
> (1) we require that any information related to atomic research and usage be *disclosed* to Japanese citizens, and
> (2) we require that our atomic research be run based on *democracy,* and
> (3) we decide to conduct our research and development with *autonomy* of the Japanese people.
> (summary/translation by author).[53]

These three pillars of the SCJ became the foundation of the Atomic Energy Basis Law of 1955. Despite of the upsurge of the anti-A /H-bomb sentiment throughout Japan as a result of the Bikini Incident, the United States, instead of acknowledging the disastrous fact, began accelerating its commercial campaign abroad to offset Japan's nuclear allergy.

## US Publicity Campaign in Japan

In line with the OCB recommendation of 30 March 1954, that urged the AEC to take action, the US Embassy and the US Information Service (USIS) began a campaign to sell nuclear materials and its related technologies in Japan. Central to this public relations activity was the participation of Matsutaro Shoriki, who ran the *Yomiuri Shimbun* newspaper, and Hidetoshi Shibata, Shoriki's facilitator and the executive of the Nippon Television Network.[54] Assisted by their co-sponsorship, US exhibits were accommodated first in Tokyo, then in Nagoya, Hiroshima, and six other major cities. The exhibitions highlighted the peaceful applications of atomic energy for generating electricity, treating cancer, preserving food, and other scientific research.[55] They were promoted by "the press and publications branch of USIS, which ran over 3,500 stories on the peaceful atom" via the Japanese media,

---

51  Committee of Genshiryoku Kaihatsu 10nenshi, ed., *Genshiryoku Kaihatsu 10nenshi* [Ten Years' History of Nuclear Energy Development], 32; *Asahi Shimbun*, 4 March 1954.
52  Ibid.
53  General Meeting Minute of the 17th Science Council of Japan, 23 April 1954. Summary and English translation by the author.
54  Hidetoshi Shibata, *Sengo Masukomi Kaiyūki* [Migration Report for Postwar Mass Media], (Tokyo: Chuo Koronsha, 1985), 41–46.
55  About 110,000 people visited the exhibits in Hiroshima. BS Asahi, "Nuclear Power Plant and Atomic Bomb: Japanese Nuclear Power and Shadow" (Genpatsu to Genbaku: Nihon no Genshiryoku to Beikoku no Kage), broadcast on 12 August 2013.

an average of almost ten items per day. The USIS-Japan radio activity totaled "500 million listeners contact during 1955."[56]

To the question whether atomic energy was a *boon* or a *curse* to mankind, 75% of 250 visitors to the peaceful atom exhibits "*before* [as original] seeing the exhibits, answered a *boon* in December 1955,"[57] whereas in December 1954 the same question might well have drawn a total of 75% toward a *curse*. "Until the beginning of 1955, many people were opposed to any understanding by Japan [sic] in the utilization of atomic energy;"[58] however, during 1955 the diffusion of atomic knowledge among the public by newspaper and other media was so decisive that it brought about this "miraculous change."[59] So successful was this public relations effort and the promise of a nuclear energy future for Japan, that the US offer appeared to be safe for the Japanese public, as long as atomic energy was intended for non-military use.

This view was shared by some prominent academics. A Marxist economist Hiromi Arisawa of the University of Tokyo evaluated the merits of atomic energy based on the following standpoint: nuclear energy fulfilled two requirements—lower costs and security of resources. Arisawa believed that the prospects for nuclear energy would be even greater.[60] He learned this lesson from the experiences that the Germans had gone through in the cruel repatriation and mass loss of jobs during the Great Depression, and concluded that building a nuclear power plant in Japan was indispensable, because this was the way Japan should attain self-sufficiency of the Japanese economy. His idea of pursuing nuclear energy for a sustainable future never changed, even in the aftermath of the Three Mile Island accident of 1979 and the disastrous nuclear meltdown at Chernobyl in 1986.[61]

Remaining problems still left unsolved were heard during this period of atomic upheaval. Dr. Kinji Shimizu, President of the Nagoya Technical University,

---

56   A telegram from United States Information Service (USIS) Tokyo to United States Information Agency, "Atoms for Peace Pay off in Japan," Country File: Japan e General, Jan–June 1956, Box 505, RG59, 21 February 1956, 1–4, NAII.
57   Ibid.
58   A telegram from United States Information Service (USIS), Tokyo to United States Information Agency, "Atoms for Peace Pay off in Japan," Country File: Japan e General, Jan–June 1956, Box 504, RG59, 21 February 1956, 1–2, NAII.
59   Ibid.
60   Hiromi Arisawa, *Nihon no Enerugī Mondai* [The Energy Issue in Japan], (Tokyo: Iwanami Shoten, 1963), 235.
61   Tetsuro Kato, *Nihon no Shakai Shugi: Genbaku Hantai—Genpatsu Suishin no Ronri* [Socialism in Japan: A Logic of Anti-Atomic Bomb and Pro-Nuclear Power Plant], (Tokyo: Iwanami Shoten, 2013), 254–255.

warned of the continuing problem with the disposal of "ash," costing billions of yen, which was part of the government budget.[62] Seitaro Nakamura, Assistant Professor of University of Tokyo, expressed a similar view. The greatest problem "at present," he said, was the disposal of "ashes" coming out of atomic piles and various countries were having difficulties in solving this problem.[63] Regrettably, though these dissenting opinions deserved an audience, they only received marginal attention.

The OCB concluded: "By the end of 1956, the atom hysteria was almost eliminated from Japanese public opinion."[64] US sales promotion for non-military use matched the Japanese people's desire for sustainable, peaceful future technology. Many other exhibitions sponsored by businesses, most notably the Yomiuri group, exerted a huge influence on the Japanese view of atomic energy during 1954–55.[65] Now the Japanese government had every reason to buy US-prepared uranium for a nuclear reactor.

## US-Japan Nuclear Agreement of 1955

The US-Japan Nuclear Agreement of 1955, formally called the "Agreement for Co-operation Concerning Civil Uses of Atomic Energy between the government of Japan and the government of the United States of America," was proposed in draft form in January, 1955, to Japanese Ambassador Sadao Iguchi in Washington. The official proposal was that the United States was ready to *allocate* 100 kg of enriched uranium 235, and that if Japan agreed to accept it, it should abide by the bilateral agreement based on the Atomic Energy Law, and that a preliminary discussion between the United States and Japan would follow.[66] Fundamentally, the Japanese

---

62  Extremely Hopeful for Power Generation: Remaining Problem, Disposal of "Ash", Chubu NIPPON (January 8. 1956), Local Edition, Country File: Japan e June–January, 1956, Box 504, RG59, 5, NAII.

63  Various Circles' Opinions on Atomic Energy, YOMIURI (Summary of Article), 8 January 1955, Country File Japan b Atomic Development Problem, Box504, RG59, 4, NAII.

64  "US Policy Toward Japan," NSC5516/1, 27 June 1956, Folder OCB091, Japan (File#5) [April–November 1956], Box 48, White House Office, NSC Staff Papers, 1948–61, OCB Central File Series. 5, EPL.

65  Shunya Yoshimi, *Yume no Genshiryoku* [Atoms for Dreams], (Tokyo: Chikuma Shobo, 2012), 186–206.

66  "A Proposal for Allocation of Fissionable Materials by the United States, and Bilateral Agreement with Other Nations," 6 May 1955. Nichibeikan Genshiryoku no Higunjiteki Riyo ni Kansuru Kyoryoku Kyotei Kankei [Related Documents for US-Civil Uses of Japan Atomic Energy], B' 5.1.0.J/U9, Reel#B'-0081, Gaiko Shiryokan, Tokyo, [Diplomatic Archives of the Ministry of Foreign Affairs of Japan (hereinafter referred to as DAMOFA)].

Foreign Office (JFO) understood that the domestic atomic energy issue needed not only further study, but also an appropriate revelation to the Japanese public to ensure that they were informed of the perceived benefits in the light of such an agreement being made. Internationally, the JFO thought it safer for Japan to follow the principle of the United Nations for peaceful nuclear use of nuclear energy. Regarding the trade for fissile materials, the JFO was unwilling to be tied to any specific nation by a bilateral agreement. Instead, the JFO preferred multilateral negotiations through Japan's International Cooperation Agency (Kokusai Kyoryoku Ka).[67]

The JFO responded that a final decision to the US offer would be made after the Atomic Energy Research Group (Genshiryoky Kaigai Chosadan), headed by Dr. Yoshio Fujioka, returned from the United States at the end of March 1955 and after careful consideration by the authorities concerned, especially by the Preliminary Council for Atomic Energy Utilization of the Cabinet (Naikaku Genshiryoku Riyojunbi Chosakai[68]).[69] In addition, the JFO unofficially sought the opinions of three men: Seiji Kaya, chairman of the SCJ, Kohei Suzue, Director-General of the Scientific Technical Administration Committee (Kagaku Gijutu Gyosei Kyogikai), and Kihachi Sanuki, Director of the Agency of Industrial Science and Technology (Kogyo Gijutuin Choseibu). The JFO presumed that these academic circles would agree in the long run, but for confirmation, sought first their opinions on an individual basis.

Concerning uranium, all three shared the view that it was in Japan's best interest for it to be allocated. The problem was, Kaya added, that the time was too early to accept it. Suzue worried that the JFO needed to adjust the timing with scientists, who were advancing their own projects for small-scale nuclear reactors.[70] In a step forward, the JFO confirmed to Otto Laporte, scientific attaché in the Embassy, its willingness to accept officially Japan's counter-offer.[71] During this course of negotiations between the American Embassy and the JFO, the *Asahi Shimbun* abruptly reported on 14 April 1955 that the United States had secretly proposed to

---

67  A cable from Foreign Minister Shigemitsu to U.N. Ambassador Sawada in New York, "Re: Peaceful Usage of Nuclear Energy," 21 January 1955, Reel#B'-0081,0015-0021, DAMOFA.
68  An ad hoc team organized on 11 May 1954 by ten academic experts, headed by Vice-Prime Minister Taketora Ogata inside the cabinet.
69  "Allocation of Fissionable Materials by the United States (draft)," 16 March 1955, Reel#B-0161-0163, DAMOFA.
70  Ibid, Reel # B-0143-0154, DAMOFA.
71  "Press Release for Allocation of Fissionable Materials by the United States," 18 March 1955. Reel #B-177–179, DAMOFA.

Japan the allocation of enriched uranium for an experimental nuclear reactor.[72] This article was embarrassing to the new Agency of Industrial Science and Technology (Kogyo Gijutuin) of the Ministry of Industrial Trade and Industry (MITI), which had already planned to apply natural uranium for its own heavy water plants (a five-year plan with a budget of ¥363,250 million) that required less sophisticated technology.[73] Similarly, this annoyed the SCJ members who were co-planners of this scheme.

## Dissenting Voices from the SCJ

The arguments disclosed by the *Asahi Shimbun* also revealed that the ongoing negotiations were based on a US-Japan bilateral agreement, which included Section 123 of the 1954 Act, stipulated in the National Security Council (NSC) 5431/1 that all bilateral agreements for sharing nuclear material would have to meet three requirements:[74]

1. No agreement could be inimical to US security.
2. No agreement could be negotiated such that either party required weapons-grade materials ... or trained personnel from nuclear weapon development in the United States. In a case in which the United States provided nuclear materials ... the AEC would require the return of all spent fuel and nuclear by-products for reprocessing in the United States.
3. The NSC wanted to ensure that the United States gained the maximum *psychological and educational advantage* [emphasis added] from its endeavors in this field.[75]

On the whole, any secrets given by the United States should be safeguarded and any data/materials provided should not be transferred to unauthorized persons without the AEC's approval.[76]

---

72  "Enriched Uranium for Nuclear Reactor: Allocation Offered from the US," *Asahi Shimbun*, 14 April 1955.
73  "A Big Change for a Nuclear Reactor Plan," *Asahi Shimbun*, 14 April 1955.
74  Hewlett & Holl, *Atoms for Peace and War, 1953–1961: Eisenhower and the Atomic Energy Commission*, 227.
75  NSC 5431/1—Cooperation with Other Nations in the Peaceful Uses of Atomic Energy, 8/13/54, White House Office, Office of the Special Assistant for National Security Affairs: Records, 1952–61, NSC Series, Policy Papers Subseries Box 12 NSC 5431—Peaceful Uses of Atomic Energy, 1–3, EPL.
76  "Be Considerate to Use of Atomic Power," *Asahi Shimbun* 16 April 1955.

Two days later, the Committee of Atomic Energy, part of the SGJ, held its 19th meeting and discussed the issue presented above.[77] Chairman Fujioka commented that we (the Japanese) felt constrained (himo-tsuki), since we had nothing to reciprocate to the United States. In this context, he added, Japan should make every effort to follow the three principles that the SCJ had created when Japan proceeded to join the recipients of uranium allocation. A member of the House of Representatives, Goro Hani, and a theoretical physicist, Shoichi Sakata of Nagoya University, rejected the bilateral agreement for fear of being monitored to see if uranium was being transferred for military use, which, the two men argued, was against "freedom of academic thought" (autonomy of the three principles). Both men concluded that the decision-making to a bilateral agreement demanded a thorough and measured consideration. Other members, Hirokatsu Ogura of Ritsumeikan University and Kakuzo Maeshiba of the World Economic Institute, criticized the United States for changing its policy from a multilateral proposal that called for creating an international agency (where atomic energy would be pooled) to a bilateral policy that offered fissionable materials only to friendly/non-communist countries. In general, many SCJ members disagreed with a bilateral agreement, because it was against the autonomy of Japan's atomic research and development.[78]

On 19 May 1955 the third meeting of the Preliminary Study Committee for Atomic Power (Genshiryoku Riyo Junbi Chosakai) was held. It decided to recommend acceptance of US allocation of uranium and related technologies for atomic-based development, because the final decision had to be made before 1 June 1955 to be ready for Senate ratification. It also recommended that, despite minor "dissenting opinions," which insisted on assigning priority to Japan's three principle policy, negotiations should be advanced.[79]

Related to this issue, the public hearing of the Budget Committee was held on 19–20 May 1955. Dr. Fujioka, a leader of the Atomic Energy Research Group, stated that he agreed to the following: a small-scale experimental nuclear reactor fueled by enriched uranium which was rather convenient for the time being.

---

77  Nihon Gakujutu Kaigi 15nenshi Hukyūban Henshū Iinkai, ed., *Nihon Gakujutsu Kaigi 25nenshi (hukyūban)* [A 25-year History of the Science Council of Japan (trade edition)], (Tokyo, 1977), 430.
78  Ibid, 57; "A more Deliberate Consideration needed for the Bilateral Agreement," *Mainichi Shimbun*, 17 April 1955; "The Reaction for Enriched Uranium: 19th General Meeting of the Science Council of Japan," *Asahi Shimbun*, 22 April 1955.
79  "Japan's Acceptance of US allocation of Fissionable Materials." Dissenting opinions means a group of the SCG who opposed to a bilateral agreement with the United States. International Cooperation Office #3 Section of Foreign Ministry, 23 May 1955, Reel #B-0158-0166, DAMOFA.

Therefore, he continued, it would be a good start for the production of atomic electric power in Japan. Specifically, his plan was to build Japan's first domestic nuclear reactor (using natural uranium for a heavy water type reactor with 1,000 kW) in parallel with a US small-scale reactor. In contrast, Koji Fushimi of Osaka University, an SCJ member, stated at the hearing that atomic weaponry and commercial use of atomic energy were traceable back to the same origin: their uses could not be mutually separated; therefore, Japan needed to be alert not to be directed to the usage of atomic energy for weaponry. For that purpose, instead of falling into a pitfall of reliance on a foreign supply of fissile materials, Japan should advance its own technology.[80] His view, although marginal, concurred with the principles of the CAHB and that of a critique by Hitoshi Yoshioka, an opinion leader of Japan's energy policy.

Two weeks later, Ambassador Iguchi in Washington received a reply from the AEC that there was no "himo" (constraint) existing in the bilateral agreement with a comment that the AEC was in no hurry, as the currently authorized programs—the pressurized water reactor (PWR: 50,000–100,000 kW power output) being built in the United States for experimental purposes—were unlikely to produce economically competitive nuclear power for a decade or more.[81] However, their long-term view gave the JFO an impression of a "take it or leave it" attitude.[82] The JFO proceeded to draft an agreement to respond to the US attitude; e.g. Commissioner Murray's address and Senator Yates' proposal,[83] based on an unwarranted assumption that the dissenting academia/scientists would soon agree in one way or another.[84] Consequently, the agreement was hurriedly initialed on 21 June 1955 in Washington.[85] It was formally signed on 14 November 1955. From that day forward to the year of expiration in 1960, fissile materials of 6 kg were allocated to Japan for experimental use. Materials related to nuclear reactors, such as facilities and equipment, were leased or bought by Japan. All spent fuels were delivered back to the United States for reprocessing at the expense of the Japanese government

---

80   "Acceptance of Enriched Uranium," the *Asahi Shimbun*, 21 May 1955.
81   National Security Council re NSC 5507, Atomic Power Abroad, Atomic Energy (2), Box 5, 28 January 1955, WHO NSC Staff Papers, 1948–61, Disaster File, 4, EPL.
82   "Allocation of Enriched Uranium," 4 June 1955, Reel#B Vol. 3, 0265-0269, DAMOFA.
83   "Allocation of Fissionable Materials by the United States," Foreign Minister Shigemitsu to Iguchi in Washington and UN Ambassador Sawada, 28 March 1955, Reel#B-0183-0184, DAMOFA.
84   "Allocation of Fissionable Materials," 10 March 1955, Reel#B-0144, DAMOFA.
85   "Press Release: Public Information and Cultural Affairs Bureau Ministry of Foreign Affairs, Tokyo," 5 July 1955. Reel#B vol. 4, 0169-0170, DAMOFA.

under safeguards against radiation hazards while in transit.[86] Without considering other choices, Japan continued to purchase enriched uranium until 1988 when the revised agreement was put in effect.

## Conclusion

The research question of "what made Japan rely so heavily on nuclear power for its power needs?" has revealed that United States' effort to offset Japanese people's nuclear hysteria turned out successfully, and that the idea of atomic energy's non-military use matched the Japanese peoples' desire for sustainable, peaceful future energy technology. Therefore, they readily accepted its role as a beneficiary of US atomic sales promotion. Accordingly, the Japanese government hurriedly responded and proceeded to conclude a bilateral agreement that offered an allocation of enriched uranium for building nuclear power plants in Japan. That was done, despite fierce opposition from the SCJ which insisted that the time was premature and that a bilateral agreement was against the interests of Japan's autonomy. This analysis has similarly revealed that the course of actions between the United States and Japan in the early 1950s is a legacy of the Cold War; therefore, the paper has suggested that Japan should have reconsidered its heavy dependence on US nuclear energy policy.[87]

---

86  "Agreement for Cooperation Concerning Civil Uses of Atomic Energy between the Government of Japan and the Government of the United States of America," (draft) 14 June 1955, Reel#B vol. 3, 0015-0024, DAMOFA.
87  Japan was considered as falling into the dependent nations grouped in #3, which needed a completely developed and proven power system. Before attaining it, Japan should utilize its limited capacities within the framework of NSC 5431 /1. National Security Council re NSC 5507, Atomic Power Abroad, Atomic Energy (2), Box 5, 28 January 1955, WHO NSC Staff Papers, 1948–61, Disaster File, 16, EPL.

# 3. Atomic Bombs and Cultural Representation in the World

# JAPAN'S COLLECTIVE MEMORY OF HIROSHIMA SEEN THROUGH THE EYES OF A CHILD: THE NATIONAL AND GLOBAL IMPACT OF "BAREFOOT GEN"

*Tomoko Masumoto*

Seven decades after the atomic bombing of Hiroshima and Nagasaki, most Japanese acquire their images of World War II through literature, art, and especially through documentary films and dramatized stories presented on television. Perhaps nothing has exerted a greater influence on the popular image of the bombing of Hiroshima than the story first told in the form of a *manga* ("comic book," or, later "graphic novel") written for adolescent boys. *Barefoot Gen* by Keiji Nakazawa, published in 1973, is today regarded by many people as a classic graphic novel. Told through the eyes of a seven-year-old boy named Gen Nakaoka, the story is loosely based on Nakazawa's own experience. He was six years old when the bomb was detonated and he lost his father, older sister, and younger brother. That same day his younger baby sister was born but survived for just a few months. And yet, his story is one of survival.

    According to a survey by NHK (Nippon Hoso Kyokai: the Japan Broadcasting Corporation), for Japanese people between the ages of sixteen and forty, *Barefoot Gen* was the principal source on which they based their perceptions of the war.[1] Remarkably, a work that has helped to shape a nation's collective memory of the war began as a manga, a popular culture genre that was, and remains, generally prohibited in schools. Today, Nagazawa's story has its place on the shelves of Japanese elementary school libraries. An anime version of *Barefoot Gen* was for many years routinely shown in middle school auditoriums. Across the globe, the ten-volume set is now part of collections in public libraries, even at the public library in Los Alamos, New Mexico, where the atomic bomb was created.[2] The graphic novel is part of peace studies curricula internationally, and holds an important place in atomic literature and peace literature programs.

---

1    Yoshiaki Fukuma, "Genbaku Manga no Media Shi" [Media History of Atomic Manga], in *Hadashi no Gen ga Ita Fūkei: Manga, Sensō, Kioku* [The Lived World of Barefoot Gen: Manga, Sensō, Kioku], ed. Yoshiaki Fukuma and Kazuma Yoshimura (Matsudo: Azusa-shuppannsha, 2006), 35.

2    Los Alamos History Society, "Los Alamos 1943–1945 Beginning of an Era" (Los Alamos, NM: Los Alamos History Society, 2007).

*Barefoot Gen* was the first Japanese manga to be translated into foreign languages.[3] Through volunteer translators, the work now appears in more than a dozen languages, including a 2015 Arabic version.[4] Over ten million copies in translation have been sold in more than twenty countries.[5] An English language translation of the series begins with an introduction by Art Spiegelman whose graphic novel about the Holocaust, *Maus,* won a Pulitzer Prize. Spiegelman praised Nakazawa's work as "extraordinary, its images unforgettable, and its message ultimately optimistic."[6]

What explains the impact of the story that first appeared in a boys' manga in the 1970s? How did this autobiographical story become a defining part of the Japanese collective memory of the Hiroshima bombing—and the war itself and its aftermath? How Nakazawa's narrative, which began in a low-brow medium, came to be elevated as a classic among graphic novels, peace literature, and anti-nuclear work—all fields that were non-existent when *Barefoot Gen* was first published—is an interesting story in itself.

Keiji Nakazawa began working as a *mangaka* (manga artist and writer) in Tokyo where he felt he could conceal his Hiroshima background. The *hibakusha* frequently experienced discrimination and lived in fear that was exacerbated every summer when Japanese media called attention to the anniversary of the atomic bombing. In his autobiography, Nakazawa confesses that he did not have the courage even to sign anti-nuclear weapons petitions that were widely circulated, especially in the weeks before the 6 August anniversary.[7] He wanted to hide and he wished he could forget. When his mother, who suffered from radiation sickness, died, he returned to Hiroshima to prepare her funeral. In Japan, after a body is cremated, members of the family gather and together remove from the ashes a few larger bones that remain and that they will place in the funeral urn interred at the

---

3   Jaqueline Berndt, "On the 'Politics' of Reading Manga: Introduction to the Special Issue," *Manga Kenkuyu* [Manga Studies] 11 (2007): 128.
4   Tadao Onaga, "Hadashi no Gen de Heiwa Uttae: Kairo Daigaku Kyoju ga Arabia-go Yaku" [Appealing to the Peace: A Professor at Cairo University Translates Gen into Arabic], *Asahi Shinbun*, http://www.asahi.com/articles/ASH2M0QCNH2LUHBI023.html.
5   NHK, "Sekai wo Kakeru 'Hasashi no Gen'" [Barefoot Gen goes around the world], http://www.nhk.or.jp/gendai/kiroku/detail02_3387_all.html.
6   Art Spiegelman, "Comics after the Bomb," introduction to Vol. 1 of *Barefoot Gen*, Keiji Nakazawa (San Francisco, CA: Last Gasp, 2004).
7   Kenji Nakazawa, *Hadashi no Gen Jiden* [Autobiography of Barefoot Gen] (Tokyo: Kyoikushiryoshuppankai, 2011), 185.

gravesite. But there were no bones among Nakazawa's mother's ashes. Radiation had consumed them all.[8]

Nakazawa wrote that he could no longer contain the anger he had suppressed for so many years. He was already upset when, right after his mother's death, someone came from the Atomic Bomb Causality Commission (ABCC), a government clinic and research center, requesting permission to take his mother's body as part of their research. Not only had the bomb immediately killed most of his family and made his mother suffer for years, now they dared to ask for her body, too. Using his skills as a manga artist, Nakazawa channeled his anger.[9] The result was *Barefoot Gen*. Nakazawa later said that he wanted to tell his story in the best way he could, as a warning to children born years after the war. Prior to that time, manga stories featured sports heroes or fantasy super heroes, but one editor of an innovative manga saw what Nakazawa had created and decided to publish it. Nakazawa recalls watching the editor turn away from him as he read the draft, and then realized that the editor was trying not to cry.[10]

It would be years before most people, even in Japan, would be aware of the full horror wrought by the atomic bombings. For seven years, strict censorship by the government prohibited photographs, drawings, or stories to be published or circulated. Films and photographs of Hiroshima and Nagasaki taken by journalists were seized by the US Occupation forces.[11] Until censorship eased, beginning in 1952 with the ending of US Occupation, all that most people heard and believed was that the atomic bombs had ended the war and ushered in a new era. Without accurate reports of its immediate impact and the people's suffering that followed, the popular impression was similar to what President Truman had announced: that the atomic bomb was dropped on Hiroshima, identified as a military target, with the intention of avoiding civilian casualties. Paul Boyer writes that Truman's statement determined the popular impression of this historical event.[12] Japanese Nobel Prize-winning novelist Kenzaburo Oe wrote that the hidden truth also set

---

8    Nakazawa, *Hadashi no Gen Jiden*, 192.
9    Kenji Nakazawa, *Hadashi no Gen: Watashi no Isho* [Barefoot Gen: My Last Note] (Tokyo: Asahi Sinbunsha, 2012), 166.
10   Nakazawa, *Hadashi no Gen Jiden*, 216.
11   Paul Boyer, "Exotic Resonances: Hiroshima in American Memory" in *Hiroshima in History and Memory*, ed. Michael J. Hogan (New York: Cambridge University Press, 1996); John W. Dower, "The Bombed: Hiroshimas and Nagasakis in Japanese Memory" in *History and Memory*, ed. Michael J. Hogan (New York: Cambridge University Press, 1996).
12   Boyer, "Exotic Resonances," 145.

unrealistic images of atomic bombs as legitimate weapons of war.[13] Thus began the Cold War, with few laypeople having any knowledge of the actual effects that nuclear bombs inflicted on human beings. This censorship, coming at the most crucial time, obscured deaths and silenced for the rest of their lives most of those who suffered from burns and the radiation that ravaged their bodies.

This censorship prevented depictions or reports of the bombs' human toll, only allowing pictures of the mushroom clouds over Hiroshima and Nagasaki that were taken safely from the air. Pictures at ground level showed the destruction of the built environment, but no images of the dead—the bodies turned to charcoal or floating in the rivers—nor of the living with their burns or with maggots emerging from their festering wounds.

With few exceptions, it was only after 1952 that pictures, stories, and poems about what happened to the people beneath the cloud began to appear.[14] In addition to the censorship of the Allied General Headquarters (GHQ), the Japanese government exerted its own control over the media. Films about the atomic bombings were not made available, as the government put pressure on Japan's major film companies. The noted critic of Japanese film, Donald Richie, described how some of the films that were released after the media control ended as conveying a *"mono no aware"* sentiment, implying that the atomic bombings were like acts of gods, beyond anything mere humans could resist.[15] Many of the films that featured stories of *hibakusha* showed protagonists acting humbly and with a gentle spirit as they endured the suffering caused by radiation; in this way, they gained the audience's sympathy.[16] Some films offered a positive ending, showing how love helped overcome seeming impossible obstacles. Others ended with the death of the main characters. In contrast, *Barefoot Gen* described a straightforward horror, and showed an anger directed not only at war and the atomic bombs, but also toward the and the Japanese authorities, including the emperor.[17] Moreover, Nakazawa showed children facing this situation with creativity and even humor.

---

13    Kenzaburo Oe, *Hiroshima Noto* [Hiroshima Notes] (Tokyo: Iwanami-shoten, 1965), 56.

14    Dower, "The Bombed," 127.

15    Donald Richie, "Monono Aware: Eiga no Naka Hiroshima" [Monono Aware: Hiroshima in Films] in *Hibakusha Shinema* [Hibakusha Cinema: Hiroshima, Nagasaki and the Nuclear Image in Japanese Films], ed. Mick Broderick, tr. A. Shibasaki and M. Wanami (Tokyo: Gendai-shokan, 1999), 29.

16    Richie, "Monono Aware," 32; Akihiro Yamamoto, *Kaku to Nihonjin: Hiroshima, Gojira, Fukushima* [Nuclear and Japanese: Hiroshima, Gojia, Fukushima] (Tokyo: Chuokoron-shinsha, 2015), 94.

17    Ferenc M. Szasz, *Atomic Comics: Cartoonists Confront the Nuclear World* (Reno, NV: University of Nevada Press, 2012), 113.

It should be noted that the motivations for translating Nakazawa's work into other languages for publication in other countries varied, as did the ways in which the story took on new significance depending on time and place. The publication of the translated work in Germany in 1982, for example, was read in the context of German attitudes towards the Cold War arms race.[18] Moreover, Nakazawa was seen as an anti-authority activist during a time of civil unrest in Germany. For those in the peace movement who opposed the deployment of US Pershing II missiles, there was empathy toward the Japanese. All the more so with the realization that the Germans could have been the first victims of the atomic bombings.[19]

Decades later in the United States, *Gen* appeals to many veterans of the wars in Iraq and Afghanistan who relate to the experience of children suffering from the consequences of war as shown in Nakazawa's work.[20] And in the Middle East, a professor at University of Cairo translated the graphic novel into Arabic, expressing the hope that *Barefoot Gen* might contribute to bringing peace to his part of the world where conflicts and wars continue.[21]

What helps explain the enduring impact of *Barefoot Gen* internationally? Here are six reasons:

## Manga, graphic novel, and anime genres can do what words, photography and most movies cannot

Author Kyoko Hayashi was exposed to the atomic bombing of Nagasaki and lived in fear of radiation throughout her life. She reports that she tried to write as factually as possible but still maintain her decision never to write about the hell that came after the atomic bombing. However, after she completed her first novel, she felt her writing was too naïve to portray fully the agony of the victims of 9 August 1945. The more she tried to express in words the reality of that August day, the more she realized the enormity of what she left out.[22] Art Spiegelman writes: "I've found myself remembering images and events from the Gen books with a clarity that made them seem like memories from my own life, rather than Nakazawa's. I will never forget the people dragging their own melted skin as they walk through the ruins of

---

18   Berndt, "Reading Manga," 130.
19   Ibid.
20   NHK, "Sekai wo Kakeru."
21   Onaga, "Hadashi no Gen de Keiwa Uttae."
22   Kazuo Kuroko, *Genbaku Bungakuron: Kakujidai to Souzouryokyu* [Atomic Bomb Literature: Nuclear Era and Imagination] (Tokyo: Sairyu-sha, 1993), 119.

Hiroshima, the panic-stricken horse on fire galloping through the city, the maggots crawling out of the sores of a young girl's ruined face."[23]

John Hersey, whose 1946 New Yorker essay and later bestselling book *Hiroshima* was the first intimate account of atomic-bomb victims, expressed a common response when he described the drawings and paintings that *hibakusha* created years after the event. In a book called *Unforgettable Fire*,[24] Hersey describes this amateur art work as being more moving than any photographs could be "because what is registered is what has been burned into the minds of the survivors."[25] John Dower also described the impact of amateurs' drawings when he saw them displayed alongside photographs of Hiroshima and Nagasaki:

> Photography, by its nature, often holds the viewer at arm's length. We have become so saturated with the camerawork of war, from World War II and all the sanguinary conflicts since then, that it becomes easier and easier to block out the full import of what the glossy print is showing and look upon wanton death and destruction as little more than clichés. By contrast, these pictures by Japanese survivors—ranging in technique from rough to skilled, with explanations attached in captions often written on the painting or drawing itself, and always telling a personal story—these pitiful graphics are infinitely varied and incomparably intimate. These pictures have voices. They draw the reader in. Death and grievous emotional and physical pain become individual and personal here, and the human dimension is restored to our retrospections and prognostications about war.[26]

Among the most important works of art in post-war Japan are the "Genbaku no Zu," the "Atomic Bomb Panels," painted over a period of more than three decades by Iri and Toshi Maruki. The painter couple went from Tokyo to Hiroshima immediately after the bombing in search of their family. What they found haunted them until they began to express their emotions and to reconstruct, over a period of thirty-two years the Hiroshima they saw and felt.[27] Nakazawa felt that the Marukis' epic work was too sophisticated to evoke horror. That sensibility may be one of the reasons that he chose the simple and strong lines of what many called his "amateur" style, considered out of date even at the time of his drawing. He believed that this particular style would best convey messages from the perspective of a seven-year-old boy as the style resonated with youth and strong will for life.[28]

---

23   Spiegelman, "Comics after the Bomb."
24   "Unforgettable fire" was originally started as a project of NHK Hiroshima, which called for drawings by the survivors of the atomic bombing in 1974. To date, more than 3,000 drawings have been contributed. The first collection was translated by Professor Schonberger at the University of Main and others. The English version was published in 1977.
25   John W. Dower, *Japan in War and Peace* (New York: The New Press, 1993), 243.
26   Dower, Japan in War and Peace, 243.
27   Ibid, 244.
28   Kosei Ono, "Focus on Gen's Eyes," *Manga Kenkyu* [Manga Studies] 11 (2007): 141.

Onomatopoeia is a feature of "comics" generally, and a particularly strong feature of Japanese manga. Many new words enter the Japanese vocabulary after first appearing in manga. Creating onomatopoeia is an art in itself, and it is a vital part of the impact of *Barefoot Gen*. Nakazawa uses onomatopoeia to intensify some of the most horrific scenes and emotions of characters. But the use of onomatopoeic words to imitate sounds—such as "Goooooo" to represent the sound of flames spreading in all directions—would later become a challenge for those who attempted to translate the work into other languages.

Manga art also allows for a range of images not accessible to other art forms. The eyes of characters send strong messages, and in *Barefoot Gen* the eyes of people who were still living but who knew they would soon die are strangely filled with black, indicating clearly the imminence of death.[29] Another Japanese popular culture critic commented that characters in *Barefoot Gen* share facial features such as large, wide eyes. Those features represent the expression of their strength and the will to protest.[30]

Nakazawa framed his manga similarly to the ways film directors choose and edit their shots, employing choice of camera angles, varying distances, and other features of the language of film.[31] This style follows the techniques of the internationally recognized *mangaka* Osamu Tezuka who would sometimes present a single scene in a layout that showed the scene from many perspectives, giving an especially strong visual impact.[32] Many of Nakazawa's frames are from the perspective of the child-as-witness telling the story. Historian Morris-Suzuki wrote of the power of graphic novels to draw simultaneously unimaginable events from various angles and perspectives, and said that dramatic sequential drawings stay in our memories and influence how we perceive, present, and reconstruct our perceptions of the past. She also notes that historical graphic novels reach a wide readership, including those who do not read documentary or historical literature.[33]

There have been many movies about the bombing of Hiroshima and Nagasaki adapted from novels. A common challenge encountered was the difficulty of

---

29    Kazuma Yoshimura, "Interview with Keiji Nakazawa," in *Fukushusuu no Hiroshima: Kioku no Sengoshi to Media no Rikigaku* [Mulitiple Hiroshima: Memories in Post-War History and Power Structure of Media], ed. Yoshiaki Fukuma, Yamaguchi Makoto and Yoshimura Kazuma (Tokyo: Seikyu-sha, 2012), 352–3.
30    Szasz, *Atomic Comics*, 113.
31    Yoshimura, "Interview with Nakazawa," 345.
32    Tessa Morris-Suzuki, *Kako wa Shinanai: Media, Kioku, Rekishi* [The Past Won't Die: Media, Memories, History], tr. Y. Tashiro (Tokyo: Iwanami-shoten, 2014), 228.
33    Morris-Suzuki, *Kako wa Shinanai*, 213.

depicting effectively the atomic effects on survivors. Animation allows for images that feature films, even with special effects and digital enhancements, cannot convincingly present. Akiyuki Nosaka, author of *Grave of the Fireflies*, refused to have his novel about the bombing of Kobe made into a film until he realized the advantage of producing it as an animated rather than a live action film.[34] In time, the anime version of his novel would rise to rank second only to *Barefoot Gen* as influencing Japanese popular images of the war.

## Nakazawa as witness and storyteller

Journalist John Hersey's *Hiroshima* was the first depiction of the effects of the bombing on the survivors, and as such made a great impact on readers who previously had no idea about what actually happened to the people who were living at Ground Zero. The author interviewed six survivors and told their stories in a calm but powerful style that was universally admired. Yet, Hersey himself did not experience the bombing. His distance from the reality of the event permitted a tone that made these stories acceptable to his American readers.

Nakazawa believed that people could not fully understand the horrors unless they experienced them directly. Some critics objected to the author's views that seemed to deny the right to talk about the atomic bombing to non-eyewitnesses. However, in his later years, Nakazawa also said that the most important thing for any author telling such a story is imagination rather than whether or not the author had lived through the experience of the atomic bombing.[35] The anger that motivated Nakazawa to create *Barefoot Gen* provided a challenge in terms of how much detail he should express when writing the manga. If he drew the awful reality he witnessed in detail, it would scare his young readers. However, if he modified reality, he would not accurately convey the real horror of the atomic bomb. He grappled continuously with this dilemma.[36]

The author of *Hiroshima Notes*, Kenzaburo Oe, describes *Barefoot Gen* as an ethnography of the experiences of the atomic bombing as reported by a *hibakusha*. Oe writes that Nakazawa did not "conceptualize" the atomic bombing, but rather reconstructed his lived experience. This, Oe writes, made it possible to overcome

---

34 Ayu Ishida, "Sensou-jidoubungaku ga Katarumono/Kataranaimono" [What Japanese war children's literature tells or does not tell us] in *"Hansen" to "Kosen" no Popular Culture* [Pacificism and Militarism in Popular Culture: Media, Gender, Tourism], ed. Takai Masashi (Tokyo: Jinbunshoin, 2011), 104.
35 Yoshimura, "Interview with Nakazawa," 350–1.
36 Nakazawa, *Hadashi no Gen Jiden*, 211.

the trick of conceptualization by which atomic manga or atomic novels may fail to present lived reality.[37]

One of the first "Internet atomic manga novels" authored by a third generation of *hibakusha* told the story of the writer's grandmother who as a young woman was a victim of the Hiroshima bombing. The young author later said that the more she learned about Hiroshima and the *hibakusha,* the more reluctant she felt to express her grandmother's actual feelings (*Chugoku Shinbun,* 7 August 2014). Her situation and feelings may be similar to those of Spiegelman whose graphic novel of the holocaust is based on the experiences of his father.

## Agency

Although it is now considered an "atomic bomb manga" or "anti-nuclear manga," the primary message of Nakazawa's work was to describe how it is possible, through the strength of will, to survive even the worst in life. Above all, *Barefoot Gen* is a story of survival. Wheat is used as a recurrent metaphor in the story. Gen's father often told his children to be strong like the fields of wheat, where even though the plants may be trampled many times, they will rise again. In the now famous original cover page of *Barefoot Gen*, Gen holds up a sheath of wheat as if showing his hope for the future.

In the story, Gen is a victim but also shows agency. Facing any hardship, he finds a way to act as when Gen and his younger brother perform on a street to earn money for their sick mother. Also, the manga includes many funny scenes and ones that show the creativity of children during these terrible times. These themes continue to appeal to the young readers in the elementary and junior high schools of Japan, and also to adult readers outside Japan. *Grave of the Fireflies* is also a deeply moving story of children during the war. However, in the novel and the successful anime film that followed, the children are powerless, tragic victims. Nosaka's work accurately described the tragedy of war and sorrow of a boy who could not help his younger sister and who himself died of hunger. *Barefoot Gen* also showed that fate was beyond children's control, but it also showed that Gen's actions could overcome hardship. Gen shows resilience, pluck, and a will to do whatever he can. In hopeless situations, Gen remains hopeful. In the later parts of

---

37  Akira Okawada, "'Kakujidai no Souzouryoku' to 'Kodomono Minwa'" [Imagination in the Nuclear Era and Folktales for Children] in '*Hadashi no Gen' wo Yomu* [Reading 'Barefoot Gen'] (Tokyo: Kawade-shobo-shinsa, 2014), 177.

*Barefoot Gen* there are scenes in which some war orphans die, and in which others—those who joined gangs, many allied with *yakuza*—were able to survive. This was also part of Nakazawa's experience. Gen himself acted criminally, but presents his own sense of what is necessary and just, and is able to control his own fate.

## Timing

The publication appeared at the time of the politically charged US-Japan Security Treaty that provoked sometimes violent demonstrations across Japan. Universities were shut down and some buildings were burned during the student protests. Another factor was a growing anti-nuclear weapons movement that began after the radioactive fallout from the 1954 Bikini Atoll nuclear tests that struck Japanese fishermen aboard "The Lucky Dragon." This event occurred not long after censorship had ended and when the Japanese public was becoming more aware of the full impact of the atomic bombs and the effects of radiation. Initiated by angry housewives, the protest against nuclear testing evolved into a national movement that by the early 1970s was very strong in Japan and globally.

In the United States, protests against the Vietnam War intensified each year in the first half of the 1970s. In light of the bombing of Hiroshima and Nagasaki, Japan had seen itself as a victim of war, but the government's alignment with the US raised fears of being drawn into another war and thus increased the anti-war sentiment in Japan right at the time *Barefoot Gen* appeared.[38] Several major publishers declined to publish Nakazawa's work because they did not want to deal with war and the atomic bombings in light of anti-government and anti-stories in the news. However, his powerful story line appealed to the many people eager to learn more about the horrors of the atomic bombings and the war that they had not been able to learn about earlier.

Even though the United States strictly prohibited the publication of anything that touched on the atomic bombings until 1952, writers who witnessed what happened that August, or who knew survivors of the atomic bombings, did begin to write, though they had to wait until the early 1950s to publish freely. In time those works formed the basis of a new genre in Japanese literature: *genbaku bungaku* (atomic literature). Leading writers included Kyoko Hayashi, Yoko Oota, Tamiki Hara, Masuji Ibuse, among many others. Each of their unique voices questioned the atomic horror, human absurdity, and the meaning of life. Above all, they wrote about the atrocity of nuclear weapons. Some of this literature was adapted as a part

---

38   Nakazawa, *Hadashii no Gen Jiden*.

of school textbooks. Collectively these works form an important part of contemporary Japanese culture as well as a field of academic study.

It did not take long for *Barefoot Gen* to be included in this new literary canon as well as in programs in peace education; but, it required an outpouring of support from many people along the way. It was support from adults who read *Barefoot Gen* in a boys' weekly magazine that encouraged the publisher to continue to publish the story. As Gen's story received attention in newspaper columns, interest in Nakazawa's work reached still wider audiences. The anime movie that is based on the manga brought even more attention to the original manga. A teachers' cooperative association encouraged parents to see *Barefoot Gen* as an important part of every Japanese child's education, and in time parents were buying *Barefoot Gen* for their children to read.[39] Elementary schools started keeping the *Barefoot Gen* series in school libraries, and, because it was available in these libraries, girls who previously would not have read boys' manga also began reading the story. In this way, Nakazawa's story became part of Japanese peace education programs endorsed by teachers and parents.[40]

The first translation of *Barefoot Gen*, in 1976, was carried out by a group of volunteers who were active in the peace movement.[41] The publication drew the attention of fans of underground comics, which published mainly on counter-cultural topics. These twin influences resonated with global trends of the late 1970s and early 1980s when fears of nuclear weapons and the Cold War were widespread and when the peace movement in relation to the Vietnam War was increasingly active. This was an era when people wanted stories about what had actually happened as a result of the only episode in which nuclear weapons were used in wartime.

Sabin wrote that while *Barefoot Gen* is admired in the and Europe, it also occupies an ambivalent position because of its representation of the tragedy of the atomic bombings.[42] For all its recognition, initially *Barefoot Gen* was not without its critics. Revisionist critics who argued that bombings were not necessary to end the war questioned some of what is implied in the story that runs counter to that

---

39   Fukuma, "Genbaku Manga no Media Shi," 33–4.
40   Ibid, 34.
41   Namie Asazawa, "About Project Gen," in *Barefoot Gen*, Kenji Nakazawa (San Francisco, CA: Last Gasp, 2009).
42   Roger Sabin, "Barefoot Gen in the US and UK: Activist Comic, Graphic Novel Manga," *Manga Kenkyu* [Manga Studies] 11 (2007): 158.

view. Other readers outside Japan were critical of the depiction of Gen's father slapping his sons, and some women objected to the ways women in the story were portrayed. Adult readers were unsure how to react to some of the political messages that were a part of that period of history. Beyond issues of content, people who were unfamiliar with Japanese manga had to deal with the extensive onomatopoeia that even translators struggled to put into other languages. Nor did the story appeal to all the fans of underground comics because "comics" are supposed to be humorous.[43] When *Barefoot Gen* was reprinted again in the 1980s—fueled by the new popularity of graphic novels—its style seemed outdated, especially when compared with the more stylish Japanese SF manga popular in the wider movement.

Nonetheless, from the late 1980s people who discovered *Barefoot Gen* found it to be a very important way of learning about the effects of nuclear weapons. After the English translation was published, *Barefoot Gen* was translated into French, German, Italian, Portuguese, Swedish, Norwegian, Indonesian, Tagalog, and Esperanto. In regions of the world where political conflict and war are a part of life, Gen's story resonates. In Ukraine, Israel, Egypt, and Iran, people were motivated to translate the manga, and so it now appears in Russian, Farsi, Hebrew, and Arabic.[44]

## The primacy of the emotional tone

Some literary critics have argued that *Barefoot Gen's* emotional impact does not provide the strong rational basis required to move a reader to demand political action. Kuroko appreciated the emotional power of the story but felt that the author cut off a direct path from feelings to the rational interpretations that are just as important.[45] He argued that the important political speeches that appear in the graphic novel may appeal to adult readers but would be skipped by children who would concentrate on the most horrific scenes.

An innovative study by Otaki, using a quantitative content analysis technique he developed, followed changes in the development of the characters in *Gen* by examining the words they used.[46] In his study, Otaki pointed out that Gen shifted from a more emotional stage to a more reasoned stage, based on his use of words throughout the ten volumes. Otaki argues that Gen shifted from the strong emotions expressed at the beginning of the story to a more ideological stance, and

---

43  Sabin, "Barefoot Gen in the US and UK," 160.
44  Onaga, "Hadashi no Gen de Heiwa Uttae."
45  Kuroko, *Genbaku Bungakuron*, 127.
46  Tomoori Otaki, "The Quantitative Analysis of 'Barefoot Gen': <Sensitivity> and <Idea> in a Process of Expression Changing," *Osaka University Knowledge Archive*, http://hdl.handle.net/11094/25895.

then again returned to his emotional stage in the final volumes. Otaki interpreted this shift as reflecting Nakazawa's own emotional fluctuations. Similarly, one critic argued that Gen's story was not intended as a "tear-jerking mother-child story," but rather Nakazawa wanted to transform these deepest feelings into action. Go, however, argued that the deep resentment expressed would not easily be channeled into any kind of action.[47] Critical inquiry of the kind provided by Otaki and Go called into question whether *Barefoot Gen* would lose its powerful appeal to readers if overt political action, such as that advocated by anti-nuclear and other movements, was seen as a goal of Nakazawa's story. Trying to appeal to a broader, more rational message—instead of staying at the level of personal emotion—would risk losing the impact of *Barefoot Gen* as an "genbaku ethnography," as Oe described it.[48] Given the horror of the atomic bombings and the suffering that followed, one can ask if it would even be possible for Gen to be objective and rational.

Just as the authors of genbaku literature who were victims of the atomic bombs were criticized, there was criticism that those authors themselves excluded others who were not *hibakusha* from writing about the atomic bombs. In addition to Nakazawa's struggle with the description of the horror to children, his emotional tones moved back and forth.[49]

## Issues of power and class

In Gen's story the anti-war, anti-authority, anti-emperor, and anti-atomic bomb messages are clear. This appears first in the attitude of Gen's father, revealed in his facial expressions as well as words. In real life, Nakazawa's father was an outspoken leftist, even appearing in amateur political dramas. As shown in *Barefoot Gen*, Nakazawa's father was arrested for his anti-establishment activities and was jailed for over a year. Szasz points out that "[Barefoot Gen] does not shy away from such crucial issues as the restriction of freedom of thought and freedom of speech in prewar Japan …" He goes on to say that part of what makes the manga special is that it not only focuses on the lives of the survivors but also offers a wider view including discrimination against *hibakusha*, the terrible situation of the war orphans, and the treatment of Korean residents in Japan.[50] From its earliest appear-

---

47  Chiei Go, "Chinpuka shita Seigi no Waku wo Koete" [Beyond the limits of Obsolete Justice], in *'Hadashi no Gen' wo Yomu* [Reading 'Barefoot Gen'] (Tokyo: Kawade-shobo-shinsha, 2014), 48.
48  Okawada, "'Kakujidai no Souzouyoku' to 'Kodomono Minwa'," 176.
49  Go, "Chinpuka shit Seigi no Waku wo Koete."
50  Szasz, *Atomic Comics*, 113.

ance, *Barefoot Gen* has drawn criticism, especially from right-wing groups. In particular, the fact that the seven-year-old Gen criticized militarism, the emperor, and other figures of authority was attacked as the voice of an adult coming from the mouth of a child.

Issues of power and class run throughout the story. In the manga there is a scene where Gen protests when he is asked to help make flags to welcome the emperor on his first post-war visit to Hiroshima. Like his title character, Nakazawa felt an intense anger toward the emperor who continued the war when he might have ended it, thereby preventing the atomic bombings. Gen's story also reflects the complexity of emotions, of anticipation and ambivalence, in post-war Hiroshima.[51] Years later a Hiroshima City official recounted the emperor's possible visit. Right before the group decided formally to invite the emperor, the representatives at the meeting fell silent. Then when the invitation was agreed upon, there was applause. The official wrote that he was shocked to realize that the silence was not because some people were opposed to the emperor's visit, but rather because they were embarrassed to have the emperor see such a devastated area. He added that he could not believe that people could have felt this way, given that the role of the emperor during the war led to the deaths of so many.[52]

Nakazawa's opinion about the emperor was actually much stronger than what Gen expresses in his graphic novels. He compared the post-war situation in Japan with that of Italy and Germany. In his final testament, Nakazawa wrote that whereas the German government had pursued Nazi officials to the ends of the earth, it was only Japan in which the emperor still survived, even if only a "symbol," and other war criminals became government bureaucrats, and one even a prime minister.[53]

Nakazawa's feelings toward the emperor were echoed by a video-recorded testimony of a thirteen-year-old atomic survivor preserved as part of the collection of audio and video testimonials archived at the Hiroshima Peace Memorial Museum. In her testimony, she says that on that morning of 6 August her school teacher instructed the students to help demolish some of the wooden houses in the area in order to prevent any fire from spreading if the US firebombed the city. Her teacher received orders from the government, and the government orders were given in the name of the emperor. Therefore, she argued that it was the emperor's

---

51  Nakazawa, *Hadashi no Gen Jiden*.
52  Motofumi Asai, *HIROSHIMA to Hiroshima* [Hiroshima as Philosophy versus Hiroshima in Reality] (Kyoto: Kamogawa-shuppan, 2011), 127.
53  Yoshimura, "Interview with Nakazawa," 333.

order that put the junior high school students in a place where nearly every one of the children would die.⁵⁴

Although *Barefoot Gen* communicates messages about the war, authority and even the emperor that might be seen as naïve and oversimplified in light of a complex background, they ring with a special clarity when expressed in the words of young boy speaking out amid his devastated surroundings. Gen voices the thoughts of people who did not have a voice to speak out in public.

After the war, Gen's friend argued with a female owner of a restaurant who commented that men started war and women and children were powerless victims. Gen's friend criticized the owner's cooperation with the national policy and her accusations against people who were patriotic during the war. This scene indicates that the majority of people who were patriotic silenced the voice of people who were against the war.

Issues of social class that are set out from the very beginning of the story are reinforced later, after the end of the war. Gen's mother talks about the war as being started by rich people in order to make themselves richer. The descriptions of Gen's family and his neighbors, including Mr. Pak, the sympathetic Korean neighbor who like other Koreans was forcibly brought to Japan and faced discrimination on a daily basis, clearly represent the proletariat. Even considering the particular wartime conditions, issues of class issue appear throughout Gen's story, and this theme is another of the reasons that *Barefoot Gen* received attention from overseas.

## Conclusion

*Barefoot Gen* is told by a child who witnessed the atomic bombing of Hiroshima, presented in a voice that speaks truth to power as only a child can. The medium of manga served to offer unique resources that were not available to writers or photographers. Together these features help to explain the enduring impact of Nakazawa's work. Just as the circumstances of time and place that destroyed the author's own childhood allowed him to create this story, in the decades that followed, the timing and circumstances in which the manga was read revealed the personal relevance of Gen's story its readers, notably those who were inspired to undertake writing translations. Many college students in the US today who encounter *Barefoot Gen* for the first time are shocked by a history that they were never taught at school, and for some this shock makes them consider in a new way their identity as Americans. Because the story is revealed through the eyes of a child, the reader

---

54   Survivor's testimony, Hiroshima Memorial Museum.

may set aside some of the political and historical considerations that are prominent in other treatments of the atomic bombings. It is the child's innocence that helps the reader to respond without all the entanglements of national identity.

If there is simplification in Gen's story, there is also an awareness of greater complexities within a historical event that for many is known through only a few iconic images, statistics, and a brief summary. Gen's feelings are complex and conflicted. He is self-loathing and feels anger toward authorities. Some who showed sympathy towards children who were victims were also those who cooperated with the military government during the war.

A special issue of the *American Journal of Public Health* reports that 90% of all deaths in wars are civilians, with about ten civilians dying for every combatant killed in battle. Since the end of the Second World War—often referred to in the United States as "the good war"—there have been nearly 250 armed conflicts just counting those involving the US itself.[55] Gen's story has resonated with many people who first encountered it in the context of other wars. The Vietnam War helped motivate a small group of volunteers to translate the manga into English. Wars in the Middle East have motivated others to translate Nakazawa's work into other languages, including Hebrew, Arabic, and Farsi. Though not a response to war, there is a translation into Russian by a Ukrainian writer who witnessed the Chernobyl nuclear disaster.

Photo-journalist Yoshio Tokuyama has said that the photo of the mushroom cloud may be seen as proudly expressing the power of the atomic bomb as it hides the people who suffer beneath it.[56] *Barefoot Gen* reveals what happened beneath that terrible cloud. Historian Ferenc Szasz singles out Nakazawa's manga as the best of the A-bomb films, graphic novels, and anime about the atomic bombing of Hiroshima:

> ... European and American cartoonists [who have attempted to tell the story of the bombing of Hiroshima] meant well, but their Japanese counterparts spoke from the heart when they constructed manga tales of nuclear power or crafted stories of the atomic bomb; they knew exactly what they were doing. And, unlike their US or European colleagues, they succeeded in placing the complex story of nuclear energy at the very heart of their culture.[57]

---

55   William H. Wiist et al., "The Role of Public Health in the Prevention of War: Rationale and Competencies," *American Journal of Public Health* 104, no. 6 (2014): 36.
56   Yoshio Tokuyama, *Genbaku to Shashin* [Atomic Bombs and Photos] (Tokyo: Ochanomizu-shobo, 2005).
57   Szasz, *Atomic Comics*, 114.

# NUCLEAR NOIR: *KISS ME DEADLY* AND POSTWAR ANXIETY IN AMERICA

*William Beard*

There is a fairly substantial literature on the presence of a nuclear anxiety in Hollywood and other popular cinema in the postwar period. The principal corpus of this literature lies in the "lower" genres of monster-movies and science fiction films. Beginning, perhaps, with the Japanese Godzilla movies and their imitators, but quickly spreading to encompass giant insects, hideous mutations of humanity, monsters without pedigree, invasions from outer space, and other abnormal and often inexplicable threats, popular cinema manifested the symptoms of a neurosis traceable in considerable part to the phenomenon of the atom bomb. In many of these films, nuclear power was not even mentioned; but the sense that it had unleashed new horrors and a general sense of apocalypse could be discerned from the widespread extent and commonalities of these movies. If destruction didn't come through direct explosion, then radiation would mutate and kill life on the planet. (Certainly, the presence of so many monsters is traceable to the science-fiction and incomprehensibly poisonous aspects of nuclear weaponry.) In addition to sensationalist and pulpy fictions, Hollywood provided soberer and more realist films like *On the Beach* (1959) and *Fail-Safe* (1964) that looked at the possibilities of atomic catastrophe in literal terms. One could also mention the absurdist, blackly comic *Dr Strangelove* [1964] as a further example. My undertaking here, though, is rather different. Its object is the 1955 movie *Kiss Me Deadly*, sometimes described as the culminating film in the original or "classic" period of film noir. And my argument will be that it represents a symptom of nuclear neurosis not only in content, but in form and style.

To begin with, though, I will make a few generalizations about film noir as a genre, or sub-genre, or style.[1] As a narrative genre, the principal characteristics of noir include a powerful destabilization of the moral certainties and guaranteed

---

[1] There has been much debate in the voluminous literature about classic film noir as to its generic status. Almost like light, which can be particle or wave, so film noir can be a narrative genre or a visual style. And amidst the taxonomic frenzy which has accompanied Anglo-Saxon discovery of the phenomenon, there has been a wide range of opinions, including the opinion that it was not a genre at all.

moral balance of classical Hollywood cinema from the 1920s onwards.[2] Instead of dramas centering on the protagonists' predicaments, struggles to overcome obstacles, and final victory, noir films very often feature confused or disoriented heroes who cannot make clear sense of the world, whose problems are anything but clear-cut, whose stature as Hollywood heroes is profoundly compromised, and whose narratives end either in costly and ambiguous victories or, perhaps more often, their failure and death. The presence in so many noir films of a *femme fatale* is noteworthy, as this sexually powerful, calculating, and predatory character's activities are seen as a kind of explanation for the failure of so many male protagonists to master the narrative in the familiar way. The genre has been described as misogynistic on this account—so many hapless innocent heroes, so many beautiful guilty women. In truth, however, there are as many noir films that lack a *femme fatale* as there are ones that have one. A better instrument for describing this gender "imbalance" in film noir is to talk instead about a crisis of masculinity. Males in ideologically comfortable narratives may have their difficulties, but they virtually always take control of events and bring them to a satisfactory outcome. They are standing upon firm ground, not half-blindly navigating some dark and confusing environment; and if a woman should present herself, she is incorporated into the patriarchal system of sexual hierarchy and can come along for the ride.[3]

This male anxiety in film noir has been accounted for in a number of ways, first of all demobilized men's discovery that their social position was not necessarily still there for them after the war. Women had been doing many traditionally male jobs in the absence of so many men. The war had given many people an experience that emphasized uncertainty, fear and death and made the easy solutions of classical narrative seem naïve. These factors may help to account for the anxiety-ridden nature of these films—counterintuitively occurring after the war had been won, and when America was entering a kind of social golden age with full employment, houses and education for many families, and a rocketing economic prosperity. But there certainly was a new streak of hysteria also running through American society, whose principal cause was the Cold War and the fear of nuclear apocalypse. International paranoia and the

---

2   For a comprehensive exposition of the "rules" of classical Hollywood narrative, see especially David Bordwell, Janet Staiger and Kristin Thompson, *The Classical Hollywood Cinema: Film Style and the Mode of Production to 1960* (New York: Columbia University Press, 1985).

3   In fact, this is too sweeping a description. It is broadly true for "male" genres (crime films, Westerns, adventure movies, etc.), but not nearly so much for "female" genres (notably domestic melodrama) or equal-opportunity forms (romantic and "screwball" comedy of the 1930s). But it will hold for film noir, which is a crime film subgenre featuring guns and violence.

fear of something so destructive that it was beyond rational accounting can be motives for the failures of certainty and good judgement amongst the protagonists of film noir as much as the troubling of gender categories and a disturbing consciousness of the weakness of classical narrative. *Kiss Me Deadly* can be interpreted from a standpoint that includes all of these elements, and of all noirs it expounds most clearly the power of nuclear anxiety as a radically destabilizing force.

On the assumption that many readers will not be familiar with the film, I will first offer some description. It was adapted from one of Mickey Spillane's Mike Hammer books. Between 1947 and 1952 Spillane wrote five of these private eye novels, all of them immensely popular (and altogether he was responsible for seven of the fifteen bestselling fictions in American publishing history). This detective, nominally a champion of justice, is an ultra-violent, sadistic vigilante figure with a strong taste for killing blondes; yet these qualities were exactly what made him charismatic and popular in the world of pulp fiction. The movie makes a major departure from the book in offering Hammer as a frankly unpleasant figure—narcissistic, unscrupulous and greedy.

Here is a brief summary of the action of the film: Hammer, a Los Angeles private detective specializing in divorce cases, is stopped on the highway one night by a young woman, Christina, standing in the road, escaped from a hospital.

**Figure 1.** Christine on the highway

He gives her a lift, but before they can reach safety they are captured: Christina is tortured and killed, and the semi-conscious Mike is put his car with her corpse and pushed over a clifftop. Surviving this crash, he determines to investigate what

Christina had that her killers wanted, in the hope of finding some gain in it for himself. His search takes him through all kinds of levels of Los Angeles society, from old and broken down to rich and new, and through cultural and social levels stretching from *lumpen*-proletariat to *nouveau-riche*. He is warned off by the cops, who regard his sleazy divorce work with utter contempt, and, when he penetrates to the circles of organized crime that were involved in Christina's death, he is menaced with physical danger. He persists, in the manner of all private-eye heroes, shrugging off threats and batting away sexually aggressive young women.

At last he retrieves a clue left by Christina in her own corpse and traces the object of everyone's obsession to a locker in the Hollywood Athletic Club. It is a metal box in a leather suitcase, somewhat bigger than a breadbox. It is hot to the touch, and when Hammer cracks it open, it emits an alarming roar and burst of blinding light. Before he can shut the box, it has left him with a nasty burn on his wrist. Both the local mafia and the government are in desperate search for this item. When Hammer next meets his police friend Pat, he is told that the enormous thing he is mixed up with can be described using only a few "harmless words": "Manhattan Project," "Los Alamos," "Trinity." This information finally cures Mike of his wish to turn this unknown object into some kind of material advantage for himself. But now his secretary and girlfriend Velda has been kidnapped by the crooks, and Hammer has to go and rescue her.

The final scene takes place at a beach house, where the leading villains, a doctor Soberin and *his* girlfriend Gabrielle, have taken the box. Gabrielle shoots Soberin and also wounds Hammer, and then, despite the severest warnings, opens the box. The dazzling light and heat convert her into a human torch, and as Mike and Velda drag themselves out onto the beach the house explodes with an extreme and extended violence. In some released versions, the film ends simply with the explosion, without survivors. The "atomic" element in the story is not in the original novel—there, the object of pursuit is a quantity of drugs. It is a rather important change, since a nuclear device (if that is what it is) does not belong to that set of interchangeable treasures that serves to motivate the action of so many crime films: it is not a shipment of drugs, a cache of stolen diamonds, or anything else of that kind, but a thing that is so much bigger that it dwarfs all of these quests for riches or power.

This summary has really only skimmed the surface of the intricacies of *Kiss Me Deadly*'s events. Indeed, the whole style of the film is notably abstract, fragmented, and self-conscious—especially for a rather low-budget production that went into release as just another B-movie crime film, and was reviewed by American and English critics largely as a piece of worthless and sleazy sensationalism. (For the French, and especially the young critics of *Cahiers du cinéma* and *Positif*, it was an outstanding work of art that formed an important model for the impending New Wave.) Perhaps the film's extraordinariness was camouflaged by more than a decade of moody, arty, and increasingly violent commercial crime movies that now form what we identify as classic film noir—a category that constituted a kind of "family" in which *Kiss Me Deadly* could pass as a recognizable member.

Film noir itself was of course an extraordinary development in mainstream Hollywood movies, and even more remarkably so in that it was never recognized in its native land until fifteen or twenty years after it had ceased (once again, it was a Hollywood phenomenon that had to be discovered by the French). There is an enormous literature surrounding film noir—exactly what it was, when it began and ended, what caused it, whether it is a genre or a style, and many other questions—that sometimes seems to rival that of Medieval Scholasticism in its theological zeal. For this author, Hollywood film noir began in 1944 and ended in 1955, and its ending was most clearly marked exactly by *Kiss Me Deadly*, a movie that takes everything to such extremes that it is impossible to go any further down this path.

The bulk of "classic film noir," as it has come to be called, is distinguished by a singular interference with the clean, open-and-shut narratives of the classical style characteristic of studio pictures of the 1930s, with their clearly identified good guys and bad guys, plot goals, obstacles and successful resolutions unfolding in orderly and efficient manner. Noir complicates all this: heroes are compromised and often do not achieve their goals—goals that are themselves murky and questionable; the world around them is ambiguous and troubling rather than classically clear; and tropes of personal disorientation, social darkness, and a dreamlike sense of uncertainty are everywhere. All of this, of course, exists within the framework of mainstream Hollywood crime cinema. Early noir tends to be atmospheric, murky, and oneiric, and to show a kinship with German Expressionism. But as noir progresses towards its burnout conclusion, it takes on what Paul Schrader has called qualities of "psychotic action and suicidal impulse." Violence is pushed to an extreme under the Production Code, and tension and hysteria tended to displace moodiness and shadowy menace.

*Kiss Me Deadly* represents, in this context, the extreme of the extreme. The *chiaroscuro* black-and-white photographic style of noir changes here into a visual world just as full of dark shadows and white light, but now in a completely unblended combination of deep blacks and glaring whites, sharp edges, and aggressively angular compositions—a harsh assault on the viewer. Canted camera angles and arbitrary viewpoints are added to the mix. In the auditory realm, the dialogue track is full of panting, gasping, and screaming, while the music track presents a wildly heterogeneous collection of styles.

**Figure 2.**   **Noir office scene**

Altogether the effect of these strong stylistic gestures is to push the film away from the death-loving Romantic warmth of earlier noir and towards a flatter, more abstract and high-modernist set of aesthetic parameters. J. Hoberman comments:

> Kiss Me Deadly is sensationally baroque, eschewing straight exposition for a jarring succession of bizarre images, bravura sound matching, and encoded riddles the likes of which had not been seen in Hollywood since Orson Welles kissed the industry goodbye.[4]

Raymond Durgnat adds:

> The photography is cold, hard, steely. Its strongest tones are black and a shiny, acid grey. ... Everything has the coldness of stainless steel; most of the faces are reduced to the same metallic grey. The world is devoid of sensuousness, each person is the idea of a person, an impersonating android ... A [De] Chirico light bathes staircases and corridors which become tunnels and galleries.[5]

---

4   J. Hoberman, "The Thriller of Tomorrow," The Criterion Collection Blu-Ray Edition booklet, 2011.
5   Raymond Durgnat, *Eros in the Cinema*. London: Calder and Boyars, 1966, 84.

And again Durgnat:

> It is the stark, abstract style of writer (A.I. Bezzerides), cameraman (Ernest Laszlo) and director [Robert Aldrich] which spans the space dividing the 'mere' detective story from the pure, intense, violent nightmare mood. A sexuality of terror and violence (breathing, running, kicking out, exploding) pervades the frozen film.[6]

To which David Thomson adds, *à propos* Mike Hammer himself, that he is "so hard he's impotent," and "too tight for fucking."[7] The mood is one of a suppressed hysteria, a kind of panic held at bay by the numbness of alienation and reification.

The art direction and set design are extraordinary. There is a remarkable emphasis on modern art as such. Hammer's apartment is very up-to-date in its severe rectangles and spareness of decoration. It is furnished with abstract paintings and African sculpture, as is Velda's. A later scene takes place in a modernist art gallery, where, as Elizabeth Willis says, "sham versions of Picasso, Braque, Matisse, and other modern masters sail past in the darkened exhibition hall like monsters of the modern imagination."[8] Other cultural commodities are equally modern: Hammer has a desktop transistor radio and a reel-to-reel tape recorder attached to his phone that features automatic call-answering and voicemail many years before such devices became widespread. He drives exotic convertible sports cars: first a Jaguar that gets wrecked, then an MG, then a brand-new Corvette that has to have two separate explosive devices removed from it. His clothes are casual but modish and well-tailored, his hair carefully cut. The mafia boss's house and swimming pool have a similar flatness and modernist elegance—though similarly counterposed with the boss and his hoods listening to race results on another transistor radio and brushing away women who try to get some attention ("these dames is worse than flies," one of them complains).

---

6  Durgnat 1966, 94.
7  David Thomson, "Dead Lily," *Film Comment* 33.6 (1997), 16–19.
8  Elizabeth Willis, "Christina Rossetti and Pre-Raphaelite *Noir*," *Textual Practice* 18.4 (2004), 529.

**Figure 3.    Mafia boss's home**

There is a large gap between the rather affected narcissism of Hammer's personal style and the crude and sordid strategies of his business. But his violence is so sudden and direct that it bridges the gap. In fact, his violence is in itself abstract. He paralyses one thug and kills another with his bare hands using some technique that is so occult that it isn't even shown—all we get are the screams of the victim, followed by reaction shots of the victim's buddy backing away in superstitious terror. Altogether the flatness and abstraction of this visual regime, together with the jaggedness of camera and editing, creates a sense of shallow frenzy, something that one commentator even describes as being postmodern.[9] The utter materialism of the environment, a materialism completely epitomized in the hero, is yet another symptom of a condition of alienation.

There is another side to the film—one that looks backward from this desert of meaningless lives and actions. That is an older form of living associated with Europe and the past, and also with the ramshackle shabbiness of proletarian life in the poor part of town. This is Bunker Hill, the down-and-out neighbourhood of Los Angeles that contrasts so strikingly with Bel Air and Malibu. Huge flights of stairs in concrete or in wood take us up to and down from tenement buildings, decaying wooden rooming houses, and dangerous streets. These are all presented in the first, pre-modernist, style of noir: soft dark shadows, maze-like passages and

---

9    Russel Meeuf, "Nuclear Epistemology: Apocalypticism, Knowledge, and the "Nuclear Uncanny" in *Kiss Me Deadly,*" *Literature Interpretation Theory* 23 (2012): 286.

stairwells, ageing and unlovely *décor* and inhabitants, cluttered *mise en scène*. This is the world of authentic traditional noir, something with history and experience, and it is a kind of foreign country for the modernist hero Mike Hammer to penetrate and interact, often savagely, with its denizens. Here we find, amongst several other idiosyncratic characters, an old Italian who carries heavy trunks up and down the long stairs and utters homilies about life. Here also we encounter a retired Italian tenor, living amongst hanging laundry and a boiling pot of spaghetti while belting out less-than-impressive sing-alongs with his Caruso records.

 Also inhabiting this older world are a pair of other characters. The first victim, Christina, has an apartment decorated with real art and featuring a radio tuned to classical music, while her posthumous clue to Mike is a reference to a poem by Christina Rossetti that refers to the darkness and putrefaction of death. The other character, who is a kind of Prime Mover of the narrative, is Dr Soberin. He is apprehended for most of the film only as a pair of expensive two-tone saddle shoes and a solemn voice intoning Truths drawn from Greek mythology. He refers to the contents of the box as a Medusa, compares Gabrielle with Lot's Wife and Pandora in her wish to open it, and finally conjures her, to no avail, with the barking heads of Cerberus. Soberin may be felt to be a pompous blowhard, but his emphatic self-identification with the philosophic voice of wisdom makes him the spokesman of all of Western thought and meaning. And in his failure to master the bomb which he in his detached philosophic fashion is helping to peddle to somebody, all his posturings in the realm of meaning are blown away with everything else when it explodes.

 There is a crisis of meaning in the film. Commodity fetishism, cultural shallowness, the absence of any kind of human love anywhere, the flat *presentness* of everything—these fractured abstractions of modernity express not simply an alienation from the humanism of the past, but from any meaning at all. The flat and sharp-edged aesthetic of the film perfectly answers the flat and sharp-edged nature of postwar alienation. Nothing here is even real—nothing except, eventually, the box, and the bomb. The box itself, that thing that Hammer chases doggedly without knowing the faintest thing about it, that murderous gangsters and mad doctors are grasping at, is aptly labelled by the at least partly detached and sarcastic Velda as "the great whatzit—what is it? who cares?" It is out of place in a hardboiled crime narrative, and seems instead like something out of a horror movie: it roars fiercely when its cage is opened, it burns with an incandescent fury that has nothing in common with the prosaic mechanisms of ignition and firing sequence and suggests instead a primal power that has nothing to do with science.

**Figure 4.    The box**

But when it explodes it becomes the only thing with meaning in this unreal world.

The meaning is apocalyptic, the annihilation of all history and experience. Jack Shadoian notes the way in which it obliterates in particular the genre of hardboiled crime movies in which it is nested:

> *Kiss Me Deadly*'s use of the atomic box puts the genre's iconography into a futile, sardonic perspective. If the world is going to blow up, what can guns, fast cars, being tough with women, or any of it mean? … The genre's standard equipment seems beside the point in an era of nuclear hazard. The explosions at the end of the film make all that has preceded—the 'mystery,' the tough action, the investigation, the gangster/crime and private eye film's entire sign system—meaningless.[10]

The nihilism of the film is reflected also in its absurdist sense of humour. The whole surreal juxtaposition of hardboiled low culture and self-conscious high art is constantly ironic. The end of the world is found in a locker at the Hollywood Athletic Club. Hammer's attempt to give the third degree to an art gallery owner is foiled because, having desperately swallowed a handful of sleeping pills, the man falls asleep actually while Mike is beating him up. The movie is full of such absurdities. At the end, when the eerily childlike and affectless Gabrielle is trying to find out what's in the box, her unthinking acquisitiveness could hardly be clearer. After all the treachery and torture and killing, it all comes down to this for her: "What's in

---

10    Jack Shadoian, *Dreams and Dead Ends* (Cambridge: MIT Press 1977), 266–267.

the box? Whatever it is, I want half!" (That, however, is also pretty close to Hammer's interest in the thing.)

The atomic bomb, then, is the logical endpoint of this society, and this narrative action—the embodiment of the indiscriminate power to destroy everything.

**Figure 5.    The explosion**

It is the thing that will efface every material appetite and cultural emblem, will render every coarse desire moot, will finally *be* the end of this world so bereft of significance or value. In this context, it seems like an utterly appropriate presence, the perfect endpoint of the death-spiral of Western humanity; and the radioactive desert wasteland it will produce is nothing more than a mirror of the wasteland of values in which this society is already living. Can we also say that this social wasteland has in some way been *produced* by the fact of nuclear destruction? That the consciousness of man-made apocalypse hanging over the head of every person who reads the newspapers and watches the newsreels has created that desert of human meaning? And that the frenzied style-chasing and object-chasing, the blank reduction of human desires to mere affectless appetite, is a norm which follows on from the suppressed knowledge that the end of everything is just around the corner? Perhaps so, to a degree. But there is also the equally powerful sense that the Bomb is somehow a punishment for such gross spiritual impoverishment. Also, we may ask whether it is the literal fact of atomic weapons or the mere idea of them that creates this two-headed beast. Either way the fit is perfect. In *Kiss Me Deadly*, the Bomb is both literal and metaphorical.

One further perspective on femininity and sexuality in the film, and in atomic discourse. In the first place—as we have briefly seen—the crisis of masculinity at the heart of film noir very much includes a crisis of sexuality. When noir heroes lose their "classical" power, one prominent reason is their inability to remain calm and in control when confronted by a beautiful woman. Sexual desire is often a profoundly destabilizing force for them. It may then be easier to understand the metaphorization of this sexual desire in terms of explosion and physical devastation. The clearest iterations of this metaphor, however, occur not in film noir but in what we may call noir's antitype: the robust and unfettered "wolf-whistle" expressions of a masculine sexual desire that is anything but confusing or soul-robbing. Examples of the phenomenon can be found throughout Hollywood films of the 1940s and early 1950s, and are very often connected with the sexual discourse of servicemen long deprived of female company and consequently ravenous for it. "Discourse" seems an odd word to describe the howls of desire, the broad lecherous grins, the tongue drooling, and the various other manifestations of an appetite that is, by later American cultural standards, amazingly frank and anxiety-free. The trio of postwar MGM musicals starring Gene Kelly (*Anchors Aweigh!*, *Take Me Out to the Ball Game*, *On the Town*) provide crystal-clear examples. In fact, in *On the Town* frank female sexuality is as widespread as the male variety. The *ne plus ultra* of this modus undoubtedly lies in the 1940s MGM cartoons of Tex Avery, a subcategory of which repeatedly features a wolf character driven to prodigies of impossible excess in his reaction to a luscious torch singer.

It may seem that we are far from *Kiss Me Deadly* and nuclear anxiety here, but there is a connection. It is appropriate to express sexual desire for these healthy, red-blooded 40s Americans in exaggerated terms (Avery exaggerates to the point of surrealism), and to equate it with explosive power: she is "dynamite!", she is a "blonde bombshell." Doubtless it was in this spirit that technicians loading the fourth ever atomic bomb explosion stencilled onto its side the name GILDA, accompanied by a picture of Rita Hayworth in the film noir of that name that was current at the time.[11] The ravishing Hayworth is a force that none of the males in *Gilda* can control. The target was going to be bombed by a film noir heroine.

---

11   Operation Able took place at Bikini Atoll on July 1, 1946. Documentation of the Rita Hayworth labelling may be found at:
http://conelrad.blogspot.ca/2011/07/atomic-goddess-rita-hayworth-and-legend.html
http://conelrad.blogspot.ca/2013/08/atomic-goddess-revisited-rita-hayworths.html

**Figure 6.** **Gilda adorned with a photo of Rita Hayworth**

That test occurred at Bikini Atoll in 1946, and inspired the inventor of the women's two-piece bathing suit named it after that event, so that women's mostly-unclad bodies will forever be associated with the atomic bomb. This lighthearted representation of sexual appetite as "atomic" is, of course, entirely inappropriate for an event that caused the death of so many people, however characteristic it is of a boyish male devotion to cartoon-like representations of destruction.

This postwar world of sexual frankness is seen also in *Kiss Me Deadly*, where women are constantly throwing themselves at indifferent men, and one of Hammer's basic qualities is an indifference to anybody's appetite but his own. In this respect, he spends most of the movie as a very atypical noir protagonist, a figure of focus and certainty, only to fall headlong into powerlessness in the face of the incalculable destructive power of the box. The women in the film are equally atypical as stereotypes. None of them has a conventional character—perhaps the closest would be secretary Velda. Christina, this naked-under-her-trenchcoat woman running barefoot down the highway, develops a nice line in sarcasm with respect to Hammer's power masculinity, is summarily tortured to death, and of course contains the key to everything in more senses than one.

The most curious specimen is Gabrielle (who goes through most of the movie under the alias of Lily): she is an infantile creature who also spends a lot of time in a housecoat over nothing, and who speaks in a childlike singsong even as she is shooting people and blowing up the world. She is in Soberin's lexicon all too obviously Pandora, the female who looses every evil upon the world. In a sense Gabrielle is the last of all the film noir femmes fatales, the one who destroys not just the man and herself but the whole world. But the Gabrielle who destroys the world with the bomb now reinstitutes, at the end of the movie, the noir paradigm of the female who destabilizes everything, and creates an association between the apocalyptic destruction of nuclear weapons and the male sense of profound and threatening power of heterosexual attraction buried deep in the self.

It only remains to emphasize the fact that *Kiss Me Deadly*, for all its artiness in many respects, is a genre film—and that genre is not the genre of social problem movies. Contemporary viewers, or thoughtless ones today, would never see the film as having anything of interest to say on the subject of nuclear power. Heavy, serious movies like *Fail-Safe* and *On the Beach* clearly did so: they offered their viewers a straightforward picture of the dangers and consequences of nuclear war. On the other hand, the plethora of teen and drive-in movies in the science-fiction and horror genres could give some kind of expression to fears of the unimaginable consequences of atomic weapons, especially in the climate of open hysteria they both represented and embodied. *Kiss Me Deadly* is a deeper movie than any in either of these categories. Perhaps it has something in common with *Dr Strangelove*, which came along almost a decade later, in its murderous irony and ice-cold representation of catastrophe. But *Dr Strangelove* is essentially an art movie, not a genre movie. *Kiss Me Deadly*, instead, is another testament to the power of the most intelligent genre films to create implications and complexities without wearing their importance like a badge.

# "HIROSHIMA" IN FRANCE: FORGETTING "HIROSHIMA" TO ACCEPT FRENCH ULTRA-MODERNITY AND ITS NUCLEAR POLICIES.

*Chris Reyns-Chikuma*

## Introduction

Although France was America's ally during the Second World War and was directly affected by the Japanese invasion of its Indochinese colonies,[1] documented reactions from French intellectuals and ordinary citizens to the atomic bombings of Hiroshima and Nagasaki are scarce. This is peculiar considering the central role the atomic bombs played in ending the war in the Asian-Pacific theatre, where France held significant stakes (economic, territorial, etc.), defeating an ally of Nazi Germany, and therefore also in completely ending the war. Similarly, there are very few works of fiction dealing directly with "Hiroshima" in France.[2] One can say that "Hiroshima" is almost totally absent from French culture in general.

In this chapter, I will use the few examples of French fiction about "Hiroshima" available and put them in their French context in order to explain why "Hiroshima" is almost entirely absent from French collective memory.[3] After briefly identifying several general possible causes that explain this quasi-absence, including non-involvement in the bombings themselves, the Cold War, Eurocentrism and its various orientalist forms, French colonialism, and neo-colonialism, I will focus on three main factors. These three factors overlap and reinforce each other. The first is the traumatic centrality of "Auschwitz" in Europe and the Vichy syndrome in France, including the misinterpreted Adornian position; the second is De Gaulle's nuclear policy and its continuation by the French state until today, with its official and unofficial forms of censorship. Lastly, I will explore forms of self-

---

1   See Philippe Grandjean. *L'Indochine face au Japon.* Decoux-De Gaulle: un malentendu (Paris: L'Harmattan, 2004).
2   I will use "Hiroshima" with quotation marks to refer not to the city but to the bombing of both Hiroshima and Nagasaki and as a metaphor for the horror and the difficulty of its representation. Similarly, I will use "Auschwitz" with quotation marks referring to the extermination camps. Also, all translations into English are mine.
3   The concept of collective memory is complex, but I here use Pierre Nora's definition in "La Mémoire collective" in *La Nouvelle histoire*, Jacques Le Goff (Bruxelles: Ed. Complexe, 1978), 398–401.

censorship around nuclear power that seem to have prevailed in France until today. My argument is that if "Hiroshima" is a reminder of the horrible suffering that nuclear energy can cause, a nation as obsessed with maintaining its "grandeur" as France has been, first through colonization, then through modern technological advances, may deem it best to forget such a horrific event. Hence, one finds very few and ambivalent occurrences of fictions about "Hiroshima" in France. The scope of this chapter is limited only to France and to fiction and will cover the seventy years after the event.

Next to scientific reports, documentaries, and journalistic interviews, fictions that deal with catastrophic events like "Hiroshima" are key to understanding people's mentality. However, very quickly after 1945, some intellectuals opposed fiction as a relevant way to represent events such as "Hiroshima." For example, Theodor Adorno, a philosopher-sociologist and very influential intellectual during the post war period, wrote that "Poetic art after Auschwitz is a barbarity."[4] This statement has often been misinterpreted as a testament to the impossibility, futility, and immorality of writing fiction about "Auschwitz."

The same interpretation has also been applied to fiction about "Hiroshima": for example one of the points made in the French film *Hiroshima mon amour* (1959) is to affirm that "No fiction or even no representation can do justice to what happened in Hiroshima]."[5] Nevertheless, many artists, writers and executives in the culture industry (e.g., movie producers) disagreed with this conclusion for various reasons. The popularity of cultural productions on horrific historical events suggest that the demand for fiction about apocalyptic-like topics has been high. Of course, one might argue that this demand encourages the vulgarization and commodification of suffering.

Although it is justified to question the validity of these fictional representations, especially in some popular commercial forms, some researchers and intellectuals have shown that, even if limited in its real impact, fiction could also be a powerful tool with which to create and maintain useful debates about key topics. Similarly, in several of her acclaimed books,[6] Martha Nussbaum, points out the importance of the Humanities—including works of fiction—in inducing empathy.

---

4   See Elaine Martin, "Re-reading Adorno: The 'after-Auschwitz' Aporia," *Forum* 2 (Spring 2006): 1–13.
5   The question, although quite rhetorical in this case, has still been used in 2002 in a short article by controversial bestselling French author Michel Houellebecq, "Can one write science-fiction after Hiroshima? The Exit of 20th century literature" *NRF* 561 (April 2002): 117–121.
6   See *Cultivating Humanity* (1997) and *Not for Profit: Why Democracy needs humanities* (2010).

This empathy facilitates the understanding of Others' problems and suffering and of difficult issues. Furthermore, Communication Studies specialist Marc Lits shows how fiction continues to play a critical role in our lives:[7] in much the same way as did myths in ancient societies, fiction provides stories that help us make sense of chaotic realities. Consequently, it is important to discuss these omnipresent stories with their readers and viewers in order to jointly participate in necessary and democratic public debates about key issues such as nuclear power. Conversely, the absence of fiction on a given topic makes the possibility of the debate in broad public space less likely. It follows, then, that some lobbies would prevent publication of or condemn fiction that deals with controversial issues. The almost total absence of "Hiroshima" in French culture could be interpreted as such a form of censorship.

## Japan's Key Role in French Culture

Japan has had a strong impact on French culture. Initiated by 17th-century missionaries, who were fascinated by Japanese society and aesthetics, then propagated by exchanges between diplomats and scholars, this influence culminated with *Japonisme* in the 1880s. Although *Japonisme* was an international phenomenon, it was first and foremost French, permeating French culture and especially aesthetics in painting, literature, arts and crafts.[8] While this growing trend was stunted during the Second World War, Japanese influence quickly resurged after 1945. It began among other cultural products, namely Japanese films from Yasujiro Ozu and Kenji Mizoguchi,[9] as well as Shohei Imamura's *Black Rain* (1989) and Akira Kurosawa's *Dreams* (1991). The latter two films deal with "Hiroshima." This neo-japonist wave also included popular martial arts and yakuza movies and American interpretations of Japanese reactions to "Hiroshima." Ridley Scott's version of *Black Rain* (1989) is one such film.

The movement spread to literature, with the impact of 1968-Nobel prize-winning author Yasunari Kawabata, the French president's commitment to boost and support translations of Japanese literature into French in 1982, and Kenzaburo Oe's fame in France from the early seventies onwards, which culminated with his

---

7   Marc Lits "La médiation du politique ou le passage d'un espace public délibératif à un espace public symbolique narrative," *A Contrario*, Vol. 12, no. 2 (2009): 85–100.
8   On japonisme, see Jan Hokenson, *Japan, France, and East-West Aesthetics: French Literature, 1867–2000* (Madison, NJ: Fairleigh Dickinson University Press, 2004), and Chris Reyns-Chikuma, *Images du Japon en France et ailleurs: entre japonisme et multiculturalisme* (Paris: L'Harmattan, 2005).
9   Japanese names will be written in the Western order: first name first.

Nobel prize in 1994. Neo-japonism continued with manga (Japanese comics), which have been extremely popular in France since the late 1980s. Of course, "Hiroshima" played a key role in the Japanese collective memory, and in each of these media (movie, literature, manga), "Hiroshima" was a recurrent topic that should have been to some extent visible in France. Given that the neo-japonisme movement took place from about 1955 to 1995,[10] it is even more surprising that "Hiroshima" has had such little impact on French culture.

## Intellectual Reactions

On 8 August 1945, the headline of the centrist and well-known French newspaper *Le Monde* read "A Scientific Revolution: Americans launch their first atomic bomb on Japan." Fifty years later, French philosopher Alain Brossat wrote: "One cannot conceive of a more obvious inauguration, and to say it frankly, a more vulgar one, of what is going to interminably be the rule in the village France: the ignorance of Hiroshima in its dimension of a historical, political, and cultural catastrophe."[11] On the same day of 1945, Albert Camus, then an editorial writer for the leftist newspaper *Combat*, reacted vehemently against the many positive newspapers headlines declaring the victory of France's American ally. In his editorial, he wrote: "I will summarize what I think in one sentence: mechanical civilization just reached its last degree of barbarity."[12] However, after this strong condemnation there were no other clear references to "Hiroshima" in his writings while he addressed many other contemporary controversial issues directly and indirectly.[13] This absence of references in Camus' work is symptomatic of the French disinterest in "Hiroshima" and could be found in most French intellectuals' publications when these French intellectuals were still considered central pillars of public discourse not only in France but even worldwide.

---

10  Rafoni, 113–123.
11  "On ne saurait concevoir inauguration plus voyante, et pour tout dire vulgaire, de ce qui, dans le village France, va interminablement faire loi: la non-prise en considération de Hiroshima dans sa dimension de catastrophe historique, politique et culturelle" in Maya Morioka-Todeschini (Paris: Autrement, 1995), 217.
12  "Nous nous résumerons en une phrase: la civilisation mécanique vient de parvenir à son dernier degré de sauvagerie"; the editorial was reprinted in the leftist newspaper, *L'Humanité*, 5 August 2015, at: http://www.humanite.fr/albert-camus-sur-hiroshima-leditorial-de-combat-du-8-aout-1945-580990.
13  See la peste [the plague] as an allegory of Nazism in Camus' *La Peste* but also the absent voice of the colonized Arab in spite of the fact that it takes place in Oran, Algeria (see Kamel Daoud's postcolonial rewriting of the story of *L'Etranger* finally giving voice to the absent Arab).

## The French Movie *Hiroshima Mon Amour* (1959)

Many intellectuals, mostly on the left, opposed nuclear power and the nascent French policies on atomic research and testing. In 1957, this opposition had created an atmosphere that made the production of a French feature film entitled *Typhon sur Nagasaki* possible.[14] However, this first movie on the topic is less about "Hiroshima" than about a love story that fits within the Orientalist *Madame Butterfly* frame of mind.[15] It tells a very (stereo)typical romance about a French man who went to Japan and fell in love with a Japanese girl. To add to what was already an orientalist plot, the movie became even more entertaining and popular when his French ex-lover comes to visit. The orientalist perspective in this movie, understood as a way to portray the other in a stereotyped and inferior manner, prevents any empathy and understanding of issues related to "Hiroshima." Moreover, because the word "typhon" [typhoon] refers to a real typhoon that is central in this story, it supersedes the Nagasaki bombing, to which the film only alludes, hence replacing the human-made disaster by a natural one. One can see how the Nagasaki bombing is just a sideshow in this movie. Although successful then, *Typhoon over Nagasaki* is completely forgotten today in France and abroad.

In 1959, *Hiroshima mon amour*, a more sophisticated version of this type of orientalist love story, was released. This film is the most famous one about Hiroshima, in France and beyond, in spite of (or maybe because of) being avant-garde. It was made by film director Alain Resnais and novelist Marguerite Duras who both became internationally acclaimed artists after this film. Numerous articles, many academic, have reviewed and analyzed this film from many angles, the majority of which employed various theories of film studies and trauma studies.[16] However, the film has also been dismissed for its highbrow style and more recently, for alleged Orientalism. For example, Endymion Wilkinson, a British sinologist and diplomat, wrote in *Europe vs Japan*:

> At a slightly more highbrow level, take Resnais' Hiroshima mon amour (1959), an influential film, sometimes even picked as one of the ten best films of the

---

14   This movie was directed by French film director Yves Ciampi with some Japanese input in the writing, directing, and financing.
15   On Orientalism, see Edward Said's *Orientalism* (1978), and for Madame Butterfly as a typical example of Orientalism, see Jan Van Rij. *Madame Butterfly: Japonisme, Puccini, and the Search for the Real Cho-Cho-San* (New York: Stone Bridge Press, 2001).
16   Among the many studies on *Hiroshima mon amour*, see Nina Varsava, "Processions of trauma in Hiroshima mon amour: Towards an ethics of representation," *Studies in French Cinema* 11.2 (2011): 111–123.

century. The plot is little more than the chrysanthemum theme in modern clothing. The main difference is that the European having a passing affair in Japan is a woman, not a man. [...] [Riva] the heroine picks up a Japanese lover in Hiroshima, who in the best tradition of Loti's oriental love-objects, merely acts as a foil to Riva's moods.[17]

It is difficult to know precisely why Wilkinson is so dismissive about this movie,[18] but he rightly emphasized two of its weaknesses, which are rarely addressed by the film's fans: its Orientalist bias and its limited social and cultural impact beyond avant-garde circles. These two overlooked points confirm our hypothesis of the weak presence of "Hiroshima" in French culture.

The film received much attention in leftist and highbrow artistic circles. It was shown many times in French *cine-clubs*.[19] In addition, its influence in film circles is still visible today among the filmic elite with its Japanese "remake" *H-Story* (2001) by Nobuhiro Suwa. This movie uses *Hiroshima mon amour* as a subtext, and was also quite well received by French film critics.[20] However, its impact, although strong, is limited to a niche which is encapsulated in the French idiom also used to classify *Hiroshima mon amour*: "film culte" [cult film]. So, on the one hand, it is still present in French memory for two reasons. First, because it still is regarded as one of the most interesting films in terms of its innovative techniques, it is constantly presented as a masterpiece. Second, because it is a critique of the supposed objectivity of documentaries as a reliable way to represent horrors such as "Hiroshima," it reaffirms a point of view that remains common among many intellectuals, that is, that such horrors were ultimately un-representable. However, on the other hand, this type of critique shows that in spite of the movie's fame, its impact has to be relativized within a broad French culture. In effect, *Hiroshima mon amour* is a highbrow product more famous for its avant-garde style than its "Hiroshima" topic and with literally no impact on a broader general audience for whom the film is unknown, except maybe through its title.

Another critique might be even more justifiable. In spite of its title emphasizing "Hiroshima" and its main plot reversing the typical Orientalist topic (since

---

17  Wilkinson, *Europe vs Japan* (Tokyo: Chuokoron-sha, Inc, 1982), 84.
18  This dismissive opinion might be due to a typical British anti-French opinion and/or to an anti-avant-garde attitude.
19  The movie could be seen in a cine club as recently as 2016, see: http://www.cineclubdecaen.com/realisat/resnais/hiroshimamonamour.htm
20  Olivier Amour-Mayeur, "*H-story* ou pour une esthétique du 'remake relevant'" in *Orient(s) de Marguerite Duras*, ed. by Florence de Challonge (Amsterdam: Rodopi, 2014), 237–250.

it features a white Western woman seducing a Japanese man), the film is still Eurocentric by contemporary standards. Although the main story seems to be about "Hiroshima" and the impossibility of representing its horrors, the dialogue focuses more on French memories. For example, part of the film is about French "horizontal collaboration."[21] Although very briefly, it also alludes to the Japanese army as victimizer, as an imperialist power invading and mistreating some Asian countries (which it undeniably was). It therefore relativizes Japanese suffering in a movie that presents itself as essentially compassionate about "Hiroshima" agony. For these reasons, *Hiroshima mon amour* does not play the defining role that one might first think it would in French collective memory about "Hiroshima."

The script of *Hiroshima mon amour* was written by Marguerite Duras, a writer who became an icon of French culture over the next forty years. To what extent her birth in Indochina in 1914 had shaped her interest in the topic "Hiroshima" is difficult to evaluate. She wrote other fiction taking place in "Asia" such as *Un Barrage contre le Pacifique* (1950), *India Song* (1975), and *L'Amant* (1984; *The Lover*, 1986; made into a film, 1992). In fact, this last work provoked another debate around her "orientalism."[22] However, interestingly enough, apart from *Hiroshima mon amour*, "Hiroshima" is never mentioned in any of her other books or films. One can also conclude then that the topic was never central to her work or her devoted readers.

Similarly, Alain Resnais, the filmmaker of *Hiroshima mon amour*, never returned to a Japanese topic either. However, it is worth noting that two years before, Resnais had made a documentary entitled *Nuit et Brouillard* [Night and Fog] about "Auschwitz," which was partly censored in different ways.[23] Various forms of censorship were quite common in France at the time. As shown by Henry Rousso in *Le Syndrome de Vichy* (1987; *The Vichy Syndrome*, 1991), self-censorship was imposed in the late fifties where the specificity of the Holocaust (targeting first Jewish people) and the French state's collaboration with Nazism were concerned. General De Gaulle and the myth he successfully created about French "résistancialisme"

---

21 "Horizontal collaboration" is collaboration of a woman who accepted to sleep with a German soldier for whatever reason (food and/or love).
22 See for example Karen Ruddy, "The Ambivalence of Colonial Desire in Marguerite Duras' *The Lover*," *Feminist Review* 82 (2006): 76–95.
23 See Sylvie Lindeperg, *Nuit et brouillard, un film dans l'histoire* (Paris: Odile Jacobs, 2007); in that documentary, the first form of censorship is now readable since Resnais does not once mention the word "Jew." The second form is the fact that the government forced Resnais to cut a scene showing a French policeman taking part in the roundup of prisoners.

(i.e. almost all French resisted) were at the center of this censorship system.[24] Similar forms of censorship (the state and self) after De Gaulle's coming to power were applied to other topics such as nuclear issues, discussed hereafter.

## The Nuclear Centrality of De Gaulle's Policies

*Hiroshima mon amour* came out in 1959, which was also the year in which General De Gaulle returned to power after over ten years of absence. The political instability of the Fourth Republic (1946–58), which produced twenty-one administrations in twelve years, was over. The Fifth Republic he helped create (1959) became a semi-presidential system in which the president played a central, powerful role. De Gaulle strongly supported civil and military nuclear programs that he felt would return France to the status of a great power.[25] As early as 1960, the desert in Algeria was used for nuclear testing and French nuclear testing moved to France's Pacific territories after Algeria's independence in 1962. From this point onward, France quickly developed a potent state nuclear industry. In the 1970s, the program was further accelerated due to the oil shocks. To help demonstrate the impact of French nuclear power in France, it is noteworthy that nuclear scientists such as Marie Curie and some members of her family are presented as heroes in French popular fiction and in popular history books. This popularity culminated in 1999, when the Curies' ashes were transferred to the Pantheon.[26]

This pantheonization is one more example to illustrate how and why nuclear issues, including "Hiroshima," are rarely addressed in French culture and French fiction. On the one hand, from its beginning, the nuclear industry in France has been mostly a state business. On the other hand, until Giscard d'Estaing's more liberal presidency in 1974, the French state played a strong role in controlling and censoring part of the press and various media.[27] It is then hardly surprising that it is difficult to find fiction in various media on the nuclear industry since its very existence and the debates about its justification were mostly hushed up in the name of state security and job creation. Gabrielle Hecht writes that "Proportionally,

---

24   See Henri Rousso, *Le Syndrome de Vichy* (Paris: Seuil, 1987).
25   After the US and the USSR, Great Britain had just successfully tested its first atomic bomb in 1952.
26   See Mona Ozouf, "Le Panthéon," in *Lieux de mémoire*, t.1, ed. Pierre Nora (Paris: Seuil, 1984), 139–166.
27   For censorship in France, see for example Frédéric Hervé, *Censure et cinéma dans la France des Trente Glorieuses* [1945–1975] (Paris: Nouveau monde, 2015); for a broader discussion of the complexity of the concept and realities of censorship, see Helen Freshwater, "Towards a Redefinition of Censorship," in *Censorship and Cultural Regulation in Modern Age*, ed. Beate Müller (Amsterdam: Rodopi: 2004), 217–237.

France is now [1998] the world's largest producer of nuclear energy. It derives 75–80 percent of its electricity from nuclear power, and even exports electricity to neighboring European countries."[28] Over more than twenty years of "Gaullism" (1959–1981), state security was the main argument used to silence debates over nuclear topics. After De Gaulle's death (1971) and the enormous impact of the oil shocks that followed (the first in 1973), national energy independence, unemployment, and job creation replaced state censorship with self-censorship in a more liberal and globalized France.

## Fiction in Various Genres and Medias but Still None on "Hiroshima"

As shown by specialists of the genre, science fiction (sci-fi or SF) stories have often been a way to question nuclear policies.[29] However, in France, if sci-fi has a relatively strong tradition, very few works have addressed nuclear issues. For example, only a handful of stories deal with nuclear apocalypse and those that do use nuclear issues only as a backstory for a post-apocalyptic society rather than approach these issues directly. Such is the case of Robert Merle's *Malevil* (1972), a bestselling novel adapted for French TV in 1981. Similarly, although in the series of novels about *Madame Atomos,* published from 1964 to 1970 (and then as a comic book series until 1980), creator André Caroff does address nuclear issues, the impact of his series was limited since it was categorized as popular fiction, which was looked down upon by cultural gatekeepers (critics, teachers, etc.). Furthermore, and strangely enough, its villain, Madame Atomos, is the eponymous Japanese scientist looking for revenge for what happened in Hiroshima. Hence, the only reference to "Hiroshima" one could find in French SF is a negative (evil) Japanese character who, thirty years after the event, still cannot accept the fact that nuclear power helped defeat her country.

In a short article entitled "Nucléaire et télévision française" (1989 [Nuclear Issues and French Television]), Hélène Puiseux confirmed the limited interest in "Hiroshima" in the television world which has been a very popular media since the 1960s until recently:

---

28   Gabrielle Hecht, *The Radiance of France: Nuclear Power and National Identity after World War II* (Cambridge, Mass.: MIT Press, 1998), 328–329.
29   For example, a lot of superhero stories of the 1960s staged monsters produced by nuclear accidents or mad scientists trying to control nuclear power, see http://www.sf-encyclopedia.com/entry/nuclear_energy.

In February 1985, I wrote to the 3 television channels to ask how they planned to commemorate August 6th and 9th. The first one did not reply. Over the phone, the second told me that they would air a special program during their usual 'Dossiers de l'écran' [i.e., a film followed by a debate] and the third channel wrote in a letter that they had not planned anything.[30]

Similarly, in 1991, in an article entitled "La seconde guerre mondiale à la télévision française, actes du colloque 'Les Echos de la mémoire'" [WWII on French TV, proceedings of the colloquium 'Echoes of Memory'], Isabelle Veyrat-Masson (professor of history and specialist of French media), wrote:

> … but what about Hiroshima? To parody the most beautiful film on that topic [Hiroshima mon amour] 'I have seen nothing on Hiroshima on the French TV. Only one program, well done, by Jacques Nahum and Roger Stephane aired in 1961 (for 30 minutes in the middle of August [a month when half France was on vacation]) and an English program some years later settles the nuclear military issue'.[31]

One can thus conclude that there is no French TV fiction about "Hiroshima."

In contrast, *bande dessinée* (or BD, that is, French "comics") might have played a slightly more important role than other media in shaping French memory of "Hiroshima" and of nuclear issues. This might have been possible for two reasons. First, BD was a media that was not recognized as part of official or (high) culture until the mid-1980s. Second, it was mostly produced and considered entertainment for kids. Given its target readers, BD was not pressured to respond to topics such as nuclear issues in the same way that high culture products were.[32] Nevertheless, nuclear issues in general and "Hiroshima" in particular were very rarely addressed.

In an article published in 1989, French comics specialist, Jean-Louis Tilleuil, confirmed how belatedly French comics came to be interested in nuclear issues. Tilleuil only mentions one very early comic, *Le Secret de l'espadon* [*The Secret of the Swordfish*], which was published in three volumes in 1950.[33] However, this publication was before 1959 and published in Belgium, that is, outside the period of De

---

30  163; Puiseux, 1989, 163–167; in this special issue of *Cahiers du GRIF* dedicated to "L'Imaginaire du nucléaire", 4 articles out of 20 are written by French people (2 by Marguerite Duras).
31  "… mais qu'en est-il de Hiroshima? Pour parodier le plus beau film sur ce sujet: 'Je n'ai rien vu sur Hiroshima' à la télévision française. Une seule émission, très belle, de Jacques Nahum et de Roger Stephane diffusée en 1961 (trente minutes en plein mois d'août) et une émission anglaise quelques années plus tard règlent cette question et la question du nucléaire militaire," Veyrat-Masson, 1991, 161.
32  French comics were actually censored, like in many Western countries, for other reasons, such as "morality" (references to sexuality, divorce, …); see "On tue à chaque page!" La loi de 1949 sur les publications destinées à la jeunesse, coordonné par Thierry Crépin et Thierry Groensteen. Paris: Éd. du temps; Angoulême, Musée de la bande dessinée, 1999.
33  Translated in 1986 and republished in the US in 2013.

Gaulle's decisive support for nuclear policies and its government's efforts to control French culture. In 1967, there was also *Alerte atomique* [Atomic Warning], an adventure of the very popular pilot, Buck Danny. However, if the aforementioned BD could be sold and read in France within the larger context of the Franco-Belgian comics publication world, one has to remember that it was actually produced (created, published and printed) in Belgium where the contexts, both in the comics and in the nuclear worlds, were slightly different.[34] Finally, we have to mention that although many American comics, mainly through the superhero genre, addressed "atomic" issues,[35] for various reasons, they were never mainstream in France until fifteen years ago and mainly through American globalized blockbuster movies, which means outside the French government's and French lobbies' control.

## Translations of Fictions about "Hiroshima"

During the same fifteen years, the translation business grew considerably. In spite of language barriers and cultural pride, French culture is of course not impermeable to foreign influences. In fact, contrary to its stereotype of an excessively proud culture, France has one of the highest percentages of French translated foreign books in the world.[36] Therefore, one might assume that through globalization, numerous other non-French cultural products about "Hiroshima" would have influenced opinions about nuclear issues. In the 1940s–1950s, few people in France knew Japanese; therefore, English texts written by those who did not experience or witness the nuclear bombings were often translated more quickly than texts written by Japanese who had directly or indirectly lived through "Hiroshima."[37] Such was the case of *The Flowers of Hiroshima*, written in English by Swedish author Edita Morris in 1959 and translated into French in 1961. However, the degree of sentimentalism of such fiction is not without ethical problems, taking the reader away from the real issues (the horror itself and human responsibility).[38] If some Japanese fiction such as *Kuroi Ame* (1965; *Black Rain*, 1966, and *Pluie noire*, 1972) were translated slightly quicker than other Japanese texts (although still only seven

---

34  See "Nuclear energy in Belgium," by Sabine van Depoele & Benoît Lance, *Revue des Questions Scientifiques*, Vol. 172, Issue 2 (2001): 149–156.
35  See Szasz, *Atomic Comics*, 2013.
36  For numbers and trends in translations in France, see Sapiro, 2012.
37  For an extensive reflection on, and bibliography of works on "Hiroshima" written in Japanese, and their translation/s into English, see Treat, 1995.
38  For ethical problems about Hiroshima, see Darrell J. Fasching, *The Ethical Challenge of Auschwitz and Hiroshima: Apocalypse or Utopia* (Albany, NY: State University of New York Press, 1993).

years after the original!), many Japanese books were often translated with great delay and moreover printed in small numbers. For example, an anthology like *Pika Don* published in 1965 was translated as *Pika Don: la leçon de Hiroshima* only in 1985.[39]

Not until Kawabata received the Nobel Prize in literature in 1968 did the number and speed of translations of Japanese texts increase, even more so during the presidency of François Mitterrand (1981–1995). The books written by the radical opponent of nuclear power, Kenzaburo Oe, may have had the greatest impact on public opinion since his novels were well received in France. However, because of the challenging avant-garde aspect of his writing, his popularity was limited to small literary circles. Hence, *Hiroshima Nooto* published in 1965 was only printed in French in 1985 (*Notes d'Hiroshima*). Oe first gained notoriety when he received the Literary Nobel Prize in 1994, then rose to fame again in 1995, when a vicious debate about nuclear power erupted between him and a famous French writer in the national newspapers. Although rates of translations are relatively high in France compared to, for example, the United States, except for some bestsellers, the impact of translations is restricted in terms of sales numbers and the size of its reading audience. Hence, the impact of translations, mostly first of American books, and then of the few Japanese texts on "Hiroshima," was very limited.

## Translations of Mangas and Animes

By definition, popular cultures reach a much broader audience. Manga in France gained popularity from the mid-1980s onwards, beginning with *Akira*, a story set in a post-apocalyptic Tokyo. While the cause of the apocalypse is left unclear in this story, several clues hint at a nuclear catastrophe. *Akira* is part of a great number of Japanese mangas, animes, and films like *Godzilla* or *Japan Sinks*, which reflect what anthropologist-Nipponologist Susan Napier calls the "Japanese imagination of disaster."[40] However, while this fiction make sense in Japanese historical and political contexts in which "Hiroshima," tsunamis, and earthquakes, are major components of Japanese reality and imagination, they are less relevant in a French context since France never experienced such disasters. There is a lack of empirical studies that explain why French kids, teens and young adults like this catastrophic fiction and it is therefore difficult to explain their success in France. Yet, in her studies,

---

39  Also published by Autrement.
40  Napier, 2000, 193–218.

Napier shows how "orientalism" plays a role in this fascination with "things Japanese" beyond Japanese borders.[41]

For this particular type of apocalyptic fictions, fascination might also be explained by pure entertainment and enjoyment of sensationalism in general, and/or by concrete catharsis (release of mental tensions). However, if any fiction can be at least partly educational,[42] we must be skeptical about the teaching role and any empathetic impact these "Hiroshima" works have in the French context. Most French people would not know much, if anything, about Japanese society and history, and therefore would not be able to connect these regular and strong references to Japanese realities through Japanese popular fiction. As a counter example, the success of these catastrophic, more sensational works of fiction is countered by the failure of the French translation of the Keiji Nakazawa's contextualized realist story *Hadashi no Gen* [*Barefoot Gen*]. Originally published between 1972 and 1983, only portions of the series were combined and translated in 1983 by the comic book publisher Les Humanoïdes Associés under the title *Gen d'Hiroshima*. It was a commercial failure. A new attempt at marketing the series was made in 1990, under the problematic title *Mourir pour le Japon* [To Die for Japan]. This time, the work was distributed by a larger mainstream publisher, Albin Michel. It was also released during the graphic novel movement, which favored such serious fictions, but still failed.[43]

## Tourism and Dark Tourism

As shown by sociologists of tourism like Jean-Michel Decroly and Saskia Cousin,[44] variants of tourism, such as educational or heritage tourism, are another way to heighten public awareness of foreign and, subsequently, domestic issues. Visits to Hiroshima could be part of this awareness about nuclear issues. This had already been represented in the film *Hiroshima mon amour* with a critical perspective of the role of the Hiroshima museum, but, as we have seen, with a very limited impact

---

41   Ibid, 239–256.
42   For more about informal learning, see Fabienne Thomas (dir.), *Recherches en communication* 15 (2001): 11–17.
43   The reason for that failure is not clear. Manga and anime were criticized in the 1980s–90s for their violence. Hence, Jean-Marie Bouissou, japonologist, writes: "story […] whose graphic violence repulsed the Western audience" (online). A third attempt was made in 2007.
44   Jean-Michel Decroly, et al, *Tourisme et société: mutations, enjeux, et défis* (Brussels: Editions de Université de Bruxelles, 2006), and Saskia Cousin and Bertrand Reau, *Sociologie du tourisme* (Paris: La Decouverte, 2009).

on the general population. The number of French tourists who visit Japan is relatively very high. Yet it is still not significant compared to the overall French population. These tourists quite often include Hiroshima in their tour among the few other sites they visit (after Tokyo, Kyoto, etc.) sometimes referred to as "dark tourism," that is, a tourism of sites associated with dark events such as war, genocide, assassination, etc.[45] However, even if there are few empirical studies of this type of tourism, one can be skeptical about the ambivalent motivations for visiting such sites and their lasting educational effects.[46]

## Late Recurrences Due to Nuclear "Accidents"

There have been several nuclear "accidents" in France, and in places close enough to affect it directly, the most infamous one being Chernobyl (1986). One might think that these nuclear accidents would have revived various types of activism against nuclear power, and then would also have been reflected in debates and in works of fiction. However, except for anti-nuclear movements which are notoriously weak in France in terms of size and impact (compared to the German ones for example), very few fictional accounts have dealt with nuclear issues, even after Chernobyl. Radical leftist and feminist Chantal Montellier created a challenging alternative bande dessinée interestingly entitled *Tchernobyl mon amour* (2006; as a reference to the previously reviewed fiction entitled *Hiroshima mon amour*). Yet again, this bande dessinée had a very limited impact since it was an alternative type of BD and not a mainstream publication. It does not seem to have inspired more of such fiction on nuclear issues, certainly not in the mainstream field. So, one can see that even in a field such as French comics that is less subject to [self-]censorship for these issues, nuclear topics including "Hiroshima" are almost totally absent. This brings us to a complementary explanation for the lack of "Hiroshima" in French culture.

## Beyond "Censorship from Above"

I have already mentioned some factors which played a role in this quasi-absence, such as De Gaulle's nuclear policy, the French state industry and their explicit and

---

45   For a critical overview of the topic with multiple references to Hiroshima and Nagasaki, see J. John Lennon and Malcolm Foley, *Dark Tourism: The Attraction of Death and Disaster* (London: Intl Thomson Business Pre, 2000).
46   There are no studies on French tourists in Hiroshima but a study of this type of tourism in Auschwitz leaves humanists skeptical, see Hodgkinson, 2013, 22–32.

implicit censorship. However, as emphasized by Michel Foucault, censorship from above no longer justifies the absence of a topic, especially in liberal democracies, and even more so with the advent of social media.[47] We therefore have to look for other factors. To this primary Gaullist cause, it is important to include Nazi concentration camps as a central metaphor for human horror in France. "Auschwitz" plays in Europe a similar role that "Hiroshima" plays in Japan. Hence, the "Auschwitz" trope plays the central role for questioning but also screening and selecting memories. As shown by Henry Rousso in *Le Syndrome de Vichy* (1987; *The Vichy Syndrome*, 1991), issues such as the French state's involvement in the Holocaust, and specific targeting of groups such as Jewish people, were quasi-absent from cultural representations and popular memories from at least 1959 until 1973. This is the same period, as seen above, that under the Gaullist regime, strong nuclear policies and its accompanying discourse-quasi-propaganda supporting them were implemented, and consequently, its tendency to silence any opposition to them. Following that era, "Auschwitz" took center stage for the next fifteen years.[48] In the 1990s, newly discussed traumas relating to French colonization displaced Holocaust fiction. Once again, little room was left for "Hiroshima" in French cultural representations.[49]

On top of this "Auschwitz" central factor, one has to consider how much nuclear power in France has become a key part not only of the French economy but also of French identity. This is remarkably shown by Gabrielle Hecht in *The Radiance of France: Nuclear Power and National Identity* (1998). In her book, Hecht traces "the multiple links between technological prowess and national identity."[50] To demonstrate how this connection between nuclear power and identity in France is strong I will give two different examples: one involving a French intellectual, the other, ordinary citizens working in or around a power plant.

In 1994, Kenzaburo Oe received the Nobel Prize in literature which enabled him to speak out as an intellectual on a large international public forum for at least a year. Among other intellectual commitments,[51] Oe was a radical anti-nuclear activist and on several occasions he criticized France's nuclear testing in the Pacific. In 1995, Oe refused to attend a conference in France, in protest against these

---

47  See Freshwater, "Towards a Redefinition of Censorship," 217–237.
48  See also Brossat, 1995, 217–233.
49  See Jan Jansen, "Politics of Remembrance, Colonialism and the Algerian War of Independence in France," in M. Pakier and Bo Strath (New York: Berghahn Books, 2010), 275–293.
50  See Hecht, 1998, 3.
51  For Oe as a committed intellectual, see Michiko Wilson, *The Marginal World of Oe Kenzaburo* (New York: M.E. Sharpe, Inc., 1986) 8–9.

French nuclear tests. In response, French writer Claude Simon, who had received the same prize in 1984 and was also known for his liberal positions, wrote a rather harsh critique of Oe in the newspaper *Le Monde* on September 21. In "Uses of Aesthetics after Orientalism," Japanese intellectual Karatani Kojin commented on the debate between these two intellectuals as follows:

> Simon recalled his experiences during the German occupation of World War II and insisted that nuclear weapons and tests were necessary to protect France from future invasions. What is remarkable, however, was that he invoked Japan's past—its invasion of Asia—to refute Oe. Furthermore, making this argument, Simon totally omitted reference to France's own past, to its colonization of many regions of the world before World War II, and especially to the fact that the nuclear testing took place near a particular island of the south pacific that is a vestige of its colonial past. But even more noteworthy was a twist in his reasoning: at the same time as he reproached Japan for its past invasion of Asia, Simon did not neglect to add that he was moved by Japanese calligraphy.[52]

Beyond Simon's shocking criticism of an honest intellectual like Oe who is also known for his anti-imperialist positions in his essays, fictions and public discourses,[53] Karatani's criticism is interesting for two reasons. On the one hand, it shows how sensitive and even taboo the subject of nuclear power still was in France in 1995, and how it was felt even by critical intellectuals as part of the discourse on security and identity in France. On the other hand, it shows how prevalent orientalism still was in France in 1995. It therefore partly explains why many French intellectuals would have had such a hard time integrating an empathetic perspective on "Hiroshima" and a less Eurocentric position in spite of its humanist-universalist claims. Such a sampled reaction helps to understand the absence of "Hiroshima," which was not only an event that was far away geographically and empathically from French concerns but one that was also working against French imagination as reconstructed around nuclear power.[54]

Coincidentally, in 1995, and without any direct connection to this debate between these two intellectuals, an anthology of seventeen texts from various authors entitled, *Hiroshima, 50 ans: Japon-Amérique: Mémoires au nucléaire* [Hiroshima, 50 years: Japan-US: nuclear memories], was published by Autrement, which was

---

52   Karatani Kojin, "Uses of Aesthetics after Orientalism," *Boundary 2* 25.2 (1998): 145–160.
53   Oe is certainly an honest and courageous intellectual who several times has criticized Japanese imperialist positions during and after the Second World War. See, for example, Michele Mason, "Seventeen's Battle with the Cult of Masculinity: Reading Ōe Kenzaburō's 1960s Critique of Rightist Resurgence in the Age of Abe," *Asia-Pacific Journal* 15.4 (2017): 4.
54   Again, see Brossat's "Si loin, si près: Hiroshima et Auschwitz," cited above.

at that time a socialist-reformist publisher.[55] Notably by not mentioning France in these "nuclear memories," the title is very explicit about France's non-involvement: it emphasizes that it is a matter between Japan and the United States. The book, however, contains several chapters by French authors and about French nuclear issues. For example, there is a chapter entitled "La Hague: le nucléaire au quotidien,"[56] which is relevant to our thesis. Its author, Françoise Zonabend, a professor of ethnography in Paris, applies ethnography (a "science" traditionally reserved for the study of the others/Other) to a French small peninsula called La Hague in Normandy. She describes this piece of land as a place where "are gathered all possible types of nuclear factories—a nuclear reprocessing plant, a nuclear power station, a factory producing nuclear submarines, and a center where to stock nuclear waste" (196–197).

Zonabend starts by reminding us that France is one of the nations with the highest density of nuclear power plants. She then concludes: "To live with the nuclear, one has to forget it and the best way to do so is not to talk about it" (199). This might explain why even after State censorship was weakened, especially after De Gaulle's death (1971),[57] the economic lobby censorship (led to some degree by French-state partly-owned nuclear companies like EDF and Areva), another type of censorship is now partly replacing the previous one. This more recent type is also typical of a democratic system but not yet well researched. As explained by Michel Foucault, while speaking on other topics, this is not a top-down censorship but one coming from each citizen's interest. In a country where the Gaullist state has disappeared and France's grandeur is challenged by an increasingly globalized and "flat world," either positively (by the European Union) or negatively (with unemployment being one of the biggest and uninterrupted issues since 1973), some topics have become, if not taboos, very sensitive matters. In this context of nuclear issues, "Hiroshima" is a good example of these tabooed subjects in France.

---

55  *Autrement* (it could be translated as: otherwise, in other ways) was first a magazine created in 1975 that would become a full publisher in 1985, then http://www.lexpress.fr/informations/celui-qui-edite-autrement_641736.html; the same year of the 50<sup>th</sup> anniversary, other books were published such as Béatrice Failles, *Hiroshima oublié* but without any critical perspective.
56  This chapter is an excerpt of a book published in 1989 entitled *La Presqu'île au nucléaire* [The Nuclear Peninsula].
57  See William Broad, "Hydrogen Bomb's Physicist's Book Runs Afoul of Energy Dept," *The New York Times*, 23 March 2015.

## Conclusion

It is difficult to evaluate "Hiroshima"'s impact in France with qualitative and quantitative precision. The few works of fiction analyzed above played a role in the French representation of Japan, but not enough to make up for the quasi absence of "Hiroshima" in French collective memory. Moreover, one can see also how French culture was until recently split between its high culture productions and low culture products (SF and other genres, French comics, manga, popular movies, etc.). If some high cultural products dealt with "Hiroshima" (like *Hiroshima mon amour*), they were limited in their impact; if they were popular, they were not included in the official process of memorization and therefore more susceptible to be forgotten. Furthermore, notwithstanding the importance of Japan, Japanese culture, and the nuclear industry in France, quantitative studies integrating all types of media (songs, radio plays, etc.) would show that almost nothing about "Hiroshima" survives in contemporary French culture. It seems that French collective memory, like any memory, is selective, and has "chosen" to silence and/or erase "Hiroshima" and nuclear issues.

However, "Hiroshima" could have been part of collective memory without being memorialized because of the lack of recognition by official French institutions. As argued by Sonja Kmec and Benoit Marjerus in "Methodologie et interdisciplinarité," *lieux de mémoire* [memory sites] exist also outside official *Lieux de mémoire*.[58] But letting "Hiroshima" enter or stay in French collective memory would probably have provided opponents of the nuclear industry stronger arguments in favor of their cause. Huge debates would have erupted and complex problems concerning energy independence, national security and unemployment would have arisen. Hence, all (government, technocrats and the large majority of ordinary citizens) seemed to have agreed that it might be better to forget about "Hiroshima."

Each government involved in building and maintaining nuclear plants on its own territory has its own way to hush fears about and opposition to nuclear energy. Daniel Aldrich (Professor of Political Science at Purdue University) showed in an article entitled "With a Mighty Hand," that even in a country where nuclear disasters happened at least three times (Hiroshima, Nagasaki, and Fukushima, the Japanese government influences and manipulates the way in which the

---

58   In Kmec and al. (eds), *Dépasser le cadre national des 'lieux de mémoire': innovations méthodologiques, approaches comparatives, lectures transnationales* (New York: Peter Lang, 2009), 25–31.

risks of commercial nuclear power are portrayed.[59] In spite of a strong anti-nuclear movement in Japan, most Japanese citizens seem to accept nuclear energy and its "accidents" as inevitable.

Most recently in France, a few books such as *Pourquoi Hiroshima? La décision d'utiliser la bombe atomique* [Why Hiroshima? The decision to use the atomic bomb] have used the case of "Hiroshima" to question the ethics of using nuclear weapons in war. These works have not, however, critically evaluated nuclear power as a commercial energy source. "Fukushima" (2011) does not seem to have changed anything in France around nuclear taboos in popular debates and fictional representations, or, for that matter, in Japan.

---

59   Not counting "incidents" like the 1954-Lucky Dragon ship one; Daniel Aldrich writes: "power companies have often targeted rural, depopulated coastal communities, where the population of local fishermen are declining. […] The government has created an extensive framework of policy instruments to manage and dampen anti-nuclear contestation. […] for example, students in Japanese middle schools may take science courses emphasizing the safety and necessity of nuclear power plants, with curricula written by government bureaucrats rather than teachers," in "With a Mighty Hand" in *The New Republic*, 18 March 2011.

# 4. Memoirs and Medicine: Japan, Ukraine, USA

# MY PATH FROM HIROSHIMA TO HOUSTON

*Ritsuko Komaki*

## Introduction

How did I, a Japanese woman raised in Hiroshima, come to be a radiation oncologist in the United States? My decision to become a cancer researcher and physician was made very early in my life, through my experiences with my family in Hiroshima and with one of my best friends, Sadako Sasaki, who died of acute granulocytic leukemia at the age of eleven after having survived exposure to atomic bomb radiation. I knew that I wanted to be a leukemia researcher or physician so that I would be able to help those with illnesses like hers in the future. Today, I am a Professor of Radiation Oncology at MD Anderson Cancer Center in Houston, Texas, and treat patients with thoracic malignancies. My interests include clinical trials, multidisciplinary treatment, normal tissue toxicities, and translational research.

## Family Background

My parents and their experiences greatly influenced my childhood and later my choice of career. Both of my parents were born and raised in Hiroshima. My father, Isao Udea, was the youngest of seven children. His family owned a Sake Brewery on one of the small islands near Hiroshima. My grandfather died when my father was ten years old, and his oldest brother had assumed leadership of the family business. When a typhoon hit the Inland Sea,[1] the family-owned ship carrying Sake barrels sunk, leaving the business and the family bankrupt and with no insurance coverage. Thus, at the age of thirteen, my father had to work delivering Sake bottles for his oldest brother's new liquor store in Hiroshima.

    My father decided to take a scholarship at the Hiroshima University School of Education. This meant that he had to commit to teach 7- to 12-year-old children in a small village for four years after completing his education. He later described that period as the most boring time of his life, but although he developed a peptic ulcer he was also able to save money and to pass the entrance examination for admission to Kyoto University, where he majored in Economics.

---

[1] The Seto Inland Sea (often shorted to the Inland Sea) is a body of water in southern Japan framed by Honshu, Shikoku, and Kyushu.

After he graduated, my father married my mother and went to work in Osaka, a city approximately 250 miles northeast of Hiroshima and then, as now, the second largest city in Japan (after Tokyo). Our family home was in Amagasaki City, near Osaka. My father was working at Hanshin, a highly prestigious company in Osaka, on 6 August 1945, when the atomic bomb was dropped on Hiroshima at 8:15 am. The following day, he went to Hiroshima to look for members of his and my mother's family, where he was exposed to "black rain" containing high doses of radiation. Although we lost many family members, and others became very ill from the radiation effects, some managed to survive the exposure. If we had been in Hiroshima at the time, none of us would have survived.

At that time, my father decided to move the family back to Hiroshima to help his and my mother's families, and he found work in the Hiroshima Bank. One of my most vivid memories from those days was that every time my father was promoted to various satellites of the bank, we had to move to a different city. I had to change schools four times while I was still in elementary school, although I never complained. When we moved to Matsuyama, a small city on Shikoku Island, my classmates used to laugh at my Hiroshima accent when my teacher asked me to read aloud from the textbook. This made me furious.

My father's job kept him very busy; banks then courted new clients by entertaining them after 6 pm, so he routinely came home very late at night. I only saw him on Sundays; I always missed him and was puzzled by the Japanese work system. Although he was the leader of the bankers' union, he eventually retired at age 55 when he was not promoted to a senior position in the Hiroshima Bank. He eventually died of disseminated bladder cancer at age 72, possibly from his exposure to the atomic bomb radiation and probably from his tobacco smoking. He smoked one to two packs per day of Peace, a Japanese cigarette brand, for at least forty years.

My father was a very hard-working man, but he was deeply disappointed by his first child's (and only son's) incurable illness, and was very distant from his three daughters. Because my father was so remote, I always felt that his daughters did not mean much to him, and I wished that I had been born a boy so that I could have fulfilled his desire for a son.

**Figure 1.** Isao Ueda and Yukiko Obata Ueda, parents of Ritsuko Komaki

My mother's background was quite different from my father's. My mother, Yukiko Obata, was the oldest daughter of an old samurai family. Her father, my grandfather, graduated from Tokyo University and was once an officer at the Ministry of Agriculture in Japan. Upon his retirement, he served as a secretary to Mr. Asano Nagakoto, a *daimyo* of the Hiroshima Prefecture. My grandparents had a huge samurai house with several maids and secretaries to serve them. My grandmother was my grandfather's second wife; after he had lost his first wife to tuberculosis, he decided he wanted to marry "the strongest woman in town." A striking woman, my grandmother was six feet tall, with red hair and fair skin, and everyone said that she must have had "Russian blood." Men found her imposing height intimidating, and she had not previously found a husband because men considered her "too tall to marry." But marry my grandparents did. My grandmother was at the bomb's epicenter in Hiroshima. Although she suffered every side effect of atomic bomb radiation, she survived the exposure and never developed leukemia or any other kind of cancer. She died at age 72 of Alzheimer's Disease and severe osteoporosis.

So, when my father graduated from Kyoto University, he and my mother were married by arrangement, by *omiai* (matchmaking). My mother was amazingly well read; her father's position allowed her access to a huge library, with hundreds of books on European and Asian history. By the age of seven, my mother had read almost all of them. She read many Chinese and Russian history books and all twelve volumes of Pearl Buck's "Big Earth," about China. She had memorized the genealogies of European royalty and the history of the Chinese dynasty when she was still a child. Unfortunately, this incredible knowledge of world history did not help to support her family when the atomic bomb destroyed everything. But she maintained her passion for reading, especially history, for the rest of her life.

My mother was a very strong and prideful person. She lived in fear of what would happen to her and her children if my father was called away to fight in World War II, and she encouraged her daughters to become capable women who could support the family in case anything should happen to their husbands. She was also very kind; the only affection I remember receiving as a child was from her. (My father did not show affection to his wife or children by kissing or hugging, as was typical of Japanese men at that time.) My mother, however, always hugged me when I did well in school. She was also extremely kind to those less fortunate. She told me to give my extra pencils and notebooks to some of my classmates who were orphaned after the atomic bomb or to those whose fathers had died in the war. For her entire life, my mother loved to cook for us and to compose Haiku (Japanese poems). After my father died and she traveled with my husband and I, her knowledge of European and Japanese history and her ability to compose beautiful Haiku amazed us continuously. My mother died of stomach cancer at the age of 80. I still miss her very much.

My brother and sisters and I felt very lucky because my parents loved us and supported us in all our dreams and aspirations. My mother in particular, despite her encyclopaedic knowledge of world history, would tell us how very difficult it was to get a job with the kind of knowledge she had. She really wanted her daughters to have more technical skills. I think part of the reason my father wanted me to become a doctor was because he had wanted to become one, too, but could not afford to attend medical school. His next oldest brother, only a year older, became a physician because he was adopted by a doctor's family. My father always envied him and wanted one of his own children to be a physician. My father had only one son, who was the oldest of his four children, but that son, as noted, became ill with hepatitis and died young. Hence, I am the middle of my parents' three surviving children: my older sister is a veterinarian, I am a physician, and my younger sister is a pharmacist.

## Childhood in Hiroshima

My parents decided to return to Hiroshima to care for my grandmother and my mother's younger sister, who had survived the bombing, when I was four years old. I was raised in Hiroshima. It was so important for all of us to focus on doing something positive during this awful time of death and disaster. About 75,000 people died immediately after the atomic bombing, while another 75,000 died within about three months. Still more died thereafter, especially babies or young children who had been exposed to lower-dose radiation from the bomb and developed leukemia years later. Women who were in their first or second trimester of pregnancy at the time of the bombing generally experienced miscarriage or premature delivery; those in their third trimester who were relatively close to the epicenter had babies with microcephaly. Still others developed thyroid cancer, breast cancer, stomach cancer, or multiple myeloma. It kept going on and on, the awful sequelae of the atomic bomb.

In my own family, one of my cousins died of leukemia due to radiation exposure. My grandmother had already lost her husband, my grandfather, to asthma and then lost her large house and so much of her family after the bombing. At that time, there was no paperwork or other documentation of homeownership, so my grandmother ended up in a very small house just outside of Hiroshima. My grandmother was very bitter about not having enough space in which to live and not enough food to eat. My parents told me, though, that the only thing they could give me was education, and that I should focus on that and look to the future.

## Meeting Sadako

I met my friend Sadako Sasaki in the Nobori-Cho Elementary School in Hiroshima when we were both ten years old and in the fifth grade. Although Sadako and I were the same age, we were in different classes, and we competed in running events in the fall athletic meet. Sadako was very fast, and I had a hard time keeping up with her.

**Figure 2.** **Ritsuko and Sadako, running mates**

Sadako had been exposed to radiation from the atomic bomb when she was two years old. She eventually developed shortness of breath and anemia, and was diagnosed with leukemia when she was ten years old. She was hospitalized and died of leukemia nine months after her diagnosis. Before she became ill, she had registered to attend Nobori-Cho Junior High School; sadly, she did not live long enough to do so. While Sadako was hospitalized, she attempted to fold 1,000 origami cranes. In Japan, the crane is a symbol of longevity and happiness. It is said that if you can fold 1,000 cranes, you can recover from illness. So Sadako would take her medication, which came wrapped in waxed paper, and then fold that paper into origami cranes. Sadako wanted to live! However, despite prayers from her family, and help from her friends to fold cranes, she passed away at the age of 11.

When Sadako died, my classmates wanted to memorialize her, but we had little idea of what to do. I was so moved by her death, and I thought, "we should never forget what she had to go through." By that time, I had seen so many children who had lost their parents, their siblings, and their homes. I felt very blessed to still have my parents, and my sisters, and my brother. I also remember thinking I wanted to make sure that people did not forget Sadako, and that that they would never forget this horrible disaster of atomic catastrophe.

Two years after her death, I became the student president of the Nobori-Cho Junior High School, the same school in which Sadako enrolled but never attended. I began corresponding with Sadako's older brother, and we started making plans to build a memorial statue for her. We wrote many letters to deans of schools in Japan asking for donations for in her memory. We decided to go gather donations from Hiroshima's citizens. Even though everyone at the time was struggling to survive—no one had enough food or room to live—people were still so touched that they donated what little they could. It is still amazing to me that within two years, we—just children ourselves—had collected enough to build the statue.

**Figure 3.** **Asking for donations in Hiroshima for a statue to commemorate Sadako Sasaki**

We also engaged a young man, Mr. Kawamoto, to help us gather a public educational film-making group to create "Sadako's Story." This later became a hit film, "One Thousand Cranes," which was shown in many movie theaters. Within two years, we had collected enough funds to hire an architect to create a statue, "Atomic Bomb Children," to commemorate Sadako and the thousands of other child victims of the atomic bombing. This ten-foot statue is located in the Peace Memorial Park in Hiroshima, at the bomb's epicentre. Sadako stands atop a stylized bomb shell, holding a large crane in her raised arms, praying for world peace.

**Figure 4.** Ritsuko Komaki standing in front of the Atomic Bomb Children statue, or Children's Peace Monument, in Hiroshima Peace Memorial Park, in 1980

Sadako's death had a profound influence on me. Although I was very sad, I also came to realize that I now had a mission: to make sure that her death would not be forgotten and to send a message to younger generations that atomic war should never happen again.

Following my parents' exhortations to focus on education and look to the future, I began thinking about college and medical school. I was deeply curious about the effects of radiation on people, since my grandmother had been in Hiroshima when the bomb was dropped. In fact, her house had collapsed due to the "suction effects" from the bomb. She had been trapped underneath her house but was rescued from the ruins and taken outside the city. In the next few months, she experienced every side effect of total-body radiation, hair loss, severe diarrhoea, anorexia, and bone marrow suppression. However, she recovered from these effects and lived a near normal life without developing leukemia or any malignancy. Why did my grandmother, who had been exposed to total body radiation in Hiroshima, never develop leukemia, but Sadako did? Why were some people seemingly more susceptible to radiation, and some less so?

My parents encouraged me to find answers to these and many other questions. Understandably, they wanted me to stay close to home. After I finished my secondary schooling, I began a six-year program at Hiroshima University's School of Medicine.

## School and Medical Training

During the summers when I was a medical student, I volunteered to work at the Atomic Bomb Casualty Commission, a research institute originally supported by the United States to investigate the effects of immediate and long-term radiation. They studied people who were exposed when the bomb was dropped, people like my father and grandmother, and people who came to Hiroshima afterwards, like my younger sister, who has now been living in Hiroshima for nearly sixty years. The Atomic Bomb Casualty Commission has since been renamed the Radiation Effects Research Foundation, and its research is supported by both Japan and the United States. It has close ties with the National Council of Radiation Protection in Washington, DC.

During my time in medical school, I also became interested in new research on the causes and effects of chromosomal abnormalities. But at that point, my studies took an unexpected turn. After I graduated from medical school, Japanese medical students and interns staged a walk-out to demand for a better medical system and to be paid during our first postgraduate year. This walk-out effectively closed forty-seven university hospitals. If no university hospitals were open, my postgraduate education would have to take place somewhere else—so I signed on for a one-year internship at the Radiation Effects Research Foundation. At the end of that year, the Chair of the Foundation's Radiology department, Dr. Walter Russell, recommended that I move to the United States to continue my postgraduate education. And that's how I found myself in Milwaukee, at the Medical College of Wisconsin, in 1970.

## Postgraduate Training and the Medical College of Milwaukee

In Milwaukee, I began a general internship at St. Mary's Hospital and then completed a one-year fellowship in hematology/oncology at the Wood Veterans Administration Hospital. During my fellowship, however, I became interested in radiation oncology, when I saw that some of the patients who received radiation therapy for cancer of the larynx had been cured. I thought, "wow, as long as the cancer is in an early stage and confined to a certain area, radiation can actually cure cancer." This was truly a counterintuitive thought for someone raised in Hiroshima. Many Japanese people still ask me how I could possibly be a radiation oncologist after the devastation wrought by atomic bomb radiation in Japan.

But I was coming to think this seeming dichotomy as being a matter of balance. Radiation, like chemotherapy, can kill people when used the wrong way. When used properly, radiation and chemotherapy can help cure cancer. So, everything we use, and how we use it, must be in balance. This was, and has been, a guiding principle throughout my life.

At that point, I decided to become a radiation oncologist and spent the next four years in the radiation oncology residency program at the Medical College of Wisconsin. When I finished my residency in 1979, I went to MD Anderson Cancer Center in Houston to do a fellowship in gynaecologic oncology with Dr. Gilbert Fletcher, who was then Chair of the Department of Radiotherapy, as it was known at the time. I was deeply impressed with MD Anderson, the way everyone works together—surgeons, medical oncologists, and radiation oncologists—to consider a patient's best treatment. After my fellowship at MD Anderson, I returned to the Medical College of Wisconsin as an Assistant Professor, where I married another radiation oncologist, James D. Cox, M.D., in 1980. In 1985, after having been at the Medical College of Wisconsin for fourteen years, I accompanied my husband to Columbia University in New York, where we stayed for three years before returning to MD Anderson, where we have been ever since.

## Columbia Presbyterian Medical Center

I was given the tempting opportunity to work with Dr. Eric Hall, a renowned expert on the biological effects of radiation on humans. With kind and persistent recruitment efforts from Dr. Chu Chang, Jim and I went to Columbia Presbyterian Medical Center in 1985, he as Chair of a new Department of Radiation Oncology and myself as clinical chief and Associate Professor of Radiation Oncology. The last medical department created at Columbia, anaesthesiology, was created forty years earlier. Establishing a new department, from the ground up, was quite a challenge. While Jim worked to develop and implement an infrastructure for clinical trials and a strong research program, I treated many patients with breast, gynecologic, and lung cancer. I introduced conservative surgery followed by radiotherapy for early-stage breast cancer, which was not routine at Columbia at that time. Three years later, when MD Anderson offered Jim a position as Vice President of Patient Care and Physician-in-Chief and myself a position as an Associate Professor and section chief of thoracic radiation oncology, we decided to return to Houston, where we have been ever since.

## The University of Texas MD Anderson Cancer Center

Our years at MD Anderson have been enormously productive, as well as personally and professionally satisfying for us both. Jim accepted the position of Division Head in Radiation Oncology when Dr. Lester Peters, the previous Head, returned to Australia. I have had the privilege of working with many luminaries in the field, including Dr. Elizabeth Travis, who taught me so much about the biological basis for radiation pneumonitis; Dr. Kie-Kian Ang, on the importance of radiation timing and fractionation for head and neck cancer, and later the transformative discovery of biomarkers such as human papillomavirus status; and Drs. Luka Milas and Ray Meyn, on the importance of fundamental cancer biology and translational research, bringing discoveries from the laboratory bench to the bedside and back again. I have been privileged to indulge my passions for teaching, patient care, and research, and to be able to share the knowledge I have gained with my patients and trainees around the world.

Professionally, I am proud of being awarded a Distinguished Endowed Professorship in 1998. With fondness, I reflect on my time as President of the American Association of Woman Radiologists in 2001. I was the first radiation oncologist to hold this position. I am also proud to have received the Marie Sklodowska-Curie Award from the American Association of Women Radiologists and the Society in Tribute to Marie Sklodowska-Curie in Warsaw in 2005. Growing up, Marie Curie was my role model. I read her story many times, about how she studied in Poland and then in Paris when she was only twenty-four, and became an incredibly well recognized scientist and professor in France. Her journey was surely difficult, but she persisted. And persistence is so very, very important in life. I have received many awards and gold medals for my work in the years since then, but the Marie Sklodowska-Curie Award still holds a special place in my heart.

## Proton Therapy Center—Houston

In 2006, we realized another major milestone—opening the MD Anderson Proton Therapy Center, where the first patient was treated in May 2006. Intensity-modulated radiation therapy was the most sophisticated radiation technology of the late 1990s and early 2000s. Although a considerable improvement over the previous technique, three-dimensional conformal radiation therapy, intensity-modulated therapy still required that multiple photon (X-ray) beams enter the radiation field, hit the tumor, and then exit the field. The healthy tissues lying between the tumor and the entry and exit boundaries of the radiation field still absorb radiation, and the so-called "normal tissue damage" can often have serious long-term consequences. Proton therapy, on the other hand, has the advantage that most of the radiation is deposited precisely at the tumor site—the beam stops at the distal margin of the tumor without passing through healthy tissues. Thus, proton therapy has the potential for very closely targeted treatments that can kill tumors without harming surrounding tissues. This is especially important for treatment of children, whose developing tissues are quite sensitive to the effects of radiation. We would not be satisfied if we gave a child and their family a cancer-free diagnose at the cost of suppressing growth or causing other kinds of long-term damage.

We also began to think of difficult-to-treat adult cancers, like lung cancer. The current standard therapy for locally advanced non-small cell lung cancer, which is the most common type aside from metastatic disease, is a combination of chemotherapy and radiation, sometimes with surgery if the tumor can be removed safely. Yet this therapy can be quite toxic; even those patients who are healthy enough to withstand the treatment can be left with damage to the oesophagus that makes eating and drinking painful and difficult. Others are left with radiation pneumonitis, which generally requires supplemental oxygen and occasionally kills patients even if their cancer has been controlled. Consequently, the thinking is: if patients are suffering and dying from the effects of treatment-related toxicity, how can we reduce or eliminate that toxicity? Will this help extend people's lives?

The next hurdle was cost. Building a clinical facility dedicated to treating patients with proton therapy (rather than, say, a physics research facility) is extremely expensive, and so in addition to identifying sources of capital, we needed to counter the criticisms of skeptics that the cost would never justify the potential benefit of this new treatment. So, bearing in mind our goal of minimizing toxicity from radiation-based treatment, we traveled around the world, to South Africa, Europe, and Japan, to look at the different equipment that was available elsewhere. With the generous help of several manufacturing companies, Hitachi in particular, the facility was finally built, and the Proton Therapy Center opened for business in 2006. Currently, we have treated more than 6,000 patients with protons, and MD Anderson is one of very few institutions in the United States to use proton therapy to treat lung cancer. We also use proton therapy to treat children with cancer and adults with prostate cancer, head and neck cancer, breast cancer, gastrointestinal cancers, among others.

**Figure 5.**   The Proton Therapy Center at MD Anderson Cancer Center

## Fukushima Accident, 16 March, 2011

The spectre of the "dark side" of radiation exposure was again raised in 2011, when the Tōhoku earthquake and tsunami led to the nuclear disaster at the Fukushima Daiichi Nuclear Power Plant, the worst such disaster in twenty-five years. Not only were entire towns destroyed by the tsunami, but many thousands of households were displaced after radioactive material leaked into the air, soil, and sea after breaches of the reactor containment vessels at the power plant. The Japanese authorities implemented a 20-km exclusion zone around the power plant, which as of early-2013 had resulted in the continued displacement of approximately 156,000 people. Trace quantities of radioactive particles from the incident, including Iodine-131 and Cesium-134/137, have since been detected around the world.

When the earthquake and tsunami struck on Friday, 11 March, 2011, I was in an airplane that was attempting to land in Tokyo. The extent of the devastation was an eerie reminder of events that had taken place more than seventy years earlier.

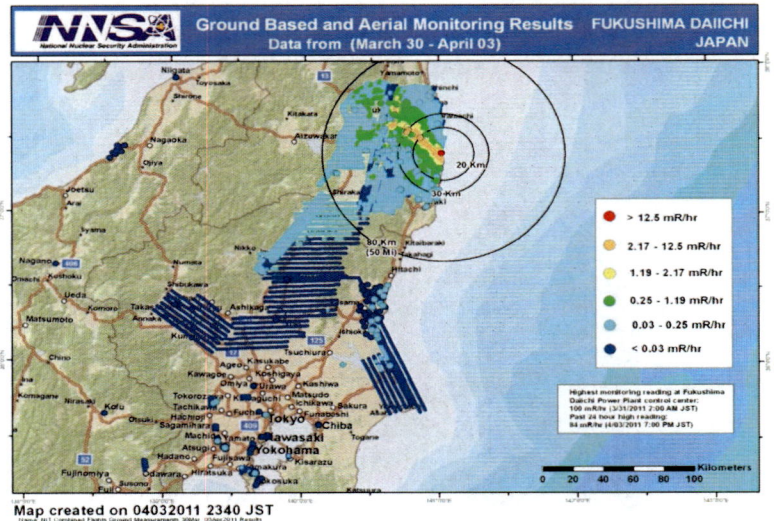

Figure 6.  Map of contaminated areas around the Fukushima Daiichi plant, 22 March–2 April 2011

Although the total radiation doses arising from this incident are generally thought to be relatively low, the risk of specific types of cancer is expected to increase among certain subsets of the population within the Fukushima Prefecture. According to a 2013 report from the World Health Organization, risks for exposed infants were 70% higher for developing thyroid cancer (for girls, raising the lifetime risk from 0.75% to 1.25%), 7% higher for leukemia (for boys), 6% higher risk for breast cancer (for girls), and a 4% higher risk, overall, of developing solid cancers (for girls).[2]

---

2  See http://www.who.int/mediacentre/news/releases/2013/fukushima_report_20130228/en/ (accessed 10 January 2018), 28 February 2013.

It will take years for the radioactive particles that still exist around the Fukushima Daiichi plant to decay. Unfortunately, the scarcity of land in Japan means that people will of necessity return to Fukushima before the area becomes completely safe. This was also true in Hiroshima. Desperation and a lack of knowledge about the long-term effects of radiation led, by early 1946, many people to return to Hiroshima to rebuild their lives. This occurred despite the fact that people were told that no one should live in the city for twenty-five years.

Thus, in many ways, my dreams have come true. I learned a lot from Sadako about facing death, and I feel that it's my turn, for the children's sake, to share what I have learned so that people don't need to suffer and die from radiation exposure. We have learned so much about the acute and long-term effects of radiation from the survivors of the Hiroshima and Nagasaki atomic bombs, as well as survivors of the nuclear accidents at Three Mile Island, Chernobyl, Fukushima, and elsewhere. We need to remain positive. The terrible experiences I had while growing up are already helping to turn radiation to our advantage by using it to treat cancer.

**Figure 7.** Jim Cox and & Ritsuko Komaki with four of their five grandchildren

# "ATOMIC SOLDIERS AND DOWNWINDERS": HEALTH LEGACIES OF THE NEVADA TEST SITE

*Susan L. Smith*

In 1961, a young Canadian folk singer named Bonnie Dobson wrote a song called "Morning Dew." It was the first song she ever wrote, composed during a visit to Los Angeles. It is a haunting song about the arrival of the apocalypse and the end of the world. It is a snapshot of something beautiful that was lost. Over the years, the song has been covered by a range of singers, from the Scottish pop singer Lulu to the punk rock band Devo, as well as the rock bands Nazareth and the Grateful Dead. This protest song proved to be relevant for many different times.[1] "Morning Dew" is also anti-nuclear and anti-war, created in a particular time and place. The phrase "morning dew" is a reference to radioactive fallout from a nuclear bomb explosion. The song reflected public concern about the possibility of a nuclear holocaust. The song, and the fears it represents about the dangers to human health and well-being, are part of the larger historical legacy of the American atomic bombs dropped on Hiroshima and Nagasaki in 1945.

In the 1950s and early 1960s, many Americans worried about what was in the morning dew. One reason for their fears was awareness of the tests of nuclear weapons that took place at the Nevada Proving Grounds, also called the Nevada Test Site. This facility became the main continental nuclear weapons test site in 1951.[2] Nevada, a western state, offered what appeared to be isolated, unlimited

---

[1] Bonnie Dobson was a student at the University of Toronto. As a youth, she had attended summer camps where union songs and protest songs were performed, including by the Americans Paul Robson and Pete Seeger. This experience taught Dobson the power of music in social change. In 1960 she went to the United States and started a singing career. She wrote "Morning Dew" after watching the film *On the Beach*, which is about a nuclear apocalypse. CBC, "Inside the Music," 2010, http://www.cbc.ca/player/RADIO+HOLDING+PEN/Inside+the+Music/ID/1620416361/, last accessed 12 July 2017. Thanks to Professor Bruce Ziff in the Faculty of Law at the University of Alberta for introducing me to this song at Folkways Alive!, now known as the Sound Studies Initiative, at the University of Alberta. This initiative maintains a partnership with Smithsonian Folkways Recordings in Washington, D.C.

[2] Barton C. Hacker, *Elements of Controversy: The Atomic Energy Commission and Radiation Safety in Nuclear Weapons Testing, 1947–1974* (Berkeley: University of California Press, 1994), 40–42. See also Howard Ball, *Justice Downwind: America's Atomic Testing Program in the 1950s* (New York: Oxford University Press, 1986); and Carole Gallagher, *American Ground Zero: The Secret Nuclear War* (New York: Random House, 1993), which discusses the impact on workers, soldiers, and residents through the stories of individuals.

space within miles of desert with only a sparse population living nearby.³ However, by the mid-1950s, scientists and the public came to understand that the greatest health dangers from atomic testing were not from the blasts, but from the fallout as the winds carried the airborne radioactive particles across the land. In particular, they worried about the carcinogenic potential of fallout, which coated the farms and towns of residents who lived downwind of the test site. The particles travelled eastward across the continent, with some of the heaviest concentrations in Arizona, Utah, and Nevada. To many of the residents, the fallout looked like morning dew on the grass.⁴

This essay uses an historical, case study approach to investigate some of the health consequences of the Atomic Age for servicemen and civilians. The nuclear weapons testing program at the Nevada Test Site left a notorious legacy for these "atomic soldiers" and "downwinders." They became casualties of the Cold War on the home front as a result of the 100 above-ground atmospheric tests in Nevada from 1951 to 1963. The impact of these tests reveals the human costs of nuclear weapons development in the United States.

Health issues have long been an essential theme of nuclear history and medical historians have shown a growing interest in the nuclear story. Scholarship has investigated the ideas and actions of scientists, activists, and military and government officials. For example, Susan Lindee, Angela Creager, and Katherine Zwicker have documented the work of scientists who were eager to understand the health effects of nuclear weapons in Japan and the United States, including the potential medical benefits of radioisotopes. Lindee, for instance, addresses the work of American bioscientists and physicians in Japan who were sent by the Atomic Bomb Casualty Commission (ABCC) to study the effects of radiation exposure on the Japanese people in Hiroshima and Nagasaki. Her book reveals important connections and parallels between the work of the scientists with the ABCC and the work of scientists in nuclear medicine.⁵

---

3   Scott Kirsch, "Watching the Bombs Go Off: Photography, Nuclear Landscapes, and Spectator Democracy," *Antipode* 29, no. 3 (1997): 227–55.

4   Paul Boyer, *By the Bomb's Early Light: American Thought and Culture at the Dawn of the Atomic Age* (Chapel Hill: The University of North Carolina Press, 1985, 1994), 352–53; Scott Kirsch, "Harold Knapp and the Geography of Normal Controversy: Radioiodine in the Historical Environment," *Osiris*, 19 (2004): 167–81; Kirsch, "Watching the Bombs Go Off," 227–55.

5   Susan Lindee, *Suffering Made Real: American Science and the Survivors at Hiroshima* (Chicago: University of Chicago Press, 1994); Angela Creager, "Nuclear Energy in the Service of Biomedicine: The Atomic Energy Commission's Radioisotope Program, 1946–1950," *Journal of the History of Biology* 39, no. 4 (2006): 649–84; Angela Creager, *Life Atomic: A History of Radioisotopes in Science and Medicine* (Chicago: University of Chicago Press, 2013); Katherine Zwicker, "Radiation, Researchers, and

David Jones and Robert Martensen have investigated the role of health physicists and medical scientists who conducted the now infamous human radiation experiments, risking the health of a wide range of individuals from vulnerable groups in the process. The government-funded health physicists and medical scientists conducted more than 4,000 radiation experiments from the 1940s to the 1970s. These nontherapeutic experiments were later judged as ethically questionable, even horrific. The human subjects, including orphans and people with mental disabilities, were exposed to radiation for the purpose of measuring its effect on their health. The Advisory Committee on Human Radiation Experiments, appointed by President Bill Clinton in 1995, concluded that "people who were used as research subjects without their consent were wronged even if they were not harmed."[6] Other scholars like Gerald Kutcher and Ellen Leopold have explored the complex links between war and cancer research.[7] As historians of medicine have demonstrated, developments in science are not politically neutral events but directly tied to the priorities of a given society, including in times of war. Although the politicization of science and medicine was not unique to the Cold War, it was pervasive.

Finally, Susan Lederer has examined the campaign for medical civil defence. Her study explored the work of medical researchers in the 1940s and 1950s who investigated ways to prevent and treat atomic casualties, especially thermal injuries from atomic bomb explosions. The medical scientists hoped to provide civilian physicians useful information about flash burns in order to aid the American public in the event of a nuclear attack.[8]

---

the United States Atomic Energy Commission: Biomedical Research from the Early Twentieth Century to the Early Cold War" (PhD thesis. University of Alberta, 2012).

6   David S. Jones and Robert L. Martensen, "Human Radiation Experiments and the Formation of Medical Physics at the University of California, San Francisco and Berkeley, 1937–1962," in Jordan Goodman, Anthony McElligott, and Lara Marks, eds., *Useful Bodies: Humans in the Service of Medical Science in the Twentieth Century* (Baltimore: Johns Hopkins University Press, 2003), 81–108; Advisory Committee on Human Radiation Experiments (ACHRE), The Human Radiation Experiments: Final Report of the President's Advisory Committee (New York: Oxford University Press, 1996), quote 493 and see also 136, 345, and 497. See also Jonathan D. Moreno, *Undue Risk: Secret State Experiments on Humans* (W.H. Freeman, 1999; New York: Routledge, 2001), Chapter 5.

7   Gerald Kutcher, *Contested Medicine: Cancer Research and the Military* (Chicago: University of Chicago Press, 2009); Ellen Leopold, *Under the Radar: Cancer and the Cold War* (New Brunswick, NJ: Rutgers University Press, 2008). On cancer research during the Second World War, see Susan L. Smith, *Toxic Exposures: Mustard Gas and the Health Consequences of World War II in the United States* (New Brunswick, NJ: Rutgers University Press,2017), Chapter 4.

8   Susan E. Lederer, "Going for the Burn: Medical Preparedness in Early Cold War America," *Journal of Law, Medicine, and Ethics* 39, no. 1 (Spring 2011): 48–53.

The Cold War between the United States and the Soviet Union marked a time when the threat of nuclear warfare felt very real for Americans and nuclear weapons development seemed to be the solution. In 1947, the Atomic Energy Commission (AEC) became the government agency in charge of nuclear bomb development during the arms race. The civilian agency grew out of the Manhattan Project, which built the first atomic bombs during the Second World War. 0After the war the United States had two main nuclear testing sites: Bikini Atoll in the Marshall Islands in the Pacific Ocean and the Nevada Proving Grounds near Las Vegas. Atomic weapons testing in the Pacific Ocean displaced many Indigenous people from their island homes. The American military relocated the inhabitants to a nearby island where they and American sailors were exposed to radioactive fallout. From 1946 to 1963, more than 200,000 American soldiers and sailors participated in one or more of the 235 nuclear weapons tests in the Pacific Ocean and the American West.[9]

## Atomic Soldiers

Many of the servicemen who participated in military training exercises in connection with the atomic bomb tests worried about radiation exposures. The atomic soldiers in Nevada voluntarily and involuntarily put their bodies on the new front lines in the Atomic Age. Many of the men were proud of their wartime service and wanted to participate in these exercises, but the hierarchical system of the military meant that others were ordered to volunteer and had no choice. The Department of Defense used the troop maneuvers and training exercises, which sometimes included Canadian and British servicemen, to address soldiers' anxieties about radiation and fighting an atomic war. The military used the atomic exercises to reassure the soldiers that radiation did not linger after a bomb blast and that they need not fear for their safety as long as they followed the proper procedures. Military officials believed that such indoctrination was important because men were worried about the health effects, including for their reproductive health. The young soldiers feared that the radiation would make them sterile and later, as veterans with children, they

---

9   Kirsch, "Watching the Bombs Go Off," 227–55; ACHRE, *The Human Radiation Experiments*, 302; John F. Lauerman and Christopher Reuther, "Trouble in Paradise," *Environmental Health Perspectives* 105, no. 9 (September 1997): 914–19; and Merissa Daborn, "'Blown to Hell': The Health Legacies of US Nuclear Testing in the Marshall Islands," *Constellations* (University of Alberta) 5, no. 1 (2013): 26–35.

wondered if it was the cause of health problems that emerged later in their offspring.[10]

The military sent troops to the Nevada Test Site for both training and research purposes. Scientists used about 3,000 servicemen in human radiation experiments in connection with the atomic bomb tests. These Cold War experiments were similar in procedure and purpose to that of earlier chemical warfare research. During the Second World War, thousands of soldiers and sailors were deliberately exposed to mustard gas and other chemical warfare agents to expand knowledge about the effects on military performance and to test protective clothing. Much like the mustard gas veterans of World War II, the atomic veterans later reported that they were warned never to discuss their military activities. Also, like earlier mustard gas researchers, radiation researchers focused on the short-term health effects and showed no interest in potential long-term health consequences for the servicemen. According to the 1995 findings of the Advisory Committee on Human Radiation Experiments, "researchers sought to measure the psychological and physiological effects of participation in bomb tests, the levels of radiation to which individuals who flew in and around atomic clouds were exposed, and the effects of intense light from the bomb blast on the eyes."[11]

It has been hard for atomic soldiers and later scholars to distinguish between the military training exercises and outright human experiments. In fact, some atomic soldiers and their family members believed, and still do, that the atomic bomb tests themselves constituted experiments and thus the men should receive compensation for any health problems. In particular, they have fought for government assistance and compensation for cancers that developed later.[12]

It is difficult to determine whether hazardous exposures caused veterans' illnesses and, if so, which ones, especially for those men who had a long military career. For example, N.G.B. of Kansas was in the military from the Second World War through the 1960s. He participated in chemical warfare training, including

---

10 One of the earliest books on the experiences of atomic soldiers was by the investigative reporter Howard L. Rosenberg, *Atomic Soldiers: American Victims of Nuclear Experiments* (Boston: Beacon Press, 1980). See also ACHRE, *The Human Radiation Experiments*, Chapter 10, especially 286 and 302. See also Brian McAllister Linn, *Elvis's Army: Cold War GIs and the Atomic Battlefield* (Boston: Harvard University Press, 2016). On soldiers' concerns about reproductive health problems from chemical exposures in World War II and the Vietnam War, see Smith, *Toxic Exposures*, 6, 123, and 127.
11 ACHRE, *The Human Radiation Experiments*, quote 505, and see also 137, 284–316, and 505. For discussion of the mustard gas experiments, see Smith, *Toxic Exposures*, especially Chapter 1.
12 ACHRE, *The Human Radiation Experiments*, 30–31, 284–85.

field tests with mustard gas, as well as nuclear weapons tests in Nevada. He remembered that he was monitored for years due to his exposure to radiation. By the early 1990s his health concerns, including the eye and respiratory problems typically associated with mustard gas exposures, led the Department of Veterans Affairs to provide him with full disability benefits.[13]

## Civil Defence and Atomic Tourism

In 1949, when the Soviet Union tested its first atomic bomb, many Americans began to feel vulnerable and wanted the federal government to do something to protect them. Americans feared that they could become the target of atomic attacks. As a result, President Harry Truman decided to invest in an arms race and create the Federal Civil Defense Agency. The task of the agency, created in 1950, was to "naturalize" the bomb and teach the public that survival was possible. The goal was to make people believe that they could live through a nuclear war as long as they took the appropriate measures. By 1955 public anxiety about radiative fallout led the agency to promote the construction of public bomb shelters in communities throughout the United States. It also encouraged people to buy or make their own "fallout shelters" and soon more than one million American families had one.[14] Even the Canadian city of Edmonton had a fallout shelter, built in 1954, for its civic leaders.[15] As Laura McEnaney argues, in this new world of citizens and civil defence, the front line was now the front lawn. Civil defence during the Cold War led to the "militarization of everyday life."[16]

Yet, American critics of the nuclear arms race did not accept the government assurances. For instance, in the 1950s, after the development of the hydrogen bomb or thermonuclear bomb there were increased concerns about nuclear fallout from these larger bombs. There were also acts of civil disobedience, including by mothers who argued that civil defence drills were pointless and thus refused to engage

---

13    N.G.B., 1992, veterans' testimony, National Academy of Sciences, records of the National Academy of Sciences, Washington, DC. I use the veteran's initials in the interest of protecting his privacy, even though HIPAA (Health Insurance and Portability and Accountability Act) US regulations do not apply to these records.

14    Laura McEnaney, *Civil Defense Begins at Home: Militarization Meets Everyday Life in the Fifties* (Princeton, NJ: Princeton University Press, 2000), 3, 42, and Chapter 2. See also Kenneth D. Rose, *One Nation Underground: The Fallout Shelter in American Culture* (New York: New York University Press, 2001).

15    Gordon Kent, "Bomb Shelter Touted as Memorial to a War that Never Happened," *Edmonton Journal*, May 1, 2011, A1.

16    McEnaney, *Civil Defense Begins at Home*, quote 152, and see also 5 and 70.

in evacuation exercises with their children. As Amy Swerdlow explains, women used the banner of motherhood to protest the bomb. In 1961, the organization Women Strike for Peace began as a group of women who were opposed to the resumption of nuclear testing after a three-year moratorium (1958–1961) by the United States and the Soviet Union.[17]

Public anxiety about nuclear weapons testing led the Atomic Energy Commission to carefully control public information. As a result, the agency was sometimes more concerned about public relations than public health. For example, it publicized developments in nuclear medicine as a positive use of the health effects of radiation. Such medical research was part of the agency's efforts to use potential civilian benefits to justify bomb building.[18]

Furthermore, the AEC contributed to the emergence of "atomic tourism" in Nevada in the 1950s. The government agency had encouraged some types of media coverage of atomic testing. For instance, in 1952 AEC officials invited about 200 reporters to witness an atomic test at the Nevada Test Site. It was the first time the media had been allowed to broadcast a nuclear explosion conducted in the United States. The journalists were posted only ten miles from ground zero. The television broadcast awed Americans. It helped to promote atomic tourism in Las Vegas, which was only sixty-five miles from the Nevada test site. John F. Cahlan, a journalist who worked in Las Vegas in the 1950s, remembered: "People started in telling us that the tourist flow would be lessened by the announcement that they were setting off atomic bombs here, but that did not prove to be true. In fact, it was just the opposite: a lot of people came up here to see the bomb go off."[19] Witnessing nuclear tests became one of the attractions of the city. Tourists brought their lawn chairs and watched bomb tests from as close as government restrictions would allow. Businesses in Las Vegas began to advertise their town as the "atomic city" and

---

17   The United Kingdom, which also tested nuclear weapons beginning in 1952, did not resume atmospheric testing after its moratorium in 1958. On the United States, see Amy Swerdlow, *Women Strike for Peace: Traditional Motherhood and Radical Politics in the 1960s* (Chicago: University of Chicago Press, 1993), 1 and 3; McEnaney, *Civil Defense Begins at Home*, 48, 50, and 81–82.

18   Kirsch, "Harold Knapp and the Geography of Normal Controversy," 167–81; Creager, "Nuclear Energy in the Service of Biomedicine," 649–84.

19   "John F. Cahlan: Fifty Years in Journalism and Community Development," interview of John F. Cahlan by Jamie Coughtry in 1986–1987, published in 1987, by the University of Nevada Oral History Program, Reno, UNOHP Catalog #137, Chapter 15—Covering the Nevada Nuclear Test Site in the 1950s, quote 222, http://digital.library.unlv.edu/ntsohp/, accessed 9 July 2017.

there was even a Miss Atomic Bomb beauty contest. There were many opportunities for atomic tourism throughout the 1950s due to regular nuclear bomb detonations.[20]

The public and the media were fascinated by nuclear weapons. Many residents in Nevada accepted and even welcomed the development of the Nevada Test Site. It brought much needed money to the state, as well as publicity for Las Vegas. According to John F. Cahlan, the local people accepted it and many reacted positively and "would get up to see the bombs go off, because you don't see that sort of a spectacle very often. It was quite a thrill."[21] W. Wallace White, a state health official, recalled that initially many residents woke up early to watch the tests, which often took place at or just before dawn. He also remembered all the media attention the tests garnered. At one point, in his capacity as an official at the Nevada State Department of Health, White was required to provide the verbal approval from the state for a bomb test. He was fast asleep and received a telephone call from the military early in the morning. White recalled,

> I rambled over to the phone, and a very precise, "This is Colonel So-and-So. Beg permission to fire an atomic blast at such-and-such a time," which was the next thirty minutes, or some blamed thing, "the wind direction is this, the forecast is that." I was never so tempted to say, "Permission denied," and hang up, because all of the networks, the radio, the newspapers, everyone was standing by for the damned thing. They knew they were going to do it. I have been sorry ever since that I didn't make headlines and say, "Permission denied" and hang up, and go to bed; I'm sure I would have caused a sensation.[22]

In addition, public interest in nuclear weapons contributed to the emergence of atomic kitsch, which included atomic clothing styles, including the "bikini" swimsuit named after the Bikini Atoll, atomic jewelry, cocktails, cakes, and comic books.[23]

---

20  Kirsch, "Watching the Bombs Go Off," 227–55. See also more than 150 interviews conducted between 2003 and 2008 as part of the Nevada Test Site Oral History Project, University of Nevada, Las Vegas, http://digital.library.unlv.edu/ntsohp/, accessed 6 July 2017.
21  "John F. Cahlan," quote 222, http://digital.library.unlv.edu/ntsohp/, accessed 9 July 2017.
22  "W. Wallace White: Caring for the Environment: My Work with Public Health and Reclamation in Nevada," interview of W. Wallace White by Mary Ellen Glass in 1968, published in 1970 by the University of Nevada Oral History Program, Reno, UNOHP Catalog #041, 90–92 and quote 90, http://contentdm.library.unr.edu/cdm/ref/collection/unohp/id/2549, accessed 7 July 2017.
23  See, for example, the essay by historian Donna Bilak, "Blast from the Past: Atomic Age Jewelry and the Feminine Ideal," Chemical Heritage Foundation, Spring 2015, https://www.chemheritage.org/distillations/magazine/blast-from-the-past-atomic-age-jewelry-and-the-feminine-ideal, last accessed 9 July 2017. For images of atomic popular culture, see http://www.historyonthenet.com/authenticchistory/1946-1960/4-cwhomefront/4-atomicculture/index.html, accessed 7 July 2017; and exhibits

Atomic tourism continues in Las Vegas today, but in a new form. In 1998, the city began an effort to preserve the history of the Nevada Test Site through the creation of the National Atomic Testing Museum, which opened in 2005. The museum, which is associated with the Smithsonian Institution, is designed to preserve atomic testing history and artifacts. However, as reviews have pointed out, not everyone accepts the museum's message that nuclear testing was essential to national security. As a result of the museum's tone of justification, even celebration, the exhibits do not adequately address the consequences of atomic testing. As I observed during my own visit, there is insufficient coverage of the human and environmental health costs of nuclear weapons development.[24]

## Downwinders

In the 1950s and 1960s, scientists were concerned about the potential health effects of atmospheric tests on "downwinders," the people who lived in the path of the radioactive fallout.[25] Information about fallout was classified during the early years of the nuclear weapons program. However, in 1957, the Congress held the first public hearings on the dangers of fallout following the emergence of an anti-nuclear movement, which included some scientists, and following Presidential candidate Adlai Stevenson's 1956 call for an end to nuclear bomb tests.[26]

Scientists at the Nevada Test Site were aware that there were some health risks from the fallout and so they deliberately scheduled atomic bomb tests to coincide with weather patterns that would blow the particles away from Las Vegas and the city of Los Angeles in southern California. However, as former public health official White explained, AEC officials were frustrated. They had deliberately selected this desert location because of its sparse population, yet the problem of people remained. According to White, government officials told him, "Instead

---

at the National Atomic Testing Museum, http://nationalatomictestingmuseum.org/, last accessed 24 February 2016.

24 National Atomic Testing Museum, http://nationalatomictestingmuseum.org/, last accessed 24 February 2016; W. Patrick McCray, "View America's Bomb Culture: The Atomic Testing Museum," *Public Historian*, 28, n. 1 (Winter 2006): 152–55.

25 For a recent study of the narratives of downwinders and uranium-affected people, see Sarah Alisabeth Fox, *Downwind: A People's History of the Nuclear West* (Lincoln: University of Nebraska Press, 2014). See also Philip L. Fradkin, *Fallout: An American Nuclear Tragedy* (Tucson: University of Arizona Press, 1989; Boulder, CO: Johnson Books, 2004).

26 Boyer, *By the Bomb's Early Light*, 353; Mike Moore, "Forty Years of Pugwash," *Bulletin of the Atomic Scientists*, 53, n. 6 (1997): 40–45; ACHRE, *The Human Radiation Experiments*, 405.

of finding no one in these areas, we found someone under every bush or up every canyon."[27]

Former journalist Cahlan remembered that most local people were not too worried about the effects. He observed, "We knew there was going to be radiation, but they said that the radiation that would affect people on the ground was about twice as much as you get when you take an X-ray picture. That calmed all the doubters for a while."[28] The gamblers in the casinos also paid little attention. According to Cahlan, "We were not afraid of the bomb. People out on the Strip who were gambling when the bomb went off—and you could feel it and see it here in Las Vegas—would all say, 'Well, there goes another one.' They'd continue on in the crap game or the roulette. It didn't bother anybody."[29]

Nonetheless, some scientists began to conduct research to better understand the health effects of fallout on residents in nearby counties. In the early 1960s Harold Knapp challenged the safety assertions that the AEC made to the public. Knapp, a mathematician with a PhD from MIT, conducted research for the AEC. He insisted that the agency had greatly underestimated the radiation dose that the public received. In 1962, Knapp worked for the Fallout Studies Branch of the agency's Division of Biology and Medicine. He was working on a report about radiation exposure from fallout when he realized that an important aspect was missing.[30]

In the 1950s health concerns focused on Strontium-90, which is a long-lasting external emitter of radiation from fallout and has a half-life of almost thirty years. The half-life is the time required for half of the atoms of a radioactive substance to disintegrate.[31] Some of the most alarming findings of its pervasiveness came from the health awareness campaigns focused on Strontium-90 and children. For example, in the late 1950s and early 1960s, physicians and activists conducted a baby tooth campaign, which collected thousands of children's baby teeth and identified traces of Strontium-90 in them. As far north as Edmonton, Canada, there were warnings about contamination in the city's water as a result of fallout from

---

27  "W. Wallace White," quote page 92, Reno, http://contentdm.library.unr.edu/cdm/ref/collection/unohp/id/2549, accessed 7 July 2017.
28  "John F. Cahlan," quote page 224, http://digital.library.unlv.edu/ntsohp/, accessed 9 July 2017.
29  Ibid," quote 225, http://digital.library.unlv.edu/ntsohp/, accessed 9 July 2017.
30  Kirsch, *Proving Grounds*, 127–28.
31  Ibid; Richard L. Miller, *Under the Cloud: The Decades of Nuclear Testing* (New York: The Free Press, 1986; The Woodlands, TX: Two-Sixty Press, 1991), 361–64; Creager, *Life Atomic*, 167.

the Nevada bomb tests. Strontium-90 is hazardous because, like calcium, it gets deposited in the bones of human beings and animals.[32]

In the early 1960s, Harold Knapp ended up at the centre of a scientific controversy about the health effects of fallout when he turned his attention to a different set of hazards—short-term internal emitters of low levels of radiation in the fallout. Radioactive iodine, or Iodine-131, has a half-life of only about eight days, but it moves quickly through the food chain. Like Strontium-90, it was a product of fallout and an "invisible danger."[33] In 1962, Knapp wrote a report about the health risks of low-level radiation by focusing on milk. Local dairy cows ate the fallout-contaminated grass and people drank the cow's milk, producing an increased risk for cancer, especially thyroid cancer. Infants and children were especially vulnerable because they consumed the largest amounts of milk. It was a time when bottle feeding rather than breast feeding was heavily promoted as healthier and more scientific.[34] The Iodine-131 present in the milk accumulated and concentrated in the thyroid gland, which was smaller in the young.[35]

Knapp's research demonstrated that the AEC had misrepresented the health risks of low-level radiation for people living downwind of the atomic bomb tests in Nevada. He drew on local knowledge and consulted with public health officials in Nevada and Utah, as well as people living in the nearby communities.[36] As the Las Vegas journalist John Calhan later asserted, "I think that the AEC was negligent in not warning the people of the state if there was any possible chance that radiation was going to hit some of the communities here and in Utah. They just [told] us that the bomb was going off. They told you not to look at the bomb at the time of the explosion, because it was so bright it would hurt your eyes."[37]

Physicians and scientists like Knapp and organizations like Women Strike for Peace were part of the public and scientific activism that tried to end nuclear testing. They helped to push it underground as a first step in addressing the health

---

32  Paul Boyer, *Fallout: A Historian Reflects on America's Half-Century Encounter with Nuclear Weapons* (Columbus: Ohio State University Press, 1998), 83–84 and Chapter 5 on the medical profession and activism; Scott Kirsch, *Proving Grounds: Project Plowshare and the Unrealized Dream of Nuclear Earthmoving* (New Brunswick, NJ: Rutgers University Press, 2005), 127–28; Jenna M. Loyd, *Health Rights Are Civil Rights: Peace and Justice Activism in Los Angeles, 1963–1978* (Minneapolis: University of Minnesota, 2014), 1–2, and 121–22.
33  Creager, *Life Atomic*, quote 167; Kirsch, "Harold Knapp and the Geography of Normal Controversy," 167–81.
34  Kirsch, "Harold Knapp and the Geography of Normal Controversy," 167–81.
35  Kirsch, *Proving Grounds*, 127–133.
36  Kirsch, "Harold Knapp and the Geography of Normal Controversy," 167–81.
37  "John F. Cahlan," quote 225, http://digital.library.unlv.edu/ntsohp/, accessed 9 July 2017.

hazards.[38] Atmospheric nuclear testing in Nevada ended in September 1963, when the US, along with the Soviet Union and the United Kingdom, signed the Partial Test Ban Treaty. The nations agreed to stop conducting nuclear weapons tests above-ground, underwater, and in space. Instead, the US moved its nuclear detonations underground, mostly at the Nevada test site, but also in Colorado, New Mexico, and Mississippi, and even on Amchitka Island, which is part of the Aleutian Islands.[39]

Unfortunately, underground testing did not entirely eliminate the health hazards. For example, in 1970 an underground nuclear weapons test in Nevada spewed radioactivity that was tracked as far away as Canada. From 1951 to 1992 there were a total of 928 nuclear tests above ground and underground at the Nevada Proving Grounds. In 1992 the US conducted its last underground nuclear weapons test and joined a world-wide nuclear testing moratorium. Nonetheless, nations have conducted over 2,000 nuclear weapons tests around the world from 1945 to the present. The winds and ocean currents carried the airborne radioactive particles as fallout circled the globe.[40]

## Health Consequences and Compensation

The health effects of nuclear testing often only showed up decades later. Diseases appeared in former soldiers, nuclear test site workers, and in the bodies of the tens of thousands of Americans who lived downwind from weapons testing and production sites in the American west. Downwinders and atomic soldiers sought federal government compensation for the health consequences but it would take additional years of activism to obtain it. Some people are still fighting for assistance, in part because many of the military records and government documents necessary to prove their claims are inadequate or missing.[41]

---

38   Kirsch, "Harold Knapp and the Geography of Normal Controversy," 167–81; Swerdlow, *Women Strike for Peace*, 3, 10, 15–16, 80.
39   The 1963 treaty was signed after the Cuban Missile Crisis of 1962. Boyer, *By the Bomb's Early Light*, 355; William Burr and Hector L. Montford, eds., "The Making of the Limited Test Ban Treaty, 1958–1963," the National Security Archive, 8 August 2003, http://nsarchive.gwu.edu/NSAEBB/NSAEBB94/, last accessed 26 February 2016.
40   In 1996, the Comprehensive Test Ban Treaty was established. It prohibits any nuclear weapons testing. For a visual representation of the global testing, see the multimedia artwork created by Isao Hashimoto, video titled "1945–1998," http://www.ctbto.org/specials/1945-1998-by-isao-hashimoto/, last accessed 9 July 2017.
41   See interviews in video and news story in Clyde Haberman, "Veterans of Atomic Test Blasts: No Warning, and Late Amends," 29 May 2016, *The New York Times*, Retro Report, https://www.nytimes.com/2016/05/30/us/veterans-of-atomic-test-blasts-no-warning-and-late-amends.html, accessed 8 July 2017.

Health concerns have centred on the risks of developing cancer and demands for government compensation for radiation-related disabilities and illnesses. Finally, in 1990 Congress passed the Radiation Exposure Compensation Act. Although the act was an important achievement, compensation was limited to people who lived in certain counties during specific years and were diagnosed with eligible or "compensable" diseases. The act provided people $50,000 if they lived in one of twenty-one counties in Nevada, Utah, and Arizona at the time of atomic testing above ground. Not only was the money insufficient to cover medical expenses, it did not go to people living in Colorado, Idaho, and South Dakota who received the highest levels of Iodine-131. Furthermore, some activists have argued that aiding those people affected by nuclear fallout would actually require compensating all people who lived in the US during the 1950s and early 1960s because everyone lived "downwind." Indeed, federal mapping reports of fallout showed that it drifted across the entire nation, and much of the continent.[42]

The compensation act provides payment to a range of individuals, including soldiers, miners, and downwinders. Uranium miners, who faced high rates of lung cancer and respiratory diseases, are eligible for $100,000 and atomic soldiers for $75,000. As of March 2015, the government has paid out over $2 billion in successful claims. Native Americans, including the Navajo, Hopi, Yavapai, Apache, and Spokane nations, are among the people who have filed claims as downwinders and workers in the uranium industry throughout the West. The compensation act, which was updated in 1997 and revised in 2004, currently has a deadline that requires that all claims be filed by 2022.[43]

As early as 1946, following the first postwar atomic test in the Pacific Ocean, officials at the Veterans Administration had warned military officials that veterans might one day demand financial assistance for service-connected disability claims due to their participation in atomic weapons testing. Finally, after years of activism, some veterans have received assistance through the Veterans Dioxin and Radia-

---

42   Miki Meek, "Compensating Life Downwind of Nevada," *National Geographic Magazine*, November 2002, including map of Iodine-131 fallout path, http://ngm.nationalgeographic.com/ngm/0211/feature1/online_extra.html, accessed 9 July 2017.
43   Department of Justice, "Radiation Exposure Compensation Act," http://www.justice.gov/civil/common/reca, accessed 15 September 2015. On uranium miners, see ACHRE, *The Human Radiation Experiments*, 354–66.

tion Exposure Compensation Standards Act of 1984, the Radiation Exposed Veterans Compensation Act of 1988, and the Radiation Exposure Compensation Act of 1990.[44]

Investigations of the health consequences of nuclear weapons testing expanded in the 1980s and continues to this day. In 1980 the Centers for Disease Control (CDC) reported higher rates of leukemia among atomic soldiers engaged in military exercises at a 1957 nuclear bomb blast at the Nevada Test Site. A report by the National Academy of Sciences in 1985 studied the fate of 46,000 atomic soldiers and also found an excess of leukemia, but deficient military record-keeping made it hard to determine the radiation exposures of specific participants.[45] In 1997 the National Cancer Institute released a report that concluded that people living downwind of atomic bomb tests in Nevada faced increased risks for developing thyroid cancer due to exposure to radioactive iodine. It also confirmed that the atomic soldiers who participated in nuclear exercises faced higher cancer rates.[46] A study conducted in 1999 for the Veteran's Administration also observed that there was a higher risk of death from leukemia in atomic soldiers.

Today the current Department of Veterans Affairs recognizes that atomic veterans and veterans who engaged in "radiation-risk activity" are vulnerable to several types of cancer, including thyroid cancer and leukaemia. They are eligible to apply for disability compensation, although there is no guarantee that they will get it.[47] Furthermore, in 2005 the Centers for Disease Control and Prevention and the National Cancer Institute completed a report documenting the public health implications for residents in the US from nuclear fallout from the Nevada Test Site and nuclear weapons tests around the world. The report concluded that a substantial portion of the external doses of radiation from 1951 to 2000 came from global

---

44  ACHRE, *The Human Radiation Experiments*, 299–300, 303, 518 and 540. Haberman, "Veterans of Atomic Test Blasts," https://www.nytimes.com/2016/05/30/us/veterans-of-atomic-test-blasts-no-warning-and-late-amends.html, accessed 8 July 2017.
45  ACHRE, *The Human Radiation Experiments*, 301.
46  Devra David, *The Secret History of the War on Cancer* (New York: Basic Books, 2007), 416. See also Institute of Medicine, *Exposure of the American People to Iodine-131 from Nevada Nuclear-Bomb Tests: Review of the National Cancer Institute Report and Public Health Implications* (Washington, D.C.: National Academy of Sciences, 1999).
47  Department of Veterans Affairs, "Diseases Associated with Ionizing Radiation Exposure," http://www.publichealth.va.gov/exposures/radiation/diseases.asp, accessed 15 September 2015. See also, Department of Veterans Affairs, "Post-Service Diseases Related to Exposure to Ionizing Radiation," http://www.benefits.va.gov/compensation/claims-postservice-exposures-ionizing_radiation.asp, last accessed 26 February 2016.

fallout. This exposure would have affected all Americans and not just those downwind from the Nevada Test Site, now called the Nevada National Security Site.[48]

American preparation for nuclear warfare produced a boomerang effect. US national security efforts to protect people through weapons development ended up harming American soldiers and polluting communities near and far with radioactive fallout. The American science writer Rachel Carson popularized the concept of a "boomerang effect" in her 1962 book *Silent Spring*, which was a study of the human and environmental dangers of the misuse of chemical agents like DDT.[49] In the early 1960s Carson raised the profile of toxic chemicals by comparing them to the dangers of nuclear weapons and fallout.[50]

Health matters remain defining features of the nuclear legacy. In the case of the Nevada Test Site, the health consequences continue to affect atomic soldiers and downwinders. They also endure in the ongoing medical interest in how to harness radiation for the diagnosis and treatment of cancers. Finally, nuclear power plants have added to the environmental and public health dangers of nuclear technology, including how to safely dispose of 50,000 tons of nuclear waste that will remain radioactive for the next 10,000 years.[51] Despite military and scientific reassurances at the time that there was nothing to worry about, public concerns about the health risks proved to be warranted.

---

48  Centers for Disease Control and Prevention and that National Cancer Institute, "Report on the Feasibility of a Study of the Health Consequences to the American Population from Nuclear Weapons Tests Conducted by the United States and Other Nations," final report, 2005, Chapter 4 on the health consequences, especially 113, https://www.cdc.gov/nceh/radiation/fallout/default.htm, accessed 9 July 2017.
49  Rachel Carson, *Silent Spring* (New York: Fawcett Crest, 1962; Boston: Houghton Mifflin Co., 1994), 80.
50  Carson, *Silent Spring*, 6.
51  Historian of science Peter Galison and filmmaker Robb Moss co-directed a film about the issue of the safe disposal of nuclear waste from the nuclear power industry. See *Containment* (LEF foundation, 2015), http://containmentmovie.com/, accessed 6 September 2015.

# CHERNOBYL AND ITS LEGACY: A MEMOIR

*David R. Marples*

## Introduction

The date 26 April 2016 marked the thirtieth anniversary of the Chernobyl disaster, the world's worst civilian nuclear disaster, and an occasion for many scientists and scholars to review its effects and ramifications. What follows is a personal story of my association with the event, and its Belarusian and Ukrainian contexts in particular. Over time one's views change and obviously the passage of time allows for more sober reflection of the dramatic changes that ensued. Moreover, one's views are never static. Consequently, it seemed most useful to offer a retrospective look in light of three decades of information and personal experience. Thus, the paper will combine my findings with events in which I took part at the time and end with some conclusions as to the lessons earned, particularly in light of the subsequent major accident that followed a tsunami at the Fukushima-Daiichi nuclear plant in Japan in 2011.

Though study of and interest in the disaster faded with time, Chernobyl has enjoyed a noted renewal of public interest, first because of the appearance of two popular books intended for a broad readership and second, through an HBO-Sky Television 5-part series that caused a sensation and was promptly banned in Russia, ostensibly for its stark portrayal of the late Soviet landscape and social life. The books in question are Serhii Plokhy's *Chernobyl: The History of a Nuclear Catastrophe* and Adam Higginbotham's *Midnight at Chernobyl*.[1] The HBO series premiered in the United States in early 2019 and was reportedly based on stories related in the book by Svetlana Alexievich,[2] as well as by residents of the reactor town Pripyat, which was evacuated on 27 April 1986.

---

1  Serhii Plokhy, *Chernobyl: The History of a Nuclear Catastrophe* (New York: Basic Books, 2018); Adam Higginbotham, *Midnight at Chernobyl: The Untold Story of the World's Greatest Nuclear Disaster* (New York: Simon and Schuster, 2018).
2  Svetlana Alexievich, *Voices from Chernobyl* (Maclean, IL: Dalkey Archive Press, 2005, translated by Keith Gessen).

## Background

The study of Chernobyl and nuclear power in the USSR began for me in Munich, (West) Germany, in 1985 at the American radio station Radio Free Europe/Radio Liberty, based there between 1949 and 1995. I had started a job as a young researcher in 1984, linked to the Ukrainian program under the nebulous title Research Analyst. There were two of such positions in the Ukrainians section occupied by Roman Solchanyk, a New Yorker with a quick wit that belied a very dedicated scholar, not always in tune with the wishes of his superiors, and myself.

Our focus was contemporary Ukraine. Roman's area was the church and the national question, we both delved into Soviet politics, and that left me with the economy and energy issues. I found the latter most appealing, and set to work eventually on a study of Ukraine's energy options, which generally signified what Moscow believed were in the best interests of Ukraine and how they were to be introduced. It soon became evident that nuclear power was—as I wrote in one of my first papers for Radio Liberty—the "wave of the future." The radios had a reputation as a US propaganda organ, but they were also a repository of a vast amount of information as well as a "Red Archive" that provided valuable information. By the end of the year I had compiled several files of information about Soviet nuclear stations in Ukraine. I had also decided to leave the radios and return to Canada.

Bohdan Krawchenko, then director of the Canadian Institute of Ukrainian Studies (CIUS) at the University of Alberta, who visited Munich during this same period, had offered me a new job as a Research Associate. The pay was somewhat lower than the attractive salaries at RFE/RL but conditions less onerous—RFE/RL was a somewhat fractious environment in which to work, as one can imagine when Soviet dissidents and others of various nationalities are all assembled under one roof in a building of narrow corridors that was formerly an asylum.

## The Disaster, April 26, 1986 and the Aftermath

Four months after I returned to Canada, the Chernobyl disaster occurred, though it was only after a couple of days that news began to filter through to the world. It was while watching two prominent American Sovietologists talking on television about Chernobyl—they knew almost nothing though they reappeared on several different channels—that the thought occurred to me to pursue the issue further and keep a close watch on the events. Krawchenko was not only encouraging; he released me from all other duties to follow the news reports from around the world.

He recognized far more quickly than anyone else I knew the importance of the event.

Though little was known at the time, the accident was a result of an experiment on the safety equipment of Chernobyl's fourth reactor, one of four graphite-moderated reactors in operation at a large edifice on the Uzh and Pripyat rivers, about 80 miles north of Kyiv, the Ukrainian capital of 2.5 million people. The goal of the experiment, conducted by a senior engineer in the absence of the plant director and chief engineer (it was a holiday weekend), was to see how long spinning turbines could generate enough power during a shutdown before the safety equipment activated. In order to prevent an automatic shutdown, the various safety mechanisms were dismantled beforehand. One of the operators began to pull out control rods to raise the reactor's power, which caused a violent surge blowing off the roof over the core and causing a graphite fire.[3]

Chernobyl was the only graphite-moderated station (the Russian acronym was RBMK) in Ukraine—there were others at Leningrad, Kursk, and a large station with 1500 MW reactors in Ignalina in Lithuania, as well as a new modern plant under construction near Smolensk. Much later the Kurchatov Institute of Atomic Energy acknowledged an inherent flaw (one of 32) in the RBMK reactor in that it became unstable if operated at low power. The Soviets boasted in 1985 that their nuclear program had remained accident-free, a statement that was later demonstrated to be a blatant lie—there had been a previous very serious accident at Chernobyl in September 1982 that was revealed when the archives of the Ukrainian KGB were published in the 1990s.[4]

For the next 3–4 days after hearing of the disaster, there was no opportunity to do much other than answer the telephone at CIUS as one media source after another called asking for information. I had nothing other than the background to the event, and details about the construction of the Chernobyl nuclear plant. But that was more than most people in late April 1986. Reports coming to Kyiv from contacts in Kyiv suggested that the situation was more serious than it appeared from the Soviet media.

On the ground around the station, events moved rapidly though dissemination of news was fragmentary. The graphite fire spread from the fourth to part of

---

3   See Victor G. Snell, 'Introduction' to David R. Marples, *The Social Impact of the Chernobyl Disaster* (Houndmills, Baskingstoke: Macmillan Press, 1988).

4   The author discussed these findings in David R. Marples, "Chernobyl: A Reassessment," *Eurasian Geography and Economics,* Vol. 45, No. 8 (2004): 588–607.

the third reactor. Firemen arrived from Kyiv to try to contain it, and first-aid workers attended to the early victims. All three categories suffered heavy casualties though the official total never rose from about 28 dead, and 2–3 instant deaths from the explosion. Helicopters flew over the fourth reactor dropping sand, boron, and lead pellets into the interior. The eventual weight derived pushed the reactor down toward the water table and coal miners from the Donbas were brought for the gruelling task of constructing a concrete shelf to prevent its further fall.

The reactor was entombed eventually in what was termed a *sarkofag*, a concrete covering, prior to which a massive decontamination exercise began to remove the irradiated topsoil in the 30-kilometre zone and cut down the forested areas. Initially "volunteers" from all over the USSR took part in the operation, but within a month the authorities ordered military reservists to the zone for initial periods of one month that were soon extended. They had a few Geiger counters but the measurements soon went off the scale. The evacuation encompassed over 120,000 residents on both sides of the border. Eventually the figure would rise to 250,000 as levels for acceptable living standards were raised over time. Some residents refused to move; others, mainly elderly, returned without permission. The Soviet media featured disasters at US nuclear stations but eventually revealed more information.[5]

## Researching Chernobyl

On 30 April 1986, I flew to New York at five hours' notice for a press conference organized by some Ukrainian activists, including a former employee of RFE/RL who knew of my work, followed by an appearance on CBS News, and another press conference in Montreal the following day. By then an unconfirmed report from UPI had spoken of 2,000 dead.[6] The Soviet side acknowledged two deaths, appointed a Government Commission to "eliminate the consequences of the accident," and *forty* hours after the explosion that blew the roof of the fourth reactor

---

5  The Chernobyl disaster received a lot of attention from Western scholars. Aside from those in medical and health journals some of the best known in English are, in alphabetical order by author: Alexievich (2006); David R. Marples, *The Social Impact of the Chernobyl Disaster* (Basingstoke: Macmillan Press, 1988); Grigori Medvedev, *The Truth About Chernobyl* (New York: Basic Books, 1991); Mittica Pierpaolo, *Chernobyl: The Hidden Legacy* (London: Trolley Books, 2007); Yuri Shcherbak, *Chernobyl: A Documentary Story* (New York: St. Martin's Press, 1989); Alla Yaroshinskaya, *Chernobyl: The Forbidden Truth* (Omaha, NE: University of Nebraska Press, 1995); and Zhores Medvedev, *The Legacy of Chernobyl* (New York: W.W. Norton, 1992).

6  https://www.upi.com/Archives/1986/04/29/Chernobyl-reactor-still-burning/9981572611428/

building, evacuated the population of Pripyat, estimated at 45,000, which housed the workers of the station and their families.

I used my files from RFE/RL to produce my first book entitled *Chernobyl and Nuclear Power in the USSR*, which was published in August 1986 by the Macmillan Press. Only the final chapter discussed the accident, insofar as the details were known. Around the time it was published, a Soviet delegation, led by Valery Legasov, arrived in Vienna for a meeting of the International Atomic Energy Agency (IAEA), delivering a report in which it blamed the accident primarily on human error. The IAEA and much of the Western world were so taken aback by the frankness of the report that they paid little attention to its dubious nature.

It was evident that the real story remained to be told. I felt that way even as other books arrived on the market. One was actually out before mine, a sensational epic by reporters from the British *Observer* newspaper. The Ukrainian National Organization (UNA), founded in USA in 1894 agreed to support a new study and offered me a grant of around $26,000, which was a small fortune by the standards of the time. I immediately applied to the Soviet Embassy in Ottawa to visit Chernobyl but received no response. In the fall of 1986 Gorbachev had called the 27th Party Congress of the Central Committee of the Communist Party and buzzwords like Glasnost and Perestroika were in circulation. But there was no clear indication of fundamental change in the Soviet system.

Further, Chernobyl appeared to many, including myself, as a cover-up operation, whereby information on health and casualties was classified and the authorities provided bland announcements to local and international media about sacrifice and bravery, as well as concocting a success story—the Soviet system had responded to a catastrophe efficiently and well. Most of these suppositions about concealment turned out to be accurate. At the same time, many observers from afar were largely unaware of the scale of the problem. With the help of a talented student from University of Pennsylvania, Leda Hewka, I started to investigate the impact of the accident on the surrounding villages and environment, wading through the Soviet media at the national and republican levels.

I completed the resultant second book called *The Social Impact of the Chernobyl Disaster*, with which I was much more satisfied than my first publication. It was made the feature review in *The Los Angeles Times Book Review* (by James Oberg), and I gleaned information from various sources, including incidentally a former RFE/RL colleague Toomas Ilves, later the president of Estonia, who provided information on executions of some Estonian clean-up workers who had refused to stay in the zone beyond their mandatory term of one month, and had downed tools in protest. Roman Solchanyk forwarded a vast quantity of information from various Soviet sources at Radio Liberty. Glasnost permitted such stories, though in the case of the clean-up workers' strike, the Soviet leaders likely could not monitor the Estonian press.

In 1988 I was in Moscow, attending a press conference of the Soviet Academy of Sciences where I had an opportunity to ask a question of Evgeniy Velikhov, Vice-President of the Soviet Academy of Sciences and shortly to be appointed Director of the Kurchatov Institute. He was the chief scientist at Chernobyl in the early months after the accident. I recall that his response was honest and detailed. I had also evidently spoken ahead of turn and there were numerous mutterings of "Who is he?" "Where did he come from?" around me. Only in early 1989 did I receive a response to my letter to the Ukrainian Foreign Ministry, receiving permission to visit Chernobyl in May or June of that year.

## Kyiv 1989

The spring of 1989 was a pivotal moment in the history of the Chernobyl accident. At that time *Pravda* and other newspapers published the first detailed maps of the radioactive fallout based on Cesium-137 (and to some extent Strontium-90), extending well beyond the officially designated 30-kilometre zone around the reactor. The dark patches on the map extended almost to the Polish border in the west, over swathes of Belarus in the south, east, and central part of the republic, and over the Russian border into Bryansk and Orel. In some parts of Zhytomyr region of Ukraine there were hotspots of radiation that were higher than most parts of the 30-kilometre zone. In the wake of this information, which infuriated local activists and journalists, I finally arrived in Kyiv in May as the guest of the Foreign Ministry of Ukraine, the second Canadian allowed to tour the Chernobyl site after a professor of Physics from Manitoba, Jovan Jovanovich.

There followed the sort of anti-climactic lull typical of the time: I was left to explore Kyiv and remained at the Hotel Dnipro for two full days before anyone from the Ministry appeared. At that point, a man called Valery Ingulskyi, First Secretary at the Foreign Ministry, sauntered into the lobby, addressing me in French, and asked me to make a list of the places I wanted to visit in the vicinity. It turned out that he knew no English and the Ukrainian Foreign Ministry had assumed that anyone from Canada must speak French. The trip to Chernobyl was set for two days ahead. I spent a couple of days visiting various Ukrainian media to get their views on the situation, as well as other information.

The time at Chernobyl was simply astounding, in every respect. It is hard to imagine today the degree of central control over every facet of industry and the combination of secrecy and shabbiness behind every Soviet institution. My host for the day was Yuri Risovanny, a Kyiv native and senior engineer (a word that means nothing like its western equivalent); he knew several Western languages and had been designated the host for any foreign delegations visiting the station. He later became a close friend and subsequently immigrated to the United States with his family.

At the village of Chernobyl, about ten kilometres south of the nuclear plant, we stopped at a prefabricated house. I was given a cross examination by Pavel Pokutnyi, head of the Kombinat association, a hard-talking bull of a man with a deep voice and a suspicion of foreigners to match. He was very interested in my first book and why it appeared so critical of the Soviet system. He and others asked me why I had worked at Radio Liberty, which they associated with the CIA—it *had* been under the control of the CIA until 1971 when it was placed under the Board for International Broadcasting. Without doubt it was a Cold War institution. Thus, while not unfriendly, there was an atmosphere of suspicion throughout our discussion and there was no doubt that I had read everything I had written. There was also some tension between Pokutnyi and my host Risovannyi.

Chernobyl was within the 30-kilometre zone but some 16 kilometres (10 miles) south of the plant. I was taken to the nuclear plant in a bus used to transport clean-up workers, who were still much in evidence, sitting on the ground eating sandwiches or smoking, oblivious to the 'Danger! Radiation!' signs all around them. We had Geiger counters and it was clear that the background radiation was 60–100 times the background norm, and higher closer to the reactor. The workers appeared not to care. The Chernobyl nuclear power station called "V.I. Lenin" was always visible in the distance.

The plant director, a small serious man in his fifties, Mikhail Umanets,[7] was civil and courteous but perhaps understandably defensive. He talked about Western propaganda and anti-nuclear protests taking place in Ukraine and Russia with evident disgust. Yuri took me around the first and second reactor units (they had

---

7   Mikhail Umanets, born 1938 in Kazakhstan of Ukrainian parents, is an electrical engineer who was director of the Chernobyl plant between 1987 and 1992. In a recent interview, he explains how he took the position voluntarily after the previous director Erik Pozdyshev became ill, and no one else seemed willing to take on the task. Though he is not opposed to ending nuclear power, he feels that Ukraine cannot survive without the industry. http://rian.com.ua/interview/20170426/1023541499.html

shut down by the end of 1987), and as far as the wall of the "sarkofag" in the fourth. I even ate lunch at the Chernobyl plant, a solid meal of pork chops, which was better than anything I had eaten in the Kyiv hotel.

Yuri then took me to Pripyat, about three kilometers to the north, and we visited the deserted apartments and an experimental glasshouse where shoots of pine trees had been taken from the irradiated forest around the station (soon destroyed) and grown alongside shoots from clean areas. They were around three times larger and their growth was unnatural. I was asked to sample tomatoes and cucumbers grown in the glasshouse. The local gardener did so with some relish, but I declined. Instead I took a cucumber, naively intending to take it back home to Canada to get tested. But my suitcase went astray somewhere in Montreal and when it arrived two days later, the cucumber had disintegrated among my clothing. Everything ended up somewhere in Edmonton landfill site.

The following day I visited the Centre for Radiation Medicine where grim-faced scientists, including I.P. Los, and O.A. Pyatak, scoffed at sensational reports from journalists and in recent films about mutations in wildlife and the situation at Narodychi, in the highly irradiated zone of Zhytomyr.[8] They provided information on the 238 seriously affected victims who had been hospitalized in Moscow and Kyiv, 85% of whom had returned to work, before giving me a dull volume of their own findings, published in Moscow, written in typical technocratic language with radiation averages per oblast rather than hotspots or highly contaminated zones. They also dismissed radiophobia and concurred with the IAEA that fear and stress had caused more sicknesses than Chernobyl radiation.[9]

It became evident by now that there was a rift between Ukrainian and Russian scientists on the one hand and the media on the other. The latter, in the early throes of Glasnost, were on a mission to unearth 'the real truth' about Chernobyl, a phrase I heard uttered frequently. The scientists regarded them with contempt and dismissed their findings as sensationalism calculated to cause panic among the population. I found this then and subsequently to be one of the tragedies of the event, namely that those reporting were so alienated with those supposedly best placed to reach conclusions about its effects. The population as a whole was firmly behind the journalists and deeply distrusted the IAEA, which it regarded as little

---

[8] For more details, see the book by Alla Yaroshinskaya, *Chernobyl 25 Years Later: Crime Without Punishment* (London" Transaction Publishers, 2011), 110; and V.M. Chernousenko, *Chernobyl: Insight from the Inside* (Berlin: Springer Verlag, 1991), 234–235.

[9] Both contributed to the 1988 IAEA Report *Medical Aspects of the Chernobyl Accident* (Vienna, Austria: IAEA, 1988). See http://www-pub.iaea.org/MTCD/Publications/PDF/te_516_web.pdf

more than a propaganda organ closely allied to the Soviet Moscow-based ministries who ran the nuclear industry. An additional problem was that the general public, though generally well read, could not comprehend the scientific volumes being produced as authoritative investigations of the medical effects of the accident.

These were unusual times, however, and at the Centre I was also allowed to meet a fireman from the Chernobyl crew (he had fought the fire from 2am until 5am on April 26), Vladimir Pryshchepa, who was confined to his bed and very sick. The scientists were obviously reluctant for there to be anything approaching a private conversation, but the short meeting was much more revealing than the formal interview with the "experts." Ironically, a memorial plaque in the grounds to the firemen and first-aid workers who had died from the graphite fire that enveloped the third and fourth reactors had been donated by the IAEA, the UN agency established to promote nuclear power.

The same rift became further evident in 1991 at a conference in Kyiv sponsored by the 'Green World' environmental association (later the Green Party), led by Shcherbak and others. One of the few offers of Western aid to Chernobyl accepted by the Soviet authorities was that of businessman Armand Hammer, who had developed personal friendships with all Soviet leaders from Lenin onward. Hammer's designate was Dr. Robert Peter Gale, a forty-year old bone marrow transplant specialist and Associate Professor from the UCLA School of Medicine.[10] Gale had conducted several transplants after the accident though ultimately all the patients died. He became a prominent voice, meeting with Gorbachev. In 1990, he was invited to speak at the Kyiv conference held by Green World, which I also attended.

Gale cut an unusual figure in 1990s Kyiv, wearing clogs and sockless. As he walked down the aisle to deliver his speech, the clogs made a considerable noise. His speech focused on the bad habits of Ukrainians, particularly smoking, which he declared was far more dangerous to them than anything linked to excess levels of radiation. His speech was marked by a chorus of booing and thereafter he became identified among Ukrainian environmentalists with the 'scientific establishment', someone who tried to water down the health effects of Chernobyl in line with the two UN agencies, the World Health Organization and the IAEA. In 2012,

---

10 Gale wrote a book about his experiences: Robert Peter Gale, *Final Warning: The Legacy of Chernobyl* (New York: Warner Books, 1989).

he also spoke about the effects of Fukushima at a meeting organized in Washington, DC, by the Health Physics Society, declaring that the risk of contracting cancer for the general public of cancer had increased by 0.002%.[11]

## The Nineties: Belarus

Subsequently I gave many talks on Chernobyl, particularly to government agencies. It was on the fifth anniversary, in April 1991, that I found myself in Washington, DC. If I recall correctly, I had been part of a gathering of anti-nuclear activists headed by Helen Caldicott, as well as a talk at the Institute of Strategic Studies at Georgetown University and a hearing at the US House of Representatives. On that same visit, I was invited to a meeting that included the Belarusian gymnast Olga Korbut. There I met a man called Yourie (his own rendering of his Christian name) Pankratz, who instantly regaled me, quite rightly, for focusing solely on Ukraine in my work on Chernobyl. The fallout in Belarus had been very severe. He invited me to a conference (it was termed a Congress) in Minsk the following April, at which, he said, I would be invited to speak.

Thus, I flew to Minsk for the first time in the spring of 1992. It was a unique period in the history of Belarus. The Soviet period had ended but there was a power struggle between the Prime Minister Viachaslau Kebich, who supported a military-security union with Russia, and the Chairman of the parliament Stanislau Shushkevich, a noted physicist, who had found himself suddenly elevated to state leader after the failed putsch in Moscow in August 1991 but lacked popular support or the backing of a political party. The Popular Front (BPF) was large and active and mounting a petition for new elections to replace the old assembly elected in 1990. The BPF placed the problems caused by Chernobyl in Belarus at the top of its agenda.

My host was an association called "Children of Chernobyl"—a very familiar name in this period as there were probably a dozen similarly named organizations. This particular one was under the leadership of Gennady Grushevoy (Hienadz Hrushavy), an ethnic Russian and a professor of philosophy, who had been part of the Popular Front and the Belarusian national revival movement. The event was held in the Yubileinaya Hotel, on the street then adorned with the name Masherau Praspekt. On the podium in front of the Children of Chernobyl, Grushevoy presided, young (he was 42) but balding and with a moustache and what seemed at

---

11  https://blogs.wsj.com/japanrealtime/2012/03/02/fukushima-health-impact-minimal/ (Accessed 26 July 2019).

that time a brusque and somewhat condescending attitude, though subsequently I realized this description was a complete misrepresentation of his character.

The Congress was a little disappointing, for the same reasons as in Kyiv, namely that there were no attempts by the scientists speaking to make their findings comprehensible to a lay audience. Many would rush through overhead charts and graphs claiming to show the impact of additional radiation on various parts of the body. There were also more politically oriented offerings opposing nuclear power—in fact an anti-nuclear power sign hung in the background for the duration of the congress. Belarus did not have a nuclear power station of its own, but the Moscow Ministry of Power and Electrification had authorized the construction of a nuclear-powered heating station on the road between Minsk and its international airport.[12]

The occasion was an eye opener in terms of contact between locals and the few selected Westerners in attendance. We (Germans and Canadians were prominent) were in big demand for social occasions and it was wonderful to be invited to the homes of various attendees. I stayed at the home of two professors at Minsk Linguistic University, Uladzimir and Tamara Tiomkin, and met numerous people who later became close friends, including Lyuba Pervushina, at that time a violinist with the State Orchestra, Yourie and his wife Mila Pankratz, Katya Stulova, and Seriozha Lapteu.

Grushevoy held another congress in 1994, notable because that time in Minsk also featured the campaigning for the first presidential election campaign, eventually won by Alexander Lukashenka. The organization lent its support to the campaign of Shushkevich, one of two democratic candidates—the other was Zianon Pazniak—who inevitably split the vote of the democrats, thus allowing Lukashenka a comfortable lead on the first ballot, and then a run-off against Kebich in the second round, an event of significance for the future study of the Chernobyl disaster. A third congress in 1996 proved to be too sensitive for the authorities (attendees included Ali Hewson, wife of Bono, the lead singer of U2, and Adi Roche, who lead the Irish Chernobyl Children International group). The atmosphere was quite tense. One doctor was refused permission to deliver his paper, and at one point the microphones were abruptly switched off. By then I had become much more aware of Chernobyl-related problems in Belarus having visited various hospitals and clinics, and interviewed doctors and scientists.

---

12  This project was abandoned shortly afterward. Today, however, Belarus has its own nuclear plant, based on Russian technology, located at Astraviec on the border with Lithuania, and discussed below.

In December 1993, I teamed up with a University of Alberta Hospital pediatrician, Dr. Ernest McCoy, and we visited several Minsk clinics. At the Belarusian Republican Centre for Cancers of the Thyroid Gland, director, E.P. Demidchik provided us with detailed evidence of the spread of thyroid cancer among children, noting that its cause, radioactive iodine, had spread through the air in the first days after Chernobyl, embracing most regions of the republic. Only Viciebsk in the north was outside its range. Around 5,000 children had fallen victim to this cancer by the early 1990s. Most scientists concur that this illness among children was the most discernible medical consequence of Chernobyl, and caused from fallout in the first few days after the accident. Belarus lacks iodine in the soil so children's thyroids took it in through the air.[13] The children most susceptible were conceived and under the age of five by April 1986, thus providing a readily discernible group for future monitoring.

Grushevoy labored on long after his former friends from the Popular Front had departed the scene (Zianon Pazniak emigrated to United States in 1996, for example). On one occasion, his staff arranged for me to visit families in the contaminated zones of Mahilou region, accompanied by some members of the Fund. It was evident that these families had been living off the land since 1986. A few of their children had traveled abroad in the summers through the Fund, but most people had remained in their villages, though the local factory, which produced flax, had shut down.

There was general poverty in evidence and most of the males I encountered were drunk or sleeping. In one place, seven people slept in one room in the middle of the day, most of them ill, though not as a result of radiation brought from the Chernobyl reactor. In almost all the cottages, the reception was uniformly warm with tables set for a feast in each one—I forget how many 'lunches' we ate but it was at least three. The fear of radiation was manifested everywhere, as was the sentiment of gloom and hopelessness. I took a photograph of a more cheerful family of seven, which appeared in my first book on Belarus, *Belarus: From Soviet Power to Nuclear Catastrophe*, published in 1996. I was later reprimanded by a member of

---

13    Demidchik and colleagues wrote several scientific papers on their findings. See, for example, E.P. Demidchik, et al, "Thyroid Cancer in Belarus," International Congress Series 1234 (2002): 69–75, available on line at https://www.researchgate.net/profile/Yuri_Demidchik/publication/223167962_Thyroid_cancer_in_Belarus/links/0deec51f0d975067a4000000.pdf. Demidchik passed away in 2010. His biography is available at http://nasb.gov.by/rus/members/memoriam/demidchik.php.

the Belarusian Society of Friendship and Cultural Relations with Foreign Countries, where I presented the book, for presenting too gloomy a picture, as highlighted by that particular photograph.

Grushevoy, in one of the many long conversations I held with him, attributed the pessimism less to radiophobia and more to the tradition in Belarus in depending upon state direction and largesse. Gorbachev's Soviet Union from 1986 to 1991, in the victims' view, had betrayed this trust by concealing the dangers of radiation and declining for three years to reveal the scope of its dissemination. Grushevoy's goal, which he emphasized most fully at the 1999 Congress of Children of Chernobyl, attended among others by the future Nobel Prize for Literature winner Svetlana Alexievich, was to set up self-help organizations at the grassroots level, something he had started to do in the early 1990s.

In 1997, however, his organization had fallen under government scrutiny and a special commission of the KGB was set up to investigate its operations. For several months, the KGB officials simply sat in the offices in Starovilenskaya Street in a restored older part of central Minsk and carried out audits (especially of its links with German organizations, where many children were sent for the summer months for recreation) while monitoring all facets of business. Ultimately the Fund was evicted from the building and forced to operate, under a different name, out of a hotel room. Some of its leaders moved to Germany, with the help of partner organizations.

The Irish 'Chernobyl Children's Project' members of which I had met in 1996, incidentally, formed ties with government organizations and thus was permitted to continue. But despite its name its main work today is less with Chernobyl victims than in mental asylums where it has carried out fundamental changes as well as medical operations on the sick, either by flying in teams of doctors or transporting children to Ireland. In 2003, its leaders helped to produce the documentary *Chernobyl Heart*, directed by Maryanne DeLeo, which won an Academy Award for Best Short Documentary. The film focused on cardiac degradation among children, though there is no verifiable link of this condition to additional radiation from the disaster.

Therein, however, lies a fundamental issue arising from the Chernobyl disaster: how many people did it actually affect through death, illness, or evacuation? That question pervaded the dozens of conferences and meetings I attended in places as far-flung as Tokyo, Kyiv, Minsk, Ottawa, London, Berlin, Munich, and throughout North America from Los Angeles to the White House. It was difficult to separate the issue from that of the future of nuclear energy and fiercely antithetical organizations such as the IAEA and Greenpeace, which disagree profoundly on the number of deaths to date from Chernobyl-induced radiation and the impact of low-level radiation.

## After Three Decades

The Gorbachev years were a special period in the history of Belarus, Ukraine, and Russia. Chernobyl's consequences catalyzed Glasnost but also were exposed by it. Underneath all the bitterness, accusations, and recriminations, it needs to be acknowledged that this deeply flawed empire had become a debating society; nothing was sacred any longer. It was like a door to a secret kingdom being opened briefly, then further, before finally being slammed shut again, and that kingdom in the meantime having split into its various parts, each with their own particular problems and the only unifying factor being the extraordinary difficulty of building something new to replace the old system.

Chernobyl was a disaster of epic proportions, especially in terms of contamination of land (over 90,000 square kilometres), but it also suffered because of the lack of affinity between its victims and those assigned to assess and take measures to overcome it. It tested the Soviet Union to the limit, and the Communist system proved inadequate for the task. That may not have been a result entirely of the weakening structure; the Japanese had similar problems after the earthquake and tsunami that caused the Fukushima disaster in March 2011. The financial load, however, was excessive, and proved even more so for the newly independent republics of Belarus and Ukraine that had to take on the burden of Chernobyl recovery after the collapse of the Soviet Union.

For Ukraine, the influence of Chernobyl has remained but it is no longer a priority issue. Rather it is perceived as one more tragedy in the 20$^{th}$ century, imposed on Ukraine by outsiders—in this case central ministries of the USSR based in Moscow. These 'tragedies' all involve excess loss of lives, commencing with the revolution and Civil War, famines of 1921–23 and especially 1932–33, the Purges, and the Second World War, and more recently the war in the Donbas and clashes with Russia. There is a tendency to see Ukraine as an innocent victim of the nuclear accident, though the archives of the Ukrainian KGB reveal earlier accidents at the same nuclear plant, including ones that resulted in the release of radiation from the reactors. In short, the problems of the RBMK type reactor were well known not only in Moscow but also at the republican level.

In Belarus, the suffering was especially acute because it was a secondary, indirect victim of the explosion, which happened ten miles south of its border; Belarusians were unaware of its scale; the party leader Mikalai Sliunkau took an active role in responding to the disaster in the parts of the zone in Belarusian territory in the first months but likely knew little about its influence. It was estimated in the 1990s that the cost of Chernobyl to Belarus in terms of damage, health, and evacuations, as well as continued monitoring of the irradiated zones, was equivalent to thirty-two annual budgets.[14] And as noted, the effects took place in a society in which local initiatives and responses were overtly discouraged. And yet it was left to NGOs to bear the brunt of the efforts to respond, with the support of foreign governments and agencies.

The number of direct deaths was probably a few hundred. If one adds the later deaths (within five years) to clean-up crews and evacuees, the figure is probably around 10–15,000. It was accompanied by a worrying rise in morbidity and general illnesses in the affected zones. What was termed "Chernobyl AIDS" appeared to be a consequence of deficiencies of the immune system, which in turn may have resulted from drastic dietary changes and fear of consuming home-grown vegetables. Diseases like diabetes among children or heart attacks among young clean-up workers were also prevalent. There were also and remain still numerous health problems that might be associated with contamination but without any definitive proof.

By 2004, prior to the eighteenth anniversary, the president of Belarus, Lukashenka, declared that the accident was over and the contaminated lands of Homiel, Mahiliou, and Brest, could be re-cultivated.[15] As a move to economize or dispel fears, it was an astute statement; as a reflection of the actual situation one hopes it was based on ignorance. Longer living radionuclides, particularly Pluto-

---

14   See, for example, the 1995 article by Ivan A. Kenik, then the Minister for Emergencies and Population Protection from the Chernobyl NPP Consequences, at: http://chernobyl.undp.org/spanish/otherdoc/fallout.htm.

15   See for example, Steven Lee Myers, "Belarus Resumes Farming in Chernobyl Radiation Zone," *The New York Times*, October 22, 2005, at http://www.nytimes.com/2005/10/22/world/europe/belarus-resumes-farming-in-chernobyl-radiation-zone.html. The cost of dealing with these consequences likely prompted Belarusian leader Lukashenka to declare that the problem had been resolved. The new Ukrainian president Volodymyr Zelensky expressed a similar sentiment in Summer 2019 when he signed a decree to make the Chernobyl Exclusion Zone more accessible to the public and a growth area of Ukraine. See https://www.president.gov.ua/en/news/glava-derzhavi-pidpisav-ukaz-shodo-rozvitku-chornobilskoyi-z-56321?fbclid=IwAR21a5NMQ3CEm12A6DICp-EA0i_9wXoDxRnJvnP9f44j_JJ2I7a29v4ICRA, accessed 26 July 2019.

nium, will remain in isolated areas for generations. Moreover, the statement implied that further research into the health effects of the accident was unnecessary and thereafter the government actively discouraged such studies. Much information remains classified and difficult to access.

On the other hand, Belarus and Ukraine almost immediately began to face questions on sovereignty and independence, followed by struggles for power among the post-Communist elite (and some non-elites) and their relationship with the largest power to emerge from the Soviet corpse, the Russian Federation. In perspective also, the damage caused by Chernobyl was extensive, but does not compare for mortalities even with another disastrous accident in India in December 1984 at the Union Carbide Pesticide plant in Bhopal, which resulted in over 2,200 immediate and over 1,500 subsequent deaths from a leakage of gas. About 15,000 reportedly died from related diseases caused by gas inhalation over the following years.[16] In the USSR, the earthquake in Spitak, Armenia in December 1988 resulted in a fatality total of around 25,000 according to a government report.[17] In scale, these events superseded Chernobyl. The difference is that they were instantly measurable and attributable to the specific accident. No such certainty occurred or will occur after Chernobyl.

Soviet society seems a foreign world today. There were few computers in 1986, no Internet, and no social networks. The chief forms of communication were the telephone and the postal system. When I was driven to Chernobyl in 1986 there was one paved road all the way from Kyiv and we stopped frequently for cattle crossing. The old authorities prior to the emergence of Gorbachev, were indeed *old*. Three Soviet leaders and at least four other Politburo members died between November 1982 (Brezhnev) and March 1985 (Chernenko). The leader of the Ministry of Medium Machine Building (nuclear weapons), which was responsible for running the Chernobyl plant until late 1986 was under the leadership of 88-year old Efim Slavsky. As noted by the Chernobyl-skeptic Piers Paul Reed, he had fought in the Red Cavalry during the Russian Civil War of 1918–20.[18]

Soviet students were not permitted to read Freud, but all the KGB workers in Intourist, as one informed me in Moscow in 1987, had to plough through eleven volumes of that great sage Leonid Ilich Brezhnev (recipient of the Lenin Prize for Literature), or watch the geriatrics assemble on Lenin's tomb for the latest funeral.

---

16 See, for example, Alan Taylor's article in *The Atlantic*: https://www.theatlantic.com/photo/2014/12/bhopal-the-worlds-worst-industrial-disaster-30-years-later/100864/, accessed 3 January 2018.
17 http://www.nssp-gov.am/spitak_eng.htm, accessed 3 January 2018.
18 https://www.theoldie.co.uk/article/chernobyl-the-disaster-that-never-was, accessed 26 July 2019.

Gorbachev took office at 54, almost absurdly young by these standards. Moreover, he was active and articulate, and his intelligent and fashionably dressed wife Raisa was always at his side. But he was not equipped to deal with major catastrophes and Chernobyl proved to be his greatest challenge in that category. He was clearly ill-prepared for the magnitude of the disaster and especially how to frame his initial response, resorting instead to propaganda about eliminating nuclear weapons by the year 2000. Initially he did not appear in public until May 14, nearly three weeks after the explosions destroyed the fourth Chernobyl reactor.

Attitudes to sensitive high-level industries like nuclear power—and to some extent to its military equivalent the atomic weapons industry—were incredibly nonchalant by Western standards. This was the country that tested the aptitude of the military by detonating atomic weapons between exercising army groups to monitor reactions and vulnerability (something revealed by *Moscow News* during the Gorbachev period). Earlier when a nuclear waste dump had exploded at Kyshtym in the Chelyabinsk region of the Urals in 1957, entire settlements were wiped out and the Techa River remains contaminated today.[19] The Kura site in Kamchatka Peninsula today is still heavily polluted from atomic weapons testing. Chernobyl was a tragedy but one with a lengthy history. The Soviet regime laid waste to its own country in its quest to be a Super Power and the results are only too evident today.[20]

Ironically, it was under Gorbachev, the one leader who tried to affect change—hapless though he often was—that the first disaster to elicit world attention took place. And it brought about that attention first of all because workers at the Forsberg nuclear power station in Sweden set off radiation alarms on entering the station on the morning of 28 April 1986. But the radiation came from the Soviet Union, not Sweden. Had that not happened, or had the accident's impact been limited to Soviet territory, then in all likelihood the accident would have been concealed like the smaller but still serious one at Chernobyl's number one reactor in September 1982.

Ultimately, there was also a positive side to Chernobyl, far-fetched though that may sound. First, it alerted the republics to the dangers of their industries being planned and administered from distant offices in Moscow by bureaucrats who

---

19  See Zhores Medvedev, *Nuclear Disaster in the Urals* (New York: Vintage Books, 1980).
20  The most graphic illustration of this phenomenon is to be found in the book by Murray Feshbach and Alfred Friendly Jr, *Ecoside in the USSR: Health and Nature under Siege* (New York: Basic Books, 1993).

likely had never set foot there. Second it released a surge of civil activity, environmental movements, and ultimately political parties that eventually brought down the Soviet regime that could no longer keep pace with US technological advances.[21] In Ukraine, for example, the formation of informal groups like Green World gave rise to the establishment of the Popular Movement to Support Perestroika (Rukh), which in turn pushed the ruling Communist Party to take steps toward democratization and reforms. Ultimately, that resulted in the division of the party between a reformist faction in Parliament and the more conservative rank-and-file party outside it. The USSR principally collapsed from within, not from external issues. Indeed, the United States was anxious to maintain Gorbachev's administration in power in 1991.

These are the lessons I learned, as well as making many lifelong friends and colleagues en route and paradoxically starting my own career outside my own discipline, and introducing me to Belarus and Belarusians. I should note that Gennady Grushevoy died of leukemia on 28 January 2014 at the age of 63. I hope my Belarusian-speaking friends will forgive me when I say that I miss hearing his beautiful Russian, with which he used to express his thoughts, always based on deep thinking and careful analysis. He wanted Belarusians to determine their own futures but he was never doctrinaire. In fact, he was disarmingly honest. For me he remains a symbol of the aftermath of Chernobyl in Belarus: community-minded, building bridges, working with young people, and, if not flouting authority, circumventing it at every opportunity. It is much preferable to a mindset of permanent victimhood and suffering, a state of mind that the Chernobyl disaster helped to perpetuate.

## The Future of Nuclear Power

The nuclear industry in the post-Soviet states underwent a remarkable recovery. Though the Chernobyl station was shut down in the year 2000, nuclear power continues to play a significant role in Ukraine accounting in 2016 for about 55% of electricity production. Eventually that figure is expected to rise to 70%.[22] All Ukraine's stations use Russian-made reactors, and though the country has not

---

21  See, for example, Tatiana Zaharchenko, "The Environmental Movement and Ecological Law in the Soviet Union: The Process of Transformation," *Ecological Law Quarterly*, Vol. 17, Issue 3 (June 1990): 455–475.

22  The Bellona Foundation has recently published a detailed study of the Ukrainian nuclear power industry from its inception to the present: Heorhii Lysychenko et al, *Atomna industriya Ukrainy* (Oslo: Bellona, 2017).

commissioned any new sites for nuclear power stations it has expanded existing ones at Zaporizhzhya, Rivne, and Khmelnytsky. The Zaporizhzhya nuclear power station is now the largest station in Europe, with six 1,000-megawatt water-pressurized (VVER) reactors. Overall, Ukraine ranks seventh in the world for the production of nuclear-powered electricity.

To the north, Belarus is constructing its first nuclear power plant at Astraviec (Ostrovets), close to the Lithuanian border (one-third of the Lithuanian population lives within 100 kilometres of the station), much to the consternation of the Lithuanian authorities, who decommissioned their own RBMK-1500 station at Ignalina in late December 2009 as one of the conditions for the country joining the European Union. The Belarusian station is expected to start up in 2019 and a second VVER reactor of 1200-megawatts capacity will be completed in 2020. Almost all aspects of the station are Russian, from the fuel to the reactors and turbines. Rosatom signed the contract with the Belarusian authorities. The settlement of Astraviec is undergoing significant development because of the need to create an infrastructure for the plant workers and their families. Thus, the construction of the nuclear power station, while it has brought many problems, has revived the local economy, created new jobs, and generally increased support for the atom in the republic.[23]

Russia also continued to expand its nuclear power program in 2000 after a short lull after the Chernobyl disaster, intending to provide up to 50% of Russian electricity needs by 2050 and up to 80% by the end of the century. Russia exports nuclear technology to China, India, and Iran, among other countries. Interestingly, in early 2017 Rosatom announced that there would be no further state support for the industry after 2020 and that it would rely on commercialization and private ownership. Russia is increasingly dependent on fast breeder reactors, which are regarded as safer and more reliable than either the VVER or RBMK technology used in the past.[24]

The zone itself has become the site for horror movies, such as Brad Parker's *Chernobyl Diaries* (2012) and in June 2015 in Kyiv, tourist agencies were offering trips to the reactor for $400 for an individual and around $100 for groups of four or more. Some wildlife has flourished there and the irradiated zone provides an

---

23 Anton Trofimovich, "Ostrovets v nachale atomnoy ery. Vse kak v Minske—kvartiry po 800 dollarov I probki na dorogakh" (Ostrovets at the start of the atomic era. Everything is like in Minsk—apartments for 800 dolalrs and traffic jams," Naviny, 5 February 2016, at http://naviny.by/rubrics/society/2016/02/05/ic_articles_116_190914, accessed 3 January 2018.

24 World Nuclear Association, "Nuclear Power in Russia,"

environment mostly free of human habitation, but there is a notable absence of birds and certain insects. Those that are fond are invariably found to have abnormalities, as the work of scientists Anders Pape Moller and Timothy A. Mousseau has demonstrated.[25]

## Conclusion

If one were to ask people in Belarus or Ukraine today where they would list the Chernobyl disaster as a factor in their daily lives, it would be unlikely to be listed in the top ten. That is natural and, I think, healthy. At the same time as the founder of the Ukrainian Green Party Yuri Shcherbak once wrote, it was an "epochal" event, something that defined a certain time period. Its consequences were inflated, underestimated, and debated endlessly, but ultimately one cannot discern if a clean-up worker or evacuee who died subsequently, passed away as a result of Chernobyl radiation or other causes. Nor will that information ever be revealed. That is why for families of victims there can be no closure.

The arguments over the impact of additional low-level radiation to humans will continue but radiation affects people differently, depending on lifestyle, environment, habits, the workplace, and other ways. Chernobyl should not be forgotten, yet it should be placed in perspective. It took place in a world that no longer exists but it is not as distant as the Second World War, which the Belarusian leader speaks of as though it happened yesterday. We should not blame those who made mistakes, or even those who refused to reveal information because that behaviour was ingrained in the Soviet system. One could begin with the Soviet nuclear industry, which lacked its own ministry prior to the Chernobyl accident, and which was regarded as the safest means of producing energy: accidents could not happen.

Chernobyl's simple lessons are that openness in reports to those affected is always the wisest policy, and that human error is always likely to outweigh even the most foolproof piece of technology. Scientists must plan for the worst, for all eventualities. In this case the technology was far from foolproof and the atom demonstrated its power.

---

25  Anders Pape Moller and Timothy A. Mousseau, "Biological Consequences of Chernobyl 20 Years On," *Trends in Ecology and Evolution*, Vol. 21, No. 4 (April 2006): 200–207.

# 5. Thinking on Nuclear Proficiency and Disarmament in the Current World

# NUCLEAR PROLIFERATION AND DOUBLE STANDARDS

*Jin Hamamura*[1]

## Taking "double standards" seriously

What are we to make of recurrent acrimonious debates over alleged double standards of the nuclear nonproliferation regime? For example, Iranian Foreign Minister Ali Akbar Salehi conveyed Iran's grievances to the 2012 session of the Conference on Disarmament (CD):

> I would like to highlight that the current exercise of double standards and discrimination are the main threats for the credibility of the NPT. This Treaty in no way provides the right for nuclear weapon states to keep their nuclear arsenals indefinitely and consequently the indefinite extension of the NPT does not mean in any way the indefinite possession of nuclear weapons. … The three pillars of the NPT [non-proliferation, disarmament, and peaceful use of atomic energy] should not be narrowed down to just non-proliferation.[2]

His point is that the discrepancy between the failure of nuclear weapon states (NWSs) to advance nuclear disarmament and their move to undermine Iran's right as a non-nuclear weapon state (NNWS) for peaceful use of atomic energy makes permanent the supposedly temporary "double standard" of the treaty.[3] He then criticized another tacitly approved double standard, Israeli nuclear weapons:

> The possession of nuclear weapons by the only non-party to the NPT in the [Middle East], which makes it a serious threat to the stability of the entire region and international peace and security, is the only obstacle in the way of [the] creation of [a Nuclear Weapon Free Zone.] … It is [a] matter of more concern that in its defiance of the demands of the international community, it enjoys the full support of some nuclear weapon states. Hypocrisy, selectiveness and discrimination describe well the behaviors of some major powers towards the region. The members of the NPT are punished while those who are outside the NPT are rewarded generously.

---

1 This work was supported by the Kōnosuke Matsushita Memorial Foundation and the Murata Science Foundation. An earlier version of this article with more emphasis on theoretical argument was published in Japanese as "'Kyūsen rain' to shite no kaku fukakusan taisei: Shōtotsu suru kihan no dakyō to nijū kijun ronsō," *Kokusai seiji* 184 (2016).
2 Statement by Ali Akbar Salehi to the CD, February 28, 2012, accessed 13 May 2017, http://www.unog.ch/80256EDD006B8954/(httpAssets)/01DF3A1217E91F61C12579B2004615BB/$file/Iran.pdf .
3 I use the terms *nuclear weapon states* and *nuclear powers* differently. The former concerns legal status under the NPT, while the latter concerns facts on the ground. India, for instance, is a nuclear power but not a nuclear weapon state.

In response to this criticism, US Ambassador Laura Kennedy countered by noting Iran's double standard between its "stated commitment to nuclear disarmament" and its "failure to comply with its international obligations regarding its nuclear program."[4] She also defended American actions by referring to President Barack Obama's advocacy of "a world without nuclear weapons."[5]

This is a familiar sight in international conferences on nuclear weapons, which is sometimes dismissed by "hard-headed experts" as a charade of asocial power politics. However, the social character of international politics has been so firmly established by constructivists that simply dismissing the debates out of hand is theoretically untenable.[6] Indeed, the debates should be taken seriously to understand *what is normatively at stake in the nuclear non-proliferation regime*.

Double standard debates are essentially "justice talks." According to Inoue Tatsuo, justice is a universalistic requirement that like cases be treated alike and thus logically renders unjust double standards, which apply different standards (or applies a standard inconsistently) without a universalistic reason for justification.[7]

Taking "double standards" seriously is not equal to casually denouncing or defending them, nor should it be. If we denounce everything that resembles a "double standard" and seek to impose a self-righteous conception of "justice" without due regard for its consequences, we might dangerously destabilize and polarize the international order and bring immense misery.[8] On the other hand, we cannot casually defend "injustice" as a necessary price to pay for stability and brush aside justice concerns. As long as such defence is itself a normative statement, it must be justified by a "moral cost-benefit analysis" based on a conception of substantive justice to judge whether the status quo is worth sustaining (as well as by just dispute settlement procedures); otherwise, the "normative pull" is undermined.[9] Indeed,

---

4  Statement by Laura E. Kennedy to the CD, February 28, 2012, accessed May 13, 2017, http://www.unog.ch/80256EDD006B8954/(httpAssets)/2B04B29DD70F3731C12579B2004FFD37/$file/Statement+delivered+2.28.12+by+USA.pdf.
5  Statement by Laura E. Kennedy to the CD, March 6, 2012, accessed May 13, 2017, http://www.unog.ch/80256EDD006B8954/(httpAssets)/B0F0A19DDD21ED91C12579B900406DAF/$file/USA.pdf.
6  For example, Alexander Wendt, *Social Theory of International Politics* (Cambridge: Cambridge University Press, 1999), 92–138.
7  Inoue Tatsuo, *Hō to iu kuwadate* (Tokyo: Tōkyō Daigaku Shuppankai, 2003), 16–20. A universalistic requirement is a "requirement to exclude from justificatory reasons for normative judgments the question of whether or not the judgements are subsumed under non-universalizable conditions, that is, conditions that cannot be described without ultimately referring to some specific beings (which include groups as well as individuals)." Ibid., 17.
8  Hans J. Morgenthau, "Justice and Power," *Social Research* 41, no. 1 (1974).
9  Inoue Tatsuo, *Sekai seigi ron* (Tokyo: Chikuma Shobō, 2012), 74–83.

these are not just "academic" issues because national leaders are known to be influenced by justice motives when making important foreign policy decisions.[10] Instead of casually defending or denouncing "injustice," this chapter aims to *make sense* of double standard debates by investigating their backgrounds.

## Deception, Deviation, or Ambiguity?

How to make sense of discontent with alleged double standards? There seem to be three ways to look at the phenomena, which I call models of *deception, deviation,* and *ambiguity*.[11]

The deception model treats the debate as an epiphenomenon of asocial power struggle. Actors in world politics are not bound by any normative concern and merely use arguments to deceive real self-interested motives. Although it is indeed important to recognize the element of propaganda, that is not the same as neglecting normative elements altogether.[12] As I have mentioned, such nihilistic views have been decidedly refuted. After all, no one would be tempted to use accusations of double standards for propaganda in a normative void where such accusations carry no weight.[13]

The deviation model regards contestation as a response to occasional deviation from norms by actors that are both normatively constrained and self-interested. Hedley Bull argues that "selective justice" (i.e., double standards) is inevitable in the anarchical society of states (i.e., lacking the central government) where claims for and enforcement of justice are made mostly (or exclusively) by individual states, which have self-interested motives. These motives steer the states away

---

10  David A. Welch, *Justice and the Genesis of War* (Cambridge: Cambridge University Press, 1993).
11  Mlada Bukovansky's typology of hypocrisy somewhat resembles this; cf. Mlada Bukovansky, "Institutionalized Hypocrisy and the Politics of Agricultural Trade," in *Constructing International Economy*, ed. Rawi Abdelal, Mark Blyth, and Craig Parsons (Ithaca: Cornell University Press, 2010), 74–77. Hypocrisy, which is conventionally defined as the "assuming of a false appearance of virtue or goodness, with dissimulation of real character or inclination," is conceptually different from double standards, though they are sometimes casually juxtaposed and treated as more or less the same. "Hypocrisy, n," OED Online, accessed 3 April 2017, http://www.oed.com/view/Entry/90491?redirectedFrom=hypocrisy.
12  Hans J. Morgenthau, *Politics among Nations: The Struggle for Power and Peace* (New York: Alfred A. Knopf, 1948), 174.
13  Thomas E. Doyle, II, *The Ethics of Nuclear Weapons Dissemination: Moral Dilemmas of Aspiration, Avoidance, and Prevention* (Abingdon: Routledge, 2015), 14; Harald Müller, "Justice and Peace: Good Things Do Not Always Go Together," in *Justice and Peace: Interdisciplinary Perspectives on a Contested Relationship*, ed. Gunther Hellmann (Frankfurt am Main: Campus, 2013), 50–51.

from consistently implementing justice.¹⁴ Accusations of double standards against such deviation are a disciplinary strategy called "naming and shaming."¹⁵ (Those accusers need not be saints either. It is entirely possible to selectively charge one's political opponents with double standards.)

Mlada Bukovansky and colleagues explain the nuclear non-proliferation regime along this line. They argue that the regime constitutes NWSs as states with "special responsibilities" that result from a compromise between the principle of sovereign equality, which urges nuclear abolition, and the reality of power asymmetry. Contestation over the regime pivots on the question of whether NWSs are fulfilling their responsibilities.¹⁶ This is surely one way to understand the phenomenon. But is there really a normative consensus on nuclear non-proliferation? Is deviation the only problem that matters? Interestingly, they acknowledge that sovereign equality implies both universal abolition and universal proliferation, even though their substantial argument simply contrasts the abolition urge with power asymmetry. Apparently, normative foundations of the regime are more complex.

The ambiguity model sees the debates as contestation over what is right in a normatively ambiguous environment. Hedley Bull contends that "selective justice" (i.e., double standards) also results from the current state of international society, which is only based on a *minimal agreement over coexistence* among (major or the majority of) states that *disagree over more substantial conceptions of justice* (e.g., human rights). Since issues concerning the latter can only be addressed to the extent that the former is not threatened, "justice" is only selectively fulfilled.¹⁷

That normative ambiguity provokes contestation is noted by many constructivists. Proponents of the "logic of arguing" contend that agents which face ambiguity about the types of norms applicable to concrete contexts resort to argumentation.¹⁸ For proponents of the "logic of contestedness," on the other hand, contestation results not only from ambiguity about the types of norms but, more

---

14  Hedley Bull, *The Anarchical Society: A Study of Order in World Politics* (Basingstoke: Palgrave, 1977), 86–87.
15  Martha Finnemore and Kathryn Sikkink, "International Norm Dynamics and Political Change," *International Organization* 52 no. 4 (1998), 902–04; Margaret E. Keck and Kathryn Sikkink, *Activists beyond Borders: Advocacy Networks in International Politics* (Ithaca: Cornell University Press, 1998), 24.
16  Mlada Bukovansky et al., *Special Responsibilities: Global Problems and American Power* (Cambridge: Cambridge University Press, 2012), 81–121.
17  Bull, *Anarchical Society*, 85.
18  Thomas Risse, "'Let's Argue!': Communicative Action in World Politics," *International Organization* 54, no. 1 (2000), 6–7.

fundamentally, also from prevalent ambiguity about the meaning of norms.[19] Although they offer different views, it is actually not easy to clearly distinguish between the two kinds of ambiguity. Contestation over the meaning of a super-norm (or "norm-complex"[20]) may reflect underlying tensions among compromised normative principles that are subsumed under the super-norm. For example, contestation over the meaning of the Responsibility to Protect doctrine often reflects underlying tensions between human rights and non-interference.[21]

Bull defends the nuclear non-proliferation regime along the line of the ambiguity model. He argues that while the regime obviously does not serve international justice (i.e., sovereign equality) and is vulnerable to normatively-charged criticism, such justice can only be achieved *by universal abolition or by universal proliferation*, both of which are unrealistic. Since even critics of the regime implicitly recognize that nuclear proliferation in general is undesirable, he observes, the debate is not really about the merit of non-proliferation *per se* but about where the line between NWSs and NNWSs be drawn.[22]

Although Bull's analysis is insightful, it does not go far enough. Firstly, while acknowledging that the regime is subject to normatively-charged criticism, he nevertheless underemphasizes its highly contested nature. It is normatively unstable not because it is in conflict with sovereign equality in some abstract sense, but because (1) it legalizes maldistribution of nuclear weapons, which have gravely undermined the traditional *raison d'être* of the sovereign state as the provider of protection and security to inhabitants;[23] and (2) legitimization of nuclear possession or abstention often draws on justificatory reasons that are, logically speaking, applicable to any sovereign state (e.g., self-defence, humanitarianism). Since Bull's analysis of the regime is premised on the framework that contrasts *consensus* over coexistence with *disagreement* over more substantial conceptions of justice, he logically regards non-proliferation as always taking precedence over sovereign equality. In other words, his overemphasis of the regime's stability is rooted in his theoretical

---

19　Antje Wiener, "The Dual Quality of Norms and Governance beyond the State: Sociological and Normative Approaches to 'Interaction,'" *Critical Review of International Social and Political Philosophy* 10, no. 1 (2007), 55–58.
20　Kurusu Kaoru, "Ningen anzen hoshō 'kihan' no keisei to gurōbaru gavanansu: Kihan fukugōka no shiten kara," *Kokusai seiji* 143 (2005).
21　Shimura Mayumi, "'Hogo suru sekinin' gensetsu o meguru kōdō kijun ronsō: Hokansei gensoku to hitsuyōsei gensoku no seijigaku teki bunseki," *Kokusai seiji* 176 (2014).
22　Hedley Bull, "Rethinking Non-Proliferation," *International Affairs* 51, no. 2 (1975): 178–80.
23　John H. Herz, "Rise and Demise of the Territorial State," *World Politics* 9, no. 4 (1957).

framework. To make this point clear, Section 0 offers an alternative conceptualization of the regime that emphasizes its highly contested nature.

Secondly, although he argues that the real point of contestation is often about where the line between NWSs and NNWSs be drawn, he does not elaborate on how the line drawn by the NPT can be normatively defended. Officially, NWSs are given their status based on the *fait accompli* established by the time of the treaty negotiations. This provides the treaty with shaky moral foundations. Section 0 introduces two implicit framing strategies, the combination of which naturalizes the contested line between NWSs and NNWSs.

Thirdly, the parties to the NPT did not settle all problems but "agreed to disagree" on many points by leaving the text ambiguous. On these issues, disputes were merely "postponed." Section 0 examines these postponed discontents that spark subsequent contestation.

## Nuclear nonproliferation regime as a *modus vivendi*

The nuclear non-proliferation regime has emerged as a *modus vivendi* between two diametrically opposed normative attitudes regarding nuclear weapon possession.[24] The concept of *modi vivendi* is used here to convey the contested character of the regime more vividly than other concepts such as "super-norms" and "norm-complexes." By definition, a *modus vivendi* is incapable of stilling conflict of values or principles. It is only a reluctant and unstable compromise conditionally justified by a "moral cost-benefit analysis" and lacks solid deontological foundations aside from the consideration that it was agreed and thus must be kept (i.e., *pacta sunt servanda*).[25] As we will see later, the regime incorporates various measures designed to mitigate discontent, but it remains highly contested.

---

24   William Walker's formulation of the regime is similar to mine in some important respects. He argues that the international nuclear order based on the "logic of restraint" which accepts "the presence of nuclear weapons … 'for the time being' whilst placing limits on their possession and usage, without unduly impending either deterrence or the diffusion of nuclear materials and technologies for civil purposes" has gradually emerged out of conflict between the "logic of armament" (including national prestige, deterrence, and strategic advantage) and the "logic of disarmament" (including prevention of nuclear war, strategic stability, sovereign equality, and nuclear security). William Walker, *A Perpetual Menace: Nuclear Weapons and International Order* (Abingdon: Routledge, 2012), 4–6.

25   On the concept of *modi vivendi*, see Kibe Takashi, "Seiji shisō to shite no modus vivendi," *Seiji Shisō Gakkai kaihō* 31 (2010). See also Inoue, *Sekai seigi ron*, 78–83.

A normative attitude that approves of nuclear weapon possession (*pro-nuclear-weaponism*) draws on a variety of reasons, including preservation and improvement of national security (through nuclear deterrence or nuclear warfighting) and national prestige (through demonstration of military strength and technological prowess). Among them, it is state sovereignty and the right of self-defence that can (under certain circumstances) provide the judgment with quintessential universalistic reasons for justification. A normative attitude that disapproves of nuclear weapon possession (*anti-nuclear-weaponism*) also draws on various reasons, including prospects of humanitarian, civilizational or possibly planetary catastrophe in the event of nuclear war; inherent contradictions or immorality of nuclear deterrence; prudential avoidance of provoking arms races; and health and environmental risks associated with development, production and deployment of nuclear weapons.[26]

These two normative attitudes have been present since the dawn of the nuclear age. The Manhattan Project and the atomic bombing of Hiroshima and Nagasaki were justified by the Allies with reference to waging a war the Axis powers had first started. In the early postwar years, however, the states discussed international control of atomic energy via the UN Atomic Energy Commission, reflecting generally held apprehension over the newly invented weapon. This discussion soon ended in deadlock with the superpowers unable to agree on the terms.[27]

With the intensification of the Cold War, the vision of international control was quietly abandoned by governments while the nuclear club grew—the USSR in 1949, Britain in 1952, France in 1960, and China in 1964. The US had regarded the bomb as vital to counter Soviet conventional superiority in Europe from the beginning of the Cold War, but the New Look policy of the Dwight Eisenhower administration put an extraordinary emphasis on nuclear weapons.[28] The Soviet government of Nikita Khrushchev had likewise leaned heavily on nuclear weapons while cutting spending on conventional forces.[29] It is safe to say that legitimacy to possess nuclear weapons was greatly enhanced by the superpowers' move to make their military strategies nuclear-dependent. In fact, the US government in these years

---

26  Cf. Doyle, *Ethics of Nuclear Weapons Dissemination*, 27–56.
27  McGeorge Bundy, *Danger and Survival: Choices about the Bomb in the First Fifty Years* (New York: Random House, 1988).
28  Bundy, *Danger and Survival*.
29  Vladislav Zubok and Constantine Pleshakov, *Inside the Kremlin's Cold War: From Stalin to Khrushchev* (Cambridge, MA: Harvard University Press, 1996), 193.

found it very hard to deny its allies in Western Europe the right to develop or possess nuclear weapons for self-defence when NATO strategy to defend Western Europe against a Soviet onslaught depended critically on those very weapons.[30]

At the same time, however, anti-nuclear-weaponism was emerging from below.[31] The development of thermonuclear weapons in the 1950s helped spread the view that nuclear war would mean the end of civilization. Recurring crises and wars that involved nuclear powers (e.g., Korea, Suez, Taiwan Strait, Berlin) instilled fear of nuclear war in the popular mind. In 1954, a US thermonuclear test at Bikini Atoll exposed a Japanese tuna fishing boat named *Lucky Dragon 5* (along with numerous other boats and some Marshall Islanders) to its nuclear fallout and killed one of its crew, as well as sparking a food crisis in Japan, which discovered that a large amount of unloaded tuna was contaminated. The Lucky Dragon incident taught ordinary people the danger of radioactive contamination, which poses environmental and health risks. All these developments provoked global antinuclear movements. Feeling their pressure, the US, USSR and UK entered a nuclear test moratorium and started negotiations on a test ban in 1958. In 1961, the UN General Assembly adopted Resolution 1653, which declared that, "Any State using nuclear and thermo-nuclear weapons is to be considered as violating the Charter of the United Nations, as acting contrary to the laws of humanity and as committing a crime against mankind and civilization."[32]

As seen above, the 1950s witnessed the simultaneous emergence of two contending normative attitudes regarding nuclear weapon possession. This deepening dilemma created a demand for a compromise.[33] The test ban negotiation, for one, can be interpreted as such an attempt: it constrains further development of nuclear weapons, but does not challenge the already established fact of nuclear powers. In the end, the three negotiating parties abandoned a comprehensive ban and opted for the Partial Test Ban Treaty (PTBT) in 1963 due to difficulties surrounding verification measures. The treaty was a *modus vivendi* that carved out a larger applicable domain for pro-nuclear-weaponism rather than a comprehensive ban: it was

---

30   Marc Trachtenberg, *A Constructed Peace: The Making of the European Settlement* (Princeton: Princeton University Press, 1999).
31   Lawrence S. Wittner, *Confronting the Bomb: A Short History of the World Nuclear Disarmament Movement* (Stanford: Stanford University Press, 2009).
32   UN General Assembly, Resolution 1653 (XVI), "Declaration on the Prohibition of the Use of Nuclear and Thermo-Nuclear Weapons," November 24, 1961, accessed June 20, 2017, http://www.un.org/en/ga/search/view_doc.asp?symbol=A/RES/1653(XVI).
33   By this I do not mean that the architects of the *modi vivendi* were motivated solely (or even primarily) by this demand. There were more parochial motivations.

effective in preventing radioactive fallout from causing a health hazard to the public while allowing the nuclear powers to continue the arms race with underground tests. Since underground tests are technologically more demanding than atmospheric ones, the ban also set the bar higher for emerging nuclear powers. This hidden but widely assumed intent to slow the expansion of the nuclear club became overt with the NPT.

International origins of the NPT date back to the Irish proposals to freeze the number of nuclear powers at the UN General Assembly starting from 1958. Irish Foreign Minister Frank Aiken presented Ireland's proposals as a pragmatic compromise that reduced the danger of nuclear war and was a first step toward nuclear disarmament. The 1961 General Assembly Resolution 1665 (the so-called "Irish Resolution") proved to be especially influential in establishing many of the rights and obligations of the soon-to-be-followed NPT. As Tsuzaki Naoto argues, it was precisely because the proposal came from a small nonnuclear neutral power like Ireland that a compromise that favoured existing nuclear powers gained a certain amount of legitimacy.[34] The NPT was finalized in 1968 after a series of negotiations led primarily by the superpowers.

The NPT permits NWSs, defined as those that had exploded a nuclear device before 1 January 1967, to continue possessing nuclear weapons with the obligation to pursue negotiations on nuclear disarmament in good faith while banning NNWSs from doing so. By this arrangement the treaty established a spatial-temporal compromise between the applicable domains of pro- and anti-nuclear-weaponism. That is, the compromise delimits the applicable domains of the contending normative attitudes by utilizing both the *spatial* dimension of distinguishing five NWSs (and their allies to a certain extent) from other NNWSs and the *temporal* dimension of having a transitory period leading to a total ban. The promise of eventual nuclear disarmament by NWSs (i.e., temporal delimitation) was meant to mitigate the distributive injustice of legitimizing the *fait accompli* (i.e., spatial delimitation).

In addition to this basic framework, the compromise also left some ambiguity about the precise lines of the normative delimitation, reflecting the unresolved tensions. Two kinds of ambiguity stood out on the spatial dimension. One was implications of territorial reorganization on the distinction between NWSs and NNWSs. What if a NWS merged with a NNWS to form a new state? What if a

---

34  Tsuzaki Naoto, "Kaku Fukakusan Bōshi Jōyaku no kigen (1955–1961 nen) (1)," *Hōgaku ronsō* 159, no. 5 (2006); Tsuzaki, "Kaku Fukakusan Bōshi Jōyaku no kigen (1955–1961 nen) (2) kan," *Hōgaku ronsō* 161, no. 1 (2007).

NNWS split into two separate states? In the NPT negotiation, the superpowers were unable to agree over the question of whether a fully-integrated "United States of Europe" may have independent nuclear forces by virtue of its successor state status to Britain and France and intentionally left the matter unresolved.[35] William Walker argues that the parties to the treaty could agree on where to draw the line between NWSs and NNWSs because by simply recognizing the *fait accompli* they could avoid the contentious topic of "fitness" to possess nuclear weapons.[36] Ambiguity over the question of territorial reorganization shows how contentious it really was.

Another ambiguity on the spatial dimension concerned the range of prohibited activities for NNWSs, specifically about their guaranteed right to peaceful use of nuclear energy. Since the distinction between civilian and military use of nuclear technology is not clear-cut, there was room for disagreement over the meaning of "peaceful use." To be sure, the NPT came close to resolving this ambiguity by recognizing the "inalienable right of all the Parties to the Treaty to develop research, production and use of nuclear energy for peaceful purposes" and calling for "the fullest possible exchange of equipment, materials and scientific and technological information" to that end (art. 4). Some observers interpret this to mean that NNWSs were free to build the *de facto* infrastructure for nuclear weapon production with the help of the international community as long as they did not build actual nuclear explosive devices, claimed that the investment was for peaceful purposes, and got verified by the International Atomic Energy Agency (IAEA).[37] The existence of this "loophole" can only be explained as a further effort to make the unequal treaty bearable for NNWSs. However, as we will see later, the US (along with some other suppliers of nuclear equipment, materials and knowledge) changed its course from the mid 1970s and started to deny (some) NNWSs uranium enrichment and nuclear reprocessing technologies (aka "sensitive technologies"), which are vital both for nuclear bombs and for the nuclear fuel cycle. This created (or exacerbated) ambiguity over the range of activities denied to NNWSs.

The temporal delimitation also suffers from ambiguity. The NPT stipulates that "Each of the Parties to the Treaty undertakes to pursue negotiations in good

---

35    Arakaki Hiromu, *Jonson seiken ni okeru kaku fukakusan seisaku no henyō to shinten* (Kyoto: Mineruva Shobō, 2016), 256–57.
36    Walker, *Perpetual Menace*, 76–77.
37    Roland Popp, "The Long Road to the NPT: From Superpower Collusion to Global Compromise," in *Negotiating the Nuclear Non-Proliferation Treaty: Origins of the Nuclear Order*, ed. Roland Popp, Liviu Horovitz and Andreas Wenger (Abingdon: Routledge, 2017), 26–27.

faith on effective measures relating to cessation of the nuclear arms race at an early date and to nuclear disarmament, and on a treaty on general and complete disarmament under strict and effective international control" (art. 6). This is ambiguous about when the transitory period will end and nuclear weapons will be abolished, reflecting unresolved tensions between the non-aligned states' calls for concrete steps towards disarmament and NWSs' hesitation to heed the calls. This ambiguity did not disappear with the 1995 NPT Review Conference, in which a program of action on a comprehensive test ban, a fissile material cut-off, and nuclear weapon elimination was agreed[38]; nor did it with the International Court of Justice's 1996 advisory opinion for the UN General Assembly, in which the Court unanimously stated the obligation not only to pursue nuclear disarmament negotiations in good faith but also to bring them to a conclusion.[39]

We have thus seen that the main question of the regime was how to establish a *modus vivendi* between contending normative attitudes regarding nuclear weapon possession by (clearly or ambiguously) delimiting applicable domains. Difficulty lay in counteracting the distributive injustice of differential treatment between NWSs and NNWSs by twin promises of eventual nuclear disarmament and peaceful use of nuclear energy.

However, this is not the whole story. We have thus far assumed that sovereign equality is an undisputed source of legitimacy. In fact, the next section shows this is hardly the case.

## Unjustified, unfortunate, or justified?

Some authors note that spatial delimitation between NWSs and NNWSs, which was originally just an acknowledgment of the *fait accompli* based on a specific date, is now increasingly defended in terms of differing degrees of "fitness" of states to possess nuclear weapons.[40] This change is best understood as a framing strategy to neutralize normative charges against the "double standard" of the spatial delimitation. If NWSs and NNWSs have some innate differences that make those states

---

38   1995 Review and Extension Conference of the Parties to the Treaty on the Non-Proliferation of Nuclear Weapons, Decision 2, "Principles and Objectives for Nuclear Non-Proliferation and Disarmament," 11 May 1995, accessed 28 June 2017, https://unoda-web.s3-accelerate.amazonaws.com/wp-content/uploads/assets/WMD/Nuclear/1995-NPT/pdf/1995-NY-NPTReviewConference-FinalDocumentDecision_2.pdf.
39   Legality of the Threat or Use of Nuclear Weapons, Advisory Opinion, 1996 I.C.J. 226 (8 July 1996).
40   Hugh Gusterson, *People of the Bomb: Portraits of America's Nuclear Complex* (Minneapolis: University of Minnesota Press, 2004), 24; Walker, *Perpetual Menace*, 77, 154–55.

respectively fit and unfit for responsible management of nuclear weapons, one could argue that their different status is not necessarily unjust. After all, justice requires not only that like cases be treated alike but also that unlike cases be treated differently.[41] In short, this change is an attempt to frame the differential treatment of NWSs and NNWSs as distributively just. We call this the *strategy of distributive justification*.

As we will see, however, this strategy was not entirely absent in the NPT. Nor was the strategy a peculiar phenomenon of the nuclear age.[42] The NPT should rather be seen as having inherited a long tradition of hierarchical conceptions of international society and given a particular twist, which in turn affected its subsequent evolution.

There is indeed a long tradition of differential treatment of sovereign states based on alleged differences in civilizational qualities. According to Gerry Simpson, legal notions of "Great Powers" and "Outlaw States" were established in the nineteenth century in the context of managing the Concert of Europe and "unequal treaties" with non-Western states, respectively. Although these concepts have experienced ups and downs since then, he argues, they have been inherited to this day.[43]

This tradition is also visible in the nuclear history. After the Hiroshima and Nagasaki bombing, US President Harry Truman and British Prime Minister Clement Atlee justified their intentions to keep the Anglo-American monopoly of atomic bombs by referring to the concept of "trusteeship," which had been used to justify colonial rule since the nineteenth century.[44] Various measures were also taken to deny the ex-Axis powers nuclear weapons due to their supposedly inherent bellicosity: nuclear research was severely restricted in occupied Germany and Japan;[45] Bulgaria, Hungary, Finland, Italy and Romania had to relinquish rights

---

41  Aristotle, *Nicomachean Ethics*, trans. and ed. Roger Crisp (Cambridge: Cambridge University Press, 2000), 1131a–b.
42  Postcolonial theorists are very much aware of this latter point. See Shampa Biswas, *Nuclear Desire: Power and the Postcolonial Nuclear Order* (Minneapolis: University of Minnesota Press, 2014); Gusterson, *People of the Bomb*, 21–47.
43  Gerry Simpson, *Great Powers and Outlaw States: Unequal Sovereigns in the International Legal Order* (Cambridge: Cambridge University Press, 2004).
44  Grégoire Mallard, *Fallout: Nuclear Diplomacy in an Age of Global Fracture* (Chicago: University of Chicago Press, 2014), 43. For the connection between trusteeship and colonial rule, see Igarashi Motomichi, *Shihai suru jindō shugi: Shokuminchi tōchi kara heiwa kōchiku made* (Tokyo: Iwanami Shoten, 2016).
45  Tanaka Shingo, "Genshiryoku kaku mondai ni okeru tokushu na Nichi-Bei kankei no hōga: Torūman seiken no tai-Nichi genshiryoku kenkyū kisei to kanwa 1945–47," *Kokusai kōkyō seisaku kenkyū* 17, no. 2 (2013).

concerning nuclear weapons in the 1947 Paris peace treaties; Austria had to do likewise in the 1955 Austrian State Treaty; West Germany had to promise not to build nuclear weapons in its own territory when it signed the 1954 Paris accords; many proposals in the 1950s to establish a nuclear-weapon-free zone or other similar frameworks in Central Europe had a not-so-veiled intent to contain West Germany.[46]

It is therefore not surprising that many promoters of the NPT had specific countries (or types of countries) of concern in mind. Of particular importance for the superpowers and their European allies was the nuclear status of West Germany, as noted by many authors.[47] For others like Irish Foreign Minister Aiken, nuclear weapons in the hands of small states or revolutionary groups were more (or just as) frightening.[48] It is no accident that the NPT was negotiated and concluded before those "frightening" possibilities (mostly) materialized. It was a preventive measure to head off such "calamities."

This does not mean, however, that the NPT was mere application of this hierarchical tradition. The tradition was given a particular twist because the NPT was a treaty with a universal scope that was negotiated when the sovereign equality principle was at its zenith.[49] Justification of differential treatment of NWSs and NNWSs based on a nineteenth-century-style "standard of civilization" was simply not possible.

Therefore, the NPT does not so much justify outright the differential treatment as adopts an appearance of accepting it out of necessity. Officially, NWSs are given their status only because they happened to have already created a *fait accompli* by the time of treaty negotiations; NNWSs must abstain from having nuclear weapons only because they happened not to have crossed the nuclear threshold yet. An "egalitarian façade"[50] was maintained by not singling out any particular state as unfit for nuclear weapon possession. And for the "façade" to be effective, it had to be plausible to a certain extent. Thus, China was admitted as a NWS because

---

46   Kurashina Itsuki, *Aizenhawā seiken to Nishi Doitsu: Dōmei seisaku to shite no tōzai gunbi kanri kōshō* (Kyoto: Mineruva Shobō, 2008).
47   For example, Arakaki, *Jonson seiken*; Dane Swango, "The Nuclear Nonproliferation Treaty: Constrainer, Screener, or Enabler?" (PhD dissertation, UCLA, 2009). See also a caveat in Popp, "Long Road to the NPT," 21.
48   Mohamed I. Shaker, *The Nuclear Non-Proliferation Treaty: Origins and Implementation, 1959–1979*, Vol. 1 (London: Oceana Publications, 1980), 5.
49   Simpson, *Great Powers and Outlaw States*. Indeed, Simpson sees the NPT as an exception to the general contemporary trend, which rejected legalized hegemony. Ibid., 74.
50   Swango, "Nuclear Nonproliferation Treaty," 12.

it had already established a *fait accompli* by the time of treaty negotiations, even though both superpowers viewed the revolutionary regime as excessively belligerent and dangerous.[51] The NPT adopted the logic of recognizing the *fait accompli* not only because, as Walker argues, the parties to the treaty could avoid the contentious topic of "fitness" to possess nuclear weapons but also because they could minimize frictions with the requirement of justice. According to Judith Shklar, although we respond quite differently to bad events depending on whether we frame them as injustice or misfortune, "the line of separation between ... [them] is a political choice, not a simple rule that can be taken as a given."[52] In that sense, the language of the NPT is a framing strategy to make people accept with resignation the differential treatment as unfortunate but necessary (instead of unjustified). This is distinct from the strategy of distributive justification. We call it the *strategy of necessity*.[53]

However, the strategy of necessity alone cannot stabilize the regime. If NWSs are differentiated from NNWSs solely because the former happened to have established a *fait accompli* before a specific date, that is likely to be seen as unjust, especially because the promise of eventual nuclear disarmament is not so credible. Moreover, the strategy does not adequately address discontent with the way the line between NWSs and NNWSs is drawn. If a *fait accompli* at a specific point in time is accepted as legitimate, new nuclear powers could adopt the same logic to demand recognition of their new *fait accompli*.[54] The strategy of necessity therefore needs to be complemented by the strategy of distributive justification. Or rather, these two apparently contradictory strategies somehow need to work in tandem to keep dodging accusations of the "double standard" because neither is persuasive enough as a stand-alone argument.

Indeed, the strategy of distributive justification was subtly embedded in the treaty language through the ingenious metaphor, "proliferation." As David

---

51   The United States had seriously considered preventive attacks on Chinese nuclear facilities in the 1960s because of its concern that a nuclear-armed China was too dangerous. The Soviet Union had come to see China as a military threat around the mid 1960s and apparently deliberated over attacking Chinese nuclear facilities during the 1969 Sino-Soviet border conflict. See William Burr and Jeffrey T. Richelson, "Whether to 'Strangle the Baby in the Cradle': The United States and the Chinese Nuclear Program, 1960–64," *International Security* 25, no. 3 (2000/01); Lyle J. Goldstein, *Preventive Attack and Weapons of Mass Destruction: A Comparative Historical Analysis* (Stanford: Stanford University Press, 2006), 56–66, 76–83.

52   Judith N. Shklar, *The Faces of Injustice* (New Haven: Yale University Press, 1990), 5.

53   The contrast between the strategy of distributive justification and the strategy of necessity is not intended as a statement that consideration of justice is irrelevant in the case of the latter.

54   Cf. Inoue, *Sekai seigi ron*, 77–78.

Mutimer points out, the word "proliferation" had previously been used to denote the reproduction of animals/plants and increases in the number of cells because of cell division. While reproductive activities and cell division are natural phenomena, excessive hyperactivity causes instability of the ecosystem (in the case of reproduction) and cancer (in the case of cell division), which requires outside intervention to restore equilibrium. The NPT defined "unbridled" increases of nuclear powers as a threat to international security by using this metaphor and established a cognitive framework that calls for outside intervention.[55] The metaphor thus represents nuclear possession of the five designated states as "normal" and that of others as "abnormal" and naturalizes the differential treatment based on alleged differences in qualities. Even non-parties to the NPT cannot avoid this dichotomy, because the treaty regulates the relations between the parties and the non-parties too.[56]

But what are the specific "qualities" of NWSs? Of course, the NPT stipulates that they undertake to avoid assisting nonnuclear powers to acquire nuclear weapons; to pursue nuclear disarmament negotiations in good faith; and to facilitate the international exchange of relevant equipment, materials, and knowledge for peaceful use of nuclear energy.[57] In addition, NWSs' behaviour since the 1960s has lent more substance to the representation of "responsible NWSs." Firstly, various kinds of security assurances have been made by NWSs, including pledges not to use nuclear weapons first ("no first use"), not to use or threaten to use nuclear weapons against NNWSs or nuclear weapon free zones ("negative security assurances"), and to assist NNWSs that have come under nuclear threats or attacks ("positive security assurances").[58] Secondly, NWSs forwent nuclear tests: the US, USSR, and UK renounced underwater, atmospheric, and extra-atmospheric nuclear tests with signing of the PTBT in 1963; France and China stopped atmospheric tests in 1974 and 1980, respectively; All NWSs signed the Comprehensive Test Ban Treaty (CTBT) and have refrained from conducting underground nuclear tests since 1996 at the

---

55 David Mutimer, *The Weapons State: Proliferation and the Framing of Security* (Boulder: Lynne Rienner, 2000), 58–63. See also Benoît Pelopidas, "The Oracles of Proliferation: How Experts Maintain a Biased Historical Reading That Limits Policy Innovation," *Nonproliferation Review* 18, no. 1 (2011).
56 Cf. Kurosawa Mitsuru, *Gunshuku kokusaihō no atarashī shiza: Kakuheiki fukakusan taisei no kenkyū* (Tokyo: Yūshindō, 1986), 38.
57 Although the latter two oblige all parties to the treaty, NWSs (especially the superpowers) are commonly expected to take the primary responsibility.
58 For an overview, see John Simpson, "The Role of Security Assurances in the Nuclear Nonproliferation Regime," in *Security Assurances and Nuclear Nonproliferation*, ed. Jeffrey W. Knopf (Stanford: Stanford University Press, 2012).

latest (though the US and China have not ratified it). Thirdly, Cold War *détente* and the US-Soviet arms control negotiations were perceived to have stabilized the strategic relations and lowered the risk of nuclear war. The substantiation of the "responsibility" has in turn constituted the "irresponsibility" as the negative, which justifies the hierarchical order.[59]

Nonetheless, substantive "qualities" of NWSs have been elusive. When diplomats, statesmen and commentators describe certain states or behaviour as responsible or irresponsible, they often mean different things. In that sense, it is like the nineteenth-century "standard of civilization." The civilizational standard was a moving target for those trying to join the civilized club. Part of the reason why the standard remained elusive is that it had changed with time.[60] In addition, the elusiveness served the established insiders by keeping the outsiders "pursuing belonging, but never really getting the recognition they crave," thereby sustaining a normative hierarchy.[61] The same could apply to the alleged qualities of NWSs.

Interestingly, the unholy alliance between the strategy of distributive justification and the strategy of necessity also emerged in the mid 1970s in defence of the US-led technology denial of uranium enrichment and nuclear reprocessing towards NNWSs. Since this new policy could not (or did not) roll back existing programs in Europe (Euratom) and Japan, it virtually meant introducing differential treatment between two categories of NNWSs based on their technological advancement at that time. This differentiation has been defended by referring to the *fait accompli* that were already in place in the mid 1970s as well as by a more tacit reference to alleged differences in qualities.

A good example of this is contrasting policies of the Gerald Ford and the Jimmy Carter administrations towards acquisition of nuclear reprocessing capabilities by Japan and South Korea.[62] The Ford administration differentiated the two

---

59 Nina Tannenwald, *The Nuclear Taboo: The United States and the Non-Use of Nuclear Weapons Since 1945* (Cambridge: Cambridge University Press, 2007), 19, 46, 335.
60 Barry Buzan, "The 'Standard of Civilisation' as an English School Concept," *Millennium* 42, no. 3 (2014): 580; Ayşe Zarakol, *After Defeat: How the East Learned to Live with the West* (Cambridge: Cambridge University Press, 2011), 192, 206.
61 Zarakol, *After Defeat*, 248. For a related argument in the context of inequality among human beings, see André Béteille, *The Idea of Natural Inequality and Other Essays* (New Delhi: Oxford University Press, 1983), 32.
62 Tomotsugu Shinsuke, "1970 nendai no Beikoku kaku fukakusan seisaku to kaku nenryō saikuru seisaku: Higashi Ajia takokukan saishori kōsō to Tokai-mura shisetsu o meguru gaikō kōshō kara no kōsatsu," *Ningen kankyōgaku kenkyū* 7, no. 2 (2009). See also Takeda Yū, *"Keizai taikoku" Nihon no tai-Bei kyōchō: Anpo, keizai, genshiryoku o meguru shikōsakugo, 1975–1981 nen* (Kyoto: Mineruva Shobō, 2015).

East Asian allies by their "qualities." In response to ROK Vice Minister of Foreign Affairs (Acting Foreign Minister) Roh Shin-yeong's complaint about the American double standard of allowing Japan to operate the Tokai Reprocessing Plant while denying South Korea the same technology, US Ambassador Richard Sneider cited Japanese anti-nuclear-weapon sentiment and the fact that Korea was a "critical area where NK [North Korean] and Sino/Soviet reaction needed to be considered."[63] It may seem at first glance that Sneider merely spoke in terms of avoiding misperception of nuclear intent, but upon closer examination what he actually implied here is the US's contrasting evaluation of the two countries' likelihood to be tempted by nuclear weapons. Indeed, the ROK did have a secret nuclear weapon program at that time and the US was already aware of it.[64] Note that difference in "qualities" is substantiated in this context as strength to resist temptation of the nuclear bomb. Such substantiation was made possible by the NPT which had constituted the "responsibility" of NNWSs too.

By contrast, the Carter administration expressed unease with the Tokai plant because it saw the issue in the context of a universal scheme of technology denial and reappraisal of the nuclear fuel cycle. Since it was unrealistic to expect Japan to abandon reprocessing altogether, the US accepted it as a *fait accompli* with certain conditions.

## Discontent with the *modus vivendi*

We have seen the basic formula of the *modus vivendi* and then the subtler framing strategies behind it. While the regime has obviously succeeded in quelling some discontent through these measures, as testified by the current NPT membership of 191 (or 190, depending on the status of North Korea), it has also been roundly criticized for its "double standards." We are going to examine various forms of discontent that spark contestation below.

Contestation over alleged double standards of the regime can be divided into two types. One concerns disagreement over the need for a compromise that accommodates both pro- and anti-nuclear-weaponism. Here, *rejectionists* who deny any such need (and favour nuclear *laissez-faire* or an immediate nuclear ban) are

---

63   US Embassy Seoul telegram 8278 to Department of State, "ROKG Rejects Our Representations on Nuclear Reprocessing," October 24, 1975, in "Stopping Korea from Going Nuclear, Part 1," National Security Archive Electronic Briefing Book no. 582, ed. William Burr, https://nsarchive.gwu.edu/briefing-book/henry-kissinger-nuclear-vault/2017-03-22/stopping-korea-going-nuclear-part-i (Accessed October 10, 2019).
64   Burr, "Stopping Korea from Going Nuclear."

joined by *revisionists* who accept that need but are dissatisfied with the way the normative domains are delimited in the regime and deceptively adopt rejectionist rhetoric to denounce it as a double standard, as Bull had observed.[65] Note that this debate does not always pit the parties to the NPT against the non-parties. The non-parties do not necessarily deny the need for a compromise, nor are they free from the framework established by the treaty. Likewise, some states might have been forced to join the treaty even though they are not convinced about the necessity of a compromise.

The other kind of contestation concerns disagreement over subsequent applicatory practices of the regime, which stems from its ambiguities. As we will see, applicatory contestation often betrays continuing tensions between the contending normative attitudes regarding nuclear weapon possession. Accordingly, contestation over application of the regime should not be understood as entirely distinct from contestation over the *raison d'être* of the regime.[66] The remainder of this section examines four specific types of discontent that spark applicatory contestation.[67]

Firstly, the question of how to cope with a new nuclear *fait accompli* established by a non- or withdrawn party to/from the NPT (Israel, South Africa, India, Pakistan, North Korea) is controversial. In the case of non-compliance by a NNWS party to the NPT, the IAEA can respond in accordance with the safeguards agreement state, including making inspections, demanding corrections, and halting nuclear transactions with the state. The IAEA can also refer serious breach of the agreement to the UN Security Council (e.g., North Korea, Iran).[68] However, the NPT (or other relevant agreements) does not have any provision to deal with a new *fait accompli* created by a non- or withdrawn party.[69]

---

65   Bull, "Rethinking Non-Proliferation," 180.
66   I am not convinced, therefore, by Nicole Deitelhoff and Lisbeth Zimmermann's argument that contestation over application of norms has stabilizing effects on the norms while contestation over validity of norms has destabilizing effects. See Nicole Deitelhoff and Lisbeth Zimmermann, "Things We Lost in the Fire: How Different Types of Contestation Affect the Validity of International Norms," PRIF Working Paper no. 18 (Frankfurt am Main: Peace Research Institute Frankfurt, 2013).
67   The author does not claim that this section exhausts all possible discontents over "double standards" in application of the regime. For other issues, see Glenn Chafetz, "The Political Psychology of the Nuclear Nonproliferation Regime," *Journal of Politics* 57, no. 3 (1995); Liu Huaping, "Guoji Yuanzineng Jigou de juxian: Yi Yilang he wenti wei li," *Waijiao pinglun* 3 (2010).
68   Abe Tatsuya, *Tairyō hakai heiki to kokusaihō: Kokka to kokusai kanshi kikan no kyōdō o tsūjita gendai teki kokusaihō jitsugen purosesu* (Tokyo: Yūshindō, 2011), 222–42.
69   Cf. Peter D. Feaver and Emerson M. S. Niou, "Managing Nuclear Proliferation: Condemn, Strike, or Assist?" *International Studies Quarterly* 40, no. 2 (1996), 212. Note, however, that the Security

The orthodox position is obviously non-recognition. However, the NPT itself legitimized NWSs' status based on the *fait accompli* established before January 1, 1967. That the NPT settled with five NWSs, instead of, say, four or six, is essentially an accident. As I noted earlier, both superpowers in the late 1960s would have preferred four (i.e., five *minus China*), if that was feasible. Likewise, if Israel had detonated a nuclear explosive device it presumably assembled in haste on the eve of the Six-Day War of June 1967, as contemplated by some of its leaders at the time,[70] the superpowers might have had to take that into consideration and propose a date later than June 1967 in their separate but identical draft submitted to the Eighteen-Nation Committee on Disarmament on August 24, 1967, in which they introduced the watershed date January 1, 1967, for the first time.[71] The point is that the concept of non-proliferation has no natural affinity with the number *five*. Even if the line of the spatial delimitation is revised and a new status quo is established in which the membership of the nuclear club has grown but its exclusivity is maintained, the concept of non-proliferation has no difficulty in supporting it. Lack of intrinsic reasons to privilege the current number of NWSs makes the spatial delimitation vulnerable to revisionism.

If one is to recognize the nuclear status for newcomers, the strategy of distributive justification (i.e., differentiating states based on alleged civilizational qualities) would probably become more prominent in both decision-making and justificatory rhetoric than when the NPT was negotiated or when the spatial delimitation of the treaty is defended. This is because on this occasion one tries to enlarge the membership of the nuclear club while maintaining its exclusivity. The strategy of distributive justification is useful for defending such changes. It is therefore in

---

Council adopted a presidential statement in 1992 which stated, "the proliferation of all weapons of mass destruction constitutes a threat to international peace and security." UN Security Council, S/23500, "Note by the President of the Security Council," 31 January 1992, accessed 20 June 2017, http://www.securitycouncilreport.org/atf/cf/%7B65BFCF9B-6D27-4E9C-8CD3-CF6E4FF96FF9%7D/PKO%20S%2023500.pdf.

70  Avner Cohen, *Israel and the Bomb* (New York: Columbia University Press, 1998), 273–76; Cohen, "The 1967 Six-Day War: New Israeli Perspective, 50 Years Later," 3 June 2017, accessed 7 June 2017, https://www.wilsoncenter.org/publication/the-1967-six-day-war.

71  Counterfactual analysis on this question is difficult. In March 1965, the US and Israel signed a memorandum of understanding in which the US reaffirmed its commitment to independence and integrity of Israel and Israel pledged "not to be the first to introduce nuclear weapons into the Arab-Israeli area." Cohen, *Israel and the Bomb*, 207. An Israeli nuclear test would breach this promise and thus might have angered the US. On the other hand, the US acknowledged in the memorandum a link between Israel's non-introduction pledge and its security. This might have made the US less unsympathetic to the Israeli decision, given that Israel perceived itself as existentially threatened by Arab neighbors on the eve of the Six-Day War.

the interest of a new nuclear power to represent itself as a "responsible" state if it wants recognition from NWSs. If the state behaves "irresponsibly," that would probably make attainment of nuclear status more difficult.[72]

The US first unofficially revised the spatial delimitation when it gave secret approval to Israeli nuclear possession in 1969, which Iranian Foreign Minister Salehi denounced as a double standard, as seen in the introduction.[73] The John Kennedy and Lyndon Johnson administrations had tried in vain to force Israel to surrender its nuclear weapon program with a combination of coercion and inducement. Israel had persisted in the face of American pressure and crossed the threshold by the eve of the Six-Day War in 1967 without a declaration or nuclear testing. Seeing the new *fait accompli* on the ground, President Richard Nixon is believed to have given approval at the 1969 summit with Israeli Prime Minister Golda Meir in exchange for Israel's promise to refrain from disclosing the fact of nuclear possession. Meir had always insisted that Israel should acknowledge the existence of its nuclear weapon program to the Americans and explain why it needed one—the memory of the Holocaust and the geostrategic vulnerability of being surrounded by antagonistic Arab neighbors who denied the existence of Israel—instead of hiding it like her predecessors David Ben-Gurion and Levi Eshkol. Although the meeting minutes are still classified, it is natural to assume that Nixon accepted this argument. National Security Advisor Henry Kissinger, anxious about possible Arab and Soviet reactions, justified the American policy change two months before the meeting as follows: "While we might ideally like to halt actual Israeli possession [of nuclear weapons], what we really want at a minimum may be just to keep Israeli possession from becoming an established international fact."[74] It is safe to say that the US redefined its Middle East non-proliferation policy as preventing the region's other states from developing nuclear weapons.

---

72    Interestingly, North Korea's leader Kim Jong-un recently declared that his country acted as "a responsible nuclear state," specifically making commitments "not [to] use a nuclear weapon unless its sovereignty is encroached upon by any aggressive hostile forces with nukes, ... [to] fulfill its obligation for non-proliferation and [to] strive for the global denuclearization." "Kim Jong Un Makes Report on Work of WPK Central Committee at Its 7$^{th}$ Congress," Korean News Service, May 7, 2016, accessed June 15, 2017, http://www.kcna.co.jp.

73    The following account of Israeli nuclear history is based on Avner Cohen's two books, *Israel and the Bomb* and *The Worst-Kept Secret: Israel's Bargain with the Bomb* (New York: Columbia University Press, 2010).

74    Henry A. Kissinger to Richard Nixon, "Israeli Nuclear Program," White House Memorandum, July 19, 1969, accessed June 7, 2017, https://www.nixonlibrary.gov/virtuallibrary/releases/nov07/071969_israel.pdf.

Although this policy change might have been partly motivated by a sense that the NPT is arbitrary or ineffective in setting a specific date after which crossing the nuclear threshold is delegitimized—Nixon and Kissinger at that time were no fans of the NPT[75]—, unilaterally revising the line of the spatial delimitation probably made the revised line look even more arbitrary, thus further weakening the regime. In the Middle East and North Africa, Iraq, Libya, Syria, and Iran had (or are/were suspected to have) pursued nuclear weapons despite their NPT membership. While nuclear weapon programs are often driven by multiple motivations,[76] a sense of injustice engendered by the regional precedent of Israeli nuclear possession might have been a contributing factor to these programs.[77]

The US policy toward India and Pakistan faced a similar problem. George W. Bush's controversial nuclear deal with India was especially notable in this regard. In contrast to the secret Nixon-Meir understanding, the US-India deal was an overt attempt to revise the spatial delimitation and thus generated fierce debate. In order to publicly defend the deal, Secretary of State Condoleezza Rice emphasized that India qualified as a "responsible" state for nuclear possession:

> India is a democracy, where citizens of many ethnicities and faiths cooperate in peace and freedom. India's civilian government functions transparently and accountably. It is fighting terrorism and extremism, and it has a 30-year record of responsible behavior on nonproliferation matters. Aspiring proliferators such as North Korea or Iran may seek to draw connections between themselves and India, but their rhetoric rings hollow. Iran is a state sponsor of terrorism that has violated its own commitments and is defying the international community's efforts to contain its nuclear ambitions. North Korea, the least transparent country in the world, threatens its neighbors and proliferates weapons. There is simply no comparison between Iranian or North Korean regimes and India.[78]

It is also notable that the Bush administration treated India and Pakistan differently, even though both conducted nuclear tests in 1998 and subsequently cooperated with the US on the War on Terror. In the words of Rice, "their behavior was

---

75  Cohen, *Israel and the Bomb*, 324–25.
76  For an influential typology of the motivations, see Scott D. Sagan, "Why Do States Build Nuclear Weapons? Three Models in Search of a Bomb," *International Security* 21, no. 3 (1996/97).
77  Middle Eastern leaders have often legitimized their nuclear programs by referring to the need for an "Arab bomb" or an "Islamic bomb" against nuclear-armed Israel. See, for example, Wyn Q. Bowen, *Libya and Nuclear Proliferation: Stepping Back from the Brink* (Abingdon: Routledge, 2006), 22; Lucien S. Vandenbroucke, "The Israeli Strike against Osiraq: The Dynamics of Fear and Proliferation in the Middle East," *Air University Review* 35, no. 6 (1984), 37.
78  Condoleezza Rice, "Our Opportunity with India," *Washington Post*, 13 March 2006, accessed 8 June 2017, http://www.washingtonpost.com/wp-dyn/content/article/2006/03/12/AR2006031200978.html.

different ... Pakistan—well, it was the home of the nuclear proliferation entrepreneur A. Q. Khan, who had spread nuclear enrichment technology to North Korea and Iran, among other places."[79] Commentators have often explained the deal with India as an example of Bush's unilateralism or his unique approach to South Asia. While it is indeed the case, the deal was probably also motivated by the same awareness that the NPT is arbitrary and ineffective in setting a specific date after which crossing the nuclear threshold is delegitimized even for a non-party to the treaty.

Secondly, ambiguity over the range of prohibited activities by NNWSs regarding the peaceful use of nuclear energy breeds problems that spark controversy over a double standard. As we have seen, there is room for disagreement over the meaning of "peaceful use." Although the NPT explicitly rules out "peaceful nuclear explosions" (i.e., detonation of nuclear explosive devices for non-military purposes) by NNWSs, other uses of nuclear technology such as uranium enrichment and nuclear reprocessing are presumably guaranteed. Some therefore interpret the NPT as virtually allowing NNWSs to build the *de facto* infrastructure for nuclear weapon production in the name of peaceful use.

Indeed, many states—parties as well as non-parties to the treaty—have adopted (or seem to have adopted) this strategy, which keeps nuclear intentions opaque. This does not necessarily mean that they are all cynically disguising nuclear weapon programs as peaceful ones. Some of them indeed are (e.g., Iraq), but others are ambivalent or undecided about whether they should build nuclear bombs (e.g., India).[80] Nevertheless, those activities do look like an attempt to redraw the line between NWSs and NNWSs by stealth, thus *spatially expanding the applicable domain of pro-nuclear-weaponism*. One might find a "double standard" on the part of those states in their criticism against NWSs for failing to advance nuclear disarmament—i.e., *criticism against temporal expansion of the same domain* (more elaboration on this point later). As seen in the introduction, US Ambassador Kennedy made sarcastic remarks about the Iranian "double standard."

Thirdly, emergence of these "opaque" nuclear programs in turn gave rise to another "double standard" by the US and other suppliers of nuclear equipment, materials, and knowledge. As noted before, in the mid 1970s they started to deny (some) NNWSs technologies of uranium enrichment and nuclear reprocessing in

---

79   Condoleezza Rice, *No Higher Honor: A Memoir of My Years in Washington* (New York: Crown Publishers, 2011), 437.
80   Itty Abraham, *The Making of the Indian Atomic Bomb: Science, Secrecy and the Postcolonial State* (London: Zed Books, 1998); Abraham, "The Ambivalence of Nuclear Histories," *Osiris* 21, no. 1 (2006).

order to prevent covert nuclear arming and virtually created a division between privileged (Euratom countries, Japan) and unprivileged NNWSs. Iranian indignation at foreign pressure on its uranium enrichment program, as we saw in the introduction, probably reflected a sense of injustice against this background.

Fourthly, ambiguity over the temporal delimitation (i.e., having a transitory period leading to a total ban) sows the seed of discontent. Because the NPT is ambiguous about when the transitory period ends, NWSs can virtually extend that period indefinitely and keep possessing nuclear weapons. (Moreover, nuclear-armed non- or withdrawn parties to/from the treaty—Israel, India, Pakistan and North Korea—are not even bound by this vague obligation.) As the hierarchical conception of international society underpinning the strategy of distributive justification has spread, this virtual erosion of the temporal delimitation becomes much easier. After all, if NWSs are "responsible" enough to be allowed to keep nuclear weapons for some time, allowing them to keep nuclear arms indefinitely does not seem terribly risky. If anything, extension of the transitory period can be presented as a necessary hedge against possible nuclear blackmail by some "outlaws."[81]

When NWSs build up (or modernize) nuclear arsenals, conduct nuclear tests, or adopt more nuclear-reliant strategies, NNWSs are obviously incensed because such moves are seen as the clearest sign of NWSs' intent to cling to nuclear weapons. When NWSs maintain existing policies, they still raise suspicion by not doing something positive. Even when NWSs actually make some "progress," like nuclear arms reduction or call for a nuclear-weapon-free world, critics might nonetheless dismiss such actions as a smoke screen to obviate pressure for "real" disarmament.[82] While moderates might think such criticism unfair, critics also have a point: the fundamental gap that divides NWSs from NNWSs does not disappear with "quantitative" progress (i.e., nuclear weapon reduction); it does only by a "qualitative" change (i.e., nuclear weapon abolition).

The debate between Iranian Foreign Minister Salehi and US Ambassador Kennedy quoted in the introduction reflects this gap. While Kennedy defended her country by referring to the vision of "a world without nuclear weapons," the Iranians were not impressed. This is due to the ambiguity of the temporal delimitation.

---

81   This argument was actually made by one of the most important political philosophers in the twentieth century. See John Rawls, *The Law of Peoples: With "The Idea of Public Reason Revisited"* (Cambridge, MA: Harvard University Press, 1999), 9. For an analysis of Rawls's stance against sovereign equality, see Gerry Simpson, "Two Liberalisms," *European Journal of International Law* 12, no. 3 (2001).

82   Anne Harrington de Santana, "The Strategy of Non-Proliferation: Maintaining the Credibility of an Incredible Pledge to Disarm," *Millennium* 40, no. 1 (2011).

NWSs are seen as practicing a double standard: attempting to *temporally expand the applicable domain of pro-nuclear-weaponism* while *accusing some NNWSs of spatially expanding the same domain.*

In India's case, this frustration with NWSs had resulted in obstruction of the 1996 CTBT negotiations at the CD and eventually a nuclear test in 1998. As Mutimer points out, this was an about face for India, which had supported a nuclear test ban since 1954 when Indian Prime Minister Jawaharlal Nehru became the first head of state to call for that idea. Indian delegates defended this reversal by criticizing the finalized CTBT for being framed by non-proliferation concerns instead of disarmament. Actually, the CTBT does have the same restraining effects on nuclear buildup and modernization as what India had long demanded. But its entry-into-force provisions, which require ratification by those states that were members of the CD and were recorded by the IAEA as having nuclear reactors (i.e., potential proliferators), were indeed influenced by non-proliferation concerns.[83] Moreover, NWSs did not commit to a time-bound framework for nuclear disarmament, just as they did not when the NPT was extended indefinitely in 1995. Seeing all these as NWSs' cunning attempts to maintain the "nuclear apartheid" for a foreseeable future under the guise of disarmament, India refused to sign the treaty.[84] Of course, that New Delhi had already covertly crossed the *de facto* nuclear threshold in the late 1980s[85] must have been a significant factor. Nonetheless, India had continued to support a nuclear test ban even after that; many of its leaders (e.g., Rajiv Gandhi, Narasimha Rao, Deve Gowda) had also continued to express Nehruvian discomfort at nuclear weapons.[86] Thus India's rhetoric should not be understood as mere expediency.

## Conclusion

This chapter highlighted the contested character of the nuclear non-proliferation regime by conceptualizing it as a *modus vivendi* between pro- and anti-nuclear-weaponism. It also shed light on the two contrasting framing strategies, combination of which defends the regime's "double standards" at a deeper level. Lastly, it examined various forms of discontent that nonetheless spark contestation over the

---

83   Mutimer, *Weapons State*, 119–125.
84   Ibid; George Perkovich, *India's Nuclear Bomb: The Impact on Global Proliferation*, updated ed. (Berkeley: University of California Press, 2001), 379.
85   Perkovich, *India's Nuclear Bomb*, 293–295.
86   Ibid, 287, 347–48, 365–66, 376–77.

regime. It has thus showed the heavy normative strain the regime has been put under.

The tensions could be solved in three clear-cut manners. One is decisive triumph of the strategy of distributive justification under which the regime is unquestionably justified by a standard of civilization. This is actually in line with resurgence of hierarchical conceptions of international society in contemporary world politics.[87] Another possibility is the NPT's total collapse succeeded by nuclear *laissez-faire*, which has been warned against many times. The third scenario, "a world without nuclear weapons," is supposedly the vision the NPT endorses. This vision remains the most appealing, as evidenced by President Obama's Prague speech in 2009.

This does not mean that the regime will necessarily take one of these paths. Conversely, the regime might possibly "muddle through" without directly solving the inner tensions. More specifically, it may successfully keep defending itself as a "lesser evil" by repetition of moral cost-benefit analyses, each of which gives conditional justification. If it manages to endure in such a manner, that endurance itself might perhaps gradually and spontaneously turn the *modus vivendi*, which would by then lose any credibility of the disarmament promise, into a full-fledged norm (i.e., a socially accepted normative principle), making moral cost-benefit analyses virtually unnecessary.

This chapter does not tell us which is the most likely scenario. Rather, it tells us that we should not be surprised by realization of any scenario.

---

87   Simpson, *Great Powers and Outlaw States*.

# UKRAINE'S NUCLEAR DISARMAMENT, 1990–2015: OVERVIEW AND HISTORIOGRAPHY

*Jordan Vincent*

## Introduction

In 1991, following months of eroding influence and a failed putsch, the Soviet Union peacefully collapsed. Ukraine, as one of the former constituent Soviet republics, inherited the third largest strategic missile and nuclear warhead stockpile in the world. Within a short time, it was put under intense international pressure—mainly by the United States and the Russian Federation—to relinquish this newfound arsenal of mass destruction. Specifically, the Americans wanted Ukraine to ship the nuclear weapons situated within its borders to Russia for dismantlement and destruction. Ukraine, however, did not easily comply with these wishes. This paper will outline how Ukraine ultimately came to relinquish its nuclear arsenal in 1994. It will begin with a brief narrative account of Ukraine's path towards nuclear disarmament, which will serve to highlight some of the reasons behind Ukraine's nuclear weapons relinquishment and what has been done since 1994 to help Ukraine sustain its commitment to disarmament.

Independent Ukraine did not come to possess its arsenal by choice; rather, it was an inheritance. Despite initial pledges to renounce its nuclear arsenal and maintain a status as a neutral state, Ukraine's geopolitical situation and historical relations with its neighbours would result in it altering this initial path. This narrative will be followed by a short historiographical overview in order to help highlight the nature of interest in this subject over the previous two decades and what gaps remain in the scholarship on this issue. Alongside Belarus, Kazakhstan, and South Africa, Ukraine is amongst a small handful of nations who have willingly renounced their nuclear weapons. Unlike these other states, however, Ukraine is currently engaged in a conflict directly related to its disarmament process. The import of this situation will be discussed in this paper's final section as it is likely to affect the future direction of scholarship on Ukrainian nuclear disarmament.

## Ukraine's Path to Disarmament

During the Cold War, in order to maximize its intake of foreign currency (namely American dollars) from the sale of oil, the Soviet Union constructed many nuclear power stations during the 1960s and 1970s to supply its domestic needs.[1] Many of these nuclear plants were located in Ukraine and the nuclear materials created in these plants helped construct the USSR's vast nuclear arsenal. As Ukraine adapted to the changing political structure of the Soviet Union during the late 1980s and early 1990s, first through a declaration of sovereignty and then independence, it committed itself to being a neutral, non-nuclear state and to shipping its nuclear wares to Russia. However, Ukraine's geopolitical situation soon forced it to renege on these idealistic commitments and instead of shipping its nuclear weapons to Russia—like the other former Soviet republics with nuclear weapons Kazakhstan and Belarus—Ukraine chose to keep its atomic arsenal. So, what happened?

After the collapse of the USSR in 1991 its nuclear arsenal was divided amongst four new states: Russia, Belarus, Kazakhstan, and Ukraine. In May 1992, the three former Soviet republics agreed that Russia would become the inheritor of all Soviet nuclear weapons. Ukraine, however, did not immediately agree to such a transfer and instead took a different approach. It inherited 2,500 tactical nuclear weapons and 1,240 nuclear warheads located on 176 intercontinental ballistic missiles. Including Ukraine's inherited bomber fleet, the number of inherited strategic warheads was close to 1,900.[2]

Shortly after Ukraine's declaration of independence on 24 August 1991, Boris Yeltsin's press office released a statement claiming that Russia maintained the right to review its borders with any non-Baltic state.[3] When pressed on what this

---

1 Paul Josephson, *Red Atom: Russia's Nuclear Power Program from Stalin to Today* (New York: WH Freedman and Company, 1999), 8–9.
2 Steven Pifer, "The Trilateral Process: The United States, Ukraine, Russia and Nuclear Weapons," *Brookings Arms Control Series*, 6 (2011): 3, http://www.brookings.edu/~/media/research/files/papers/2011/5/trilateral%20process%20pifer/05_, accessed 23 August 2015, trilateral_process_pifer. See also "Country Profile: Ukraine," Nuclear Threat Initiativ, accessed 28 September 2013, http://www.nti.org/country-profiles/ukraine/nuclear/.
3 Roman Solchanyk, "The Politics of State Building: Centre-Periphery Relations in Post-Soviet Ukraine," *Europe-Asia Studies* 46 (1994): 46–48, accessed 18 July 2015, http://www.jstor.org/stable/153030. This was a press statement, and did not reflect formalized Russian Government policy, though it did indicate fairly common attitudes towards Ukraine, as further evidenced by the statements of Luzhkov and Solzhenitsyn. Realizing the outrage caused by his press secretary's statements, Russia's Foreign Ministry and Yeltsin himself soon clarified that Russia would respect the borders of its neighbours and seek to settle territorial issues peacefully. Mariana Brudjeryn, *The Power of the NPT: International Norms and Nuclear Disarmament of Belarus, Kazakhstan and Ukraine, 1990–*

signified, Yeltsin's press secretary stated that the release referred to the Russian populations located in northern Kazakhstan, the Donbas, and the Crimea.[4] Given that these last two were Ukrainian territories, such claims emanating from Russia were particularly worrisome to Ukrainian politicians. Similar claims came from Moscow's mayor, Yuriy Luzhkov, and renowned Russian writer (and nationalist) Aleksander Solzhenitsyn.[5] Adding to this tension was the major stumbling block concerning the status of Crimea, Sevastopol, and the Black Sea Fleet (BSF), with both Ukraine and Russia laying claims to portions of the fleet. Disputes concerning the BSF would not be resolved until 1997 and ultimately with Russia's annexation of Crimea in 2014.

Leonid Kravchuk, elected Ukraine's first president in December 1991, recognized the threat posed to Ukraine if nationalistic politicians were to replace Yeltsin as Russian president.[6] This predicament derived from the long and complicated interrelated histories of both Russia and Ukraine. Because of the cultural similarities and geographic proximity of the two countries, many Russians tended to view Ukraine as an integral part of their nation and even its identity. Since the 1930s, the Soviet Union employed the same historical narrative used in the Tsarist Empire: Ukraine, Russia, and Belarus all shared a common historical origin and nationhood that dated back to the founding of Kyivan Rus' in the tenth century.[7] In this perspective, the history of Ukraine for centuries was marked by its struggle to re-unite itself completely with the Great Russian nation. Only through Soviet rule was this accomplished and in celebration of this achievement, then premier Nikita Khrushchev transferred the traditionally Russian-administered Crimea to Ukraine in 1954 in celebration of the 300th anniversary of the Treaty of Pereyaslav.

---

*1994* (PhD dissertation), Central European University, Budapest, 2016, 112, accessed 20 May 2017, www.etd.ceu.hu/2016/budjeryn_mariana.pdf.

4   Roman Solchanyk, "The Politics of State Building: Centre-Periphery Relations in Post-Soviet Ukraine," 46–48.

5   Ibid. On the eve of Ukraine's referendum on independence in early December 1991, Solzhenitsyn remarked that Ukraine's independence should not be decided on a national level, but instead on a regional (*oblast'*) level. Another leading Russian figure to express skepticism concerning Ukraine's territorial integrity was Moscow's mayor, Yuriy Luzhkov, who consistently voiced his opinion that the 1954 transfer of the Crimea was illegal and that Sevastopol was a Russian city.

6   John Morrison, "Pereyaslav and After: The Russian-Ukrainian Relationship," *International Affairs* 69 (1993): 683.

7   Andreas Kappeler, "'Great Russians' and 'Little Russians': Russian-Ukrainian Relations and Perceptions in Historical Perspective," in *The Donald W. Treadgold Papers in Russian, East European, and Central Asian Studies* (Seattle, WA: University of Washington Press, 2003), 22–24.

There were several results of these modern disputes with Russia, burdened by the history of these two countries. Ukraine asserted administrative control over its nuclear weapons in April 1992, shortly before it signed the Lisbon Protocol (this protocol would make Ukraine party to START-1, see below). Administrative control signified that Ukraine had jurisdiction over the officers involved in the maintenance and operation of the weapons, giving the affected service members the option to quit the military, continue in Ukraine, or move to Russia.[8] Ukraine also claimed the technical ability to block unauthorized use of the weapons on its territory, but not the ability to launch or use them itself.

Another important consequence of these jingoistic Russian claims was that Ukraine had halted the shipment of its tactical nuclear weapons to Russia in early 1992 (though Ukraine did resume and complete the transfer soon thereafter due to American consternation over the matter). In the spring of that same year, while Ukraine's then President Leonid Kravchuk was in Washington D.C, Ukraine's parliament (the *Verkhovna Rada*) approved the signing of the Lisbon Protocol. This protocol, signed between Russia, Ukraine, Belarus, and Kazakhstan, ensured that Ukraine would inherit Soviet responsibilities stemming from the Strategic Arms Reduction Treaty (commonly known by its acronym START-1) and that moreover, the nuclear weapons of the former USSR found on the soil of these states would be placed under one authority (Russia) and destroyed.[9] The most important aspect of this protocol was that Ukraine, Belarus, and Kazakhstan had to adhere to the 1968 Non-Proliferation Treaty (the NPT) as non-nuclear weapon states in the shortest possible time. In return for adhering to START-1 and the NPT, Ukraine would receive $100–$150 million in aid though the Nunn-Lugar Program (see below).[10]

However, the Ukrainian parliament, swayed by the arguments of its large right-leaning voting bloc, refused to acknowledge that Ukraine was a non-nuclear state—and would therefore not dismantle all its weapons—because the NPT had

---

8 Steven Pifer, "The Trilateral Process: The United States, Ukraine, Russia and Nuclear Weapons," Brookings Arms Control Series 6 (2011): 9.

9 Nadia Schadlow, "The Denuclearization of Ukraine: Consolidating Ukrainian Security," in Ukraine in the World: Studies in the International Relations and Security Structure of a Newly Independent State. Harvard Ukrainian Studies 20 (1996): 274, accessed 20 January 2016, http://www.jstor.org/stable/41036694.

10 Sara Z. Kutchesfahani, *Politics and the Bomb: The Role of Experts in the Creation of Cooperative Nuclear-Non Proliferation Agreements,* New York: Routledge, 2014, 120; Sherman Garnett, " Ukrainian Relations: Past, Present, and Future," Harvard Ukrainian Studies 20 (1996): 107, accessed 28 September 2013, http://www.jstor.org/stable/41036686.

no provisions for the USSR's successor states. The NPT stated that a "... nuclear-weapon State is one which has manufactured and exploded a nuclear weapon or other nuclear explosive device prior to 1 January 1967."[11] Ukraine's parliament felt that since Ukraine had helped produce the nuclear weapons, it should be compensated for their removal. Moreover, as long as Ukraine's security was not guaranteed by Europe and the West, it should retain its strategic arsenal, which after the removal of its tactical nuclear weapons consisted of 176 ICBMs with multiple warheads.[12] Notwithstanding this interpretation, it should be underlined that a top priority of President Kravchuk and the Ukrainian diplomatic corps was to proceed with negotiations on nuclear disarmament and that Ukrainian intransigence on the matter was largely due to nationalists within its parliament.[13]

The Ukrainian parliament was roughly split into two voting blocs: the Communists and *Narodna Rada* (People's Council). These blocs, however, frequently changed composition and until the 1994 election, there was little variation in the platforms of most parties save that some could simply be labeled communists and others national-democrats. These voting blocs would merge with coalitions that either supported the president or voted against him, thus further complicating the Ukrainian political scene.[14] Some of the major parties at this time included *Rukh*, the Peasant Party of Ukraine, the Agrarian Party, the Socialists, and the Communists.[15] The left leaning parties in parliament, namely the Communists, Socialists, and Agrarians were particularly prone to infighting and shifting loyalties, more so after the 1994 elections.[16] Conflicts arose because the Socialists and Agrarians,

---

11   The Treaty on the Non-Proliferation of Nuclear Weapons, Article IX-3, United Nations (1968), accessed 2 September 2015, http://www.un.org/en/conf/npt/2010/npttext.shtml.
12   Nadia Schadlow, "The Denuclearization of Ukraine: Consolidating Ukrainian Security," 278.
13   Mariana Brudjeryn, *The Power of the NPT: International Norms and Nuclear Disarmament of Belarus, Kazakhstan and Ukraine, 1990–1994* (PhD dissertation), Central European University, Budapest, 2016, 120–126.
14   Bohdan Harasymiw, *Post-Communist Ukraine* (Edmonton, AB: University of Alberta Press, 2002).
15   More specifically, the Ukrainian far-left, such as the Communists, had their highest support in Ukraine's eastern industrial cities. Support for other radical leftist parties and central-left parties was also localized in Eastern and Southern Ukraine. Centre-right, radical right, and liberal parties had their support bases in Central and Western Ukraine. For a more detailed summary of Ukraine's complex political landscape during this period, see Taras Kuzio, *Ukraine under Kuchma: Political Reform, Economic Transformation and Security Policy in Independent Ukraine* (London: Macmillan Press Ltd., 1997), 8–26.
16   Andrew Wilson, "The Ukrainian Left: In Transition to Social Democracy or Still in Thrall to the USSR?" *Europe-Asia Studies* 49 (1997): 1293, accessed 28 September 2013, http://www.jstor.org/stable/154086.

though they bemoaned the breakup of the Soviet Union, still nominally supported Ukraine's independence. The Communists did not.[17]

Though the left was more divided than the right, this does not mean that rightist forces could easily pass legislation. As evidence, political legislation was 10 to 15 percent more likely to be passed than legislation concerned with economic reform.[18] This discrepancy was because of Ukraine's numerically stronger leftist parties, which were opposed to extensive privatization. Legislation dealing with political issues, such as the armed forces, changes to the constitution, or citizenship, was less ideologically disconcerting to the totality of the Ukrainian left than changes to Ukraine's command economy. For this reason, the *Verkhovna Rada* was capable of garnering enough support to delay, modify, or block treaties submitted to parliament by President Kravchuk. In terms of defence policy, the multitude of changing coalitions and vague ideological convictions hindered the development of a clear conception of Ukraine's security needs.[19] Unclear defence requirements proved to be beneficial to Kravchuk. Unable to endorse an ethnic definition of Ukrainian citizenship and thereby gain more support from nationalists, Kravchuk was more aggressive in his negotiations over Ukraine's strategic forces.[20] However, the international community, particularly Russia and the United States, viewed such policy negatively. In relation to actions of Ukraine's *Rada* and its conditional acceptance of START-1, President Kravchuk stated "if we were rich, we would never pose such questions ... But our economy is in crisis. There is a fall in production. Can we independently decide this problem? No, that's clear to all.[21]"

Prior to Ukraine initiating its half-hearted START-1 ratification, negotiations concerning Ukraine's disarmament were primarily a bilateral affair between Russia and Ukraine. These negotiations throughout 1992 and 1993, however, bore relatively little fruit. As Russia became frustrated with a series of failed negotiations, it became apparent that the United States would have to become more involved.

---

17  Ibid., 1298–1301.
18  Leonid Finberg, "Les Problèmes Majeurs de la Société ukrainienne en 1995," *Cahiers du Monde Russe* 39 (1995): 501, accessed 28 September 2013, http://www.jstor.org/stable/20170981.
19  H.M Perepelytsia, *Beziadernyy status i natsional'na bezpeka Ukrainy* (Non-nuclear status and the national security of Ukraine), (Kyiv: Natsional'nyy instytut stratehichnykh doslidzhen' [National institute of strategic studies], 1998), 8–10.
20  Charles F. Furtado Jr. "Nationalism and Foreign Policy in Ukraine," *Political Science Quarterly* 109 (1994): 93, accessed 28 September 2013, http://www.jstor.org/stable/2151661.
21  Serge Schmemann, "Ukraine Finds Nuclear Arms Bring a Measure of Respect," *The New York Times*, 7 January 1993, accessed 8 August 2015, http://www.nytimes.com/1993/01/07/world/ukrainefinds-nuclear-arms-bring-a-measure-of-respect.html?pagewanted=all&src=pm.

After impressing upon the Ukrainian government the important relationship between START-1's ratification and future financial and security aid, the US persuaded Ukraine to ratify START and also to sign an umbrella treaty that tied Ukraine to the Nunn-Lugar program by the fall of 1993. This program, shepherded by two American senators—Sam Nunn and Richard Lugar—sought financial aid for the nuclear-inheritor states of the former USSR so that they could secure, and if need be, dismantle their strategic stockpiles.[22] The Nunn-Lugar program had five major goals: to safeguard and eliminate nuclear stockpiles within the former USSR; to prevent the proliferation of nuclear weapons; to prevent the proliferation of nuclear expertise and scientists; to support the de-militarization of Soviet defence industries; and finally, to expand military defence contracts between the US and former Soviet states.[23]

During the summer and fall of 1993, when the Americans agreed in principle to compensate Ukraine for the highly enriched uranium within its warheads (including from those tactical nuclear weapons already shipped to Russia), the Americans, Russians, and Ukrainians crept slowly towards a mutually acceptable agreement. Finally, on 14 January 1994, the presidents of all three states met in Moscow and signed the Trilateral Statement. Under this new treaty, Ukraine would accede to the Lisbon Protocol and sign the NPT as a non-nuclear state as soon as possible. In return, the Americans agreed to give Ukraine financial aid to help defray the cost of protecting and shipping the weapons to Russia. Ukraine would also receive security assurances from Russia, the USA, and Britain once it became a non-nuclear state, party to the NPT and once START-1 entered into force without caveats. Building off of the earlier promise of $150 million, by 1994, of the $800 million available through the Nunn-Lugar program devoted to the former-Soviet republics, Ukraine was now to receive a revised figure of $175 million for its cooperation.[24] Insofar as Ukraine continued to ship its strategic missiles to

---

22   Ashton B. Carter, Kurt Campbell, Steven Miller, and Charles Zraket, *Soviet Nuclear Fission: Control of the Nuclear Arsenal in a Disintegrating Soviet Union*, (Cambridge, Mass.: Center for Science and International Affairs, Harvard University, 1991); Cited in Philip Taubman, *The Partnership: Five Cold Warriors and Their Quest to Ban the Bomb* (New York: Harper Collins Publishing, 2010), 273–275.

23   United States Congress 22 § 5951, "Findings on Cooperative Threat Reduction," accessed 28 September 2013, http://www.law.cornell.edu/uscode/text/22/5951.

24   Ukraine would go on to participate in the Nunn-Lugar program until its memorandum of understanding with the USA expired in late 2013. As such, between fiscal years 1993–2014, Ukraine received $593 million through the Nunn-Lugar program. Please see United States Congress, Congressional Research Service, *The Evolution of Cooperative Threat Reduction: Issues for Congress*, Washington D.C.: 2014, 21, accessed 1 September 2015, https://fas.org/sgp/crs/nuke/R43143.pdf.

Russia, it would receive lightly enriched uranium to power its nuclear reactors. In addition, Ukraine had ten months to remove the warheads from its sophisticated SS-24 missiles, thus rendering them impotent.[25] By the summer of 1996, Ukraine had shipped all of its nuclear warheads to Russia and thus concluded its tenuous status as a possessor of nuclear weapons.

Nearly a month after Ukraine ratified the NPT in mid-November 1994, thus becoming a legally bound non-nuclear state, Russia, Britain, and the United States fulfilled their commitments made in the Trilateral Agreement by providing security assurances to Ukraine in what was known as the Budapest Memorandum.[26] These three nuclear-weapon states reaffirmed their commitment to respect Ukraine's sovereignty and territorial integrity in addition to renouncing the use of force against Ukraine, except in self-defence. Similarly, they promised not to deploy any form of economic coercion that would interfere with Ukraine's internal decision-making process and violate Ukraine's sovereignty. The final major point of the Memorandum was that in the event that nuclear weapons were used against Ukraine, then the three powers would seek immediate Security Council assistance.[27] Ukraine would long seek wording that went beyond "assurances and commitments"; it wanted instead guarantees. Twenty years later, as Russia was annexing Crimea and invading Eastern Ukraine, this slight difference in wording would have very important repercussions.

Unlike in Ukraine, the nuclear disarmament of Belarus and Kazakhstan never became a major issue. Similar to Ukraine's declaration of state sovereignty, Belarus' declaration also stated a commitment to neutrality and denuclearization. Certain Belarusian politicians, such as Defence Minister Pyotr Chaus and Foreign

---

25  U.N Office at Geneva, Conference on Disarmament, "Letter Dated 26 January 1994 From the Permanent Representative of the Russian Federation to the Conference, the Representative of the United States of America to the Conference and the Permanent Representative of Ukraine Addressed to the President of the Conference on Disarmament Transmitting Texts of the Trilateral Statement by the Presidents of the Russian Federation, the United States of American and Ukraine, as well as the Annex to the Trilateral Statement, signed in Moscow 14 January 1993," (CD/1243) 4 February 1994, accessed 01/09/2015, http://daccess-ddsny.un.org/doc/UNDOC/GEN/G94/602/55/IMG/G9460255.pdf?OpenElement.

26  *Pro pryyednannya Ukrainy do Dohovoru pro nerozpovsyudzhennya yadernoi zbroi vid 1 lypnya 1968 roku* (Concerning the joining of Ukraine to the Non-proliferation treaty of 1 July 1968), 16 November 1994, N. 47, accessed 2 September 2015, http://zakon1.rada.gov.ua/laws/show/248/94-%D0%B2%D1%80.

27  "Memorandum on Security Assurances in Connection with Ukraine's Accession to the Treaty on the Non-Proliferation of Nuclear Weapons," Article 1–4, Russian Federation, United Kingdom, United States of America, Ukraine, signed in Budapest 5 December 1994, accessed 15 December 2014, http://en.wikisource.org/wiki/Ukraine._Memorandum_on_Security_Assurances.

Minister Pyotr Krauchanka intimated that Belarus should not hastily relinquish its share of Soviet nuclear weapons (1,220 at the time of independence), though after 1992 Belarus did not seriously consider retaining any of its weapons.[28] Only in 1996, under the Lukashenko administration, did Belarus arbitrarily halt the shipment of its missiles and warheads to Russia, citing that the shipments of these weapons was unnecessary given that Belarus and Russia would soon be united.[29] Nonetheless, shipments were soon resumed and completed in November 1996.

The fourth state to inherit Soviet nuclear weapons was Kazakhstan. Immediately following independence, Yasser Arafat and Iraq, in addition to several other Middle Eastern states, all made overtures to the new Kazakh state in hopes that it would sell some of the weaponry, or if not, at least link itself more closely to Middle Eastern affairs.[30] Kazakhstan did not acquiesce to these demands and decided to ship its weapons to Russia if the US would pay the cost. In order to transport the warheads, the US built special rail cars that would be used throughout the nuclear-inheritor states for transport.[31] The Americans would also successfully launch Project Sapphire, a covert mission whose goal was to collect stray Kazakh uranium and ship it via plane to the USA.[32] However, less secretive methods would result in Kazakhstan being nuclear free by May 1995, by which time it was clear that the problem of post-Soviet nuclear proliferation had been adequately handled.

## Ukraine's Economic Crisis

Now that we have seen the general history of Ukraine's disarmament process (and to a lesser degree those of Belarus and Kazakhstan), it bears mentioning that the collapse of the Ukrainian economy during the 1990s was a consequential factor in Ukraine's decision making. The industrial directors in charge of post-independence Ukraine's state enterprises formed a powerful political lobby and helped influence the course of reforms pursued by the Ukrainian government. Managers and lobbyists pressed the government to increase the nominal money supply and, in this way, allow agricultural and industrial output to remain high due to state

---

28    Ruth Deyermond, *Security and Sovereignty in the Former Soviet Union* (London: Lynne Rienner Publishers Inc., 2008), 90–92.
29    Ibid, 92–93.
30    Richard Rhodes, *The Twilight of the Bombs: Recent Challenges, New Dangers, and the Prospects for a World Without Nuclear Weapons* (New York: Alfred A Knopf, 2010), 118–119.
31    Ibid, 119–122.
32    David E. Hoffman, *The Dead Hand: The Untold Story of the Cold War Arms Race and its Dangerous Legacy* (Toronto: Doubleday, 2009), 452–456.

purchases. This reform emphasized industrial production at the expense of needed monetary reform. The state, immersed in the legacy of central planning, was happy to oblige.[33] As a result, most Ukrainian enterprises were being subsidized by government funds. The state budget was likewise based not on central bank forecasts (which were left out of the decision-making process), but on projected production figures. When these quota-based budgets were found to be several times smaller than what was actually spent, the Ukrainian government took the actual budgetary figures and at the end of the year claimed them as the official budget. The only monetary reform introduced in Ukraine initially was prompted by actions in Russia. Once Russia liberalized price controls, Ukraine passed similar reforms, though they were not very far reaching.[34] The combination of across the board subsidies and unrealistic budgets led to rampant inflation.

As inflation spiralled out of control in 1992 and 1993, Ukraine began experiencing serious problems in its balance of payments, especially regarding its imports of gas and oil. The combination of pre-existing infrastructure (pipelines, refineries etc.), inefficient industries, and heavily subsidized energy prices inherited from the USSR ensured that it would be reliant on Russian and Central Asian oil and gas.[35] The price of gas imports was also a point of contention between Russia and Ukraine as much of Ukraine's gas imports from its neighbour during this period were accrued as debts.[36] As Ukraine's foreign currency reserves dwindled, in August 1993 it chose to force exporters to hand over a portion of their hard currency at a fixed rate well below market levels.[37] From this point, inflation turned into hyperinflation as the *karbovanets* (coupon) lost much of its value and the price of imports increased drastically. By the end of 1993, inflation for the year stood at 10,235 percent.[38]

---

33  Viktor Pynzenyk and Vira Yakusha, "How to Find a Path for Ukrainian Reforms," in *Russian and East European Finance and Trade* 36 (2000): 60, accessed 28 September 2013, http://www.jstor.org/stable/27749515.
34  Ibid, 60.
35  Margarita M. Balmaceda, "Gas, Oil and the Linkages between Domestic and Foreign Policies: The Case of Ukraine," *Europe-Asia Studies* 50 (1998): 258, accessed 28 September 2013, http://www.jstor.org/stable/153460.
36  Josef C. Brada and Gregory V. Krasnov, "Implicit Subsidies in Russian-Ukrainian Energy Trade," *Europe-Asia Studies* 49 (1997): 827, accessed 28 September 2013, http://www.jstor.org/stable/153487. Payments for oil and gas shipments were to use convertible currency. In mid-1993 Ukraine and Russia agreed on a price for oil. Disputes over gas prices have continued.
37  Vasily Zorya, "Panic on Ukrainian Currency Exchange: 19,000 Karbovantsy to the Dollar," *Izvestia*, 21 August 1993, in *The Current Digest of the Russian Press* 45 (1993): 26, accessed 28 September 2013.
38  Viktor Pynzenyk and Vira Yakusha, 62.

Ukraine's severely strained financial situation in turn adversely affected its military spending during the early 1990s (and very plausibly even to this day). The 1992 budget promised the military 15.8% of state expenditures; in actuality, it was 9% and by 1995, the Ukrainian military budget was three times smaller than it had been in 1992.[39] Functional nuclear weapons, in Ukraine's case its SS-19 (liquid-fueled) and SS-24 (solid-fueled) missiles, are not single mechanisms, but are part of an intricate system that must work in perfect precision if they are to operate properly. Needless to say, nuclear arsenals are also very expensive. Notwithstanding that Ukraine already had much of the necessary infrastructure to create nuclear weapons, it would still cost Ukraine $25 billion ($43 billion in today's figures) to produce its own warheads. Such a figure would have represented the sum of Ukraine's military budget for the next fifteen years.[40]

Juxtaposed to the enormous financial costs of nuclear weapons, post-disarmament Ukraine began to experience noticeable diplomatic and economic benefits after signing the Trilateral Agreement. In 1995, the World Bank agreed to offer Ukraine a loan ($1 billion) on condition that it continued efforts towards economic privatization.[41] In a similar vein, Canada's Minister of Foreign Affairs Lloyd Axworthy offered Ukraine $550 million of credits in 1996, while Canadian businesses agreed to invest $425 million in the Ukrainian economy.[42] Though Ukraine's relations with the West—and the US in particular—improved after 1994, relations with Russia continued to be difficult. After the resolution of the outstanding nuclear weapons problem, the next stumbling blocks in Russian-Ukrainian relations were the related issues of the Black Sea Fleet and Sevastopol, though this too was resolved, for the time, in the 1997 Treaty on Friendship.

---

39    H.M Perepelytsia, *Beziadernyy status i natsional'na bezpeka Ukrainy* (Non-nuclear status and the national security of Ukraine), Kyiv: Natsional'nyy instytut stratehichnykh doslidzhen' [National Institute of Strategic Studies], 1998), 12.

40    Perepelytsia, 19. The estimated price is in 1991 dollars. Adjusted to inflation this figure would be $42.85 billion in 2015 dollars.

41    Ustina Markus, "World Bank Offers Credit Package to Ukraine," *Radio Free Europe*, 20 November 1995, accessed 27 August 2015, http://www.rferl.org/content/article/1141054.html; Chrystyna Lapychak, "Ukrainian Economic Update," *Radio Free Europe*, August 31, 1995, accessed 22 July 2015, http://www.rferl.org/content/article/1141008.html.

42    Ustina Markus, "Canada to Offer Some $550 Million in Credit to Ukraine," *Radio Free Europe*, 25 October 1996, accessed 13 July 2015, http://www.rferl.org/content/article/1141282.html.

## The Crimean Question

After independence, Ukraine and Russia soon began to argue over ownership of the fleet, with Russia claiming that it was Russian property and Ukraine claiming that a portion of the fleet belonged to itself. Until a permanent solution could be found, Russia and Ukraine agreed to joint command of the fleet. Linked to the issue of the fleet was the division of fleet property in Sevastopol and the emergence of a Crimean separatist movement during the early 1990s. These issues were settled in the 1997 Treaty on Friendship between Russia and Ukraine. Given that Russia had never officially recognized Ukraine's borders, of crucial importance for Ukraine were Articles 1–3 of the treaty, which enshrined official Russian recognition of Ukraine's sovereignty and territorial integrity.[43] Articles 5–7 were designed to help normalize relations, calling for increased inter-governmental and inter-bureaucracy cooperation and for immediate consultation in the event of an emergency.[44] At the time, this treaty represented a broad attempt by both Russia and Ukraine to resolve several issues, most importantly territorial disputes, the Black Sea Fleet, and the question of outstanding Soviet debts (to be assumed by Russia), all of which seemed to promote a more constructive framework for future relations.[45]

## International Aid to Ukraine

Since the Trilateral Statement did not deal with Ukraine's strategic weapon delivery systems and the complex technology behind their construction, Ukraine needed to sign the pre-existing, multilateral Missile Technology Control Regime (MTCR) of 1987 to help prevent any potential proliferation. This treaty was designed to maintain control and surveillance over the export of missile equipment and its re-

---

43  Treaty on Friendship, Cooperation, and Partnership between Ukraine and the Russian Federation, Russia and Ukraine, Art. 1–3, 31 May 1997, accessed 28 September 2013, http://www.jstor.org.login.ezproxy.library.ualberta.ca/stable/pdfplus/41036701.pdf?acceptTC=true&; The only other treaty of this sort signed between Russia and Ukraine dated from Soviet times (Treaty between the Ukrainian Soviet Socialist Republic and the Russian Soviet Federative Socialist Republic of 19 November 1990). See Article 39. The Russian Duma did not ratify the treaty until 1999, see, "Russia Ratifies Friendship Treaty with Ukraine," *BBC World Service*, 17 February 1999, accessed 28/ September 2013, http://news.bbc.co.uk/2/hi/europe/281231.stm.
44  Ibid, Art. 5–7.
45  "Ukrainian, Russian Presidents Sign Political Treaty," *Radio Free Europe*, 2 June 1997, accessed 28 September 2013, http://www.rferl.org/content/article/1141420.html.

lated materials and technologies in order to prevent the proliferation of WMD delivery vehicles.⁴⁶ Through American cooperation and encouragement, Ukraine joined the MTCR in 1998 and through this treaty, also acceded to the 1978 Antiballistic Missile Treaty. The year 1998 also marked the signing of a treaty of cooperation concerning the peaceful use of nuclear energy and research between the United States and Ukraine. The agreement, entitled "Atomic Energy: Peaceful Uses of Nuclear Energy," allowed for the transfer of information and research and further prevented Ukraine from enriching any of its uranium.⁴⁷

In 2004, Ukraine began to receive funding to improve the training of its border services and customs in the detection of nuclear materials in order to deter smuggling and the proliferation of nuclear material and technologies. The Defence Threat Reduction Office (the focal point for the Nunn-Lugar program implementation in Ukraine) bolstered Ukrainian border services by providing funds for sophisticated inspection equipment, upgrades to maritime/river patrol craft, and an enhanced technical presence in the Chernobyl exclusion zone and along the Ukrainian-Moldovan border (given the potential for smuggling along these countries' borders).⁴⁸ This program, which ran from 2004 until its completion in 2013, provided Ukraine with $144.45 million and trained 7,372 border guards and 1,870 customs officers.⁴⁹ The Nunn-Lugar program also aided in the construction of the requisite training facilities, such as the George Kuzmycz Training Centre in Kyiv, named after the American Department of Energy official initially in charge of overseeing American aid to Ukraine's border services and nuclear industry. Another aspect of the Nunn-Lugar program in Ukraine was to provide funding for the State

---

46   US State Department, "US-Ukraine Missile Agreement," *State Department Fact Sheet on the Ukraine-US Memorandum of Understanding on the Transfer of Missile Equipment and Technology*, 13 May 1994, accessed 6 September 2015, http://www.fas.org/nuke/control/mtcr/text/940803-355651.htm.

47   Atomic Energy: Peaceful Uses of Nuclear Energy—Agreement Between the United States of America and Ukraine, United States, Ukraine, 6 May 1998, Art. 3, accessed 6 September 2015, http://www.nti.org/media/pdfs/StateandUkrainePeaceNucMay1998.pdf?_=1316627913.

48   US State Department, "WMD Proliferation Prevention Initiatives," *Embassy of the United States, Ukraine: Defense Threat Reduction Office*, accessed 11 August 2015, http://ukraine.usembassy.gov/dtro/wmd.html. Located along Ukraine's border, Moldova's break-away Trans-Dniester Republic would be a likely area for smuggling to occur.

49   Ibid; "Ambassador Tefft Celebrates the Successful Completion of the Weapons of Mass Destruction-Proliferation Prevention Program," *Embassy of the United States, Ukraine*, accessed 11 August 2015, http://ukraine.usembassy.gov/events/wmd-ppp2013.html.

Space Agency of Ukraine and the Pavlohrad Chemical Plant in the destruction of SS-24 missiles—specifically their motor casings and missile propellants.[50]

In December 2008, the US-Ukraine Charter on Strategic Partnership was signed in Washington. This new agreement reaffirmed the commitment of both states to limiting the proliferation of weapons of mass destruction and any associated technologies through currently existing international agreements.[51] The United States also reconfirmed the importance of—and its continued adherence to—the Trilateral Statement and the Budapest Memorandum, in which it offered security assurances to Ukraine.[52] After his re-election, President Barack Obama announced his commitment to the continuation of the Nunn-Lugar (also known as the Cooperative Threat Reduction Program).[53] By the end of 2012, the U.S had released an estimated $8 billion in aid to Soviet nuclear inheritor states and had destroyed over 7,500 nuclear warheads. Ukraine's portion of this total was $1.3 billion.[54]

In its aid to Russia, Canada established a bilateral working relationship and could provide aid directly, while in its aid to Ukraine, Canada "piggybacked" on existing American programs, such as the Nunn-Lugar program.[55] Like their American counterparts, Canadian officials recognized the practicality of finding employment for former Soviet physicists and scientists and therefore helped fund technology centres in Moscow and Kyiv. In this way, Canadian aid managed to

---

50   Ibid., "Strategic Nuclear Arms Elimination," *Embassy of the United States, Ukraine: Defense Threat Reduction Office*, accessed 16 August 2015, http://ukraine.usembassy.gov/dtro/snae.html.
51   US-Ukraine Charter on Strategic Partnership, United States and Ukraine, Section II, Art., 4, 19 December 2008, accessed 16 August 2015, http://ukraine.usembassy.gov/strategic-partnership.html.
52   Ibid, Preamble, Art. 4.
53   Barack Obama, "CTR 20th Anniversary—President Obama's Commitment," *YouTube Video*, posted by NunnLugarCTR, 15 December 2012, http://www.youtube.com/watch?v=3820TKBcTK8&feature=youtu.be.
54   Mark Thompson, "Nunn-Lugar No Longer?" *Time*, 16 October 2012, accessed 6 September 2015, http://nation.time.com/2012/10/16/nunn-lugar-no-longer/; US State Department, "Senator Lugar Visits Ukraine," *Embassy of the United States, Ukraine: Defense Threat Reduction Office*, accessed 6 September 2015, http://ukraine.usembassy.gov/press-releases/lugar2012.html
55   Canada, Department of Foreign Affairs and International Trade Canada, *Summative Evaluation—Global Partnership Program Nuclear and Radiological Security*, Ottawa [2008], Section 4.1, Accessed 6 September 2015, http://www.international.gc.ca/about-a_propos/oigbig/2008/evaluation/nrs_snr08.aspx?lang=eng&view=d. For information on other American programs through which Canada operated, see U.S Department of Energy, "Second Line of Program," *National Nuclear Security Administration*, accessed 6 June 2015, http://www.nnsa.energy.gov/aboutus/ourprograms/nonproliferation/programoffices/internationalmaterialprotectionandcooperation/se.

find employment for over 2,300 former Soviet nuclear weapons scientists.[56] Other forms of Canadian assistance were $100 million to Russia for decommissioning nuclear submarines and $5 million for Ukrainian border security and detection equipment, particularly at Kyiv's Boryspil airport.[57] France and the European Union also gave extensive aid to Ukraine. In 1998, Ukraine and France signed an Agreement on the Development of Peaceful Uses for Nuclear Energy, scheduled to last for twenty years unless renewed. This agreement echoed the peaceful energy use agreement signed by the United States and Ukraine that same year.[58] In 2005, Ukraine signed an agreement with the European Atomic Energy Community (EURATOM) on Cooperation in the Peaceful Uses of Nuclear Energy. This agreement called for nuclear safety, the exchange of research and personnel, and for measures to prevent nuclear proliferation.[59]

## Ukraine's Conflict with Russia

Though post-disarmament Ukraine was successful in integrating itself into the international community, (having even succeeded in its fundraising efforts for its aging nuclear reactors at Chernobyl), it did not realize all of its goals. It still has not received adequate security guarantees, and was left with only the assurances of the Budapest Memorandum. Since the ousting of President Viktor Yanukovych, the Russian seizure of Crimea in early 2014, and the ensuing "uprisings" in Luhansk and Donetsk, these assurances have amounted only to economic sanctions and the financial isolation of Russian elites and banks. Russia itself, a signatory of the Budapest Memorandum, has ignored Ukraine's invocation of the Budapest Memorandum and has stated that since it did not sign the memorandum with Ukraine's

---

56    Canada, Department of Foreign Affairs and International Trade Canada. *Summative Evaluation—Global Partnership Program*, Ottawa [2008], Section 2.3.

57    Ibid; See also Department of Energy, "Ukraine, and Canada Complete Major Joint Border Security and Non-proliferation Effort," *National Nuclear Security Administration*, 8 December 2008, accessed 6 June 2015, http://www.nnsa.energy.gov/aboutus/ourprograms/nonproliferation/program offices/internationalmaterialprotectionandcooperation/se.

58    Accord de Coopération entre le gouvernement de la République Française et le gouvernement de l'Ukraine pour le développement des utilisations pacifiques de l'énergie nucléaire, France and Ukraine, 3 September 1998, Art., 2, accessed 19 August 2015, http://www.nti.org/media/pdfs/91_1.pdf?_=1316627913. This agreement did not come into force until 13 June 2000. See Articles 16 and 17.

59    Agreement between the European Atomic Energy Community and the Cabinet of Ministers of Ukraine for Co-operation in the Peaceful Uses of Nuclear Energy, European Union and Ukraine, 28 April 2005, Art., 4–8, accessed 26 September 2015, http://ec.europa.eu/world/agreements/down loadFile.do?fullText=yes&treatyTransId=10181.

current government, it did not have to recognize the agreement.[60] Moreover, Ukraine's current government allegedly came to power in a coup, and therefore need not be entirely recognized.[61]

Attempts to ease the hostilities in Eastern Ukraine have centered around the Minsk Agreements. The first, implemented in September 2014, quickly broke down as fighting resumed between Ukraine, Russia, and the Russian-backed separatists. In February 2015 a new Minsk agreement was reached, wherein Ukraine would decentralize its control over the breakaway provinces, which in turn would rejoin Ukraine.[62] In order to do this and change its constitution, Ukraine would need the approval of its parliament—a feat not likely to occur given the current conflict. Russia, for its part, is treated as a mediator rather than a participant in the conflict. Bearing in mind Russia's control of the separatist regions and the de facto veto this gives it on Ukraine's stability, Russia has done little since 2015 to seriously pursue the implementation of Minsk II.[63] To this day the conflict continues in Eastern Ukraine, albeit less intensely than during the summer of 2014.

## Historiography of Ukraine's Disarmament

Having provided an overview of the timeline surrounding Ukraine's nuclear disarmament, Ukraine's post-disarmament non-proliferation agreements, and the country's security environment during recent years, this paper will now turn to how Ukraine's nuclear disarmament has been treated by other authors. Russia's invasion of Ukraine will serve as a dividing line of sorts between authors who examined Ukraine's nuclear disarmament before 2014 and those who have done so subsequently. From this divide, gaps in this issue's scholarship will be identified and the full impact of Russia's violation of the Budapest Memorandum will be explored.

---

60  Mariana Brudjeryn, *The Power of the NPT: International Norms and Nuclear Disarmament of Belarus, Kazakhstan and Ukraine, 1990–1994*, 182.
61  Shaun Walker, "Russia Will Recognize the Outcome of Ukraine Poll, Says Vladimir Putin," *The Guardian*, 23 May 2014, accessed 8 September 2015, http://www.theguardian.com/world/2014/may/23/russia-ukraine-vote-vladimir-putin-president.
62  "The Economist Explains: What are the Minsk Agreements," *The Economist*, 14 September 2016, accessed 25 July 2017, https://www.economist.com/blogs/economist-explains/2016/09/economist-explains-7.
63  Judy Dempsey, "Judy Asks: can the Minsk Agreement Succeed? A Selection of Experts Answer a New Question from Judy Dempsey on the Foreign and Security Policy Challenges Shaping Europe's Role in the World," Carnegie Europe, 22 February 2017, accessed 25 July 2017, http://carnegieeurope.eu/strategiceurope/?fa=68084.

Ruth Deyermond, in *Security and Sovereignty in the Former Soviet Union*, concentrates not only on the process by which Ukraine dealt with its nuclear arsenal, but also other security issues involving Russia's relations with Georgia and Belarus. She argues that in order to understand properly the evolution of security relations between these new states and the conflicts that erupted, one must examine how different definitions of sovereignty came into conflict following the collapse of the Soviet Union in 1991.[64] Ultimately, Ukraine and Georgia based their definition of sovereignty on those widely used in the West, such as the inviolability of borders and equality under international law. In contrast, Belarus and Russia continued to approach the notion of autonomy using a Soviet model of state sovereignty.

Ukraine, the most successful state in terms of having its views and demands implemented within the framework of the CIS, took a decidedly Western interpretation in how it defined its sovereignty. Deyermond points out that there is no one set definition present in the Western political tradition that can absolutely define sovereignty. However, she does point out that most definitions share several commonalities, namely that: sovereignty is often founded upon a people or nation; that the existence or raison d'être of the state is derived from these groups; that the power derived from this, both in terms of internal and external sovereignty—though sometimes shared in some spheres with sub-state actors—ultimately resides in a centralized government; and finally, that on the international level all states are equal.[65]

The Soviet model on which Russia based its diplomatic relations with its post-Soviet sister republics, though superficially similar to that produced through the Western political tradition, had several profound differences. Whereas the Western model held all actors to be equal, the Soviet version in essence allowed for a multiplicity of hierarchy in the application of sovereignty.[66] Once the USSR collapsed and Russia declared itself to be the USSR's legal successor, it was only a matter of time before conflict erupted over the division of the Soviet Union's most cherished institution—its vast military, including nuclear weapons.[67] Since Russia viewed itself as the regional hegemon entitled to a deferential sense of sovereignty from its neighbours, it was likely that it would enter into conflict with Ukraine, a

---

64 Ruth Deyermond, *Security and Sovereignty in the Former Soviet Union* (London: Lynne Rienner Publishers Inc., 2008), 1–2.
65 Ibid, 19–22.
66 Ibid, 26.
67 Ibid, 55–56.

state with the intentions and means to ensure that it was treated according to Western principles of sovereignty.

Hryhoriy M. Perepelytsia of the Ukrainian National Institute of Strategic Studies, a state-funded presidential advisory body, analyzes the factors that influenced Ukraine's nuclear disarmament and the foreign policy options available to a non-nuclear Ukraine in his 1998 report *Beziadernyy status i natsional'na bezpeka Ukrainy* (Non-nuclear status and the national security of Ukraine). Perepelytsia's work reads as a policy report, outlining the pitfalls facing Ukraine during the 1990s and the rationale for why Ukraine would have wanted to pursue various foreign and domestic policy courses. Russia's historic links with Ukraine and the perceived loss of a vital part of Russian nationhood, combined with the fact that most of the USSR's air defences and much of its military-industrial complex were based on Ukrainian and Belarusian territory, put Ukraine in a precarious position from the outset of its independence. [68] Perepelytsia examines the series of agreements through which Ukraine de-nuclearized itself (i.e. the NPT, START, the Budapest Memorandum) and how Ukraine should navigate foreign affairs, primarily with the West, Russia, and its other neighbours (with whom it could seek potential alliances).[69] He stresses that Ukraine's security assurances obtained during the 1990s were superficial at best and that the main requirement for Ukraine's new defensive model would centre on flexibility.[70]

Steven Pifer's brief summary of the process of nuclear disarmament involving Ukraine and Russia, from the perspective of an American diplomat, clearly summarizes the main events of the complicated years 1992–1994. Steven Pifer, on behalf of the Brookings Institute, wrote "The Trilateral Process: The United States, Ukraine, Russia and Nuclear Weapons" as an easily accessible summary of the processes that led up to the Trilateral Agreement and with it the end of overt nuclear proliferation in the former USSR. Pifer, the former US ambassador to Ukraine, explains the dominant interests of USA, Russia, and Ukraine during the early 1990s. American goals could be summed up by the State Department motto at the time: "it's the nukes, stupid." [71] In other words, the United States was most concerned with the proliferation of nuclear weapons in some of the new states of the former

---

68 Perepelytsia, *Beziadernyy status i natsional'na bezpeka Ukrainy* (Non-nuclear status and the national security of Ukraine), 4–7.
69 Ibid, 17–23, 40–46.
70 Ibid, 100–103.
71 Steven Pifer, "The Trilateral Process: The United States, Ukraine, Russia and Nuclear Weapons," Brookings Arms Control Series 6 (2011): 3.

Soviet Union. Eventually, the conditions of Ukrainian nuclear disarmament would come down to a few main points: assurances of Ukrainian territorial integrity and sovereignty; compensation for the highly enriched uranium in its weapons; financial aid for the dismemberment of Ukraine's weaponized nuclear infrastructure; and finally, the question under what conditions would Ukraine's weapons be destroyed.[72]

Pifer concludes with a discussion of the lessons learned by this entire ordeal. First, he notes that the Trilateral Agreement provided solutions to the needs of all three involved parties. Second, there was the importance of practicality: all sides, despite some tense moments, were in the end willing to listen to the needs of the others and seriously consider compromises. By bringing the presidents of each government together for a fixed meeting, the Trilateral Agreement forced the bureaucracies of each state to work more quickly and efficiently than usual. American financial aid, through the Nunn-Lugar program, facilitated negotiations at crucial moments.[73] These lessons, according to Pifer, are still applicable today to such nations as North Korea and Iran.

Oleh Kondratenko's 2011 article, "Protses yadernoho rozbroiennya i Ukrainy (The process of nuclear disarmament and Ukraine)," examines in a chronological fashion the role Ukraine played in post-Cold War nuclear disarmament efforts and centres around START-1 and START-2. Kondratenko writes that as a topic (and save for a few authors), nuclear weapons as a means of achieving goals in international affair receives little attention. He begins his article by recounting the history between the United States and the Soviet Union that lead to START-1 and introduces Ukraine to his recount by emphasizing the role that this new nuclear power played in delaying this new arms reduction treaty.[74] For the remainder of the article, Kondratenko examines the negotiation process between Ukraine, Russia, and the USA that led Ukraine to being nuclear weapons free. He portrays Ukraine as having always acted in good faith, and brushes over some of the acts taken by Ukraine to frustrate the negotiation process. Russia's main motive in this process was to first try and keep Ukraine in its political orbit, and failing this,

---

72  Ibid, 7–8.
73  Ibid. 30–32.
74  Oleh Kondratenko, "Protses yadernoho rozbroyennya i Ukrainy (The process of nuclear disarmament and Ukraine)," in *Naukovi zhurnaly Natsional'noho Aviatsiynoho Universytetu, Seriya: ekonomika, pravo, politolohiya, turyzm* (The Scientific journals of the National Aviation University, economics, law, political science, and tourism series), Volume 2, issue 4 (2011): 75–77, accessed 10 May 2017, http://jrnl.nau.edu.ua/index.php/IMV/article/viewFile/3265/3218.

to punish it. The goal of the United States was to prevent further nuclear proliferation, while that of Ukraine was to secure economic assistance, limit Russian influence, and gain security guarantees.[75] Kondratenko's conclusion highlights why it would have been impractical for Ukraine to have kept its arsenal and notes that despite these impracticalities, a nostalgia for a nuclear past has nonetheless entered into Ukraine's political discourse.[76]

Like Kondratenko, Oleksander Potyekhin's 2016 article "Iaderne rozbroyennya Ukrainy u konteksti ii vidnotsyny z SShA ta RF (The nuclear disarmament of Ukraine in the context of its relations with the USA and the Russian Federation)" provides an overview of Ukraine's path towards denuclearization and incorporates the author's analysis of the relevant history with the opinions of other scholars who have examined this subject. Potyekhin notes that the goals of Ukraine's nuclear diplomacy were to attract the attention of the leaders of the international community, receive compensation for its warheads and their related missiles, and finally, to receive external security guarantees.[77] Interestingly, the article also rightly points out how little work has been done to analyze Ukraine's of its tactical nuclear weapons article (19).[78] However, unlike the work of Kondratenko or the other authors listed thus far, Potyekhin's article was written following the Russian invasion and is as a result framed by these events and provides an *ex post facto* analysis of Ukraine's decision to de-nuclearize. After spending the first portion of his article briefly outlining the history behind Ukraine's nuclear disarmament and the special role played by the USA in the process, Potyekhin analyzes the consequences resulting from Ukraine's inability to secure security guarantees.

The impression that Potyekhin gives is that Ukraine received insufficient funds for denuclearization and that the country had been influenced by fears of not receiving anything for its nuclear stockpile. In the absence of security guarantees, Nunn-Lugar did very little to assist Ukraine's conventional military capabilities or the country's dire domestic situation during the 1990s. Further to this point, the author stresses that the West had not done enough to assist Ukraine in its fight against Russia (i.e. provide lethal assistance or aid for Ukraine's war migrants) and that due to this shortcoming, the West, and the USA in particular, owe it to

---

75   Ibid. 76–79.
76   Ibid, 79.
77   Oleksander Potyekhin, "*Iaderne rozbroyennya Ukrainy u konteksti ii vidnocyny z SSHA ta RF,*" in *Ahora,* Issue 16 (2016), 20, accessed 15 May 2017, http://kennankyiv.org/wp-content/uploads/2016/04/Potehin_Agora_V16_final-3.pdf.
78   Ibid, 19.

Ukraine to provide more financial and military assistance.[79] According to Potyekhin, in the absence of nuclear weapons there was only so much that security assurances could do for Ukraine given the state of that country's military in the face of Russian aggression and the Americans' unwillingness to become too closely involved (21–22).[80] The consequences of Ukraine's denuclearization, Potyekhin concludes, will likely serve as a dampener on future enthusiasm for nuclear disarmament.

Mariana Brudjeryn's 2016 dissertation, *The Power of the NPT: International Norms and Nuclear Disarmament of Belarus, Kazakhstan and Ukraine, 1990–1994*, examines the normative mechanisms of the NPT and how these norms influenced the denuclearization processes and narratives of these three post-Soviet states.[81] Brudjeryn's use of archival and primary sources renders her work one of the most substantial studies on nuclear disarmament in the former Soviet Union in recent years. For Brudjeryn, given that Ukraine contested most of the norms and expectations of the NPT, it serves as the base case for analysis and the foundation on which comparisons can be made between it, Belarus, and Kazakhstan.[82] Ukraine's national democrats, according to Brudjeryn, were the driving force behind Ukraine's drive to keep its nuclear weapons for the purpose of maintaining statehood and sovereignty, especially given the potential for Russian aggression. Brudjeryn only touches upon Russia's modern-day aggression in Ukraine, noting that as a result of the conflict there has been a renewed interest in Ukraine's denuclearization.[83] She instead focuses mainly on the time frame outlined in her dissertation's title.

Echoing observations made by Oleksander Potyekhin, Brudjeryn notes that as a disintegrating all-union military shipped Ukraine's tactical nuclear weapons to Russia after the collapse of the USSR, the need to maintain control of the new republic's nuclear arsenal became further apparent. As Ukraine dealt with the USA and Russia over the status of its arsenal and the process of its denuclearization, three competing narratives emerged within Ukraine that muddied the negotiation process. The first of these narratives, advocated primarily by Kravchuk and Ukraine's Ministry of Foreign Affairs, was that ownership of nuclear weapons

---

79   Ibid, 20–21.
80   Ibid, 21–22.
81   Mariana Brudjeryn, *The Power of the NPT: International Norms and Nuclear Disarmament of Belarus, Kazakhstan and Ukraine, 1990–1994* (PhD dissertation), Central European University, Budapest, 2016, accessed 20 May 2017, www.etd.ceu.hu/2016/budjeryn_mariana.pdf.
82   Ibid, 42.
83   Ibid, 6.

could be used as means towards financial aid.[84] The second, put forth by *Rada*'s national democrats, was that possession of nuclear arms could be used by Ukraine as a means of political hedging. They admitted that though Ukraine would eventually disarm, nuclear weapons could be used as negotiating tool towards security guarantees or other ends.[85] The final narrative, advanced by a narrow part of Ukraine's military, was that these weapons should be kept and used for deterrence.[86]

Belarus on the other hand never contested the NPT, while Kazakhstan only did so briefly and both ultimately shipped their weapons to Russia based on the belief that maintaining closer and more positive relations with that country would increase their security.[87] The net result of the disarmament process in the former USSR was that despite all the geopolitical changes of the early 1990s, the non-proliferation norms that underpinned the NPT maintained their ability to wield power and frame the disarmament discourses of Ukraine, Belarus, and Kazakhstan.[88]

Though scholarly output has been significant on American and Soviet nuclear problems, comparatively very little Western research has examined independent Ukraine's nuclear weapons era (1991–1994). Since Ukraine delivered its last nuclear warhead to Russia in 1996, the issue of Ukrainian nuclear disarmament has continued to receive little interest, other than as a case study by modern nuclear disarmament NGOs. Even less scholarly attention has been paid to the aid Ukraine received after independence and the treaties signed between Ukraine and other states concerning its nuclear industry and related technologies. This applies equally to international efforts at preventing nuclear materials from exiting Ukraine's borders. These last two points are significant for though Ukraine has the infrastructure and know-how necessary to construct nuclear weapons, it has signed numerous post-1994 treaties which preclude it from developing or possessing nuclear weapons or exporting any enabling/supporting technologies. Moreover, other treaties have tied the Ukrainian nuclear industry to those of Western Europe and the United States and in this way have made it much more difficult for Ukraine, even covertly, to move towards arming itself with a new generation of nuclear weapons.

---

84    Ibid, 148–152, 183–184.
85    Ibid, 152–155.
86    Ibid, 155–157.
87    Ibid, 215, 295–297.
88    Ibid, 310–311.

What the above examined works all have in common is that they show Ukraine was an active participant in its disarmament process, striving its best to maximize the benefits—both in fiscal and national sovereignty terms—that it could accrue through negotiating away its nuclear arsenal. Moreover, they make clear that an overwhelming majority of Ukrainian decision makers did not seriously think Ukraine could become a true nuclear power like Russia, China, France, or United States. More comprehensive works examining Ukraine's nuclear disarmament, such as those of Ruth Deyermond and Mariana Burdjeryn, include it as a section in an overarching analysis of a broader issue. Deyermond focuses on how conceptions of sovereignty have influenced the evolving relations of post-Soviet states, while Brudjeryn frames it as a means of analyzing the non-proliferations norms of the NPT and only briefly touches upon how Ukraine's example has been affected by its conflict with Russia.[89] Perepelytsia examines Ukraine from the perspective of policy advisor, providing ample analysis on the economic, diplomatic, and defence policy options available to Ukraine in the 1990s. The articles of Kondratenko and Potyekhin highlight Ukraine's nuclear disarmament from a Ukrainian perspective, with Potyekhin's emphasizing the obligations owed to Ukraine by the West and, in passing, what effect Ukraine's example is likely to have on future disarmament efforts. Steven Pifer's account also touches upon how Ukraine's example can serve as a guide for ongoing negotiation and disarmament efforts with Iran and North Korea.[90]

## Conclusion

Ukraine serves as a good case study for showing that international disarmament efforts do not cease once a state has merely renounced and removed the enabling technologies and resources from its territory; rather, it is an ongoing process that depends on a state's willingness to be an active and respected member of the international community. Save for outright invasion, in the absence of even some willingness to compromise or pull back from developing a nuclear arsenal—as is arguably the case with North Korea—it is difficult to see how a truly recalcitrant state can be forced to comply with international non-proliferation norms. Before 2014, Ukraine could have been viewed as a non-proliferation success story. Post-2014,

---

89 Brudjeryn, 6, 182. Brudjeryn's mentions that the Russia-Ukraine conflict has renewed interest in Ukraine's disarmament history. Otherwise she mentions only that the consultation mechanism of the Budapest Memorandum has only been invoked once, this being by Ukraine in 2014.
90 Pifer, "The Trilateral Process," 32.

however, that conclusion becomes much more debatable. Of the two authors writing on Ukraine after 2014, only Potyekhin analyzes the serious implications for disarmament caused by Russia's invasion of Ukraine and violation of the Budapest Memorandum. Several non-governmental organizations, such as the Brookings Institute, the Arms Control Association, and the Carnegie Institute, have all released papers or touched upon the significance of post-2014 Ukraine.[91] This area, along with future research into the haphazard removal of Ukraine's tactical nuclear weapons and post-1996 non-proliferation compliance measures, presents a likely future avenue through which Ukraine's nuclear disarmament can be both researched and interpreted.

In summary, Ukraine inherited its nuclear weapons after the fall of the USSR in 1991 and ensuing territorial claims emanating from Russia convinced Ukrainian nationalist-minded parliamentarians of the need to retain a nuclear arsenal. In turn, the combination of economic collapse and American diplomatic and financial pressure eventually prompted Ukraine to relinquish them and since 1994, the United States and Europe have aligned Ukraine's nuclear industry with internationally accepted standards, thereby helping fight the possibility of nuclear proliferation. As one of only a handful of examples of a state that willingly and voluntarily renouncing its nuclear arsenal, Ukraine is a little studied historical case in terms of non-proliferation. However, following the events of 2014 it is likely that Ukraine will be more closely examined by scholars and policy experts alike given the chimerical nature of its disarmament legacy.

With the events that have unfurled since the Euromaidan protests, it remains to be seen whether in the coming years the failures of the Budapest Memorandum will affect the decision-making of states considering to cross the threshold from non-nuclear to nuclear powers. It is to be hoped that for states debating whether or not to build nuclear weapons, economic considerations and international social standing will outweigh the need for protection against possible dire

---

91   Daryl G. Kimball, "Arms Checks Unaffected by Ukraine Crisis," Arms Control Association, Arms Control Today, Volume 44 (2014), accessed 15 July 2017, https://www.armscontrol.org/act/2014_04/Arms-Checks-Unaffected-by-Ukraine-Crisis; Steven Pifer, "The Budapest Memorandum and Obligations," Brookings Institute, 4 December 2014, accessed 8 August 2017, https://www.brookings.edu/blog/up-front/2014/12/04/the-budapest-memorandum-and-u-s-obligations/;
Elena Chernenko et al., "2015 NPT Review Conference: Tragedy, Farce, or Unexpected Success?" Carnegie Endowment for International Peace, 23 March 2015, accessed 4 May 2017, http://carnegieendowment.org/2015/03/23/2015-npt-review-conference-tragedy-farce-or-unexpected-success-pub-58889.

security threats in the future. For those states pursuing nuclear weapons development willing to cooperate and bargain, Ukraine stands out as an example of how a state can attempt to maximize its benefits without antagonizing the international community. Conversely, Ukraine may just as easily serve as an example of how international security assurances, given in exchange for nuclear deterrence, can amount to very little in an actual conflict.

# CONTRIBUTORS

**William Beard** has published books on David Cronenberg and Guy Maddin, and articles on some of the films of Atom Egoyan. He has studied the cinema of Clint Eastwood, with a book and a number of articles and book chapters. He contributed as an expert commentator to the Warner Brothers issue on DVD and Blu-ray of the complete Dirty Harry films, and was invited to provide full-length expert commentary tracks for Blu-ray reissues of films by David Cronenberg (*Rabid*, *The Brood*, *Scanners*, and *Dead Ringers* to date).

**Aya Fujiwara** is Director of the Prince Takamado Japan Centre for Research and Teaching at the University of Alberta. She is the author of *Ethnic Elites and Canadian Identity: Japanese, Ukrainians, and Scots, 1919–1971* (University of Manitoba Press, 2012).

**Jin Hamamura** is a PhD student of international relations at the University of Tokyo, Komaba. His work focuses specifically on nuclear double standards and hierarchy in the nuclear nonproliferation regime. He won the 10th *Shakai rinri kenkyū shōrei shō* (research encouragement award for social ethics) of the Nanzan University Institute for Social Ethics for his article "'Kyūsen rain' to shite no kaku fukakusan taisei," published on *Kokusai seiji*, 184 (2016).

**James F. Keeley** is an Associate Professor Emeritus with the Department of Political Science, and an Emeritus Fellow with the Centre for Military, Security and Strategic Studies, at the University of Calgary.

**Ritsuko Komaki** is Professor of Radiation Oncology at Baylor College of Medicine, Houston, Texas. She is Professor Emerita of Radiation Oncology, University of Texas and an Executive Advisor of Sapporo Proton Center, Ohno Memorial Hospital, Hokkaido, Japan. She is the recipient of the Marie Sklodovska Curie Gold Medal from Warsaw Curie Foundation in 2005 and the Gilbert H. Fletcher Society Gold Medal for Outstanding Achievements in 2016.

**David R. Marples** is Distinguished University Professor, Department of History and Classics, University of Alberta. His most recent book is *Ukraine in Conflict* (E-International Publishing, 2017) and he has published three books on the Chernobyl disaster in Ukraine.

**Tomoko Masumoto** is Professor of Communication at Kansai University. Her publications include "Tales of Two Cities: Hiroshima and Los Alamos and the Collective Memories of the Atomic Bombing Presented in their Principal Museums," and *With Respect to the Japanese: Going to Work in Japan* (with John Condon), (Intercultural Press, 2011).

**Frederick V. Mills** is a PhD Candidate in the Department of History and Classics, University of Alberta. He is Co-Editor (with David R. Marples) of *Ukraine's Euromaidan: Analyses of a Civil Revolution* (Stuttgart: ibidem Verlag, 2015).

**Chris Reyns-Chikuma** is Associate Professor in the Department of Modern Languages and Cultural Studies at the University of Alberta. He is the author of *Images du Japon en France et ailleurs: entre japonisme et multiculturalisme* (Paris: Harmattan, 2005).

**Yuko Shibata** is a research fellow at Meiji Gakuin University in Tokyo. She is the author of *Producing Hiroshima and Nagasaki: Literature, Film, and Transnational Politics* (Honolulu: University of Hawaii Press, 2018) and *Hiroshima Nagasaki: hibaku shinawa o kaitaisuru* (*Hiroshima/Nagasaki: Debunking a Myth of the Hibakusha Narrative*) (Tokyo: Sakuhinsha, 2015). Her articles appear in both academic and popular journals in English and Japanese. She was formerly a staff writer at *Asahi Shimbun* and published four team-authored books in Japanese.

**Atsuko Shigesawa** is Associate Professor in the English Studies Department of Kobe City University of Foreign Studies in Japan. Her work focuses on censorship, propaganda, and media coverage of World War II and the atomic bomb in the United States and occupied Japan. She completed her graduate studies at Hiroshima City University. She was a Scholar in Residence through the Fulbright Dissertation Program at American University in Washington D.C. in 2014–2015, and is author of *Genbaku to ken-etsu: Amerikajin kishatachi ga mita Hiroshima, Nagasaki*, (2010), which discusses American censorship during World War II and its influence on the coverage by American journalists of Hiroshima and Nagasaki following the end of war.

**Mayako Shimamoto** is a visiting fellow at Osaka University, where she earned her doctorate in American history in 2012. An edited version of the dissertation was published as: *Henry A. Wallace's Criticism of America's Atomic Monopoly* (Cambridge Scholars Publishing, 2016). Her current research interest concerns Japan's nuclear policy in the context of US-Japan relations. Her recent works include: "US Nuclear Policy in Early Cold War Era: From Henry A. Wallace's Perspectives, 1941–1955," in *Intelligence*, Vol.14 (Tokyo, 2015); *Historical Dictionary of Japanese Foreign Policy* (Maryland, 2015), and "Japan's Dilemma over Nuclear Fuel Cycle: Is Finnish Repository a Role Model?" in *Suomi ja Japan* (Helsinki, 2019).

**Susan L. Smith** is a Professor of History at the University of Alberta. She is the author of *Toxic Exposures: Mustard Gas and the Health Consequences of World War II in the United States* (Rutgers University Press, 2017).

**Jordan Vincent** received his MA in History from the University of Alberta in 2013. He is currently Project Lead Trans Mountain Expansion Project, Government of Alberta, working on the development and coordination of Alberta's energy policy in British Columbia.

***ibidem**.eu*